HOUGHTON MIFFLIN REPRINT EDITIONS

SIR ROBERT WALPOLE

The King's Minister

Van Loo

SIR ROBERT WALPOLE

J. H. PLUMB

SIR ROBERT WALPOLE

VOLUME II

THE KING'S MINISTER

AUGUSTUS M. KELLEY · PUBLISHERS

CLIFTON 1973

TO

H. E. HOWARD

First Published 1961

(Boston: Houghton Mifflin Company)

RE-ISSUED 1973 BY
AUGUSTUS M. KELLEY · PUBLISHERS
Clifton New Jersey 07012
By Arrangement with HOUGHTON MIFFLIN COMPANY

Library of Congress Cataloging in Publication Data
Plumb, John Harold, 1911—
    Sir Robert Walpole.
    (Houghton Mifflin reprint editions)
    Reprint of the 1956–61 ed.
    CONTENTS: 1. The making of a statesman.
                      2. The king's minister.
    Includes bibliographical references.
    1. Walpole, Robert, Earl of Orford, 1676–1745.
    [DA501.W2P522]   942.06'9'0924   [B] 72–128080
    ISBN 0–678–03551–2 (v. 1)
    ISBN 0–678–03572–5 (v. 2)
    ISBN 0–678–03550–4 (set)

Printed in Great Britain by
Fletcher & Son Ltd, Norwich

CONTENTS

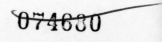

ILLUSTRATIONS

ix

ILLUSTRATIONS

A NOTE ON DATES

Unless otherwise stated all dates in this book are Old Style,
except that 1 January, not 25 March, is taken as the
beginning of the new year.

PREFACE

M Y MAJOR debt in this volume as in the first is to the Marquess and Marchioness of Cholmondeley, without whose help and encouragement this volume would not have been written. Each time that I return to Houghton, the stronger grows my conviction that Sir Robert Walpole possessed superlative taste in the visual arts. My account of his house, furniture and pictures is all too brief; but I hope that, short as is it, it will establish him as one of the most significant figures in the history of English taste in the early eighteenth century.

During the years that I have spent writing this life of Walpole I have been amazed by the kindness and generosity of those who own manuscripts, those who look after them, and those fellow scholars who work on them. By gracious permission of Her Majesty, Queen Elizabeth II, I was able to consult the Royal Archives at Windsor and I am grateful to Sir Owen Morshead and Miss Smith for the help that they gave me during my visits. I am also indebted to the Duke of Marlborough, the Trustees of the Chatsworth Settlement, the late Dowager Marchioness of Bristol, the Earl of Harrowby, the Earl of Lovelace, the Earl of Mar and Kellie, the Earl Waldegrave, the Lord Brabourne, the Lord Walpole, Sir Hughe Knatchbull-Hugessen, Major-General Sir Eustace Tickell, Bt., Mr H. L. Bradfer-Lawrence, and Mr T. R. C. Blofeld for giving me access to their papers and kind permission to quote from them. Professor Robert Halsband and Dr Aubrey Newman have drawn my attention to a number of references and I am particularly indebted to Captain T. T. Barnard for his help with the early life of Maria Skerrett. Once again Mr R. W. Ketton-Cremer has been my mentor on Norfolk affairs, for which I am most grateful. The advice of Dr Ragnhild Hatton and Dr John Owen has saved me from many slips, but I am entirely responsible for those that remain. I have benefited greatly from the criticisms of Mr John Hayward, Mr Neil McKendrick, Dr J. P. Kenyon and Sir Charles Snow. Mr John Guinness has been most helpful with the iconography of Sir Robert Walpole.

My debt to librarians and archivists is again large, particularly to those at the University Library, Cambridge, the Public Record Office, the British Museum, the Register House, Edinburgh, Archives Etrangères Quai d'Orsay, the Rijksarchief at The Hague, the John Rylands Library, the Pierpont Morgan Library, the Fitzwilliam Museum and the Record Offices of Berkshire, Essex, Hertfordshire, Lincolnshire, Northamptonshire and West Suffolk.

Only those who have struggled with my handwriting will appreciate the gratitude which I feel for the work of my secretary, Miss Margaret Parry.

INTRODUCTION

IN 1722 Robert Walpole stood on the threshold of success. His great rival, Charles Spencer, Earl of Sunderland, was dead. George I, who did not like him, knew him to be indispensable for the security of the government. His enemies, although far from defeated, lacked capable leadership. His position at the Treasury provided him with vast resources of patronage and influence which he could use to strengthen his grip on Parliament. Walpole, however, did not stand alone. No one thought of him without Charles, Viscount Townshend. They had known each other from earliest childhood, shared the same struggles, enjoying office and sustaining defeat together. They had been linked so long in political purpose that they had achieved an almost common identity in other people's minds. And each certainly thought of the other as complementary to himself. Foreign affairs were Townshend's business, domestic policy Walpole's. In 1722, Walpole's experience of government was more limited than Townshend's. He had acted as Secretary at War for two years and Treasurer of the Navy for a few months; he had been Paymaster of the Forces twice, but that was an office of profit and patronage rather than affairs. He had also twice been appointed First Lord of the Treasury and Chancellor of the Exchequer, which had brought him into the cabinet. His first spell as First Lord had been brief, from October 1715 to April 1717, a mere eighteen months; by the time Sunderland died he had held the Treasury again for a year. Not only had Townshend sat in the cabinet far longer than Walpole, but also his experience, both as Secretary of State and as Plenipotentiary at The Hague, had been far wider than Walpole's. Furthermore, he had dealt with those affairs—the relations with

I

foreign states and princes—in which the royal interest was greatest. Walpole had no first-hand experience of diplomacy, which was the principal concern of all cabinets. He possessed an admirable knowledge of the Commons and its members; he was aware of the possibilities of patronage in the Army and Navy as well as the Treasury. His spells of office as Chancellor had given him considerable insight into the financial organization of the kingdom, but his stay in office had been too brief to put many of his ideas into action. The one exception had been the establishment of the Sinking Fund, but even in that Stanhope had managed to secure a part of the fame which it brought.[1] In 1722 Walpole's abilities were most clearly recognized in his political *expertise*; in the dexterity with which he managed the House of Commons. There his touch was masterly. Such arts might lead a man to greatness, but they could never be more than the foundations of power. A new and wider world beckoned to Walpole, and one which in the end could only bring him into conflict with Townshend. Indeed, its attractions were to prove irresistible. As head of the Treasury Walpole was bound to be concerned with the results of diplomacy, if not with its operation. Subsidies to foreign princes had to be found by him from taxation. Wars, or rumours of wars, involved expense and expense was his business. The longer Walpole remained in office, the more certain it became that he would be drawn into the web of diplomacy. Nor was it possible for Walpole to adopt a passive attitude to any problem of power. Yet it is most unlikely that he deliberately and consciously developed his interest in foreign affairs. These were Townshend's concern and Townshend was his most intimate friend. The first independent actions that he took resulted from anxiety which at times drove him to precipitate action. The cause was Carteret, who on Sunderland's death had become the hope of those who wished to see the power of Walpole and Townshend limited; Carteret, whose vast knowledge of the European scene made him a formidable rival for the King's ear. Once begun, how-

[1] Cf. *Walpole*, I, 147.

ever, Walpole's interest grew; his love of dominion would not let him rest. In the end diplomacy became as much his concern as the disposition of patronage or the raising of taxation. Could men be aware of the course of their lives, Townshend must have realized, even in 1722, his grave disadvantage *vis-à-vis* his brother-in-law. Townshend's political future was in a sense circumscribed; he could not, like Walpole, add to his stature by acquiring authority in the affairs of Europe. The House of Lords required little management and, although he might influence patronage, he could not control it. Walpole's world was closed to him in a sense that his world was not closed to Walpole. From 1722 to his resignation in 1730, his was a losing game. No doubt the means by which Walpole undermined his authority were unconsciously motivated, and to him the result of accident. Yet the conflict which gradually developed between them arose in rational terms in disagreements about policy. Although Walpole acted without deliberate purpose, his instinct directed him with the sureness of an arrow to its target—to power absolute and undivided.

Walpole had not shown great interest in diplomacy during his periods of high office, for they had coincided with two domestic problems of great complexity—the foundation of the Sinking Fund and the South Sea Bubble. During his first spell at the Treasury Walpole had only had time enough to make his mark as a financier, and he can have had few thoughts to spare for the intricacies of diplomacy except in so far as his position in the cabinet forced it upon his notice. The political struggles which arose from the disasters of the South Sea Company's activities had absorbed his attention. In 1722 he could look about him with a new authority and with a new security. From that time his career became entangled in questions relating to Britain's relations with foreign states. In the end it was his failure to solve them that brought about his fall; and to understand Walpole's career as the King's minister an attempt must be made to describe the baffling shadow world of European diplomacy with which Walpole had to contend.

This is essential, too, for one other reason. Foreign affairs were a major concern of the House of Commons, and they directly influenced men's judgments and men's votes. In the great opposition that arose against Walpole from 1726 to 1733, some of the gravest charges levelled against him were concerned with his handling of this country's European alliances. Diplomatic success or failure had an effect on ministerial strength in the voting lobbies. Many of Walpole's diplomatic actions arose from his political needs in Parliament, and foreign affairs and politics became inextricably intertwined. There is no understanding of one without a knowledge of the other, for during these years Walpole ceased to be a politician of mere local importance and emerged as a statesman of European significance.

BOOK ONE

THE YEARS OF VICTORY

CHAPTER ONE

WALPOLE'S EUROPE

WALPOLE HAD scarcely known a Europe at peace. Throughout Walpole's childhood, youth and early manhood Louis XIV had struggled to impose his authority on Europe, and Walpole's earliest experiences as a statesman had been with the war against France. The maritime powers, Holland and Great Britain, had combined with the Empire and with some of the states of Germany to check the French King's ambitions. To do so had required Englishmen to make war with a thoroughness that would have amazed their ancestors. Armies in Flanders and Spain, fleets scattered over the seven seas, had been raised and maintained only with the greatest difficulty. Never before had the British been so involved in war. Although the Government had hired troops wherever it could, the press gang had become a common dread, and full conscription, for which Walpole himself had pleaded, only just avoided. The financial strain had, in William III's reign, proved almost too much for the weak administrative powers of the Government. Reforms in banking and taxation and brilliant improvization and invention in administration had, however, created a remarkably flexible war machine.[1] Nevertheless, a nation, clamouring for peace, had brought the war to an abrupt end in 1713, when the treaty of Utrecht, negotiated with exceptional alacrity by Walpole's enemies, saved France from the utter ruin which further campaigning might easily have inflicted on her. Britain had finished the war with a burden of debt which, although puny by modern standards, seemed of astronomical proportions to men of the time. Many statesmen, Walpole

[1] J. H. Plumb, 'The Organisation of the Cabinet in the Reign of Queen Anne', *Trans. R. Hist. Soc.*, 5th Series, VII (1957), 137-57.

included, thought survival demanded peace, but others did not think that the problems which thirty years of war had created could be solved without further recourse to arms. In fact, apart from a little localized fighting, peace was to be maintained for nearly thirty years, in spite of frequent alarms. Peace was Walpole's constant aim but it was not his deliberate policy. After the failure of France to achieve the domination of Western Europe, there remained no power strong enough to make the attempt. Britain and the Dutch in combination might have possessed both the men and the wealth, but their lack of a highly centralized state machinery and, even more, the satisfaction derived from their overseas commerce, inhibited such ambitions. Furthermore, apart from Russia and Prussia, no country after 1715 possessed the purposeful and aggressive leadership comparable to that which Louis XIV had given to France. Prussia was as yet too small and Russia too remote to threaten Western Europe. So peace of a sort was maintained, but only just maintained, for the great peace treaties of Utrecht, Rastadt and Baden had left plenty of problems, important or trivial, for the powers to quarrel about. Nor were the Western states without ambition, or unwilling to take a chance, even at the risk of war, of snatching either a dynastic or commercial advantage at another's expense, and periods of acute crisis were typical of the Europe that Walpole came to know so well.

Yet there was no general war until a few years before Walpole's fall. This was not due to the wisdom or vision of any statesman or to a loathing of war by the ruling classes of Europe. The condition of Europe was such that a number of powers could combine to prevent any threatened aggression and so maintain the uneasy equilibrium which had resulted from the failure of France. That powers were so willing to band together to restrain ambition rather than to share the plunder of mutual victories was not due to any belief in a need for a concert of Europe but merely to the calculation of a main chance. None of the great powers could hope to win against the rest combined; no ally could be relied upon not to desert. So the countries of Europe nagged and bickered amongst themselves and directed their aggressive instincts towards their weaker neighbours or to the exploitation of primitive peoples in distant lands.

2

THE BASIC structure of Walpole's Europe was still feudal and it was rare for any man, save a lawyer, to achieve power in government or move with ease in society unless he was armigerous. Birth and rank were the only safe passports in a world of ancient, inherited rights. All governments respected the economic and social privileges of their aristocracies, even if such privileges were inimical to the efficiency of the state. The Prince of Condé ruled the Clermontois with its 40,000 inhabitants; he collected and spent the taxes raised there. The gentlemen of the Province of Boulonnais officered their own army which was separate from that of France.[1] Prince Radziwill's estates were so large that he could support a private army and his palace was run like a court. In Spain a grandee told his King that his nobility was 'made by God and time': the extent of his estates, the absolute nature of his seignorial jurisdiction, and the multiplicity of his privileges can only have made this seem like a truth rather than a delusion to all who heard him.[2] In Sweden, Denmark and Italy the aristocracy still possessed the dominant power in the state. Suicidal warfare between factions, the steady attrition which treason, plot and conspiracy exacted on their class, had weakened and in places—notably England—thinned the European aristocracy. Yet their power remained great; their traditions rooted in antiquity; and they possessed a sense of themselves as a caste apart which gave them an arrogance, a panache, and an almost unconscious egoism which allowed them to live and to die with little thought of

[1] *Cambridge Modern History*, VII (ed. J. O. Lindsay), 215.
[2] *The European Nobility in the XVIIIth Century* (ed. A. Goodwin), 43.

any standards or loyalties but their own. Sometimes these preoccupations with birth and rank bordered on the ridiculous; the passion engendered in Saint Simon by questions as to who should sit on a stool in the Royal Presence or whether the *Président du Parlement de Paris* should, or should not, raise his hat on coming into the presence of a Duke of France, seems to border on insanity. And yet they demonstrate how deep the consciousness of rank went.

They were warriors and heralds by birth, by instinct, and by education. Most monarchies had insisted, for their own safety, that they should also be courtiers. War, diplomacy, social life, these were the professions of the aristocracy. And it is not surprising that they should take questions of inheritance as a just cause for war: and that dynastic problems should seem to play an inordinately large part in the diplomacy of eighteenth-century Europe. Whether or not a Spanish prince were permitted to do homage to the Emperor for Piacenza was not a quaint lunacy of the age but a matter of moment; a part of the legal structure in which they had moved throughout their lives. And the Europe of Walpole cannot be understood, any more than his England, unless it is realized that in many ways it lay closer to the fifteenth and fourteenth centuries than to our own.

Yet another stronger tide was flowing, sapping the foundations and persistently eroding the ancient, barbaric structure of European society. Merchants there had always been. From the high middle ages town life, the erratic yet continuing growth of commerce, the questing search which had led to the great discoveries had built up in Europe a powerful merchant class. Sometimes, as in Venice, the Netherlands and the free cities of the Empire, they had acquired freedom to build societies and governments based on their own values. Mainly, however, they had forced themselves into the interstices of feudal society and by their power and wealth secured privileges and at times modified the nature of government. Many of their values and interests had come to stain feudal society like an indelible dye.

Men of great landed wealth found their riches increase and some deliberately attempted to exploit the ever-growing commerce and industry of Europe. Even if they despised all bourgeois values and activities, they could not evade the consequences of the vast traffic which bore Frenchmen, Netherlanders, Danes and Russians to the earth's extremities. Profit had long been equated in the minds of governments with power; power with ships and armies. And commercial rivalries had led to those clashes of arms for which the aristocracies had been trained. Although the government of Europe was in the hands of its nobility, its problems were created by the middle class. And the nature of Europe's increasing wealth was so well understood that Louis XIV or his great foreign minister Torcy, could express sentiments which were at one and the same time feudal in concept and bourgeois in intent. And this is why eighteenth-century wars and eighteenth-century diplomatic activity have seemed so dull and so boring. The outmoded ideas, the trivialities of the causes of quarrels often conceal the vital issues that were at stake. To the contemporary nothing was trivial, nothing astounded, because the issues were a part of his instinctive attitude.

Nothing better illustrates this intermingling of tradition, this enravelment of aristocratic and mercantile concepts, than the vast conflict between Louis XIV and the maritime powers over the Spanish Succession. Louis XIV had attempted to secure the vast dominions of Spain for his own family and the commerce of the Indies for his nation. This arose, however, not only from national ambition but from the attitude to life which Louis, and other European kings, held. Royal dynasties were called by God to rule and for any one of them not to accept the burdens and obligations of his destiny was almost akin to blasphemy. The crown of Spain had descended to Louis' family by the mysterious yet divine process of hereditary succession. This was God's edict, and treaties, laws, renunciations, testamentary bequests might be meaningless and irrelevant in comparison.

Of course, the facts of life forced on all kings and emperors—even Louis XIV—a modification of this absolutist view of the sanctity of dynastic claims; but they were always harking back to it and were for ever uneasy under the compromises which war and diplomacy forced on them. Louis XIV had warned the negotiators of the Treaty of Utrecht that his grandson Philip V's formal renunciation of the French crown was likely to prove meaningless if his young great-grandson (afterwards Louis XV) were to die. Archaic though this dynastic factor might seem, it still exerted a powerful influence in those aristocratic circles which provided the vast majority of Europe's soldiers and diplomats. After all, hereditary succession was more often than not the one sure basis of their own wealth and their own position of authority. In the early eighteenth century England's attitude to monarchy was unique and outstandingly revolutionary; indeed her social structure was more fluid than that of any other nation, including the Dutch, and this has made it difficult for Englishmen to comprehend the force—blind, instinctive, irrational—of dynastic claims based on hereditary right though even in the freer English society they were far weightier, far more compelling, than the course of its history might lead one to suppose. And it did not seem odd to Walpole that the death of a sickly boy might plunge Europe into another long and exhausting war. The health and the capacity for fatherhood of Louis XV became the concern of Europe.

When the makers of eighteenth-century treaties calmly broke up territories, ignoring social, economic, linguistic or historic factors, as they did at Utrecht, they were not motivated by a cynical disregard of what has seemed to later generations the most fundamental relations in human society. They were trying to interpret the dictates of God which, as ever, tended to prove intractable when applied to the confused condition of humanity. For unfortunately, God had in His wisdom thought fit to bless Europe with not one, but many ruling dynasties, whose intermarriages had provided a welter of dynastic claims as difficult to unravel as His own oracles. So a field of conflict existed in which the thrust of economic expansion or the needs of national power could find expression. And, of course, outside the European arena these conflicts were more simply avowed. In Africa, in India, in the Americas the battle for empire between France and England and the Dutch was accepted for what it was—a brutal struggle for wealth. This mixture of economic aggression and dynastic interest naturally varied from state to state; in the more highly commercialized and industrialized countries the search for wealth played a more conscious role in the formulation of policy. Yet both economic and dynastic aims could at times be merged with or overridden by conceptions of strategic needs. Organized professional armies, officered by the nobility and led by kings or princes themselves, were a part of the European states system. Only England had been reluctant to commit its resources to the maintenance of a large standing army, but the hope, so very generally held, that the necessity for an army would pass, had never been realized. Furthermore, no such opposition had arisen against the necessity for a fleet. Although the belief that England must maintain a naval force stronger than the rest of Europe's was accepted almost without question, so that strategic considerations were rarely absent from the minds of British statesmen, the security given by the channel prevented them from becoming the obsession that they were to so many European princes.[1]

Questions of wealth, questions of power expressed in terms of dynastic claims and backed by highly trained professional armies gave the diplomacy of early eighteenth-century Europe its curious flavour. There were, however, one or two other factors of exceptional importance: the

---

[1] The cost of armed diplomacy led naturally to a more rigorous organization of the state and to the intensive search for economic advantages. Armies and fleets, in peace or in war, were deliberately associated with the spirit of patriotism which added to their strength. Both processes weakened dynastic, and strengthened national, attitudes.

character of men could influence events profoundly, and not only the character of rulers but also of diplomats. For this reason, rulers ruled—usually in a detailed administrative sense—and, although they were subject naturally to the pressures exerted by their ministers, they were freer from restraint than rulers, royal or elected, have subsequently become, except in moments of crisis or totalitarian rule. And diplomats themselves were less subject to detailed control. Although much improved, the means of communication were still desperately slow, and time itself became a subtle weapon of diplomacy—adding as it were a new dimension in which government could fence with government. The prevarications and delays, the decisions taken only to be disavowed, the knowledge that the whole strategy of a diplomatic campaign might be changed by the changed opinion of one prince, inflated the respect in which diplomacy was held and led also to complications almost for their own sake, so that often the left hand of a prime minister scarcely knew what his right hand was doing. Naturally, monarchs and many statesmen grew to believe that diplomacy was a complex art in which success could come only to men who had grown old in its practice. Hence, some of the stranger figures who emerge in the early eighteenth century— Alberoni, the abbé of Parma, who became Elizabeth Farnese's minister, only to be succeeded by an even more flamboyant adventurer than himself—Ripperda, the Dutchman who finished as a Bashaw of Morocco—or Goertz, the German who influenced the foreign policy of Charles XII of Sweden. These were the wild, bold men brought in to take the gambles that the staid professional diplomats would not countenance. After their inevitable failure, the old hands crept back to their desks and practised their finesse on the insoluble problems of European power politics.

As men came to believe in the power of diplomacy or, at least, to be entranced by the fascination of the game, so too were those who took part in it subjected to the pressures of corruption. Bribery became endemic and spies abounded, forcing diplomacy into ever more secret and personal channels, leading often to two, three or more diplomatic exchanges being carried on simultaneously and these in their turn merely inflating the price that governments were ready to pay for treachery of another's servants. And here once more the feudal strain in eighteenth-century society is important. Until the most recent times, France, England, Germany, Sweden, the Netherlands had been a prey to factional conflicts between aristocratic groups in which the King had been a pawn. Much as they might reverence the concept of monarchy, or intrigue and quarrel for the privilege of holding the royal shirt at a levée, this did not prevent plot, treason, conspiracy from being endemic in aristocratic society. Few noble families lacked an ancestor who had gone to the block: all royal families possessed forbears who had been assassinated. Dynasties, noble as well as royal, had risen through successful treason, and this natural tendency to treachery was, of course, the cause of infinite anxiety to statesmen;[1] the reason, in fact for Walpole's obsession with Jacobitism.

At this time there was little sense of loyalty to a nation, and it is astonishing how easy it was to buy the confidence of a highly placed minister of state. The growing national consciousness in England made her diplomats far more dependable and her ministers less bribable than those of most other countries in Europe, but it was a comparatively recent development. In the reigns of Charles II and James II ministers and leaders of the opposition had held out their hands for French gold; in William's reign and in Anne's flirtations with the Pretender had taken its place—a custom which had not entirely ceased with the accession of George I. These activities were not the result of greater human depravity but of the absence of what is now considered to be morally binding attachments. Loyalty to a dynasty or to a

[1] Leganez, a grandee of Spain, excused his treason on the grounds that he refused to 'draw the sword against the house of Austria to whom my own house owes so many benefits'. *The European Nobility in the XVIIIth Century* (ed. A. Goodwin), 46.

set of ministers did exist but its operation was not universal nor held in such public veneration as loyalty to a nation has become. The cause for this may lie partly in the homogeneity of the ruling castes of Europe. Treachery and disloyalty are more frequently found in closed societies of professional men, where a person rather than a group is the victim. The aristocracy of Europe met not only on terms of equality but tastes, manners, interests and language were largely the same. It was fatally easy for coteries to form which seemed to have more in common than the state to which they belonged. Often such relationships were cemented by family alliances and marriages. The fact that Bolingbroke's wife was the Marquise de Villette made it easier for him to enter into a close correspondence with the French Government in his anti-Walpole campaigns. So too, the pro-French grandees of Spain had their relatives at Versailles with whom they could plot treason. Personal, family and clan ambitions could run as easily counter to the needs of the state as the dynastic ambitions of the monarchs themselves, with the added disadvantage that their expression was not subject to the checks of national needs. When it is remembered that these circles provided the diplomats of Europe, it is easier to understand why it was riddled with what seems to us to be treachery. Irritating and maddening as it was to those betrayed, yet such treachery was easily forgiven. Naturally, if treason reached the point of armed rebellion, men suffered; and here and there a man of no importance—like the Norfolk Jacobite, Christopher Layer—might be put to death for little worse than what his betters could do with impunity. Within the circles of government and diplomacy, treasonable activity was regarded with little more distaste than the malicious and destructive envy of colleagues will arouse in tough-fibred, power-seeking men. The Duchess of Maine suffered only a brief rural exile for her plot against the Regent of France; that, and his personal displeasure. In modern times Bolingbroke's career would have been cut short by a traitor's death, but Walpole could do nothing more than exclude him from his seat in the House of Lords. The first decade of the eighteenth century witnessed a growth of treachery; this should not generate a feeling of moral repugnance for these men. They were as trapped in the atmosphere of their day as we in ours. The ease, however, with which they double-crossed each other is a factor of great importance and was instrumental in making Walpole depend on his brother, Horatio, in diplomatic negotiations. Horatio's loyalty to his elder brother was absolute; but Walpole's foreign policy might have proved more successful had he depended on a cleverer man who occasionally sold his secrets to his enemies. These things— the dynastic ambitions of kings, the commercial rivalry of nations, the urgent needs of strategy, the treachery of men— Walpole did not have to learn. The nature of foreign governments and of the men who ran them were, however, in 1722 almost a closed book to him. He began to give the same concentrated attention to the red despatch boxes that contained the ambassadorial correspondence of half the courts of Europe as he did to questions of finance or patronage. Slingelandt, Chauvelin, Ripperda, Rottembourg ceased to be shadowy figures of cabinet debate but became real and living figures; the problems of Berg and Julich, of Parma and Piacenza, of Barrier Fortresses and Assientos his constant preoccupation. A tour of the diplomatic horizon of Europe is essential for understanding Walpole's contribution to English history.

3

THE UNITED Netherlands were the lynch-pin of English foreign policy. The two countries were united by common strategic interests—the control of the Channel, and the equilibrium in the Baltic—which had finally overridden their natural rivalry in commerce. Trade was the foundation of Dutch greatness. Holland and its big towns—particularly Amsterdam—was Europe's warehouse; the market in which all commodities, including money, were bought and sold.

Timber, hemp, tar, furs from Russia and Scandinavia
jostled with the fine damasks, silks, olive oil and wine from
Italy and Spain; tobacco, sugar, spice from the East and
West Indies, piled high on the teeming quaysides, awaited
transhipment to all Europe. Throughout this tiny country,
canals were being dug, towns built, roads paved; schools,
universities, hospitals, almshouses founded. The lofty, plain-
fronted houses belied their sumptuous interiors: beautiful
plasterwork, intricate carving and handsome plate bespoke
the solid wealth of this merchant's paradise. All travellers
were amazed by the neatness and cleanliness of Dutch
cities, the ease of transport, the absence of crime, the
excellence of their government, the care expended on the
old, the sick and the poor. Prosperity, such as Europe had
never known, blazoned the land. Dutch achievements in
science—Huygens, Loewenhoek, Boerhaave; in philosophy—
Descartes,[1] Spinoza; in art—Rembrandt, Vermeer, Hals;
were worthy of their wealth. Their technology was superior to
any in Europe. In spite of constant war and repeated invasion, their riches had grown and their arts and sciences
had continued to flourish. The Dutch remained the most
resilient nation in Europe, possessed of an excellent army
and an indomitable fleet. Each town, each province was
dominated by a closely intermarried, rich, powerful oligarchy of rich merchants and lawyers who had drawn into
their hands the economic, legal and social life of their
neighbourhoods. Each passing decade increased their
natural conservatism; considerations of wealth outweighed
those of strategy and stability attracted them more than
adventure; risk, particularly of war, became abhorrent to
them. And the vast wealth of the Dutch was leading to a
paralysis of the will.

Since 1688 the Dutch and the English had shared defeat
and victory. The alliance had been forged by William III

---

[1] A tribute—Descartes—to Dutch toleration which provided men of genius
with a shelter from the intolerance of the bigoted. Descartes was, of course,
French by birth and Catholic by education.

and proved by Marlborough. Together they had humbled France, the greatest military power in Europe; singly neither could have survived. Naturally such an alliance had suffered strain; Oxford and Bolingbroke had nearly wrecked it by their hasty peace with France in 1713—and the suspicion, strengthened by this action, that the English were always willing to sacrifice Dutch interests to their own, lingered on. The advent of Townshend and Walpole to power and the presence of Horatio Walpole at The Hague in 1714 did much to assuage it, but the suspicion never died for it rationalized a deep-seated envy which many Dutchmen were beginning to feel about the English. This made them uneasy allies.[1] Despite their jealousy of England's growing overseas trade, Dutch investments in the Bank of England, the National Debt, the South Sea Company and a host of other financial and economic ventures inhibited anything but a common foreign policy in essentials even though this jealousy made for difficulties over detail and led to endless wrangling and resentment. Many Dutchmen in power were irked by what seemed to be a position of subservience. The English decided according to their own interests, the Dutch were expected to follow suit. The critics pointed to the eager way the English had accepted a slice of the Spanish trade at Utrecht and agreed to the exclusion of the Dutch. They stressed English indifference to the vital Dutch question of the Barrier fortresses. The Dutch, tired of invasion, had secured at the end of the war a line of formidable fortresses along the border of the Southern Netherlands (modern Belgium) and France. At the same time these Southern Netherlands had been taken from Spain and given to the Emperor, who was responsible for seeing that the economic clauses of the Barrier Treaty were carried out. He tended to ignore them. The Dutch groaned and grieved and protested in the name

[1] For Anglo-Dutch relations see Ragnhild Hatton, *Diplomatic Relations between Great Britain and the Dutch Republic, 1714-21* (1950): C. H. Wilson, *Anglo-Dutch Finance in the Eighteenth Century* (Cambridge, 1951): John Murray, *The Honest Diplomat* (The Hague, 1955). Horatio Walpole's diplomatic papers at Wolterton have been of great value for this and subsequent sections.

of justice; Stanhope and Sunderland displayed little sympathy. The rancour against the English grew. The course of events between 1715–22 did little to assuage it. George I's interests in the Baltic called for effective action against the Swedish fleet. And here for once Hanoverian ambitions chimed with English commercial interests.

The Baltic trade, however, formed one of the most considerable sectors of the Dutch economy. They clung leech-like to neutrality; and tried their utmost to restrain George I and his ministers. To their primary fear of losing the actual Baltic trade was added another, that George I might make himself master of the Elbe estuary and so give the English a great port—Hamburg—as an entrepôt for their Northern European trade. Finally the English lost patience and took unilateral action. Stanhope made the position quite clear to the Dutch: he wrote to the English ambassador as follows:

'I am to acquaint you that Sr. George Byng who is to command the squadron of his Majesty's ships in the Baltic is not only instructed to attack the Swedish ships wherever he meets with them, but also to seize all vessels which come out of any of the ports of Sweden, as well ships of war as transports and merchantmen, and to take all ships of other nations which would go into the ports of Gottenburg or any other part of Sweden. The Dutch are not to doubt of these instructions being closely pursued, since His Majesty can neither in good policy nor honour, allow the subjects of the States to build their fortune on the loss and ruin of his, and to the strengthening at the same time of his enemies.'[1]

The English took the same firm line in 1719: on both occasions the Dutch trade lost. The English knew how to make trade flourish by war. Apart from secret but private negotiations with one or two leading Dutch statesmen, Stanhope secured an alliance with France without bothering to secure the support of the Dutch Government. He knew that, willy-nilly, they would be forced to follow. Again their shuffling, dilatory, suspicious diplomacy was no match for

[1] Hatton, *op. cit.*, 154.

the quick personal diplomacy of Stanhope and Dubois. Time and time again the Dutch had to adjust themselves to a *fait accompli* and to learn the bitter lesson that their voice was growing negligible in the affairs of Europe.

Their dilemma was due to ineluctable circumstance. The island security of the English had given them a golden opportunity to expand their trade when the Dutch were fighting across their devastated homeland. The structure of English economy was also more elastic; a lower standard of living and a higher rate of profit gave English goods and English freights a competitive advantage. Furthermore, the resources which England controlled, both at home and over-seas, even though they were far from being adequately exploited, made it certain that her wealth would quickly surpass that of the Netherlands. The United Provinces were moving away from an offensive to a defensive economy and that change had strengthened those cautious and conservative elements of Dutch society for which the Dutch constitution seemed to be designed.

The United Provinces were a federation of seven states all of whose consent was needed before any treaty could possess validity. The office of Stadtholder was in abeyance, partly owing to the fact that the one claimant, William of Nassau, was a child, but also because the mandarin class which governed Holland preferred the collective leadership. Although the business of the country was conducted in public by the representatives of the States, known as 'Their High Mightinesses', the real power lay with the Grand Pensionary of Holland, for, unless Holland, the richest of the provinces, was prepared to accept a policy no progress was possible.[1] Until his death in 1720 this office had been filled

---

[1] Cadogan in 1722 referred to them as 'quelques avocats, qui élevés dans les vûes reservées de leurs professions, sont incapables de gouverner une grande République, et manquent autant de lumières pour les Affaires d'Etat'. Two years earlier Charles Whitworth had formed the same opinion. 'These people have all the symptoms of a crazy Government, they are jealous, peevish, complaining, wilfull, they will have everything and do nothing'. See Hatton, *op. cit.*, 217-21, 251.

by Heinsius, the friend and ally of Marlborough, a cautious administrator who, as he grew older, preferred the discomfort of a fence to the horror of a decision. In the election of his successor, the English were skilfully out-manoeuvred by the French. Fortunately for them, the smaller states of the United Provinces disliked the mastery of Holland which the Pensionary system fostered. Furthermore, the indecisive and palsied government, whose incompetence was as great in domestic as foreign affairs, had induced a formidable opposition to itself. Add to this the hatred that all close to power feel for narrow, interbred oligarchies, and it is not surprising that many, including George I, deluded themselves with the idea of a constitutional revolution.

'Le désordre, la confusion et la désunion dans le gouvernement d'Hollande sont augmentées à un tel point, que tout le monde convient qu'il ne scauroit subsister sur le pied qu'il est,'[1] wrote Cadogan to George I in 1721 after a secret mission to the United Provinces to explore what popular support a bid for the Stadtholdership by William IV of Nassau might secure. There was much, although Cadogan wishfully exaggerated its extent, and as soon as English gold began to flow into strategic pockets, there was more. Naturally George I, an underestimated diplomat, had seen further than the mere return to power of the House of Nassau. He had already selected one of his granddaughters to be William's bride. Cadogan's secret mission had, of course, drawn attention to itself by its very secrecy, and the well-placed guineas did not require much interpretation. Within a few months English aims were common knowledge.

The French had for many years exploited amongst the Dutch the irritations and mortifications which the brusque diplomacy of England had caused, but this interference by Cadogan was a God-given opportunity which they seized with skill as well as avidity. The enormities of England's ambitions were exposed and eagerly believed by those men in power who could only lose by the elevation of William.

[1] Hatton, *op. cit.*, 250.

Doggedly they entrenched themselves in a policy of cautious inaction for which the Netherlands' constitution was peculiarly well-designed, indifferent to the steady erosion of their country's greatness. Nevertheless, the avowed championship of the cause of the Stadtholder created unnecessary difficulties for the English, and, as Cadogan belonged to Sunderland's faction, common sense and personal animosity combined to convince Walpole of the absurdity of pushing William into the Stadtholdership.

Walpole, indeed, possessed greater knowledge of Dutch affairs than of those of any other European country because of his frequent conversations with his brother, Horatio, who not without justification prided himself both on his knowledge of Dutch affairs and on the esteem in which he was held by Dutch politicians. Townshend, too, was well acquainted with the leading Dutch statesmen, above all with Slingelandt, a tough, irascible, warm-hearted man, much after Townshend's heart. Townshend, too, had been grateful for the loyal way in which the Dutch leaders had praised him to George I at The Hague when the King waited for fair weather on his way to England in the autumn of 1714. The peremptory attitude of Stanhope and Sunderland towards their Dutch colleagues had deeply disturbed Townshend, for he felt that England's closest ally was being unnecessarily alienated to gratify the King. On their resumption of power, Walpole and Townshend tried naturally to win back the Dutch and allay their suspicions of English policy. They sent Horatio Walpole over to The Hague to spread goodwill, bonhomie and useful presents. And to show the sincerity of their friendly intentions, they discharged at last the debts incurred by the English to the Dutch during the War of the Spanish Succession. It was all to little purpose. The Dutch—not only Hornebeck, the new Pensionary, but even old anglophiles like Slingelandt—had grown too suspicious of English aims to be won back to incautious friendship. They were too keenly aware of George I's ambitions for Hanover, too frightened that he might place the rich Elbe trade entirely in the hands of the English, too certain that he might sacrifice their claims for the sake of the Emperor's approval. That was an ancient grievance, but it festered and did not heal with the years. To the chagrin of the Dutch, the English still refused to exert any pressure on the Emperor to make him fulfil the economic clauses of the Barrier Treaty. To George I, whose sole concern in public affairs was to secure the investiture of Bremen and Verden and to tie more formally these territories on the Elbe to his Electorate, the constant whining of the Dutch about these trivialities seemed extremely distasteful. And the gay havoc made by Stanhope and Sunderland of Anglo-Dutch relations was accepted by the King with complete equanimity. Thus Walpole and Townshend inherited unnecessary difficulties; in the Dutch they possessed a reluctant ally whose suspicions were exploited by their enemies and one who required constant cajolery to keep in line with their common purpose—a tranquil Europe.

4

ENGLAND'S OTHER traditional ally in Northern Europe was the Empire, a curious ramshackle accumulation of territories, the result of successful Hapsburg marriage and of successful war against the Magyars and the Turks. It was ruled by Charles VI, who had failed so dismally in Spain during the great war of the Spanish Succession: a failure which he could blame on England for deserting the common cause at Utrecht and leaving him to fight alone. Like his brother, Joseph I, whom he succeeded, Charles VI lacked a male heir, for his only son died young. He became obsessed by the desire to make certain the succession of his eldest daughter, Maria Theresa, and this became the mainspring of his diplomatic activity for twenty years.

He had been urged by Eugene of Savoy, the great Austrian general, the friend and colleague of Marlborough, to back this diplomacy with a large and powerful army, which also accorded in other ways with the needs of the Imperial Government. The social basis of the Empire was agrarian and aristocratic. Over the centuries the subject peoples—Czechs, Magyars, Serbs and the like—had been battered into subjection, converted to Catholicism, and their leaders, the native nobility, uprooted to be turned into officers, diplomats and courtiers at Vienna. A sprinkling of the new wealth of Europe, together with the presence of so many aristocrats, gave Vienna a gay and luxuriant culture reflected in its splendid Baroque buildings of Fischer von Erlach and Donner and the italianate operas of Metastasio.

The vast army and brilliant Court life were deceptive. The administration was archaic and the Austrian Government failed to mobilize the riches in material and in population which it controlled. The Dutch and the English had been forced to finance the Austrian armies during the War of the Spanish Succession. In spite of one leader of genius, Eugene of Savoy, and in spite of a proud and brave officer class, the Austrian armies had achieved little. The Archduke Charles had failed miserably in Spain; reinforcements were always too few and too late. Furthermore the Empire had been involved not only in Spain, in Italy and in Germany itself; the Eastern frontier with the Turks also rarely knew peace. The slaughter of the infidel possessed a strong attraction for the Catholic aristocracy of the Empire, and armies, which Marlborough desperately needed, battered themselves against the battle-scarred walls of Belgrade. The gains of the Empire at Rastadt—the rich Bourbon lands of Italy—had, however, been considerable. And Tuscany had been added to them through failure of heirs and, more importantly, the Southern Netherlands, the only part of Charles VI's dominions which could hope to compete in commercial activity with Holland, France, or England. Realizing the intentions of his allies, Charles VI had struggled to prevent the strangulation of the commerce of the Southern Netherlands by the economic clauses of the Barrier Treaty. His dynastic fears and ambitions had in the end overpowered his reluctance, though unwillingly; afterwards he ignored what he could, paid little or no attention to the Dutch complaints and gave every encouragement to his subjects to initiate commercial enterprises that he so desperately needed to increase his wealth. The chief of these was the East India Company of Ostend—a project which George I viewed with equanimity, but Townshend and Walpole with abhorrence.

There were others. He browbeat the Venetians and obtained their consent to the development of Trieste and Fiume in the hope of securing a slice of the Levant trade. He even bought a port on the Coromandel Coast from the Great Mogul. Nevertheless these activities proved to be but pawns in the diplomatic game, means of scaring the English and the Dutch into supporting his dynastic obsessions which were the major preoccupations of his life. Nor were they confined merely to his daughter's succession: the loss of Spain cut him to the quick.

He refused for some years to recognize Philip V as the legitimate King of Spain; and even after the Quadruple Alliance in 1718 had removed that danger to European peace, there were sufficient disagreements to make a renewed conflict between Hapsburg and Bourbon likely. They ranged from the right of inheritance of some small Italian states such as Parma and Piacenza to those farcical issues which trouble the minds of princes: Who had the right to appoint Spanish grandees? Was the Emperor or the King of Spain the head of the Order of the Golden Fleece? To whom did two old tumbledown palaces in Rome belong? As idiotic and personal as these conflicts were, they were dangerous to the security of Europe. The dynastic ambitions of Spain were as great as Charles VI's and far less restrained, and it was only the determined naval actions of his ally, England, which helped him maintain his position in Italy. In 1718 this help was so quickly given because George I needed the Emperor's support for his policy in Northern Europe.

George I wished to extend the territories, power and in-

26

fluence of Hanover. Naturally he expected his new greatness as King of England to further his aims. The Emperor,
however, was not sympathetic to any increase in the powers
of any German prince; the dangers were too obvious, so he
prevaricated about George I's dearest wish—Imperial recognition of his right to the bishoprics of Bremen and Verden
(small but strategically and economically important territories at the mouth of the Elbe). The archaic and cumbersome machinery of the Imperial courts was used to keep
George I in suspense, for the ambitions of Charles VI were
in harmony with the English only in regard to Spain.
Elsewhere their conflict of aims, although unavowed, was
critical for the balance of power. George I was fundamentally
uninterested in the South. He wished to exploit the weakness
of Sweden and break her hold on her German lands. In this
he had the support of Denmark, whose King was only too
willing to be an ally so long as he could re-absorb ducal
Schleswig-Holstein. Stanhope and Sunderland, so insecure
at home, had been all eagerness to please George I and had
ordered Sir John Norris to the Baltic with a fleet sufficient
to intimidate the Swedes. Jacobite dabblings and the warm-
hearted but impotent encouragement of Spain's chief minister, Alberoni, failed to distract George's ambition. The
reluctance of the Dutch infuriated but did not deter him, in
spite of the urgent complaints of his London merchants that
the Dutch, safe in neutrality, would steal their trade. No
sooner were Sweden's ambitions scotched than Peter the
Great jeopardized the balanced security of the Baltic States.
Prussia, George I's ally, feared to use its splendid army of
giants which had become the life-absorbing monomania of
its half-crazed King. Peter offered help to Jacobites, gave a
home to the Duke of Holstein-Gottorp, the deposed heir of
ducal Schleswig-Holstein, who, conveniently enough, was
also a claimant of the Swedish throne. Charles VI viewed
the troubles and perplexities of George I in the North with
complacency and refused to use his influence to restrain
Peter.

Although by strength and by diplomatic skill George I extricated himself from his difficulties and procured a general settlement in 1720, nevertheless his relations with the Emperor were embittered. With the Dutch so hesitant and his Northern allies so unreliable, the need for a close alliance with France seemed imperative. The failure to implement properly the Barrier Treaty, the dilatory and insulting tactics employed to withold recognition of George's territorial claims, were enough to sour the King's attitude to Charles VI and to make him consider an alliance with Austria's greatest enemy, France. There were other aspects, too, of imperial policy which filled British statesmen with disquiet. The Emperor's dynastic preoccupations were matched by his devouring passion for the advancement of his religion. The weakness of France in 1714 gave him the great opportunity to intrigue unhindered in the petty states of Southern Germany and the Rhineland and the conversion of their princes to Catholicism was followed by the steady increase of those Imperial powers which had decayed over the centuries. Naturally this growth in the Emperor's authority frightened the larger and more independent states of Northern Germany. To many it seemed that the menace of the Bourbon's bid for the domination of Europe had only been overcome, after a vast expenditure of blood and treasure, by the doubtful expedient of replacing them by the Hapsburgs.

The realization of this change in the balance of power was more keenly appreciated by the Hanoverian ministers and a few skilled and long practised diplomats than by the uninformed members of the House of Commons. For as long as most of them could remember, friendship and close co-operation with the Empire and the Netherlands had been the foundation of England's European alliances. The growing hostility towards Charles VI, expressed by the King's ministers, was regarded as a further sign of the sycophancy of Sunderland and Stanhope, an attitude which Townshend and Walpole had not been slow to exploit.

These suspicions, however, turned to conviction when rumours of the sacrifices which George I was prepared to make towards Spain filtered through to London and the Commons.

5

THE GREAT Spanish Empire had been partially dismembered by the treaties of Utrecht and Rastadt, an action which both Philip V and Charles VI, the two claimants to the Spanish succession, refused to recognize.[1] The years between 1714 and 1722 had been dominated by a resurgent and vigorous Spanish effort to re-establish her control of her former Italian possessions. This great attempt had been sustained by the will of Elizabeth Farnese, one of the most remarkable women of the century. She was coarse-fibred, insatiable, a bouncing hoyden of a girl who by the lustiness of her appetites had secured the control of her priapic, half-mad husband. Her ambition was simple—principalities for her sons, for they appeared to have little chance of succeeding to the throne of Spain, as Philip V had heirs by his first wife. Naturally the principalities were to be in Italy, for Elizabeth had dynastic claims of her own in Parma, Piacenza and Tuscany, claims that were stronger than those of the House of Hapsburg. Her determination was naturally fostered by a considerable section of the Spanish Court who detested the humiliations of the peace treaties and feared the influence of the French party at Madrid, for France, owing to its own dynastic difficulties, wanted an accommodation between Spain and Austria. The hearts of many Spanish grandees had leapt with exultation when, on her journey to Spain, Elizabeth sent the King's French mistress, Madame d'Ursins, into exile, an action which Philip V (about to exchange an old mistress for a young wife) was not reluctant to confirm.

[1] For Spain see W. Coxe, *The Kings of Spain of the House of Bourbon:* A. Baudrillart, *Phillipe V et la Cour de France,* 5 vols.: Duc de Saint Simon, *Memoires* (ed. A. de Boislisle, Paris, 1918): E. Armstrong, *Elizabeth Farnese,* 2 vols.: S. Harcourt Smith, *Alberoni:* J. O. Mclachlan, *Trade and Peace with Old Spain* (Cambridge 1940): S. Conn, *Gibraltar in British Eighteenth Century Diplomacy* (Yale 1942).

The King of Spain lived close to madness. He was deeply religious and extravagantly lustful, and after a few nights of marriage Elizabeth became an obsession. A woman of strong, coarse, nerveless tastes, she settled unresentfully to her lot. The King's pastimes, no matter how singular, became hers. With him she rose at dawn for endless prayers or the massacre of woodcock or stayed with him in bed, sometimes for weeks at a time, when lust consumed him. When he refused to shave or wash or cut his nails or hair, she shared his animal world. Her gnawing fear was that his cloudy mind would sink into total darkness or that in one of his rare moments of terrifying lucidity he would abdicate his throne. To prevent this she was prepared for any sacrifice no matter how macabre, tolerating even those evenings of boisterous fun, when in the austere galleries of the Escorial, she, with her ladies in waiting, attacked the King, supported by his collection of dwarfs. Dresses were torn, wigs knocked off, hair pulled out, faces scratched in this curious regal play. At times the sport was more vigorous, and the King allowed himself to be a target for dishes hurled by his dwarfs. And at any moment of the night or day she had to be ready for the obsessive, compulsive lust. In this lunatic existence government and diplomacy had to wait—often ambassadors were kept weeks for an answer to their despatches—and it is a remarkable tribute to Elizabeth that Spain pursued a policy of such vigour.[1] For a time she was served by one of the most adroit statesmen of his age, Cardinal Alberoni, whose relation to Elizabeth bore a striking resemblance to Robert Walpole's with Queen Caroline. He, too, developed the latent political ambition of his Queen, leading her to believe that her insight and authority could control the destiny of Spain. With Caroline this was little more than illusion; with Elizabeth, as

[1] Frederick the Great had the highest admiration for Elizabeth. She had 'L'âme fière d'un romain et le courage mâle d'un anglais, la finesse italienne et la vivacité francoise faisaient le caractère de cette grande femme; elle marchait audacieusement à l'accomplissement de ses desseins, inébranlable en ses volontés, et ne se rebutant jamais: rien ne pouvait la surprendre, rien ne pouvait l'arrêter.' 'Histoire de Mon Temps', *Publicationem aus den K. Preussichen Staats archiven* (Leipzig 1879), iv 169.

Alberoni discovered to his cost, illusion became reality, for she coolly sacrificed him to the needs of her diplomacy.

Unfortunately for Elizabeth the force of her policy was vitiated by the weakness of Spain. Alberoni secured reforms against the massive obstinacy and entrenched privileges of the grandees, but they were not enough. Neither her army nor her navy nor even her wealth was commensurate with the Queen's ambition. The Spanish force which landed in Sicily in 1717 to recapture the Italian dominions was quickly cooped up in the island by the crushing blow given by England and her allies at Passaro. Nor could the Spaniards buy allies or mercenaries as easily as England for, vast as the Spanish empire was, its trade was exploited by other powers and it produced scarcely sufficient bullion to maintain the solvency of the Spanish Kings. Defeated in war, Elizabeth was forced to adhere to the Quadruple Alliance by which England and France hoped to secure a general pacification of Europe, but the acceptance of this treaty came only after months of hard bargaining, which demonstrated that the conflict between England and Spain was so violent that war alone could resolve it. The war was delayed for nearly twenty years and the delay was due not only to the dilatory diplomatic habits of the Spanish Court but also to the un-flagging optimism of Walpole and his ambassadors that the conflict could be resolved.

The enmity between England and Spain was focused on two points of conflict—the Spanish trade concessions won by England at Utrecht, known as the *Assientos*, and the possession of Gibraltar and Minorca to which Spain had agreed with the utmost reluctance and only under pressure from France. At first the acquisition of Gibraltar was not regarded by the English as more than a bargaining counter for increased trading privileges in the West Indies. Philip V refused to grant the usual licences for trade. The Spanish got it into their heads that the restoration of the *cédulas* for the Assiento trade could only be tolerated if Gibraltar were returned. George I and Stanhope wished passionately for an accommodation with Spain and neither of them had much use for Gibraltar which they regarded as expensive and profitless. In a rash moment George I promised to restore the Rock to Spain, although after the expense of the war against Spain in 1718 he refused to do so without a *quid pro quo*. The haggling was protracted, and frequently impeded by the French, who were not unwilling to compromise the English by turning tentative offers into positive statements. Unfortunately for George I and Stanhope, Walpole and Townshend, when in opposition, stirred up the Commons to a passionate protest against any concession to Spain about Gibraltar, a protest which frightened Stanhope into adding 'with the consent of Parliament' to his King's letter to Philip V which promised to restore Gibraltar. When Townshend and Walpole came to power, they held that the Spanish King was wilfully misunderstanding England's intentions by his insistence that Gibraltar should be handed back. Walpole and Townshend knew the uproar which such an act would cause in the City and were more determined than the King's late ministers to return Gibraltar only at the price of greatly increased trading privileges.

The privileges which Britain had obtained from Spain at Utrecht had brought little profit—one ship had sailed to the Indies, another, the *Prince Frederick*, had been seized at Santa Cruz during the hostilities in 1717, and that, when Walpole took office in 1721, was the total of the trade carried on under the Assiento agreement. The *Assiento des Negros* had been more extensive and more profitable. Nevertheless the slight returns and the constant obstacles which the Spanish put in the way of this trade, infuriated British merchants and made them feel that they were being cheated of the fruits of English victories under Marlborough. Naturally their coveteous imagination inflated the riches of which they felt themselves deprived. Dreams of wealth denied gave emotional force and moral fervour to their denunciations of Spanish dishonesty and decadence. Every reprisal taken by the Spanish against English piracy was magnified into an act of fiendish Catholic cruelty. In these troubled waters the French happily fished. Eager as the French Government was to avoid a general European war, it was not indifferent to the pickings of diplomacy. Not much, perhaps, can be achieved by diplomatic manoeuvres, but between 1715–40 France was more successful than any other nation had been before or has been since. And this was accomplished by two old priests, one of whom was nearly eighty when he achieved control of the French state.

6

IT IS difficult to imagine the glory of France in the early eighteenth century. At Versailles Louis XIV had created a world of sophisticated aristocratic grandeur. This palace was vaster, more ornate, than any that had been built since the days of Imperial Rome. The canals and fountains, both here and at Marly, were the wonder of the age. French painters and poets constantly harked back in their pictures and their dramas to the glories of the Roman Empire, hinting that in Louis and in France Europe had at last found an equal to the magnificence of Augustus and his Age. The polish of French society was equal to its setting and Englishmen, Germans, Russians, Austrians and Scandinavians felt raw, uncouth and provincial in comparison. It became a mark of gentility to have spent one or two years in France and to be able to speak the French language. As well as endowing aristocratic society with a new art of living, Louis XIV had created a magnificent, well-disciplined army without equal in Europe and perfected a diplomatic system the like of which Europe had never known before. Both had been used relentlessly in the pursuit of fame, dynastic ambition and commercial expansion. The mobilized wealth and power of England, the Empire and the Netherlands had with difficulty thwarted but not defeated France. Louis XIV's grandson sat securely on the throne of Spain, and ruled her scarcely diminished Empire.

A thriving commerce, an exceptionally ingenious and productive craft industry, a hard-working peasantry and a bountiful land were the sources of French strength. Its state-system, corrupt, inefficient, hampered by privilege, was strong by the standards of the time and extracted a larger income than any other European government could wring from its people. This, however, proved inadequate to support the armies of France or pay for the endless wars in which they were involved. Nor were the army and the debts of war the sole burdens of the state. A Court addicted to ostentation and luxury, an aristocracy for whom splendour was a part of existence, and a locust cloud of clerks, advocates, bankers who had battened on every financial transaction, kept the government of France on the edge between solvency and bankruptcy.

The wars of Louis XIV had laid a heavy burden on the provinces of France, a burden, indeed, whose weight was reflected in the grim poverty of their peasantry. Yet a peasant economy is always remarkably resilient. A few years of peace, a few good, but not bumper, harvests and the grim times of malnutrition and toil are soon softened.[1] The appearance of the French people deceived, however, most English travellers, used to a more apparent prosperity and to a more evenly graded wealth. Throughout the century France possessed remarkable strength and the inefficiency of the *ancien régime* has been grossly exaggerated.[2] His greatgrandson, Louis XV, came to the throne when only a sickly child of five. The nobility, many of whom had hated their political impotence during Louis XIV's reign, had reassumed its traditional role at Louis' death, but the system of

[1] A fact which Lady Mary Wortley Montagu noted. In 1739 she writes; 'France is so much improved, it is not to be known to be the same country we passed through twenty years ago . . . instead of pale, yellow faces, wrapped up in blankets, as we saw then, the villages are filled with fresh-coloured lusty peasants, in good cloth and clean linen. It is incredible the air of plenty and content that is over the whole country.' *Letters of Lady Mary Wortley Montagu*, ed. W. Moy Thomas (1893), II, 42-3.

[2] English history text-books have been responsible for giving a totally wrong impression of Louis XIV's reign. He neither failed nor ruined France. He left France richer and more powerful than he found her.

Councils, introduced by the Regent, quickly broke down through sheer incompetence, due largely to an almost insane preoccupation with questions of etiquette.[1]

The Regent, Louis XIV's nephew, the duc d'Orléans, reverted to professional advisers, selected by himself, to conduct diplomacy and finance; he was luckier in the former than the latter for he unwisely selected John Law, a Scotsman much fascinated by the potentiality of state credit. The result was the Mississippi scheme, which proved as wild and disastrous as the South Sea scheme in England which it inspired. Yet the long term effects on France were no more disastrous than those of the South Sea Bubble on England— a peasant and craft economy was basically impervious to the iniquities of high finance. In Dubois, the Regent found a man of consummate skill. The *abbé* was a worldy, cynical priest, ostentatiously loose-living, as befitted the Regent whose friends gave the word *roué* its significance. He was a cultivated man, a great bibliophile—he and Stanhope settled the preliminaries of the Anglo-French alliance in a Dutch bookshop—and exceedingly knowledgeable about the powers and personalities of Europe. Indeed he laid down the broad lines of diplomacy which France was to follow until the death of Fleury in 1743. His aim was, quite simply, to isolate the Empire, not through war or aggressive diplomacy but by breaking its traditional friendship with England and the Netherlands. Alliance with England, however, was not to be purchased by any sacrifice of French ambitions. Alongside with friendship went constant intrigue to play upon the fears of the Dutch that they were being turned into a tool of the English; for Dubois and Fleury well knew that the English would hesitate to plunge into war unless they were certain of the support of the Dutch fleet. In the North, how-

---

[1] One of the most violent storms was raised by Saint Simon, who insisted that the *premier président* of the Paris *Parlement* should doff his hat when addressing a duke as he did when speaking to a prince. The president, however, claimed equality with Dukes and refused. A row of monstrous proportions developed which excluded the consideration of other business. See *Memoires de Saint Simon* (ed. Boislisle, Paris, 1918), XXIX, *passim:* also app. IV, 504-22, L'Affaire du Bonnet.

ever, the situation which faced Dubois was of extreme complexity. Friendship with Peter the Great was essential to France, but Peter was intriguing to place a puppet on the throne of Sweden and he had given refuge to the Duke of Holstein-Gottorp, the ruler deprived of Schleswig by the King of Denmark and George I. George I feared and hated Peter, holding him responsible for his difficulties in the Baltic, and viewed the intrigues of France at Petersburg with distaste.

Conditions were easier in the South, where France was willing to make every effort to keep the Anglo-Spanish conflicts confined to the level of negotiation, for Dubois was wise enough to realize that war with Spain could only enrich England. France, whose influence at the Spanish Court steadily grew, in spite of the periodic alarms inspired by the rash and impetuous Elizabeth, wished to avoid war, at least for a generation, until the increase in her fleet and the fullness of her coffers gave her the chance to break English power in America and the East. Furthermore, England depended on French influence to persuade the reluctant Philip V to confirm the Assiento trading privileges which England had gained in the West Indies and to withstand the Spanish King's insistent demands for the restoration of Minorca and Gibraltar.[1]

Such a policy was not easy to achieve. In most Europeans, and especially in the English, there was a deep-seated distrust, based on envy, of the French; a constant fear that the sublety of French diplomacy would always outsmart the honester, if simpler, English. Also Anglo-French friendship had been the work of Stanhope and Sunderland and was therefore regarded with little favour at first by either Walpole or Townshend. Their suspicions of France's intentions had been sharply aroused by the betrothal of the Infanta of Spain to Louis XV in September 1721. Realizing their

[1] Indeed French influence helped slightly to extend these privileges, see J. Dureng, *Le duc de Bourbon et L'Angleterre* (Paris, 1911), 41. Naturally this helpful attitude was not altruistic; it was most marked when France wanted to allay England's suspicions.

alarm, Dubois acted with consummate tact. After a few months of delay, filled with protests and assurances of the innocence of this family alliance, he demonstrated his honourable sentiments to England by betraying the Pretender. Nothing could have been more opportune for the government of George I. Although the country had begun to recover from the effects of the South Sea Bubble by 1722, there was still much resentment and sufficient political discontent (as the tory victories in the local elections in London demonstrated) for the government to welcome an opportunity to display the treasonable activities of the tories.

This disclosure by Dubois of the secret intelligence which he possessed of Jacobite activity undoubtedly impressed both Townshend and Walpole and helped them to reorientate their attitude to the Anglo-French alliance which previously they had viewed with suspicion if not distaste. But a far more potent factor was at work than either policy or expediency.

Carteret, the heir of Sunderland, had declared himself to be in favour of friendship with the Empire, and thereby reverted to the traditional diplomatic pattern of England's European alliances. He was eager to please. He was well aware of George I's fears of the Czar's ambitions. He regarded a Franco-Russian alliance as likely to cause a breach in Anglo-French relations—indeed George I could hardly regard it as anything but an act of treachery in which his interests had been sacrificed to forward the ambition of France. In 1722, when Carteret, as Secretary of State for the South, began to formulate his policy, the schemes of Dubois of isolating the Empire and of securing the friendship of England seemed doomed to failure. If Carteret could check the Czar and re-establish the balance of power in the Baltic, he would, he thought, secure the absolute confidence of George I and place Walpole and Townshend at a disadvantage. Nor was Carteret playing a lone hand. By his side stood Cadogan. He could rely on the wealth and influence of the Marlboroughs. The relics of Sunderland's faction were entirely his. On the sidelines he possessed much sympathy which was likely to become more demonstrative as he proved his strength. Argyll and Islay as yet were not fully committed to Walpole; the Pulteneys were drifting towards discontent. And he himself was no mean adversary. He had to his credit a brilliant diplomatic triumph—the reconciliation, in 1719, of Sweden and Denmark and the alliance against Russia in 1720. He had strengthened the position of Hanover, and George I, therefore, was not indisposed to view him unfavourably.[1]

Walpole and Townshend as well as the Court had no doubt that he was much their most dangerous rival. They were determined on his defeat; hence any policy initiated by Carteret was viewed by them with suspicion. They searched for its weaknesses. As Carteret leaned towards the Empire, the attractions of a French alliance became ever stronger to Townshend and to Walpole. But for the next two years the struggle for political ascendancy in England was fought not in Parliament but in the chancellories of Europe.

By the time that struggle was resolved Walpole had acquired a wide knowledge of European affairs and had committed himself to a comprehensive foreign policy. As in so many aspects of his career he was led to this by a strange mixture of motives in which personal animosity and a lust for power mingled with sound sense and a grasp of immediate possibilities. The need for Carteret's disgrace drew him into the complex web of European diplomacy from which he was never again able to disentangle himself. How much and how little of that strange world he came to understand is difficult to assess. Yet one thing is certain: he never possessed that mastery of its complex detail which was almost second nature to him in domestic affairs. His greatest weakness was a lack of direct personal experience. Walpole never set foot on foreign soil. The great figures of European diplomacy

[1] Carteret also spoke fluent German and French which some historians have thought a sufficient accomplishment to endear him to George I. He was also witty, voluble, insistently cultured, eager to impress and indefatigable in the parade, if not the exercise, of his abilities, characteristics which can have been no more endearing to George I in his native, than in a foreign, tongue.

were largely unknown to him and he had to rely on the shifting impressions of other men in order to assess their characters. He was equally ignorant of the power, riches, social and military organizations of the countries of Europe, a deficiency which the quick perusal of official memoranda helped to alleviate but could not dispel. It is not surprising, therefore, that his first hesitant steps in the diplomatic world should be guided by the one principle of trying to avoid all commitments, a policy which the French viewed with cynical surprise, and that he should leave to Townshend the formulation of that detailed policy by which Carteret was to be brought to book.

CHAPTER TWO

THE DISGRACE OF CARTERET, 1722-24

SARAH MARLBOROUGH possessed a fiery temper, and enjoyed a grievance; but few of her rages equalled the one provoked by the ministry by their behaviour after Sunderland's death on 19 April 1722. Without consulting either her or the Duke, the Secretaries of State sealed up Sunderland's private study. The Duchess sent for Townshend, for Daniel Pulteney, Sunderland's brother-in-law, and for the house steward; all the ministers were besieged by emissaries insisting that she and the Duke must be represented when any papers were to be inspected or better still that the room should remain sealed until her grandson, the new Earl of Sunderland, returned from abroad. To no avail. The Secretaries, with two witnesses—the Duke of Kingston and Lord Carleton—took what they wanted without showing even the endorsements either to the domestic chaplain or to the steward who were present. The Duchess thought that it was highly remarkable that the Secretaries should leave untouched a whole cabinet full of official papers—indeed they jokingly said that it would provide good entertainment for Sunderland's son when he returned. Sarah, incensed by the whole proceeding, hinted that £1,200 in banknotes was the real quarry of the Secretaries and she dismissed as stuff and nonsense their plea of the need to recover secret service papers. Why, she asked, had no one ever thought of secret service papers when Bolingbroke had been dismissed or when Stanhope or Craggs had died?[1] Perhaps even Sarah may have realized that she was, for once, quite in the wrong when two weeks later the news of a Jacobite plot, involving Lawrence Atterbury, the Bishop of Rochester, was broken to the public.

[1] *Blenheim MSS*, G. Sarah Marlborough's dictated account of these events.

Walpole was cock-a-hoop, yet in no way surprised. Jacobitism obsessed him. He saw it everywhere. Just beyond his grasp the conspirators were at work. Jacobite agents lurked in the most unlikely places. Every suspicion, every hint needed to be tracked down. No informer was too corrupt to believe. Any ne'er-do-well, any cheat or double-crosser was sure of a careful hearing at Chelsea. Money spent on hunting down the peril was never wasted. Year after year Walpole built up a vast web of counter-espionage with his own spies in all the capitals and ports of Europe. The scantier the evidence, the more certain Walpole was; any measure was justified in bringing conspiracy to light. He could cross-examine for hours on end. He could countenance any gaoler's tactics, short of torture, if evidence might be forthcoming. The mere scent of a plot had been sufficient to excite Walpole to a restless, thrusting activity.[1] He pushed himself forward, took decisions without authority, and pursued Atterbury with vindictive hatred.

The ministers were already hot on the trail of the conspirators and their eagerness to obtain Sunderland's papers was due to their fear of a leakage at a delicate moment in their investigation. Only two days after Sunderland's death, they received further confirmation of the plot from Cardinal Dubois who revealed to them the requests for help which the Pretender had made to the Regent of France.

Carteret wrote at once on 25 April to Sir Luke Schaub, his protégé, who was acting as British ambassador in Paris. His solemn and rather breathless despatch stressed the unity of the ministry in the face of this crisis; indeed, he wrote, they were on the point of sending Colonel Charles Churchill to explain to Dubois that the death of Sunderland had not made the slightest change in their friendship towards France;

[1] Anyone who doubts Walpole's obsessional preoccupation with Jacobitism should read through the Cholmondeley (Houghton) Manuscripts: letters from agents in France, Italy, the Austrian Netherlands, etc., are as numerous as the files of reports on Jacobitism in Scotland, the Pretender's intentions to introduce Roman Catholicism, the arming of Jacobites, etc. etc. The whole subject of Jacobitism between 1715 and 1745 needs studying, especially the influence of the fears of Jacobitism on the English government.

now his visit would be doubly opportune for the Cardinal could tell Churchill all he knew.[1] On no account was Schaub to return to London, for such a visit might cause embarrassed comment. Carteret did not realize that the first threads of a skilful web were being spun around him.

Charles Churchill—bastard nephew of Marlborough— was a hard drinking, hard hunting, half-literate friend of Walpole—one of his most devoted and loyal allies. That he should take charge of these delicate negotiations and so thrust Schaub into the background was the beginning of what was to be a long campaign to undermine Carteret's credit and to belittle Schaub—a step which may not have been taken consciously by Walpole but merely on the sound political principle that any matter of importance should if possible, be controlled by oneself or one's friends. The same reason led Townshend and Walpole to pack off Horatio to The Hague on a special mission to the Dutch, although Cadogan had been sent there as ambassador extraordinary the previous year. Cadogan was a friend of Carteret and an old ally of Sunderland so the less limelight he got, the better. Horatio went to warn the Dutch that, as in 1715, their troops might be needed to quell a Jacobite rebellion.[2] The Dutch, however, were soured by recent British policy and with grudging reluctance promised only half the number demanded.[3]

The discovery of this Jacobite plot was singularly opportune. Apart from the chance it gave to Walpole of crushing the Jacobites, it also offered him, as he was quick to realize, excellent political advantages. The restoration of confidence

[1] L. G. Wickham Legg (ed.), *British Diplomatic Instructions 1689-1789*, IV, *France, 1721-7*, 30. 'Nous avons jugé aussy qu'à l'occasion de la mort de my Lord Sunderland, en qui le Cardinal avoit sa plus grande confiance il étoit très à propos de luy dépêcher quelque personne, pour luy dire de bouche de la part de my Lord Townshend, de Mr Walpole, et de la mienne, que les ministres du Roy sont entierement d'accord: et que nonobstant les disputes et contrarietez qu'il y a eües entre nous, c'est la ferme intention de tous de suivres les maximes des Comtes de Sunderland et Stanhope par rapport à la France et au Cardinal . . .'

[2] Horatio Walpole had left for The Hague by 3 May 1722 when Townshend wrote to him enclosing a copy of the information which he had received from Dubois on 2 May. See *Walpole MSS*, Letters to Lord Townshend, 1722-5. His letters of credence were sent on 4 May.

[3] *Ibid.*

after the South Sea Bubble had proved far easier than the removal of a sense of grievance in the losers. A bankrupt's rancour takes a long time to disappear, particularly when other men's chicanery has been as instrumental as one's own stupidity. Naturally enough the Jacobite agents magnified these discontents to the Pretender and urged him to exploit them by invasion. The Bubble crisis itself had blown up too quickly for the English Jacobites so they planned for an uprising to coincide with the general election of 1722.[1] Even this proved beyond their capacity. The plot had been once more postponed to the time of the King's expected visit to Hanover in the summer of 1722, when Walpole struck. At once he set about making the most of it; indeed he made almost too much of it and was in danger of over-playing his hand.

The nation was informed of the conspiracy on 8 May by a letter from Townshend to the Lord Mayor of London. The next day all papists and non-jurors were ordered from the city. And then the troops—thousands of them—marched in, setting up a great military camp in Hyde Park, where they remained for the summer giving an air of suspense and excitement to the capital. The gravity of the situation was further underlined by the cancellation of the King's visit to Hanover; and the ministry made great play of the threats of assassination which had been anonymously revealed to the Duchess of Kendal.[2] On 19 May the Reverend George Kelly, the Bishop of Rochester's secretary, was arrested, but he displayed a most unclerical skill in keeping off the King's messengers with his sword whilst he burnt the incriminating evidence in his possession. This mismanagement infuriated Walpole, for it proved a real setback to the investigation. Kelly had to be released. Nevertheless, the conspirators tripped themselves up in spite of an elaborate use of

---

[1] HMC, *Onslow MSS*, 513; Coxe, I, 168-9.
[2] The King was to be killed *en route* for Hanover. Townshend sent a copy of the letter to Horatio Walpole at The Hague but he also expressed great scepticism about the threat: *Walpole MSS*. Townshend to Horatio Walpole, 5 May 1722. A further rumour of a plot to kill the King came from France via Destouches later in the year: Wickham Legg (ed.), *Diplomatic Instructions, France, 1721-7*, 31.

fictitious names and cyphers—the break was provided by a little spotted dog called Harlequin, about whose injuries and movements everyone was willing to sign confessions, either forgetting or being ignorant, that the dog had been referred to in the treasonable correspondence. Harlequin had been sent as a present to Atterbury's wife from France; once established, this proved that *Jones* and *Illingworth* were cover names for Atterbury. A good step forward, but not con-clusive, for the letters even *en clair* hinted rather than revealed treason, and Walpole was very worried that he might not uncover enough. 'We fox-hunters,' he wrote to Horatio, 'know that we do not always find every fox that we crosse upon.' He knew the important part this plot could play in fixing the new ministry with the King, with Parliament and with the public. He was loath to see it fade away. In spite of the scepticism of both Townshend and Carteret he remained convinced that the Pretender intended to invade with Spanish help.[1] That scent, at least, proved a red herring.

The hot summer months, enlivened here and there by portentous thunderstorms, passed in endless interrogations at the Cockpit. Over and over again the Committee of the Council with Walpole in the lead bullied, threatened and cajoled the riff-raff of conspiracy—the lodging-house keepers, the drifting ne'er-do-wells eager to pick up a guinea as a courier, and the double-crossers and informers who hoped to butter their bread on both sides. And yet it was all to little purpose until a suspect called Plunket thought fit to save his own skin by turning King's evidence. What he had to say was sufficient to damn a broken-down Norfolk attorney turned barrister, one Christopher Layer, but insufficient, much to Walpole's annoyance, to arraign Atterbury accor-ding to the due processes of the law.[2]

Kelly, Layer, Atterbury, Lord Grey and North and Lord Orrery were all incarcerated in the Tower by the end of September in readiness for the meeting of Parliament. Layer

<hr/>

[1] Coxe, II, 220-2. RW.'s report on the plot sent to Horatio.
[2] For Layer see R. W. Ketton-Cremer, *A Norfolk Gallery* (1948), 125-48.

was clapped in irons, placed in solitary confinement and constantly interrogated. Atterbury and his brother peers were closely confined and subjected to harsh treatment. Atterbury, in particular, was denied the amenities which were usually granted to a peer of the realm imprisoned in the Tower. Atterbury, however, a strong, violent character, was not easily bullied. He complained to Townshend, complained to the House of Lords and on one occasion lost his temper so effectively that he knocked down General Williamson, the Deputy Lieutenant of the Tower.

Atterbury, a man of great intelligence and immense force of character, had ruined his career by constant aggression. He lacked all judgment and he had begun, after 1714, to live out his restless ambition in the delusive dreams of conspiracy.[1] If ever James were to return he might become Archbishop of Canterbury, otherwise Rochester would remain his portion to the end of his days. Unbalanced though he was, outspoken and truculent toryism had won him the devotion not only of like-minded clerics in the Universities but also of London's discontented working people. He had through his life and sermons become a symbol of protest. When the ministry rushed him to the Tower sympathetic mobs surged about his carriage; shortly afterwards he was being publically prayed for in the churches of London.[2] He had to be brought to book, but it was not easy.

The evidence that he had dabbled in treason, though strong, was insufficient to secure his certain condemnation by the usual processes of law. Neither Townshend nor Carteret felt that they could leave anything to chance and Walpole himself was determined not to do so. The imprisonment of Atterbury became very rigorous and on one

[1] For Atterbury see *The Official Diary of Lieutenant-General Williamson*, ed. J. C. Fox, 34-43, 141-58: H. C. Beeching, *Francis Atterbury*, 276-307: Coxe, II, 220-51: PRO, *SP Dom.*, 45: C(H) MSS, 69. These are Walpole's files of the papers used by the Commons' Committee for their Report of 1 March 1723 (printed in *Reports of the House of Commons*, 1715-35, I, 100-350). They contain, however, some papers not printed in the *Reports*.

[2] A. J. Henderson, *London and National Government, 1721-42* (Duke University, 1945), 72.

occasion Walpole had him peremptorily searched by Williamson without the least authority for his act—a fact which Atterbury quickly seized on and protested vociferously to the House of Lords. Williamson just escaped arrest on a charge of breach of privilege. Townshend quickly came to Walpole's rescue and gave him a post-dated authority for his action. In spite of searches and close confinement no more incriminating evidence was discovered; and Atterbury skilfully exploited the rigours of his treatment and the blundering earnestness of his gaoler to blacken the character of the ministry and to arouse sympathy for himself.

Walpole, however, took a serious view of the threatened rebellion, both from conviction and from political necessity. He always feared invasion. Throughout his life he regarded Jacobite activities as one of the most serious threats to the stability of the regime. And his letters to Horatio, in which there was no need to dissimulate, betray that fear. Even so, there was a certain ostentation about the ministry's acts to preserve the safety of the realm, and a ferocity which the situation did not demand. It would seem that Walpole and the ministry had lost all sense of proportion. The troops were kept in Hyde Park long after the necessity for their presence had passed, even if it had ever existed. When Parliament met, Walpole, refusing to realize that the crisis had not materialized, demanded two acts which the situation did not require, one being the suspension of the Habeas Corpus Act, the other the imposition of a fine of £100,000 on the Roman Catholics in order to pay the expenses which the conspiracy had inflicted on the government. Neither bill was popular and both were thought by many to be excessive and the latter vindictive. Walpole, however, was determined and the bills became law.[1]

---

[1] *Brabourne MSS*, Diary of Sir Edward Knatchbull, Bt. fo. 40. Many whigs opposed these bills, particularly that against the Catholics. Knatchbull was summoned from Kent for the third reading but had not sufficient time to get back to the House. Those whigs who voted against the Court had their names ostentatiously taken down. Knatchbull's diary is invaluable for the period 1722-30 and deserves publication.

No sooner had the parliamentary session opened than the Duke of Norfolk was apprehended and sent to join his fellow Jacobites in the Tower; then Layer was, at last, arraigned for treason. A pitifully silly tale unfolded of clandestine visits to Rome; puerile treachery in ale-houses; attempts to weaken the loyalty of drink-sodden soldiers; boastful hints and loose talk. Such were the highlights of Layer's treason and for such he was found guilty and condemned in the law's fulsome and majestic phrases to be drawn on a hurdle, hanged, castrated, disembowelled, beheaded and quartered.

Layer believed that he had been tricked. During the investigations by the Lords of the Committee he had been told by Walpole and others that nothing he said would be used against him. Two under-secretaries had nevertheless taken minutes which were used at his trial.[1] Still, he pinned his hope on the promise of Walpole and the rest that they would intercede with the King and he wrote with measured dignity to Walpole protesting at the betrayal of trust and recalling the promise of mercy.[2] The mercy he obtained was the mercy a playful and tireless cat displays to its victim. Layer's execution was delayed time and time again, but that was all the mercy he knew, for he was closely confined and kept in irons. His spirit did not break and the ministry gained no further information. On 17 May 1723, he was, at last, delivered over for execution. The more barbarous details were remitted but his head festooned Temple Bar until a gale blew it down a generation later.[3]

For the rest Walpole was reluctantly forced to admit a deficiency of evidence. There was no possibility of making Atterbury a martyr; even Kelly and Plunket could not be brought to book and made to suffer as Layer had suffered. So the ministry proceeded by the somewhat old-fashioned

[1] Walpole's copy of these minutes is C(H) MSS, Papers 69/3.45.
[2] C(H) MSS; Christopher Layer, 27 November 1723.
[3] It was picked up by Dr Richard Rawlinson, the Oxford antiquary, who became so enamoured of it that he kept the skull on his desk and was buried with it in his right hand, see Ketton-Cremer, op. cit., 148.

and suspect method of a bill of pains and penalties. Although Atterbury conducted his own defence with truculent skill, the verdict was foregone. He was banished, while Kelly and Plunket were imprisoned for life.[1] On 18 June 1723, Williamson escorted Atterbury to a waiting man-of-war and watched, to his infinite relief, the ship spread its sail and gather way towards France. There was no disturbance; only the Duke of Wharton, a recent convert to Jacobitism, turned up to wish the Bishop 'Godspeed' and in Walpole's account of this to Townshend there is a hint of disappointment.[2] He was far from satisfied. He could never shake off the feeling that he had missed a chance and had failed to ferret out the evidence which would have made crystal clear the desperate designs upon which he believed the Bishop was engaged. Until Atterbury died in 1729, Walpole spent lavishly on spies and stoolpigeons to report every movement of the Bishop. At his death he attempted to seize his papers, but in the end the evidence still eluded him.[3]

[1] Plunket died in the Tower in 1738; Kelly escaped in 1736 to become one of the seven men of Moidart who landed with the Young Pretender in the '45.

[2] Coxe, I, 171. There is one small matter in the relationship between Atterbury and Walpole to which reference must be made. H. C. Beeching, *Atterbury*, 278-9, accepts the statement of Morice, Atterbury's son-in-law, made later, that Walpole offered Atterbury, in May 1722, the see of Winchester if he promised to give up his Jacobite sentiments and join the Walpole group. The fact that Walpole openly visited Atterbury about 19 May 1722 (HMC, *Portland MSS*, VII, 324) cannot be regarded as contributory evidence. They met many times during the summer, before Atterbury's arrest on 24 August, to discuss matters arising out of the death of the receiver of the funds of Westminster Abbey (see Beeching, 325-6: Coxe, II, 223-4).

Atterbury's restless, ambitious character was not likely to make him attractive to Walpole. Atterbury was always eager to blacken Walpole's character and not nice in his methods (cf. his suggestion [Coxe, II, 226-8] that Walpole planned to bring in the Pretender after the death of George I), and, unless other evidence is forthcoming, the story must be regarded with suspicion. On the other hand, there can be little doubt that Sunderland had been in close negotiation with Atterbury before his death; in addition to the evidence quoted in *Walpole*, I, 365, the Princess of Wales also knew of Sunderland's intrigues and sent a prompt warning of them to Sir Joseph Jekyll, *via* Mrs Clayton: Royal Archives, Windsor, *Geo. Add. MSS. 28*.

[3] Walpole sent John Macky to the Austrian Netherlands on the pretence of buying pictures to organize the interception of Jacobite correspondence. The chief agent became Jaupain, the postmaster of Louvain, who sent Walpole a great deal of Jacobite material. The need to obtain Atterbury's correspondence is frequently stressed in the personal and secret correspondence between Jaupain and Walpole which Walpole carefully endorsed and preserved.

In the handling of Atterbury's plot, the ministry proved itself both ruthless and efficient. The treatment of Layer contains a deliberate brutality, difficult to condone, yet by the low standards of the time, the treatment of these conspirators was neither inhumane nor ungenerous. Knowing the subsequent course of events it is difficult to give due weight to the fears and anxieties which beset the men who ruled. They had grown up amidst threats of assassination, plots and invasion and as they learned their country's history they read of a singularly bloody tale of violence, civil war and executions without justice. By 1722, there had been one invasion and another attempted invasion in the first seven years of the King's reign, and the deep shock of the South Sea crisis had done little to encourage a sense of stability and solidarity. The evidence, although scant, would have been sufficient for the Stuarts to use the block, and the solitary execution of Layer argues in the Hanoverians and their ministers either a deeper sense of security or a greater humanity, most probably the former for they could not help but know that on broad issues of political and religious sentiment they and the majority of their subjects were at one, a situation never enjoyed by any Stuart but Queen Anne.

2

EVEN DURING the months of the Atterbury plot the harmony of the ministry had been more apparent than real.[1] In the days following Sunderland's death Carteret had written ardently, and probably sincerely, to his emissary in Paris, Sir Luke Schaub, of the need for unity at Court.[2]

Jaupain's letters are, of course, in French. See C(H) MSS; Correspondence for 1723 and 1724, letters of J. Macky and Jaupain. Jaupain's letters are very numerous, no translations exist for them, and the presumption must be that Walpole could read them without difficulty.

[1] HMC, Polwarth MSS, 250. 'If some are to be credited, the ministers, tho' well in appearance, are not intirely one, for, say they, the plot keeps them together more than they would be otherwise, being embarked in the discovery they must hold hard to one another.'

[2] Cf. supra, p. 41.

Walpole remained suspicious. He had never forgotton the great betrayal of 1717. His instinct for reality told him that Carteret would make a bid to secure George I's favour at the expense of himself and Townshend. He also knew that the prospect of Carteret's success would rally to his side the Lord Chancellor and Lord Berkeley and their clients, defections which might jeopardize Walpole's own position.[1] Cadogan was an avowed enemy; Argyll and Islay, dubious allies, secure for the moment but never dependable. And the Germans—particularly Bernstorff and Bothmar—always made Walpole acutely anxious. In the early summer of 1723 Walpole became uneasy about the future. He felt that he and Townshend needed some signal mark of the King's approval; without it, they might fail to rally the neutrals and, without a plot, the next Parliamentary session might run into serious trouble. Perhaps it was this sense of uncertainty which made him turn with such obvious delight to his new converts—the Duke of Newcastle and his brother, Henry Pelham.

Until Sunderland's death, no one had been more devoted to him than Thomas Pelham-Holles, Duke of Newcastle, a man who found it easy, and necessary, to adore authority.[2] Sometime between April 1722 and June 1723, Newcastle turned his coat. The same enthusiastic, adolescent adulation which he had shown to Sunderland and Carteret was offered to Walpole and Townshend, particularly to Walpole, who not only accepted it with alacrity but responded warmly to the Duke's devotion. His letters to Newcastle glow with a gay affection which makes a remarkable contrast to his usually dry and austere style.[3] No matter how secret the letters might be which passed between Townshend and Walpole, they were never kept from the Duke. Newcastle was nearly drunk

[1] BM *Add MSS*, 32,686, fos. 300-1: Coxe, II, 276. Berkeley was First Lord of the Admiralty 1717-27: he had replaced Orford, Walpole's patron, at the time of the Whig split in 1717. The Lord Chancellor, from 1718-25, was Thomas Parker, Earl of Macclesfield, another Sunderland nomination.

[2] For Newcastle see S. H. Nulle, *Thomas Pelham-Holles, Duke of Newcastle. His Early Political Career, 1693-1724* (Philadelphia, 1931).

[3] These are scattered throughout BM *Add MSS*, 32,686-7.

with delight. And well he might be, for this outburst of mutual adulation had a basis more solid than sentiment. If Carteret were to be removed from his Secretaryship of State, his seals would go to Newcastle. Also, at the first opportunity his brother, Henry Pelham, was to become Secretary-at-War. And in return the solid little block of Members of Parliament who owed their seats to Newcastle would be at Walpole's service. The acquisition of Newcastle as an ally strengthened Walpole's position both in the Lords and in the Commons. It was, however, quickly assimilated and it did not dispel the fear and anxiety which Carteret's close proximity to the King inspired, and which were intensified by two small victories for Carteret.

In the flush of triumph over Atterbury, Walpole had over-estimated his strength. He attempted in January 1723 to get Carteret removed, and he failed.[1] The King would not hear of it. In June, he learned that George I, eager to get to Hanover, after his absence the previous year, intended to take with him not only two mistresses but two Secretaries of State—Carteret as well as Townshend. The Northern powers, amongst which Hanover was counted, were the province of Townshend; the Southern belonged to Carteret. And usually the Southern Secretary stayed at home. Carteret, however, remembered the ease with which Townshend had been outmanoeuvred by Stanhope in 1717 and soon discovered excellent grounds for his presence at Hanover. France was intriguing with the Czar; the Czar was threatening to invade Sweden; the Empire was at logger-heads with Spain; the congress of Cambrai, which was about to meet, was likely to raise many more issues than it was likely to settle. Hanover would be the diplomatic *schwerpunkt* of Europe, where Southern as well as Northern problems would have to be solved. There was an obvious need for the presence of both secretaries and Carteret went.

[1] *Arch. Aff. Etr., Corr. Angl.*, 344, fos. 16-18, Destouches to Dubois, 7 Jan. 1723. Destouches reported that Pulteney was to replace Carteret in this scheme. He may have been mistaken; if true, it would imply that the Newcastle-Walpole alliance had not been formed by that date.

Walpole's anxiety grew obsessive; every letter to Townshend or Newcastle betrays the fear which haunted his imagination.

Although Walpole could not bring himself to realize it, his political position was exceptionally strong. He had triumphed over his enemies; his rivals had dropped dead; he had secured Argyll and Newcastle; he dominatèd the Commons; he was a master at business. Knowing this, it is fatefully easy now to overestimate his security. What Walpole did not know, (and the political world shared his ignorance) was whether or not he and Townshend enjoyed the absolute support of the King. So far no important or unmistakable gesture of royal approval had been made on their behalf; death, not disgrace, had cleared the ground of their enemies. They had won, through strength and ferocity, high stations for themselves and their friends; so far, so good, but it was not enough. They needed, at least Walpole felt that they did, an overt act of royal approval, and no act other than the disgrace of their chief rival would be overt enough for Walpole.[1]

Townshend and Walpole were rightly uneasy about Carteret. He was young, brilliant, with an excellent command of French and—sinisterly—German; a man of fine breeding and lofty ambitions, whose recent successes had dispelled his natural indolence. Later, defeat, and the passing years, led him to find consolation in burgundy, the classics, and heartsore epigrams, but in 1723 the world was before him and Europe beckoned him to solve its problems, an enterprise which he felt to be worthy of his quality. With serene arrogance he despised the political methods of his day and enjoyed too loudly a jeer at Walpole and Townshend's preoccupations. His lofty, overbearing manner, his sense of power and love for a peremptory decision, were dangerous not only for himself but also, as Walpole was aware, for his country. Walpole was willing to admit his own lack of knowledge of the complexities of European diplomacy but he knew, as few did,

[1] Walpole's letters to Townshend revert time and again to their need for a public mark of favour, see Coxe, II, 251-95.

I. ROBERT WALPOLE

II. THE MARBLE PARLOUR, HOUGHTON HALL, NORFOLK

what the Commons would, and would not, tolerate. Walpole wished to keep clear, as far as possible, of all commitments. A waiting, patient, hesitant policy seemed to him infinitely desirable—hard enough in all conscience to obtain from Townshend, impossible from Carteret. In Walpole's mind public need and personal desire combined to make Carteret's removal a necessity.[1] The danger, Walpole thought, was that Carteret might bring off a successful diplomatic *coup* and so win the King's heart. Townshend, on the other hand, never had the slightest doubt that he possessed the King's confidence to the full and that he would not have much trouble in outwitting Carteret or any of his allies, if they were foolish enough to commit themselves. Townshend enjoyed a sanguine temperament.

Always a prey to anxiety, Walpole was far less sure, and the slightest, the most unreliable, rumour made him dither with apprehension. Naturally he seized the slightest chance to disparage Carteret and his friends in the King's eyes. So obsessive was his anxiety that it betrayed him into a rash action that appalled Townshend.[2] In June 1722 the great Duke of Marlborough, who had been stricken with palsy for many years, died at last—an event for which Cadogan, friend and associate of Carteret, had long been waiting. Confident of his military eminence and secure in the knowledge that the King admired him, Cadogan confidently expected the great offices which Marlborough had held,

[1] Coxe, II, 263, Walpole to Townshend, 23 July 1723. 'In a word my politics are to keep free from all engagements as long as we possibly can. You'll forgive my sudden, and possibly very improper, thoughts upon a subject that I am but little acquainted with: but I am mightily inclined to caution', and BM *Add MSS* 32,686, fo. 285, RW to Newcastle, 25 July 1723, when sending on to the Duke a copy of the above quoted letter. 'But notwithstanding what I wrote in publick I own my apprehensions are great upon this occasion, and if an emulation or endeavour to outvye one another should transport us into any dark engagements I dread the consequences, which made me write in the manner I did, and if I had not been afraid of displeasing Lord Townshend at this distance in a point where I do not know his way of thinking, I should have inlarged a great deal more upon the topick of caution.'

[2] Coxe's account of 'this incident (Coxe, I, 188–9) is quite misleading and he suppressed a number of passages in the letters which he quotes from the Hardwicke papers (now BM *Stowe MSS*, 251) which underline Walpole's mistakes.

including the rare and singular title of 'Captain-General'.
Much to Walpole's annoyance he began to act in accordance
with his pretensions. He decided to muster the troops for
six instead of the three months which Walpole had agreed
with the King, and that meant additional expense. Walpole
persuaded the Lords Justices to refuse permission, wrote
sharply to the Secretary at War, and complained bitterly to
the King of Cadogan's behaviour.[1] At the same time the
Guards' regiments had become extremely annoyed by
Cadogan's issuing orders to them. Their commanding
officers roundly declared that they took no orders except from
the King. Walpole supported their protestations warmly.
Naturally Cadogan wrote a furious letter to Carteret.
Fortunately Townshend was able to take control of what
might have become an ugly situation and one detrimental to
their interest. The King, who usually was most sensitive on all
army matters, remained unmoved, and so displayed the great
confidence which he placed in their judgment, a confidence
which ought to have allayed Walpole's anxiety at once.
Townshend wrote to Walpole on 29 June 1723 N.S.:

'As soon as I received your letters I took care to be
first with the King whom I found entirely in the sentiments you could wish in relations to matters in dispute.[2]

His Majesty however thinks you are under a mistake
in one part of your letter in relation to the Horse Guards
and Grenadiers which he had above a year ago put under
the care and inspection of my Lord Cadogan in the same
manner as the other regiments of the army; at my coming
out from the King I found Lord Carteret in the outer
room who had received a thundering letter of complaint
from Lord Cadogan which he shewed me, and exclaimed
prodigiously against the treatment my Lord had met with.
I sayd a little towards convincing him of his error and
foretold him in some degree that the King would say to him
on that subject. He gave no attention to what I sayd, but
insisted I should go in a long with him. After having read

[1] BM *Stowe MSS*, 251, fos. 2–4.
[2] This was the question of the muster.

Lord Cadogan's letter to the King he began with making remarks on the strongest parts of your letter to the Secretary at War (of which Lord Cadogan had sent him a copy) but the King cut him short by taking all the harshest part of it on himself and saying that you did it by his express order. My Lord then would have insisted how unkind it was in you not to have given Lord Cadogan notice of this before you sent your letter to the Secretary at War, to which the King himself answered that in that also you had obeyed his orders, and thinking Lord Cadogan was at that time at Greenwich. Lord Carteret then finding that no good was to be done for his friend did, according to his usual method of proceeding, think everything very right that had been done, and when we came out, told me, that when people could be guilty of such extravagancys and blunders they could not take it ill if they were no better supported.

My good Lord is just the same man here as he was with you in England, running about and making the most servile court to man, woman and child, but hitherto without any sort of success that I can percieve.'[1]

But he begged Walpole to have no more scuffles with Cadogan about the Horse Guards. Unfortunately Walpole was too obsessed with the enormities of Cadogan, or too committed to his friends in the Horse Guards, and the next batch of letters from England raised the issue again in a slightly different form. Townshend again tried to pass this off as a minor matter and again succeeded, but Carteret now realized that Cadogan had only to stick to his pretensions and he and not Walpole would win. As he left the audience chamber he told Townshend: 'I always thought they would get a rapp over the knuckles for pretending to exempt the Guards from command.' Townshend was well aware that Carteret was right. He and Walpole had been very lucky indeed to extricate themselves so easily from a position which might have rebounded to their disadvantage. Their luck could not hold for ever, so Townshend bluntly asked Walpole

[1] BM *Stowe MSS*, 251, fos. 3-4.

that he 'might not be put under the like difficultys again by
pretending to dictate to the King in a point relating to the
government of the army which he would never bear to be
controlled in, neither in this country nor England and if you
were as well convinced, as everybody here is, of the strength
which our interest daily gains, I am sure you would agree
with me in opinion that it is no more necessary than proper
to put it to such sort of trials . . .'[1]

Although this may seem a trivial matter, it is indicative
of the desperate tension at Court and of the enormous, if
unreal, fears with which Walpole was beset during the
summer and autumn months. Although posterity has seen
him as firmly settled in the saddle by 1723, he himself expected to be thrown at any moment. The obsessional nature
of his anxiety is apparent from the fact that no sooner had the
worries about Cadogan subsided than a new phantom made
him tremble: the rumour ran that Carteret was to bring over
to England the Countess von Platen, the King's Roman
Catholic mistress, a rumour which, as it was quite baseless,
infuriated Carteret. When solemnly repeated by Walpole,
Townshend, too, was vastly irritated and snapped at Walpole.
Fears, however, luxuriated like weeds in Walpole's fertile
mind. Again he wrote urgently to Townshend: Carteret was
to be ambassador in Paris, already a house was being bought.
Once more Townshend had to allay Walpole's anxiety. Indeed, during these months it was Townshend who was carrying Walpole, laughing at his fears and boldly planning, not
only for himself but for Walpole too.

'And I am satisfied that the surest way to continue
things here on the present good foot, and to put our
credit with the King past all danger of competition or
accidents, will be to form a good scheme for the next
session, by falling on some new expedient for the ease of

---

[1] BM *Stowe MSS*, 251, fos. 17-23, and Townshend added as a postscript, 'Our
friend the *maréchal* who is here bids me tell you that provided you throw no more
rubbs in the way about Guards, *Nous nous moquons de toute ce qu'ils nous peuvent
faire*'. If Walpole did not understand French, this postscript is a curiously insulting one for a brother-in-law and close friend to write.

the nation, and the benefit of trade and credit, which points, his majesty has so much at heart, that the succeeding in them will infallibly rivet us in his esteem, and give us a greater advantage over our adversaries, than can be hoped for from carrying any particular point against any of them. For this reason I beg of you to turn your thoughts as early as you can towards bringing the supplies of the next year within two shillings in the pound,[1] and the malt; and I submit it to your consideration, whether the uniting the South Sea and East India companys, and the easing our East India trade in some such manner as I hinted in my last, would not be very popular, and at the same time divert any ill humour which may be stirring in the parliament, if they have not some such useful point to employ themselves upon.'[2]

If Townshend hoped to turn Walpole's obsessions away from Hanover, he was unsuccessful. Although he took Townshend's advice, and began to plan a programme for the next session on the lines which Townshend had suggested, he and Newcastle waited impatiently for the special couriers who sped between the two Courts. Walpole hungrily devoured their despatches, relaxed for a time in Townshend's confident optimism, and then fell once more a prey to his anxieties as a fresh rumour of Carteret's favour settled like a blight on his uneasy temperament. It is time to turn to the battle which Townshend fought with such brilliance.

3

THE MAJOR difficulty for British diplomacy was to interpret correctly the intentions of the Czar. The rumour ran that he was about to attack Sweden, depose its King, and place his own nominee on the throne. This was to be followed by the recovery of Schleswig-Holstein for his relation, the Duke of Holstein-Gottorp. Naturally the pro-German poli-

---

[1] i.e., the Land Tax.
[2] BM *Stowe MSS*, 251, fo. 257, Townshend, 28 July 1723. Townshend's interest in the East India Company arose from the fact that his son and heir had married the daughter of Governor Harrison, a leading East India merchant.

57

ticians of Sweden were highly alarmed. So was the King of Denmark. The former asked impatiently for money, the latter for ships. George I and his Hanoverian advisers had always feared Peter the Great's designs in the Baltic and their fear was intensified when they discovered that France was trying to negotiate a separate treaty with Russia. France, more concerned to isolate the Empire than placate England, seemed quite prepared to jeopardize the Anglo-French alliance in return for the friendship of the Czar. How was war to be avoided in the Baltic? How was a separate Franco-Russian treaty to be circumvented. Carteret's answer, designed to pander to George I's well-known fears, was to act forcibly—large subsidies to strengthen the Swedish senate's will to resist; mobilization of a British squadron for Baltic service. Their policy was warmly sponsored by Bernstorff in the closet and by the Countess von Platen in the boudoir. And rumours of Carteret's new favour and bold ideas were soon harrying Walpole's nerves. Townshend kept his head and refused to be rushed. He realized that, though prompt and warlike measures might please the King, they would enrage Parliament. He refused to spend a penny until the need arose, but he urged Walpole to have £200,000 ready, in case of need, and then set his face firmly against mobilization.

England must be driven into war by actions of the Czar, not rushed into it by rumours. This policy received the support of Hatorff in the closet and of the Duchess of Kendal in bed. These were the problems and these the protagonists at Herrenhausen.[1]

The Czar let Carteret down. He and Bernstorff had confidently announced that the Russian invasion fleet had sailed. Townshend refused to be ruffled, although the in-

---

[1] For the above paragraph and for the rest of this section the following books and manuscripts have been used; J. Dureng, *op. cit.*, 73-169; Wickham Legg (ed.), *Diplomatic Instructions, France, 1721-7*, 47-57; Coxe HW; Comte St Baillon, *Horace Walpole à la Cour de France* (Paris 1867): *Walpole MSS* which contain many diplomatic instructions not given in Legg; BM *Add MSS*, 22,517, 32,738: *Stowe MSS*, 247, 251: PRO *SP Regencies; France*, 179: Arch. Aff. Etr., Corr. Angl.; *Townshend MSS*, Raynham. Townshend had won the friendship of the Duchess of Kendal—as usual, through her pocket.

telligence which they quoted sounded convincing. Before any action was taken, or a penny spent, Townshend insisted on absolute certainty. He argued this policy with the King, against Carteret, and won. The days passed and turned into weeks and still the invasion did not materialize. The lead had passed to Townshend. The threat of the invasion of Sweden had, however, frightened the King of Prussia—a change of wind which Townshend quickly realized could be exploited to his own advantage. But before he could do so, Carteret suffered a more grievous blow.

For many months Dubois had been in monstrous pain from an ulcerated bladder. Terror kept him from the surgeon's knife. At last unendurable agony drove him to submit; the consequence was gangrene, delirium, death and the end of one of the more singular careers of modern times.[1] Carteret had stood well with Dubois, and his client, Sir Luke Schaub, the British representative at Paris, had stood even better. On whom would Orléans now lean? And would Schaub remain *persona grata?* The rumours which reached Townshend were highly gratifying—Orléans was about to recall Nocé, a man whose disgrace Schaub had helped to engineer. In a moment of inspired foresight Townshend saw how he and Walpole could exploit this situation to their own great advantage; but not even Townshend, brilliant, assured, confident as he was, could have guessed that his intrigue would be so astoundingly successful.

Before, however, Townshend could undertake the delicate negotiations which his scheme entailed, there were some immediate public advantages to be gained from the hesitancy which Dubois' death introduced into the conduct of French affairs. Also, a mere negative triumph over Carteret was quite inadequate for Townshend's purpose and his waiting policy towards the Czar had been that and nothing more.

[1] Father Dubois, having complacently watched the growth of a quite remarkable carnal appetite in his pupil, the duc d'Orléans, made himself indispensable by pandering to the tastes thus awakened. His reward was not only the Premiership of France but also a Cardinal's hat. He deserved the former as much as he disgraced the latter.

So, he sent for Chavigny, the French representative at Hanover, and told him roundly that George I was bitterly opposed to a separate treaty between France and Russia which could only be to the Czar's advantage. Then he struck at the heart of the matter. No encouragement, he said, had been given by the English to the Emperor; outstanding differences remained unsettled and George I had refused to listen to those who had proposed a settlement. The threat was quite clear to Chavigny. If France pursued her negotiations with Russia, a rapid rapprochement between England and the Empire, whose isolation was the main goal of French diplomacy, would follow. The interests of George I in the Baltic could not be casually sacrificed by France.[1] Townshend's timing was, of course, perfect: Dubois' death made the Regent and his advisers wish to avoid a crisis. The Franco-Russian treaty remained in abeyance.

This policy was so manifestly in the interests of George I that there was no question of a difference of opinion, except on trivialities, with Carteret. Yet a mere statement of attitude was insufficient for Townshend's purpose and alien to his nature. He loved, from time to time, a really bold stroke. And he went all out for a treaty with the King of Prussia who, alarmed by Peter the Great, was ready enough for a defensive alliance. Quick though Townshend might be to seize a chance, he was not without guile and he related with glee to Walpole the fact that he had got Carteret's name inserted in the commission for negotiating the treaty with Frederick William. George I hated the idea of a state visit to Berlin, for he detested public appearances and he loathed the King of Prussia, and it is an indication of Townshend's favour that he consented to make the journey.[2] The initiative in foreign affairs had passed completely into Townshend's hands and when, in November, the French

[1] Dureng, *op. cit.*, 76–7.
[2] George I overcame his repugnance and left for Berlin early in October. The treaty of Charlottenburg was signed 10 October 1723 (N.S.). It was at Berlin that he had his first intimations of mortality. At dinner in Charlottenburg the King fainted and took some time to recover: BM *Sloane MSS*, 4,204, fo. 325.

formally announced their decision to abandon separate negotiations with Russia, Townshend's triumph was complete. He had avoided war, expense, isolation, preserved the French alliance and acquired a powerful ally. The ruin of Carteret now seemed a matter for timing.

Others were quicker to believe it than Walpole; rumours of Carteret's influence still drained his spirits; shiftier men, however, had sensed the change of wind.[1] The summer and autumn of 1723 brought Walpole some strange visitors. Lechmere, a whig of truculent independence, came to make his peace. He was followed by Kinnoull, a tory, who was willing to pledge his friends as well as himself, a pledge which, to Townshend's great relief, Walpole declined. 'Nothing', he wrote to Walpole, 'can be more dangerous than to enter into negotiations with the tories or even labour under the suspicion of it at this time.'[2] These visitors were followed by more alarming guests—Harcourt and, of all people, Bolingbroke.

It must have been a sweet moment for Walpole to have his old rival sitting at his dinner table and begging for his favour; sweet yet disturbing. Bolingbroke was all charm, eager to help, eager to betray—particularly Carteret. And he spoke not only for himself but for the tories, for Sir William Wyndham and for Gower. Out spilled their secrets and Bolingbroke told how Carteret had pressed them during the previous winter to attack Walpole in the Lords and Commons. Everyone was willing to renounce Jacobitism; everyone eager to leap on Walpole's band waggon. Fulsome flattery, deadly exposures, wild promises poured forth without restraint. This was the Bolingbroke Walpole knew too well and heartily despised. As Walpole quickly saw, it was all too clever by half; the scheme was far too dangerous to touch. He preferred the tories to remain tories, and in the wilderness. Bluntly he told Bolingbroke that he was not interested, and for good measure, pointed out his imprudence in attempting to

[1] Coxe, II, 256.
[2] *Ibid.*, 257.

61

negotiate to bring in tories when he expected his full pardon from a whig parliament.[1] Furthermore, Walpole advised him not to go to Hanover but to return to France. And for the time being Bolingbroke meekly accepted his advice.[2]

Yet the interview worried Walpole, as it worried the friends whom he consulted. He knew that the question of Bolingbroke's future had not been settled by the pardon which had passed the Great Seal in May 1723 and which had quashed the death penalty without restoring either his estates or his seat in the Lords. Bolingbroke was determined to remake his shattered political career. He had already written letters of fulsome thanks to the King and to the Duchess of Kendal and they had been graciously received— a reaction, perhaps, not entirely surprising considering that he had paid the Duchess's niece a bribe of £11,000.[3]

Yet it cannot have been money alone which won her aunt's and the King's support. In their kindly attitude to Bolingbroke[4] there was a hint of malicious resentment at their dependence on Walpole and Townshend, casual rather than deliberate, but meant to humiliate. Walpole was well aware that Bolingbroke's full pardon might create real difficulty with his supporters, and, if obtained, Bolingbroke's charm and his wife's influence with the Duchess could lead to incalculable trouble.[5] But these were Walpole's problems, not Townshend's, who had immediate use for Bolingbroke's weakness for double-dealing.

Townshend had out-jockeyed Carteret in terms of policy. It had been a straight fight; often they went together to the King and argued out their differences in front of him. But both of them had been too long in politics to let matters rest on mere merit. Townshend started to weaken Carteret by

[1] Coxe, II, 257.
[2] Coxe, II, 264-5: BM *Add MSS*, 32,686, fo. 301, RW to Newcastle, 10 August 1723.
[3] Coxe, II, 312.
[4] And it should also be remembered, in extenuation, that Bolingbroke was a great European figure and a man of exceptional social charm, a quality for which neither Walpole nor Townshend was distinguished.
[5] BM *Add MSS*, 32,686, fo. 301.

buying off his German allies for solid cash.[1] Frightened, Carteret secretly summoned Bothmer to Hanover to repair the breach. It proved too late. On the other hand it seemed, in November 1723, that Carteret would bring off the splendid coup which he had long planned for the daughter of the Countess von Platen. The scheme was to marry her into the distinguished French family of Vrillière, for whom a dukedom was to be granted by the Regent of France at the request of George I; but, of course, the King's demand was only to be made when it was known that the Regent would comply with it. This was a gambit for more than prestige; dukedoms in France were desperately difficult to get and to obtain one would underline heavily the great influence of Carteret and Schaub at Versailles, an influence which could not lightly be set aside.

Instinctively, yet with no thought of upsetting the marriage, Townshend had realized that Paris was of far-reaching importance and the core of Carteret's strength. So long as French affairs were in his hands, he could not be dispensed with. Townshend's moment of illumination, after the death of Dubois, was to get George I to send Horatio Walpole on a secret mission to Paris to report on the personal situation created by the Cardinal's death. Originally Townshend had thought of this solely as a prestige manoeuvre. As he wrote to Walpole, although the mission was to be passed off as a private one, yet all the world would comprehend that it was a direct snub to Carteret, and, their interest, especially in France, would be set in a better light. Horatio was either to get Schaub discredited or to win him over and so 'wound them in the most vital and sensible part'. But he was to steer quite clear of the marriage project; at the end of September Townshend thought that it was so certain to take place that they must avoid at all costs seeming to obstruct it.[2]

As Horatio and his brother realized, he was, of course, placed in an exceptionally difficult position, but no sooner

[1] Coxe, II, 267.
[2] Ibid., 267–8.

was he in Paris than Townshend secured proper diplomatic credentials for him, much to the joy of Newcastle and the despair of Carteret.[1] Horatio was quickly off the mark. Within a few days he had summed up the situation at the French Court and written a private despatch which said very much what Townshend expected and wanted to hear. And even better it delighted the King. As Townshend scribbled at the end of his reply: 'You have gained immortal honour with our Master.'[2] Horatio, naturally enough, was eager to get rid of Schaub at the earliest possible moment for he realized that a situation in which there were two ambassadors, one open, the other secret, was bound to become hideously difficult the longer it was protracted. His description of Schaub's character, abilities, and influence was quite damning. Schaub loved intrigue, pursued gallantries, forgot his duties, suppressed his orders, misjudged enemies and friends. He lacked reserve, dignity, commonsense. Reckless and arrogant, he was blind to reality and busy not only digging his own grave, but his country's as well. And there remained his final effrontery—his constant boasting of his and Carteret's influence with George I. According to Schaub, Walpole and Townshend could expect their downfall at any moment. Vain and obtuse as he was, he was all eagerness to help Horatio, unaware for a time that his presence might terminate his career.[3]

Prejudiced Horatio might be, but he possessed some of his brother's shrewdness about the nature of men; he could be baffled, even outwitted, by subtle characters; Schaub, how-

[1] *Walpole MSS*, 'Duke of Newcastle's Despatches', 1723-4, Newcastle to HW., 22 October 1723. 'Upon discoursing the King upon your arrival att Paris and business there, Lord Townshend suggested that a credential from His Majesty would very much facilitate your affairs there and the pretence of the admission of the King of Portugal to the Quadruple Alliance might be a good handle for it. The King gave prodigiously into it and promised to propose it of himself the day after in the presence of Lord Carteret, which he did with so much dexterity that Lord Carteret dared not make any difficulty about it, this, you may imagine was not very pleasing to him. . . .' Also, Coxe, HW, 34.

[2] *Ibid.*, 'Despatches from Lord Townshend', Townshend to HW.

[3] Coxe, HW, 78-9: *Walpole MSS*, Letters to Townshend, 22 March (N.S.) 1724.

ever, was well within his range. Events quickly bore out the justice of Horatio's criticism. In November Schaub reported that the dukedom was a *fait accompli*. If the King formally sent his request, Orléans would comply at once. Letters were drafted. And then an express from Horatio arrived. The French, quite aware of his importance, had secured for him a secret meeting with the Regent. Orléans expressed his difficulties. He wanted to please George I, nothing would give him greater pleasure. He was aware of the deep personal interest which his Majesty took in the Countess von Platen's family. Yet to give the Vrillière family a dukedom would create immense difficulties and outrage the Court. Naturally if the King insisted, it would be done, but he wanted George I to know how awkwardly he was placed. It is odd that Orléans had not spoken earlier, until it is realized that Dubois' death had brought back Nocé to Court, that Nocé loathed Schaub and that Schaub had stupidly failed to realize that this idle, proud, sensual courtier relished his secret influence with Orléans and enjoyed to the full a tortuous revenge. Horatio had grasped at once the vital importance of Nocé who, of course, engineered his interview with Orléans, no doubt engineered it to prick the bubbling optimism of Schaub at the moment when he thought the consummation of his long negotiation was within his grasp.

George I was shocked. He hated difficulties and loathed all events which drew attention to himself.[1] And no King reverenced titles more than he did. Townshend had no difficulty in underlining Schaub's folly and Horatio's wisdom, Carteret's final disgrace was brought a step nearer. Horatio's powers were increased, and for the next few months Britain had two ministers at Versailles. Horatio was driven to distraction. He wailed and complained to Robert, he badgered Townshend. He became ill; gout flew all over him.

[1] He begged foreign powers to send ministers, not ambassadors, to his Court because he hated the ostentatious ceremonial which the reception of an ambassador involved.

He begged to be made sole ambassador or released. In every other despatch he threatened to resign, only to have Townshend and his brother remind him of his duty and implore him to be patient. Schaub was bound to go and, after the disastrous autumn in Hanover, Carteret too; but George would part with neither of them easily. He was, as kings will, exercising his power. He had done most of what had been asked of him, even returning quite early in December from Hanover at the request of Townshend and to the relief of the Duchess of Kendal. And he found it hard to let them enjoy their final victory. Furthermore the sudden death of the duc d'Orléans provided him with a reasonable excuse to keep them on tenterhooks. An immediate change at such a juncture was unthinkable. The weeks dragged by, rendering Horatio almost hysterical with apprehension, which only alarmed his brother and made Townshend short-tempered.[1] As Schaub lingered on at Paris and Carteret remained secretary, Walpole and Townshend and their friends seemed to have reached a frustrating impasse. Their anxiety was intensified by an ugly rearguard action which Carteret had been fighting with a certain skilful efficiency. A strange combination of copper coinage, the Duchess of Kendal, the Lord Chancellor of Ireland and Jonathan Swift created a situation of the utmost difficulty for Walpole and Townshend. This was almost unendurable, for final and complete victory seemed so close at hand.

4

IRELAND IN the eighteenth century was a country of growing self-consciousness, and, curiously enough, confidence. The rebellions, plots, slaughters and massacres of the seventeenth century had battered the native aristocracy into subjection. Certain reliefs from the strong pressure of a growing population on a fundamentally agrarian society were given by emigration to England and the plantations, by

[1] *C(H) MSS*, Horatio Walpole: 15 February and 11 March 1724 (N.S.).

service in the Irish regiments of the French kings and by the cultivation of the potato, which enabled more to live on less. At the same time, what there was of a middle-class was enjoying a mild prosperity owing to the increasing demands in England for Irish primary products—cattle, wool, linen, butter and horses. This prosperity was even more marked amongst the great landowners, who had taken their pickings from Cromwell's and William's wars. The upshot was the growth of a self-conscious, protestant, yet Irish upper class who possessed wealth but only limited political power. The government of Ireland did include many of the leading Anglo-Irish families, but the greatest part of the Irish patronage was used for English political purposes and there was a considerable sense of frustration in the Irish Parliament, which was kept under only by extensive jobbery and resolute action by the Lord Lieutenant and the Chancellor, at this time the Duke of Grafton and Lord Midleton, and their deputies.[1] The new wealth was leading to the embellishment of Dublin; and indeed it provided an interesting and fashionable centre which drew all that was ambitious and vocal in Irish life. Political impotence bred frustration and a sympathetic audience encouraged its expression.

This atmosphere fostered the genius of Jonathan Swift. Luck had run against him and his gifts had never earned the rewards they so richly deserved. Towards the great world, particularly London and the Court, he felt nothing but envy and bitterness. His mood struck a responsive chord in the hearts of many Irishmen. The discontent of Swift and his audience was suddenly fused to create a dangerous political situation by the manufacture of copper coinage by one Wood of Birmingham, under patent. This patent had been

---

[1] Sunderland had increased the power of the resident Irish families, see Coxe, II, 356. Grafton, 19 December 1723: 'Lord Sunderland carried the compliment to this country too far by choosing out of the natives all the chief and most of the other judges, and the bishops too, which has been attended with very mischievous consequences to the English interest.' Boulter, Archbishop of Armagh, voiced the same opinion, see *Letters of Hugh Boulter* (Oxford, 1769), I, 21–3.

granted to the Duchess of Kendal, who had sold her rights at a handsome profit.

It may be said at once that there was nothing irregular in this proceeding in a legal sense; furthermore, Isaac Newton assayed the coinage and demonstrated that the Irish were getting excellent value; the metal used was good and Wood's profit small. Truth, however, was of no importance; the deepest resentments of a subjected people and a satirist of genius were to be aroused. Carteret clutched at this opportunity to discredit his rivals, so golden in appearance, yet deceptive in reality. What was to be his salvation merely completed his ruin.

The origins of the patent are obscure. Townshend thought that Sunderland had arranged it. What is certain is that it passed the Great Seal, with Walpole's approval, on 12 July 1722. The City of Dublin immediately protested but protests from the City of Dublin were common enough; no one paid the least attention. Naturally many months passed before the coins were struck at Birmingham and shipped to Ireland and it was not until September 1723 that criticism grew sharp, bitter and vocal. The Chancellor of Ireland, Lord Midleton, failed to suppress a Parliamentary protest. He and his brother, St. John Brodrick, loathed Walpole. They detested the part which he had played in the South Sea crisis and they viewed with equanimity a situation which might lead to difficulties for him. Strongly worded addresses were allowed to pass both Irish Houses and Midleton was very quick to get in touch with Carteret.[1] Walpole was aware of the traps being laid for him. He knew that the Brodricks had done nothing to soothe the Irish Parliament. He knew also that Carteret supported them.

'You observed,' he wrote to Townshend on 1 October 1723, 'that previous notice was sent of this to Hanover; and surely in a proper time and manner the King may be con-

---

[1] The Chancellor's son, Alan Brodrick, had with singular prescience turned up at Hanover; naturally he took a letter from his father to Carteret, Coxe, II, 272-3.

vinced with whom the Brodericks are linked, and by whom influenced, which was too notorious last winter, to be at all doubted. Lord Carterett, in this attack, has different views; he slurs the Duke of Grafton, he flings dirt upon me, who passed the patent, and makes somebody uneasy for whose sake it was done; and this is one of the instances wherein these that think themselves in danger, begin to be upon the offensive.'[1]

However, at this time, Walpole thought little of this scheming; the resolutions passed by the Irish Parliament he considered to be ridiculous. They implied a demand that Irish money should be minted only in Ireland, a demand which could never be allowed, for the coinage was a matter for the King's prerogative. Yet he was aware of growing difficulties. These resolutions had been the first measures of the Irish Parliament; the necessary money bills, very much Walpole's concern, remained to be passed. He suggested a non-committal reply from the King to the Irish and wrote somewhat sharply to the Duke of Grafton, bidding him keep the Brodricks in order and get on with the King's business.[2] This, he thought, would settle the matter and he saved up his fury against Midleton and Carteret until the moment came to discharge it with effect. For the time being the sudden death of Orléans, the tenacity of Schaub and the plight of Horatio seemed far graver matters.

And there was another anxiety. Bolingbroke began to push himself forward. No sooner did the two brothers-in-law seem to have the situation under control than it escaped from their grasp. Bolingbroke's French wife was influential with the duc de Bourbon, who had now succeeded Orléans as the first minister of France; so he pressed his services on Horatio, on Townshend, on the Duchess of Kendal, and on the King himself. He knew the way the wind was blowing. He was more than willing to kick Carteret in the teeth and show his

[1] Coxe, II, 276–7; also *Townshend MSS*, Raynham. Walpole, of course, had the Brodricks' letters intercepted, opened, copied, re-sealed and despatched.
[2] Coxe, II, 279–80.

spirit by betraying Schaub and rendering him odious to the French Court. This, he speculated, would create an obligation and lead on to his full pardon, the restitution of his estates and his seat in the House of Lords.[1] The death of Orléans, of course, had given Carteret and Schaub renewed hope; the hateful Nocé lost his influence, Schaub fancied his own charm with Bourbon's mistress, Madame de Prie. Horatio Walpole soon discovered that Schaub had revived the old demands for the dukedom, much to the embarrassment of Bourbon, Louis XV and his tutor, Fleury—an influential and powerful old man of seventy who was soon to outwit Bourbon and rule France for twenty years.

Naturally Horatio Walpole wanted to check Schaub without the help of Bolingbroke who, equally naturally, was quite determined that he should not. Walpole and Townshend hovered between the devil and the deep; Bolingbroke wielded such influence that they were tempted to use him, but rightly they feared the consequences. And there was a further quandary which paralysed them and inhibited decisive action. Although Horatio was confident that Bourbon did not want to grant the dukedom, Schaub was equally confident that he did. If easily obtained, George I wanted the dukedom granted. Could Bourbon be double-crossing Horatio for the sake of Schaub and Carteret as Nocé and Orléans had formerly double-crossed Schaub? After all, Bourbon had nominated a close friend of Carteret's and Schaub's as ambassador for England. So doubts and suspicions grew rank as weeds and the pre-occupations of Townshend, Newcastle and Walpole became obsessive. Furthermore, they received a nasty jolt on the King's return to England. Walpole had devised a neat arrangement by which Cadogan was to be kicked out of his military

[1] Bolingbroke got his chance partly through Walpole's precipitate action when he learned of the death of the Duke of Orléans; he approached Bolingbroke through Harcourt on 27 November 1723 (O.S.) (5 December N.S. Orléans died 2 December N.S.), presumably to send personal assurances to Bourbon, the new first minister, with whom Bolingbroke was very friendly. Bolingbroke quickly and adroitly seized his chance to become a go-between with the French Court.

commands, Cobham to become Commander-in-Chief, and Argyll, Master-General of the Ordnance. No doubt Walpole was smarting from the resentments which his earlier mistakes about Cadogan had aroused, but they ought to have taught him to wait and not meddle with military matters. The King peremptorily refused to consider the changes. He liked Cadogan and approved strongly of his qualities as a soldier.[1]

This was a serious rebuff and was very gratifying to Carteret. Schaub, too, was quite certain that the dukedom would be granted in a few weeks and that Bourbon and Madame de Prie were his devoted friends. Also Horatio Walpole felt that his anomalous position had gone on for too long and he was beginning to grow restive. Ireland instead of quietening down, as Walpole expected, blew up. Jonathan Swift, in the guise of an anonymous linen-draper, started to publish *The Drapier's Letters*. They were a wild success and the boycott of Wood's halfpence, which he advocated, plunged the Government of Ireland into a grave crisis.[2] The winter months of 1724 were dark days for Walpole and Townshend. The final, overwhelming breakthrough seemed impossible to achieve, and before them stretched the years of chicanery and double-dealing which went hand in hand with the struggle for power.

At least Parliament proved easy to manage; the whig opposition was secret rather than avowed; and those tories who kept Wyndham and Harcourt company preferred absence or abstention at such a delicate moment, for many hoped that Bolingbroke would extricate them from the wilderness in which he had abandoned them. And following Townshend's repeated and urgent advice, Walpole provided the city merchants with a programme of taxation reform, of

---

[1] Coxe, I, 189.

[2] Swift's first letter was published early in February 1724 and its virulence may be judged by: 'These halfpence are like the accursed Thing, that, as the Scripture tells us, the children of Israel were forbidden to touch. They will run about like the plague and destroy everyone who lays his hand upon them.' The burden of Swift's argument was that the halfpence were a fraud and worthless. See Jonathan Swift, *The Drapier's Letters*, 1724-5, ed. Herbert Davis (Oxford, 1941), 12.

sufficient interest at least to keep them quiet, but of entrancing prospect for the independent country gentlemen who
hoped that increased yields from merchandise would lift
the burden of land-tax from their shoulders. Walpole's reforms, like so much of his work, were neat, practicable and
effective. Tea, chocolate, coconuts were to be placed in
bonded warehouses and freed from customs duties but subject, on sale for internal consumption, to an excise. The
aptness of the method lay in the check on smuggling, the
simplification of customs procedure, and in the encouragement of re-export from London. These, of course, were not
original ideas; the Dutch had used excise for many generations. It had even been tried in England. Walpole had
become completely converted by this method of taxation;
later it very nearly brought about his ruin.[1]

Although Parliament was all harmony and the money
bills skipped through the Commons with refreshing alacrity, demonstrating to George I, if demonstration were
needed, the excellence of Walpole's control of that difficult,
suspicious, and cantankerous body, elsewhere all was confusion, danger, plot and counter-plot. The Irish problem
grew worse and worse as winter changed to spring. Grafton
failed hopelessly to obtain any sort of control over the
situation. He was hesitant by nature and found it difficult
to commit himself strongly to decisive action. His long,
tediously self-justifying letters infuriated Walpole, who could
not comprehend the situation in Ireland. For him it was the
deliberate result of malice and intrigue; the coinage was
excellent; the Royal prerogative unexceptionable; Wood's
profit reasonable. The irrational Irish attitude defeated him.
There Walpole lacked all intuitive sense of the surge of
politics in the wider context of public opinion.

Anxiety at fever-pitch, prolonged day after day, exasperated Walpole to such a degree that he began to lose control

---

[1] For a fuller discussion of Walpole's economic policy see below pp. 233–39:
N. Brisco, *The Economic Policy of Robert Walpole* (Columbia University Press
1907) is very inaccurate and of little value.

of his temper. Grafton was deeply offended by the tone of Walpole's letter and complained to Newcastle; and even Horatio, whose patience had worn as thin as his brother's, was rated sharply for his passion and selfishness. Naturally Horatio protested bitterly.

'. . . upon the most serious and cool consideration,' he wrote on 22 March 1724 (N.S.), 'I can't recollect any step that I have taken, or any act that I have done from my first coming to this moment that has had any other view, or that deserved your reproach of passion in doing business, and that myself is always uppermost in my thoughts. I protest to God I can't comprehend what you mean by it. Whatever weakness I may have I am sure I never have had in my whole life that of making the publick or the concern of my friends subservient to my particular interest.'

Horatio had grown restive in Paris. For months he had told Walpole of his acute embarrassment. On his arrival he had been treated with great deference as England's future ambassador, but as the weeks and months passed and Schaub still remained at his post, the deference vanished and he was greeted with increasing cynicism. When he and Schaub appeared together at Court there was a scarcely suppressed titter. Over and over again he had pleaded to be released from this intolerable situation: always Walpole and Townshend begged him to stay. And now:

'I am loaded with the most unjust reproaches of passion and selfishness; and at last it has come to a certain proposition that I am entirely at a loss to execute, and it is a task never layd upon anybody before. I am now to draw Sir Luke Schaub's picture in the colours he deserves, to be sent to Lord Townshend, to be layd by Lord Townshend before the King, and then to be shown by the King to Lord Carteret, Schaub's particular freind and patron who will immediately perhaps undertake the justification and defence of him, and desire time to do it. If the particulars I have given of his character and conduct as they naturally fell in my way from time to time which might, I thought, have been made known on the proper occasions to His Majesty, had no effect towards removing the impediment to his Majesty's service here, I cannot tell how to colour and digest those particulars in a letter by itself nor do I see what good an account in general of him can do besides making a scene of contention between myself and that despicable wretch.'[1]

Nevertheless, Horatio, fundamentally so loyal and devoted, obeyed his brother and sent a long letter to Townshend, recapitulating Schaub's incompetence and cleverly stressing the way in which he had mishandled the question of the dukedom. Bourbon and Louis XV were both strongly opposed to such a grant and Schaub's continued insistence, in which he thoughtlessly involved the King, had done harm not only to Anglo-French relations but to the high esteem in which Bourbon and Louis XV had held George I. Although this had been said repeatedly by Horatio, he had never before summarized the position so forcibly or so clearly nor placed the matter in so critical a light. A decision on Schaub's future became imperative.

The King's irritation at being nearly placed in a false position with Louis XV was at last brought to such a pitch that he overcame his reluctance to anger Carteret, dismissed Schaub and appointed Horatio Walpole sole ambassador at Paris—the deliberate, ostentatious and unmistakable gesture for which Townshend had been working for so long.[2] After this the dismissal of Carteret from the Secretaryship of State was merely a matter of time. It followed a few weeks later. When it came, it was combined with a delightful piece of

---

[1] C(H) MSS, Horatio, 22 March 1724 (N.S.). Coxe suppressed this letter in both his life of Robert and that of Horatio. Horatio's letter about Schaub which he included with this letter to his brother for him to amend as he pleased is printed by Coxe, HW, 78-9. This is the only occasion on which Horatio and his brother came near to quarrelling and it is an indication of the vast strain of these months that their mutual trust should have given way to angry reproaches.

[2] The final and irrevocable dismissal of Schaub took some weeks to accomplish. Carteret naturally tried to get the blow softened for Schaub. He was allowed to return to Paris but only to attend the Platen-Vrillière marriage and to present formally his letters of recall. Whilst in Paris he made a last desperate bid—a project for marriage between Louis XV and the Princess Anne which incensed George I. Walpole MSS, Newcastle Despatches. Newcastle to HW, 14 May 1724.

irony. Carteret's allies, the Brodricks, had been as responsible as anyone for permitting the Irish situation to get out of hand. Carteret was appointed Lord Lieutenant of Ireland in the room of the Duke of Grafton. He was given a chance to prove his constantly repeated assertion that he wished not only to serve the King but live well with Walpole and Townshend. He could either break the Brodricks or break himself. He broke the Brodricks.

Newcastle, of course, had been promised Carteret's place, yet his appointment aroused great surprise and bitter disappointment in William Pulteney. Pulteney was a brilliant House of Commons man, a fine, eloquent, moving speaker of great personal charm. He had gone into the wilderness with Walpole in 1717; on their return to power in 1720 he had been fobbed off with minor, if lucrative, office; promotion had come in the reshuffle of 1722 but it had been honorific rather than political. His discontent had begun to show itself, for he was an extremely ambitious man. Walpole preferred Newcastle, a man of far fewer intellectual gifts, less confident and far more anxious than Pulteney. The burdens of state, which would have sat lightly on Pulteney's shoulders, weighed Newcastle down. He complained constantly of his labours, but he loved them to distraction. His vast, tumbling correspondence, millions of words in his own hand and tens of millions dictated, stretches like a vast *sudd* across the eighteenth century. Through the incoherent, gushing torrent of words peeps both sense and judgment, often overlaid, mostly foolishly expressed, but unmistakably there. He was intelligent enough to grasp a case, yet his lack of self-confidence in these early years made him very pliable. His formidable industry and passion for detail made him both dependable and efficient in spite of the cumbersome processes of eighteenth-century administration. And to make him almost irresistible was the fact that Newcastle influenced, almost to the point of control, the nomination of sixteen members of Parliament. Pulteney owned one pocket borough, Hedon, at which he needed one seat for himself. Really there

was no choice for Walpole and Townshend had they wished
to exercise one. Pulteney, sharp-tongued, brilliant, charming,
ambitious and very capable of arousing loyalty in others, was
not the type of colleague they sought. But his rejection did
not make for peace in politics.

Grafton, conscious of his own dignity as a second generation royal bastard, was soothed by being given Newcastle's
old office of Lord Chamberlain, which offered him the rich
field of Court life for the exercise of his talent for being on
everyone's side at the same time. More important, however,
was the elevation of Henry Pelham, Newcastle's brother, to be
Secretary-at-War. Walpole had the highest admiration for
Pelham's abilities and he rapidly assumed the position of
deputy-leader of the Commons, becoming Walpole's most
staunch and dependable lieutenant in the management of the
Commons. Like Walpole, he had a shrewd sense of men and
a passion for detail.

These changes marked a massive victory for Walpole and
Townshend for which they had persistently worked during the
two years since Sunderland's death. They had consolidated
their position at Court to a degree which many must have
thought impossible. George I, in 1722, had liked neither
Townshend nor Walpole, indeed his feeling for the latter
bordered on loathing. In the ministerial changes which had
taken place in April 1722 they had achieved no more than
parity with Carteret. By April 1724 the old Sunderland party
had been reduced and subjected. All the major offices of
state were controlled by close allies of Walpole or by his
dependants. It is easy, now, to appreciate the overwhelming
qualities which made the consolidation of their power inevitable. The Parliamentary sessions of 1723 and 1724 were
conducted with an ease that was unprecedented. Never in
the memory of any politician had there been less debate or
more alacrity in the passage of necessary bills of supply.
Those two sessions were a demonstration, if demonstration
were needed, not only of Walpole's ability but of his indispensability.

Equally magisterial had been Townshend's handling of foreign affairs. War and expense in the Baltic had been avoided; a powerful ally had been acquired in Prussia; France's intention of a separate alliance with Russia had been checked. Much of this policy had been achieved against the natural inclinations of the King, yet with his entire approval. Their struggle had not been for personal power alone, although their correspondence is full of intrigue. True, they were fighting men, but men with ideas quite opposed to their own, men whose attitude to politics and life was antipathetic to them. Time and time again Walpole had made his simple political faith crystal clear—peace and prosperity, a contented King and a contented Parliament: simple aims, yet requiring for their achievement the control of complex issues as well as the management of a myriad of contending personalities.

By the summer of 1724 they had won through. A patch of discontent remained here and there—in Ireland, in the City of London—and if dangerous problems abroad had not been settled there was a chance they would be at the Congress of Cambrai. And even those points of dispute—the Investiture, Gibraltar, the Ostend Company—were minor, not major. And sweetest of all, perhaps, their power was not shared. Newcastle was a dependant, not an ally on terms. Carteret had been outwitted and isolated but, cunningly enough, not turned into an opponent. Only Bolingbroke cast a shadow. Yet even Walpole's temperament, so obsessed by anxiety, refused to be unduly disturbed by the prospect of the return of a convicted traitor. The next few years were the most unclouded of Walpole's life and he enjoyed the triumphs of power—security, success and adulation.

CHAPTER THREE

VICTORY, 1724-26

THE NEXT three years were the happiest and most peaceful that Walpole ever knew as the King's first minister. The changed circumstances of his private life had much to do with this. From the South Sea Bubble to the fall of Carteret had been a period of great strain in which his natural anxiety was at times brought almost to breaking point. The sources of this anxiety were not exclusively political or public. The strains of his official career were often charged with an emotional force drawn from the deeper chambers of his heart. For years he had had to witness the desperate sickness of his eldest daughter, Catherine, whose daily life was a gruesome round of fever, fainting, vomiting and pain which destroyed the character before it killed the body. Though men were much more inured then to the spectacle of pain than we are today, Walpole was racked by his daughter's suffering.[1] This private grief must have taken away much of the joy which he felt in his political triumphs of 1722. The next few years brought him little consolation. He and his wife were completely estranged. She devoted herself to her young son, Horace, whom she adored, to her music, to her exotic birds, to her clothes and jewellery and, doubtless, to her lovers.[2] Her husband found consolation where he could. From

[1] BM *Sloane MSS*, 4,034, fos. 319-36: 4,046, fo. 6, for Walpole's correspondence with Dr Cheyne and Dr Hans Sloane who treated the girl. The letters and Mrs Bedford's, the girl's governess, make very grim reading. See also *Walpole*, I, 320. She died at Bath on 9 October 1722. *Historical Register*, 1722, Chronological Diary, 45.

[2] *C(H) MSS*, Account Books, 22. Her bills for the opera were very high. John Rudd was paid £94 10s. 0d. in 1723; £78 15s. 0d. in 1724; £99 4s. 6d. in 1725. There are other large payments to Heidegger and to the Academy of Music. Edward Beach, the Toyman (in the eighteenth century, toymen sold gold and enamel trinkets) figures constantly in this account book, so do jewellers, dressmakers, shoemakers and the like. Obviously Lady Walpole was quite as extravagant as her husband.

casual remarks in his correspondence with Newcastle and others it is clear that he was living hard during these years, drinking, eating, hunting, wenching.[1] This, combined with the formidable quantity of administrative business which he discharged every day of his life, proved too much for his health. He was more constantly ill during these years than at any other time of his life, and what is exceptionally rare for him, for he usually made very light of constant sickness, he complained of his troubles to Newcastle and Townshend.[2]

Yet there were consolations even in these years and even in his family. He was very proud of his eldest son, Robert, whom he had carefully brought up. Before he had been sent to Eton he had been very well grounded in French,[3] and, as soon as his schooldays were over, he had been despatched on the Grand Tour from which he returned in 1723 to find himself a peer of the realm. Sir Robert and Townshend had both obtained peerages for their sons, not only to demonstrate the favour which they enjoyed at Court, but also to strengthen their group in the House of Lords. The elevation of Robert Walpole junior to a barony also made it clear to the whole world that Walpole himself had no intention of leaving the Commons.

This decision, which was fraught with great consequence for the development of parliamentary government, must have been made either during or after the South Sea crisis. In 1720, at the time of the reconciliation of the Prince of Wales with his father, rumours had been both numerous and insistent that Walpole was to take a peerage at the next reshuffle of ministerial posts and his very heavy purchases of

[1] BM *Add MSS*, 32,686, fo. 333; the only illegitimate child of Sir Robert Walpole's, apart from his daughter by Maria Skerrett, was Catherine Daye. Her parentage is unknown: she was born about 1724. Presumably Molly supplanted her mother. For the few details known about her life, see *The Correspondence of Horace Walpole, The Cole Letters* (ed. W. S. Lewis), II, 371–2.

[2] BM *Add MSS*, 32,686, fos. 333, 361.

[3] At the age of twelve, he had either a French tutor or a French valet. *C(H) MSS*, Vouchers 1713: 'Pd Master Bobbee and Frenchman £36.' The Frenchman was living in the household as Lady Walpole paid his bills.

land in East Norfolk, about Crostwight, gives some substance to the rumours.[1]

The tradition of leaving the Treasury in Commission and linking the First Lord with the Chancellorship of the Exchequer and the Leadership of the House of Commons had not been established by 1722. Indeed the aim of all men of genius in financial affairs in the recent past had been to obtain the office of Lord Treasurer, which only a peer could hold. And Walpole, ambitious as he was, doubtless had his eye on this office, which would have given him an outstanding official status. The experience of his active political life had brought home to him, particularly sharply in 1721, the need for strong leadership in the Commons, combined with favour at Court. In the struggle firstly against Sunderland, and afterwards against Carteret, his massive strength had been derived from his capacity to manage the Commons, an ability which made George I grudgingly concede his indispensability in the difficult months after the South Sea crisis and before Sunderland's death. Once Walpole had won the full confidence of his King, the combination of these two assets—royal favour and dominion in the Commons—mutually strengthened each other and gave to Walpole's regime a stability never previously achieved in parliamentary government since the days of the Tudors. Henry Pelham, Lord North and William Pitt the Younger were to achieve a similar strength for the administration by the combination of the same offices with complete royal favour. Because of their achievement, many historians have regarded Walpole's decision to stay in the Commons as an obvious one to make and have failed to realize his acumen and his originality, just as they have overestimated his strength before the death of Sunderland and the disgrace of Carteret. No one knew how powerful this combination could be or how irresistible once achieved. And that is why it is during these years from 1724-7, when men began to realize the vast nature of

[1] See *Walpole*, I, 312, and additional reference, HMC, *Portland MSS*, VII, 281-2. RW paid £21,000 for his Crostwight estate. *C(H) MSS*, Vouchers, 1722.

Walpole's power, that he began to be widely known as the 'Great Man'. The singularity, the sheer novelty of his position needs, however, to be constantly stressed. The realization of this power was not immediately apparent to either Walpole or his contemporaries. The full extent of his victory and of his pre-eminence was revealed by events— by events and, perhaps, also by the style of life which Walpole designed for himself and his children. For Walpole consciousness of greatness needed a physical expression.

He had decided to tear down the old rambling house at Houghton in 1720; by 1724 his new house—more like a miniature palace than anything that Norfolk had yet seen— was growing fast, at least by eighteenth-century standards.[1] The conception was grand—new house, new stables, new village, new landscape. The preliminary work necessitated the fencing of the new park, the destruction of a part of the old house and stables and the construction of temporary accommodation, for Walpole could not forgo his annual Congresses. This alone had taken two years and the first stone of the new house was not laid until the end of May 1722—a fitting coincidence with Walpole's emergence as the King's first minister.[2] The house was not finished until 1735, or rather, not perfected, for it was habitable, in part, by 1726, and completely so by 1729 when the village was removed from the Park and set up afresh outside the main gates.[3] Long before it was completed the mansion had

[1] For Houghton see C. Campbell, *Vitruvius Britannicus*, III, 27–34; I. Warre, *Plans, Elevations, Sections, Chimney Pieces and Ceilings of Houghton Hall* (1735): H. Walpole, *Aedes Walpolianae*; C. Hussey, *English Country Houses, Early Georgian*, 1715–60, 72–86: *Studies in Social History* (ed. J. H. Plumb), 196–8.

[2] *Walpole*, I, 359–60; *C(H) MSS*, Jonas Rolfe, 30 May 1722: 'Dr Bland, I presume, has given an account of laying the first stone of the New House. I wish your Honour many happy yeares to enjoy it.' The brick cellars and first stone course were completed by 7 December 1722: *C(H) MSS*, R. Hardy to T. Rigby. Even in the autumn of 1723, when the confusion of building must have been very great, he had the Duke of Devonshire and Lord Godolphin to stay. 'I made them both go both fox and hare hunting.' BM *Add MSS*, 32,686, fo. 362 RW to Newcastle, 24 October 1723.

[3] Hervey, present at a large house-party, writes as if the house were completely finished in 1727, (see Ilchester, *Lord Hervey and His Friends*, 23–5). The cupolas bear the dates 1726, 7, 8, 9, but these could have been raised after the main rooms had been constructed if not embellished. The inscription on the

become an object of wonder and envy to the *dilettanti* and *cognoscenti*. The second Earl of Oxford, Harley's son, thought that it was tasteless. 'I think', he wrote in his diary, 'that it is neither magnificent nor beautiful, there is very great expense without either judgment or taste'. And after surveying the rooms and decorations he came to the conclusion: 'I dare say had the money which has been laid out here, nay and much less, been put into the hands of a man of taste and understanding, there would have been a much finer house and better rooms and greater.'[1] One would not expect a Harley to regard the work of a Walpole with anything but a critical eye, but Oxford had studied architecture and he was patron of James Gibbs who, he thought, had been mistaken in altering Campbell's design (principally of the stone turrets) for Walpole.[2] Yet Oxford's was a lone voice, save for Walpole's envious enemies. Hervey and Sir Thomas Robinson both wrote eulogies which are well known, but both, perhaps, concentrate on the convenience of the house and the richness of its ornamentation than on its outward appearance. Both of them admired William Kent, whereas Oxford detested him.

As Hervey realized, Walpole laboured under natural disadvantages at Houghton; there was no water, only ponds which dried out most summers. Nor did timber grow naturally on the bleak, windswept plateau where the house was situated. Indeed, the first step taken by Walpole had

house reads. 'Robertus Walpole Hac Aedes Anno S. MDCCXXII Inchoavit, Anno MDCCXXXV Perfecit'. *Perfecit* must, however, include stables, all minor works and furnishings, for Walpole's huge parties, the Norfolk Congresses, were in full swing by 1727, see Ilchester, *op. cit.*, 71. Hervey does, however, mention that the state dining room and bedroom were not fully completed by 1731, although the designs for chimney pieces and furniture had been decided upon. All but the dining room, however, had been completed a few months later when the duc de Lorraine visited Houghton in December 1731: HMC, *Carlisle MSS*, 85–6. The shifting of the village was thought to be of sufficient interest to posterity for the parson to make a note in the Parish Register. Under 4 July 1724 he wrote; 'The foundation was dug for the first two houses of the New Town': *Houghton Parish Register*. The new village consisted of twelve semi-detached cottages on each side of the road leading to Harpley.

[1] HMC, *Portland MSS*, VI, 160–1.
[2] B. Little, *Life and Works of James Gibbs* (1955), 86.

been to call in the famous landscape gardener, Bridgeman, to design plantations and groves, even before the house was started. They did, and still do, a little to soften the landscape; but water, in spite of the expense to which Walpole went, proved elusive, and the setting remained austere. The design of the house is singularly apt for this natural austerity. It is grand, plain, massive; yet elegance, without the slightest hint of prettiness or triviality, is given by the low-built pavilions and their curving colonnades. The decoration of the exterior is classical both in restraint and design, never distracting to the eye, and the dominant effect of the building is dignity mixed with grandeur. Against the clear, blue East Anglian skies it achieves a unity and splendour that is truly Palladian.[1]

Within there is no austerity but a riot of luxurious decoration. Walpole himself loved beautiful objects and he devoted as much time to the embellishment of his house as to the pursuit of the fox; his rustic tastes have long been remarked, whereas his aesthetic judgment is scarcely appreciated outside the circle of his descendants. He employed the outstanding craftsmen of his day and cared nothing for the cost.[2] The lovely marble chimney pieces, some luxurious, some simple, all elegant, were by Rysbrack. William Kent designed the furniture—two magnificent suites of ninety-six pieces, half in walnut and half in gesso covered with green velvet, still adorn the Stone Hall and the Saloon. His consoles and mirrors are both richly gilt and heavy with swags, yet fitting, in the magnificence of the state rooms. The plaster work by Artari is of the same quality, luxurious and grand, but never riotous, always restrained by a sense of proportion that gives to these magnificent rooms an air of reasonableness and propriety. Yet perhaps more impressive are the doors and doorcases. Walpole decided to use mahog-

[1] Christopher Hussey, *Early Georgian*, 1715–60, 72–86; also B. Little, *op. cit.*, 178.
[2] The gold trimmings of the green velvet state bed, designed by William Kent, cost £1,219 3s. 11d. Turner, Hill and Pitter in the Strand carried out the work; C(H) MSS, Vouchers, 1732.

any and he used it with a richness and profusion that was unusual in English houses of his day.[1] The doors are as thick and as massive as Walpole himself. Their decoration, however, is restrained and their craftsmanship superb; they are so excellently hung that they open and close to the slightest touch; in richness, elegance and utility they symbolize the finest qualities of eighteenth-century craftsmanship. In every detail of construction and decoration Walpole took the liveliest interest. He was responsible, against the advice of the *virtuosi*, for constructing the domed towers in stone.[2] He insisted on building the stables at a place well removed from the house. A well-concealed bawdy joke in the stucco dado of the Stone Hall could never have been made by Artari without Walpole's permission. He designed with Bridgeman his park and plantations, which in 1720 was one of the first attempts at a natural landscape setting for a house.

Houghton was designed not merely for display but also for living. It was not, as great houses went, a vast house; it could not compare with Chatsworth, Blenheim or Castle Howard. The rooms, apart from the saloon and marble hall, were commodious rather than grand, built for utility and convenience as well as for show. The bedrooms each had a small adjoining room for a servant; the offices—brew house, laundry and kitchens—were neatly grouped in one pavilion. The rustic, or ground floor, was as carefully arranged for business and pleasure as the first floor—the *piano nobile*—for state and show. The long arcade with its four chimney pieces was an admirable lounging place for men and dogs tired from a day's hunting or shooting, while the rooms, next to the kitchen, provided a profusion of food for the

---

[1] This profuse use of mahogany greatly impressed his contemporaries, see HMC, *Carlisle MSS*, 85. For an appreciation of the furniture of Houghton see S. Sitwell, *British Architects and Craftsmen*, 129-30.

[2] It is extremely doubtful whether James Gibbs had anything whatsoever to do with the design of these cupolas, see *Studies in Social History* (ed. J. H. Plumb), 207.

III. THE WEST FRONT OF HOUGHTON HALL, NORFOLK

Van Loo.

IV. MARIA SKERRETT, 2ND WIFE OF SIR ROBERT WALPOLE

hungry guests. To contemporaries the convenience of Houghton was as remarkable as its beauty.[1]

Houghton, however, was planned by Walpole to be more than a tribute to his wealth and greatness, more even than a home for his family. It was to provide an appropriate setting for his great collection of works of art, for as soon as Walpole had the money he became one of the greatest collectors in Europe, paying record prices for the work of painters to whom he was devoted. After politics, his pictures and sculptures were the constant preoccupation of his life. Children, friends, ambassadors, even spies, were expected to report on, and if need be, negotiate for pictures. He had begun in a modest way, first as a patron—to Jervas, Richardson and Wootton—and then he began to buy at auctions.[2] Before 1720 he must have acquired an interesting small collection, but mainly, if the scanty records are reliable, of family portraits. After 1720, and with increasing momentum, he began to purchase old masters. As Houghton grew, from 1722-7, his pace quickened; and Titians, Raphaels, Rubens, Rembrandts, Poussins, Domenichinos, and a host of lesser works were loaded in huge crates on the lumbering wagons which slowly dragged their way to Lynn, or were sent at greater risk by the short sea passage. They came from Italy, France, Flanders and Holland. John Macky, whilst acting as a spy on the Jacobite postal network at Brussels, secured a large Snyders to go with the four famous market scenes which Walpole already possessed, as well as a Rubens and a book of miniatures.[3] Lord Waldegrave, when ambassador at Paris, negotiated the purchase of Poussin's *Holy Family*

---

[1] HMC, *Carlisle MSS*, 84-6.

[2] He bought two pictures at the Earl of Halifax's sale, one a Poussin, in 1717; and two pictures at Greffier's sale in 1717 for £13 5s. 0d. He also purchased some years later in 1725 a very large quantity of Vandykes at the sale of the Duke of Wharton's pictures; *C(H) MSS*, Account Books, 20a; Horace Walpole, *Aedes Walpolianae* (2nd ed. 1753). A number of MSS catalogues of Sir Robert's pictures exist. The earliest is in the Pierpont Morgan Library, New York, which was drawn up in 1736. Some of the entries and attributions are in Sir Robert's own handwriting. Other catalogues are in the possession of the Fitzwilliam Museum, Cambridge and in Herts RO.

[3] *C(H) MSS*, John Mackay, 5 February 1724 (N.S.).

for the highest price ever paid for a Poussin.[1] Walpole's eldest son came back from his Grand Tour loaded with sculpture and his youngest was equally concerned for his father's taste twenty years later.[2] Friends remembered his passion when they wished to demonstrate their loyalty or good fortune. General Churchill gave him a couple of antique busts from Cardinal Albani's collection as well as a picture by Romano. Ambassadors and consuls knew their duty. Waldegrave, as well as buying pictures for Sir Robert, sent a present of a Bassano; Benjamin Keene at Madrid offered a Murillo; Tyrawley at Lisbon had the lucky chance to discover a Holbein of Edward VI. Horace Mann, who owed his consulship at Florence to his eminent cousin, marked his deep sense of obligation by sending a magnificent bronze by John of Bologna. Naturally, rich sycophants added their quota—the Dukes of Montagu and Chandos sent pictures, the Earl of Pembroke the fine bronze by John of Bologna which still stands in the well of the great staircase. And Walpole placed his own purchases most judiciously. Some of his first pictures, including a Titian, were bought from de Morville, Louis XV's secretary of state, others came from de Vrillière who occupied a similar post; perhaps the excellent prices which they obtained

[1] *Waldegrave MSS*, RW to Waldegrave, 21 March 1735; 'I will give £400 for the picture which is, I believe, the highest price that was ever given for a picture of Poussin': also RW to Waldegrave, 14 and 21 August 1735. Waldegrave got the picture for £320: *C(H) MSS*, Waldegrave, 16 August 1736. Some other prices which Sir Robert paid are as follows; Murillo, £315 for four small pictures: £203 15s. 0d. for the Ascension: £220 for The Nativity, *Fitzwilliam MSS*. Salvator Rosa; Prodigal Son, £500: Guido Reni; The Consultation of the Fathers, £700: Child in the Manger, £500: Palma Vecchia; Adoration, £300. *MSS Catalogue* Herts R.O. The collection at his death was valued at £34,975 by Horace Walpole, *Walpole MSS*.

[2] *C(H) MSS*, Edward Walpole, 15 August 1730 (NS). Naples. ' . . . I have seen every statue and piece of that kind of antiquity that is worth seeing at Rome among which there is nothing to be had that could possibly serve your purpose. Those that are valuable and most entire are either entail'd or in the hands of people that wont part with them. I have desired Mr Swinny whom I believe you must know, to procure you two such if he can meet with them nor could you possibly employ any body that would answer your expectation better either in point of integrity, I mean getting your things at a just price, or in the knowledge and judgement of those things . . .' Edward Walpole, Sir Robert's second son, was on the Grand Tour with Lord Boyne.

with such ease helped to confirm them in their anglophilia; if so, no doubt the secret service fund contributed its quota.[1] As the years passed these masterpieces of painting, sculpture and bronze became the glory of Houghton; and collections of almost equal magnificence covered Sir Robert's walls in Arlington Street, at Chelsea and even in his rooms at the Treasury.[2] Had the wanton extravagance of his grandson, George, Earl of Orford, not forced him to sell this extraordinary collection to Catherine of Russia, Walpole would be recognized for what he was, one of the greatest connoisseurs of his time.[3]

Houghton, of course, and its picture collection, was only one aspect of the ostentatious grandeur in which Walpole lived. His visits to Norfolk were rarely extensive and from

[1] Horace Walpole, *Aedes Walpolianae* (2nd ed. 1753), 38–96 *passim*. Walpole did not always get the best of the bargain; French statesmen, also connoisseurs, realized their opportunities for unloading their dubious pictures. Horace Walpole on 5 August 1724 (NS) wrote from Paris: 'I am glad you are satisfied in your pictures and I am sensible that the Titian was the worst of the kind but when I proposed an abatement of the price, my friend Nocé who is very particular and humoursome, had like to have broken off the whole bargain and it was with great management that I brought him to temper again . . .' *C(H) MSS*, HW, 5 August 1724. Two years later Horatio was still doing what he could to increase his brother's collection. 'As to the pictures,' he wrote on 5 June 1726 (NS), 'the Raphael was sold two days before I received your letter; for 1900 livres which is now about £950 ster. There remains still the Guido, the Paul Veronese and there is an old Palma that is an excellent picture . . .' *Ibid*. It was not long before the Parisian picture dealers besieged Walpole with tempting offers of old masters. *Ibid*., de Roussel, 15 April, 22 August 1733.

[2] By 1736 Sir Robert possessed 421 paintings of which he himself had acquired at least 400. *Pierpont Morgan MSS*.

[3] R. W. Ketton-Cremer, *A Norfolk Gallery*, 184. They were sold for £36,080. 'It is the most signal mortification to my idolatry for my father's memory that I could receive,' Horace lamented. 'It is stripping the temple of his glory and of his affection. A madman excited by rascals has burnt his Ephesus.' Josiah Wedgwood, who had never seen the pictures, regarded the sale as a national disaster. 'I had seen in the public prints,' he wrote to his friend Thomas Bentley on 18 September 1779, 'and lamented the approaching fate of the Houghton collection of paintings . . . Everything shows we are past our meridian, and we have only to pray that our decline may be gentle, and free from those sudden shocks which tear up empires by the roots.' I am indebted to Mr Neil McKendrick for this reference. George and Joseph Farington had been employed by Orford to make copies of his grandfather's pictures. They were afterwards engraved by Boydell and published in *The Houghton Gallery*. Most of these pictures are still at the Hermitage, Leningrad; a few were sold to Andrew Mellon and to Calouste Gulbenkian by the Soviet Government.

87

about 1725 he settled into a fixed routine. In May he spent about a fortnight, in November about a month, in Norfolk. He never came alone, however, and he used these occasions to entertain his intimate friends on a vast and expensive scale. John, Lord Hervey, who was a frequent visitor (his family lived at Ickworth, near Bury St Edmunds, and his proximity as well as his wit and charm made him a singularly convenient guest), described one of these Norfolk Congresses, as they came to be called, to Frederick, Prince of Wales.

'Our company at Houghton,' he wrote on 21 July 1731, 'swelled at last into so numerous a body that we used to sit down to dinner a little snug party of about thirty odd, up to the chin in beef, venison, geese, turkeys etc; and generally over the chin in claret, strong beer and punch. We had Lords spiritual and temporal, besides commoners, parsons, and freeholders innumerable. In public we drank loyal healths, talked of the times and cultivated popularity; in private we drew plans and cultivated the country.'[1]

The days passed in strenuous gallops after hare and fox or in visiting and viewing; William Kent was busy at Holkham and Raynham. Sir Andrew Fountaine, who had been in the same election at Eton with Walpole, had created at Narford, according to Hervey, 'the prettiest trinket I ever saw. My Lord Burleigh could not make a better ragoust of paintings, statues, gilding and virtu!'[2] Few lacked pretence to virtuosity and the qualities of architraves, pediments and orders were as frequently discussed in Houghton's rustic arcades as the finer points of horse or dog or bitch. And in the midst of the hunting and viewing and drinking and flirting there were the serious hours when Walpole retired to his library and discussed personalities and politics with Townshend, Newcastle or Henry Pelham. At the November

---

[1] Ilchester, *Hervey and His Friends*, 73–4.
[2] Ilchester, *Hervey and His Friends*, 74. Lord Oxford, however, strongly disapproved of Narford. 'It is a pretty box, a great deal of painting and gilding done by very bad hands; many pictures, most copies'. HMC, *Portland MSS*, VI, 164.

Congress the tactics were laid down for the parliamentary session, which Walpole always tried to delay until January, for, as he said, 'I allways thought the adjournments at Christmas tended more to caballs than all other occasions.'[1] And cabals, except of his own making, Walpole did not like.

Naturally the satirists cast a baleful eye on the lavish and extravagant hospitality to which Walpole treated his guests; they sneered at the wonderful food and superlative wines and brooded darkly on the horrid plots that were being concocted in the secrecy and isolation of Norfolk. Year after year the ballad makers were sure of a quick return for a bit of heavy humour at the expense of a congress.

'To keep open House for the Space of Twelve Days,
Six weeks before *Christmas* our *Wonder* should raise.
    G–d send we shall not
    Hear of a New Plot,
Tho' by such a Thing has good Money been got.
But *Englishmen, Englishmen,* look to your *Hits,*
Let no Body *bubble* you out of your *wits.*
    · · · · ·
Fat Turkeys, fat Capons, and all Things in Season,
That Hearts could desire, or wish for in Reason.
Some *Woodcocks* were there too, and *Brawn* and *Mince-
    Pies,*
And *Custards* completed the whole sacrifice.
    · · · · ·
Two hundred good Pounds were laid out every Day;
See, while *the Sun shines* what it is *to make Hay.'*[2]

The *Craftsman* jeered at the great lantern in the Stone Hall

---

[1] Coxe, II, 278.

[2] *Political Ballads illustrating the Administration of Sir Robert Walpole*, ed. Milton Percival. Oxford Historical and Literary Studies, VIII (Oxford 1916), 38–9. A New Norfolk Ballad by Sir Francis Walsingham's Ghost, first published *Daily Journal*, 17 November 1730. Other ballads on the same theme: *The Norfolk Lanthorn, Craftsman,* 28 July 1728: *The Norfolk Congress Versified, circa* November 1728, based on the *Norfolk Congress,* a prose pamphlet published on that date. This had however been composed in 1725 and handed about in Norfolk in MS. A copy with *The Quadrille as it is now play'd at Soissons* of 1725 on the same sheet is in the *Blofeld MSS.*

for which he had paid one hundred and seventy guineas. The pamphleteers derided his French dishes as well as his French policy. No opportunity was lost to pillory his grandeur, his ostentation, his extravagance, or to question from whence came the flood of necessary gold. For Walpole lived high wherever he went. Only the best claret was seen at his tables—Lafite, Latour, Haut Brion. He paid reckless prices for old burgundy, old hock and champagne.[1] His wine bill in 1733 with James Bennett—one only of the half-a-dozen merchants who supplied him, but perhaps the principal one— was £1,118 12s. 10d., and 540 dozen empty bottles were returned.[2] The same profusion was to be found in food, clothes, jewels, carriages, chairs, presents, Christmas boxes, tips. Little Horace had his footmen, French-tailored silk clothes and writing master.[3] His wife lived in the same high style and his mistress too. As soon as he obtained the Rangership of Richmond Park for his eldest son, in 1726, he became his deputy and set about the Old Lodge. An army of carpenters, plasterers, furnishers made short work of £14,000 and Walpole had another comfortable, extravagant house where he could indulge his friends with good food, good wine and excellent hunting at the weekend.[4] And Walpole loved it

[1] *Wine and Food Quarterly*, 1951, J. H. Plumb, 'Sir Robert Walpole's Wines'. The earliest reference known to a vintage hock of a particular year is derived from Sir Robert's bills.

[2] *Studies in Social History* (ed. J. H. Plumb), 201. It is not surprising that Walpole gave Bennett a very warm personal letter of introduction to Earl Waldegrave when he visited Paris. *Waldegrave MSS*, RW to Waldegrave, 30 August 1733. Walpole's extravagance was a constant theme in contemporary gossip. HMC, *Carlisle MSS*, 84. HMC, *Portland MSS*, VI, 161. Walpole was allowed 2d. a dozen on empties. It was already an established practice for a wine merchant to bottle a customer's wine. Wine was also sold by the bottle; Walpole often sent out for a couple of bottles of champagne. C(H) *MSS*, Vouchers, various years.

[3] C(H) *MSS*, Account Book 22, fos. 54, 57. His tailor, Nicolas Olivier, was paid £32 8s. 6d. on 28 January 1725; Horace was then seven years old. His shoemaker's bill was five guineas in the same year.

[4] E. Beresford Chancellor, *The History and Antiquities of Richmond, Kew and Ham* (Richmond, 1894), 218. C(H) *MSS*, Account Book 22. Walpole became deputy so that the office would remain in the family for a longer period. His son gave up all the Ranger's rights and perquisites to his father, who hunted the park regularly at weekends.

all—the wine, the food, the clothes, jewels and the palatial houses in which he was to pass his life. And, perhaps, more than these was the knowledge that he had established his family, raised it from obscurity to aristocratic magnificence. During these years of splendour and victory he not only ennobled his son but also married him to a great heiress, Margaret Rolle of Heanton in Devonshire, who brought him the control of two parliamentary boroughs—Callington and Ashburton—as well as great estates. His daughter, Mary, suitably dowered, became the bride of Viscount Malpas, heir to the Earl of Cholmondeley, one of the leading families of Cheshire. With wealth and grandeur came a secure place in society not for himself—his deliberate coarse, rustic habits were always liable to raise a snobbish smile at Court—but for his children and his children's children.

2

YET SWEETER than these things was that taste of power which he pursued with the greed and lust of a jealous lover. It was during these years that he acquired a new nickname. To his friends, to his enemies, to the world at large, he became quite simply 'The Great Man'—a title which could be used with bantering affection or spiteful hatred. Behind the wealth, the ostentation, the lavish and constant hospitality lay the reality—the queues of needy supplicants waiting through the endless hours at Arlington Street and at the Treasury; and not only needy supplicants, but dukes, marquesses, earls, viscounts, barons, knights and gentlemen haunted his levees and dogged his heels at Court; ladies, from the Duchess of Kendal to Women of the Bedchamber, sent him pressing little, ill-spelt notes, to remind him of their need for favour. Day after day, week after week, month after month, year after year, the volume of supplication grew louder and louder. Every trick, every artifice was used to inveigle his support—presents, offers of loyalty, votes at command, nominations for seats, threats of independence. The bulk of

Walpole's remaining correspondence harks upon the same theme: that the pursuit of office and pension was the right true end of politics. Walpole knew that fact, of course, from the first day that he entered Parliament, but in Anne's reign the disposition of places had been somewhat haphazard. First come was often first served; the recommendation of Mrs Masham might carry more weight than Harley's. Politicians mostly strove to make their patronage pay dividends, but they were in and out of power so frequently that the dividends were often paid to their successors. Certain fields of patronage were jealously guarded. The Commissioners of the Customs and Excise tried to evade the Lord Treasurer's recommendations and keep their numerous appointments for their own clients.[1] The Lord Chancellor controlled the livings in the gift of the Crown, but more often than not he was cajoled by an importunate bishop or courtier. Benefices in the hands of bishops or members of the administration were not always disposed of for the common good. The Commander-in-Chief, the Master General of the Ordnance, even the Secretary at War, tended to deal directly with the Sovereign for the immense patronage of the Army. And the same was true of the Navy.

Walpole set out to engross the entire field of patronage, to guard it jealously, and to make it yield a solid core of support in the Commons and victories at the elections. His view of office had always been realistic. In 1715, when he became Paymaster-General and Governor of Chelsea, he had purged every office that he controlled and placed his friends and dependants in them with the ruthlessness of a Tammany Hall boss. In 1721 he swept the Treasury clean as he could and installed his clients wherever possible. No office was too humble; Thomas Cremer, who had made him small loans in his early days as a Member of Parliament, found his reward as Inspector of the Treasure and Teller Vouchers and

---

[1] E. Hughes, *Studies in Administration and Finance 1558–1825*, 269–70, and the pertinent criticisms by S. Baxter, *The Development of the Treasury 1660–1702*, 90–104.

Deputy of the Clerk of the Cofferer of the Household. No
relative went unnoticed; all Walpoles, Townshends, Turners,
Shorters were, of course, handsomely provided for. The Manns,
likewise, did splendidly. Thomas obtained the profitable post
of Chamber-Keeper at the Treasury, worth £400 p.a. and
what he could make on the coals and candles that he
provided for the office. Robert, in addition to his Deputy-
Treasurership of Greenwich Hospital, also secured a Collec-
torship of the Port of London.[1] Distant cousins were not
forgotten—George Nayler became Usher of the Receipt—
and connections by marriage, if loyal, obtained their deserts–
Peter Leheup, allied to Horatio Walpole's bride Mary Lom-
bard, started as an under-clerk at the Treasury at £50 a
year. Ruthlessly and efficiently he placed his friends' relatives and dependants once he had secured his own. No office
within the wide-ranging grasp of his own department was
too humble for his attention. His correspondence contains
series of letters, dealing with all types of revenue officers
scattered throughout the length and breadth of the land.
Every writer that begged for a place knew the coin that he
had to trade in: he possessed political influence—it was at
Walpole's disposal; his loyalty had been, was, and would be
impeccable. Although in the past Commissioners of Excise
and Customs had exercised a certain independent patronage,
Walpole quickly stopped that and no one was appointed
except with his consent. By such means he created the
Treasury party which became the most reliable ministerial
group in the Commons. Yet influence was only one of his
methods of securing a loyal Treasury. His efficiency, his
exemplary industry, his constant availability, his willingness
to listen to new ideas and to accept what he thought good
made bonds of loyalty between him and his subordinates
that were as strong as any that patronage could create.
Nevertheless he believed firmly in patronage as the surest
foundation of political loyalty and he set about collecting

[1] Miège, *The Present State of Great Britain*, and J. Chamberlain, *Magnae
Britanniae Notitia*, various editions 1720–30.

as much as he could even in fields remote from the Treasury.

George I was very tender about appointments to, and promotions in, the armed forces, regarding them very much as a part of his royal prerogative and he needed to be circumvented rather than cajoled.[1] Walpole accomplished his aim by securing close allies in the vital offices and then making sure that he was always consulted by them. His first victory was to obtain the Secretaryship-at-War for Henry Pelham; the fall of Carteret also enabled Walpole to persuade the King to get rid, at last, of Cadogan. He was replaced by the Duke of Argyll, not easy or complaisant, but usually fully co-operative in these early years so long as due consideration was given to his demands. And once, of course, that it became known that army or navy promotions were unlikely to succeed unless backed by Walpole, the stream of applications flowed in a steady tide to his door.

The Church was less easy to manage, although during the years 1720–7 when the luck was running with Walpole, it held with the Church too. Walpole and Townshend, of course, needed the bishops; twenty-six dependable votes in the Lords was their aim. Until 1722, vacancies had run against them. Anne's tories had continued to flourish; Sunderland had slipped in his own nominees when vacancies occurred. In 1723 their luck changed; death, the joker of eighteenth-century politics, played havoc with the bishops and they dropped like leaves in Vallombrosa. Robinson of London, Harley's Privy Seal, died on 11 April 1723; Fleetwood of Ely went on 4 May, quickly followed by Winchester on the 15th and Chichester a week later; and October

---

[1] John Windus, a relative of Walpole, in May 1725 sent a petition for promotion to George I. Mahomet, George's servant and factotum, told him to apply to Henry Pelham, the Secretary at War, to whom the petition had been sent. Windus was wise enough at this point to apply to Walpole, for Pelham never acted without Walpole's advice. In July of the same year the Governor of Sheerness was on the point of death. Pelham wrote to Walpole that he had refused all promises and would make none until he could discuss the succession with Walpole on his return from Norfolk. *C(H) MSS*, J. Windus, 25 May 1725; Pelham, 3 July 1725.

brought St David's into the market.[1] Atterbury had been exiled for high treason, leaving Rochester vacant. Five deaths and one banishment of bishops mostly unsympathetic to Walpole, permitted a complete remodelling of the hierarchy. Neither Archbishop was reliable, a disaster to which Walpole, Townshend and Newcastle had given considerable thought. They needed a reliable adviser—not only whig but whig in their way. They thought that they had found him in Edmund Gibson, Bishop of Lincoln, ambitious, whig and patronless. He displayed his devotion to the administration by writing ardent pamphlets explaining its more unpopular acts, and willingly acted against the Bishop of Rochester.[2] Walpole and Townshend began to woo him. He was translated to London; his opinions were solicited on promotions as the vacancies occurred; and finally he was persuaded, after a becoming reluctance, to accept the post of adviser on ecclesiastical patronage to the ministry, thereby passing over both Canterbury and Winchester whose office as Clerk of the Closet had usually carried with it the Crown's confidence in such matters.[3] Walpole, however, with his quick and certain judgment was not taken in by Gibson's diffidence; he sensed the thirsty ambition. On 6 September 1723 he wrote to Newcastle:

'. . . I thought that I might fairly play the courtier so far as to have the meritte of my good wishes with the Bishop of London, and therefore took an opportunity of telling him what I had thought of that matter. At first he was all *nolo episcopari*; before we parted I percieved upon second thoughts he began to rellish it and the next morning *ex mero motu* he came to me, talked comically, is a mortal man, wants to be ravished, and desired me expressly to write to my Lord Townshend to prevent the King's

---

[1] N. Sykes, *Edmund Gibson* (Oxford 1926), 80–4; *Handbook of British Chronology*, ed. F. M. Powicke, *sub* various dioceses.

[2] Sykes, *op. cit.*, 79–82, HMC, *Portland MSS*, VII, 316, for Dr Stratford's acid comment.

[3] Sykes, *op. cit.*, 86–7. Coxe, II, 350. BM *Add MSS*, 32,686, fos. 300, 312, 321, for Walpole's description to Newcastle of his conversations with Gibson about vacancies.

coming to any resolution about the disposal of the Clerk of the Closetts and Lord Almoner's places. We grow well acquainted. He must be Pope, and would as willingly (be) *our* Pope as anybodies.'[1]

Gibson, indeed, proved 'mortal', but in ways, too, which Walpole found less endearing. Gibson cherished large ambitions for the Church as well as himself. He agreed that the government of the Church should be whig, and Walpolean whig. He also wanted it to be dominated by excellent and sound churchmen. The bishops were to control the Crown patronage in their dioceses and merit, not influence, was to be the touchstone. He aimed, too, to reform the universities and for this end more royal patronage was to be provided and again to be dispensed to good whigs and good churchmen. Walpole and Townshend, bombarded by memoranda of great clarity but inordinate length, took more readily to the former than the latter, creation not dispersal of patronage being their aim. They shuffled the question of Crown patronage on to the shoulders of the Lord Chancellor who controlled it in a legal sense, knowing full well that the years would be eaten up in argument. Gibson's scheme to provide regius professors in modern history and scholarships from the King for the teaching of languages and the production of diplomats at Oxford and Cambridge received Royal sanction; so did his rota of Whitehall preachers by which obscure but promising dons might display their merit at Court. Historians, linguists, learned divines, proved singularly elusive and Gibson's great scheme quickly became further grist for the mill of patronage.

Yet these memoranda showed Gibson's quality; Walpole never liked him; idealism and self-advancement fitted too blindly together in Gibson for his taste and naturally he deplored his obstinacy which was to prove doubly unfortunate when the Princess of Wales became Queen and acquired

---

[1] BM *Add MSS*, 32,686, fo. 327, 6 September 1723. Walpole was so amused by the idea of having a Pope that he continued to call Gibson 'my Pope' which can hardly have endeared him to Gibson. Hervey, I, 90.

the power to indulge her own eclectic taste in the promotion of theologians. But that lay in the future. During these years, 1723–7, thanks to the strength of Gibson and the feebleness of the Archbishops, Walpole and Townshend secured a closer control of the hierarchy and the Church than any ministry had enjoyed since the Revolution. Nor did Walpole's eye rest merely on the hierarchy; deans, prebends, archdeacons, parsons and curates were assessed in terms of their political influence and devotion but, unlike Gibson, he was more concerned for their genealogy than orthodoxy, an idea which also came a few years later to the Bishop of Killala in a moment of inspiration. He wrote to his sister, Mrs Clayton, Mistress of the Robes to the Princess of Wales.

'What occurs to me at present is the considering of ecclesiastical preferments in a political view. It has not been customary for persons either of birth or fortune to breed up their children to the Church by which means when preferment in the Church is given by their Majesties there is seldom anyone obliged but the very person to whom it is given, having no near relations either in the House of Lords or Commons but are gratified or kept in dependence thereby. The only remedy to which is by giving extraordinary encouragements to persons of birth and interest whenever they seek preferment which will encourage others of the same quality to come into the Church and may thereby render ecclesiastical preferments of the same use to their Majesties with civil employments.'[1]

Obviously Walpole's ruthlessly practical attitude to Church patronage struck an echoing chord. Nor did he forget the dissenters. They were loyal whigs. They voted. They could be a nuisance. So he made affirmation easier for the Quakers, spent a thousand a year relieving the necessities of the widows of dissenting clergymen, found a job in the Customs for Isaac Watt's brother, Enoch, cultivated Samuel Holden, bank director, Russia merchant, dissenting leader,

---

[1] A. T. Thomson, *Memoirs of Viscount Sunden*, II, 9. See also HMC *Carlisle MSS*, 55.

and passed a yearly bill of indemnity to save them all from the pains and penalties of the Test Act. That he would not, could not, repeal, but he was ready in all else to sweeten their lot.[1] And his success may be judged by the fact that, in 1727, some Quakers of Hertfordshire voted at his bidding for a Jacobite. There was no chance of a whig, and Walpole always preferred an avowed Jacobite to a Hanoverian tory so the Quakers voted to a man for Charles Cesar.[2] The only sect that Walpole was prepared to persecute, whether through ancient prejudice, intellectual conviction or their lack of influence, was the Roman Catholic.

Many of Walpole's ideas were simple and direct and no man, once convinced, pursued his aims with greater ruthless consistency. Office must be in the hands of loyal men wherever office might be. He did not make Sunderland's mistake and encourage natives in Ireland or in the plantations to expect places. Their governors, too, were made to work for the system and put their patronage at Walpole's disposal. And it is not surprising that ninety per cent of the jottings on the neatly folded pads upon which Walpole scribbled mnemonics for his daily consultations with the King should deal with patronage,[3] nor that his levees, held three times a week, should be thronged with noble supplicants, nor that his doors should daily be besieged by beggars, nor even that his porter should earn more in tips than the income many a country gentleman derived from his estates. From 1722 to 1727 Walpole seized whatever chance came his way to draw patronage under his control; no place was too small for his

[1] For Samuel Holden see N. Hunt, *Sir Robert Walpole, Samuel Holden and the Dissenting Deputies*, Oxford, 1957; for Enoch Watts, *C(H) MSS*, Joseph Gascoigne (?) 23 March 1723.

[2] Governor Edward Harrison of Balls Park, Hertfordshire, MP for Hertford, whose daughter and heiress had married Townshend's eldest son (he was also a close friend of Walpole who patronised him by making him Postmaster-General in 1727 as well as by buying his arrack from him), used his influence for Cesar, so did other supporters of the ministry. Quaker votes can be identified from the poll book for Hertfordshire for 1727. I am indebted for these facts to Mr Lionel M. Munby's unpublished article on *The Hertfordshire Election of 1722*, based on MSS in the possession of Mr Cottrell-Dormer of Rousham.

[3] *C(H) MSS*, Papers, 90, 91.

attention, no person too humble to be considered; a flattering word, a half-made promise, even the hint of future benevolence could serve a purpose; for the more patronage Walpole controlled, the less far it seemed to go, and the greater grew the clamour.

There was not enough. And some saw a sharper edge of Walpole's character. An old friend and schoolmaster up in London to try to obtain a favourable lease of Crown property for Eton was twice shown the door. James Dulle Crispe, sacked from his office in Chelsea Hospital, tried for ten wearisome years to get a fair hearing for his case and failed, a broken and destitute man.[1] Sir John Fryer, Lord Mayor of London in 1721, had served Walpole well by securing the defeat of unwelcome addresses on the South Sea Bubble from the violently angry Common Council. Almost immediately he fell on evil days and by February 1723 he was pleading for a humble post in the Customs of London.[2] Two years later he was still begging, but his condition was far more desperate. He wrote:

'After two years five months attendance on the Treasury it will be needless to repeat the many applications I have made or the frequent promises I have had from your Lordship of a Tidesman's place in the port of London. I am now reduced to that extremity that I must either soone participate in your Honour's favours or change my liberty for confinement in a Gaol. I am well satisfied your Lordship intends to extend your goodness to me for which your Honour has now a fair opportunity by the death of one, Gabriel Butcher, a Tidesman in the port of London that died yesterday morning and should not even now have troubled you with this further address but for the consideration or reminding your Honour under the

[1] *C(H) MSS*, Richard Sleech, 12 May 1724; James Dulle Crispe, 1 June 1724. Crispe was a victim of the spoils system. Walpole wanted his place for a dependant.
[2] Fryer took a more realistic view of his chances than the public at large. In November 1722, he was expected to succeed Sir Marmaduke Wyvil as Commissioner of the Excise. Miège, *Present State of Great Britain* (1723), Lists, 71.

waight of business you support, and my own extremitys which are such as render your Lordship's personal help only servisable to the most unfortunate, humble, and respectful servant, John Fryer.'[1]

Fryer was an old and broken man. What little influence he had possessed in London politics had vanished. Places were not wasted on failures and Fryer died in poverty eighteen months later.[2] Naturally, a sensitive or pitying nature would have found it quite impossible to work this patronage system with Walpole's ruthless efficiency. His method is clear. The juiciest plums went to his own relatives and dependants; offices were showered on his brothers and cousins; on his Norfolk friends; on his bankers, solicitors and agents. Then came the hordes of dependants of his close and loyal allies. The leavings were measured out amongst peers and members of Parliament in return for effective support in their respective houses. There were few, few indeed, who were great enough or influential enough to command a place without Walpole's direct intervention.

Some were excluded; some grew tired of promises endlessly delayed in fulfilment; bitterness, envy, hatred festered until men grew heartsore. During the first few years of Walpole's greatness expectancy kept men quiet; but as months grew into years, hope died and in its place burnt the need for revenge. For a time Walpole could afford to be carefree—to sweep aside with a sneer the envy of the dispossessed. But they cast lengthening shadows across his future and they were bound to grow in number, for there were too many men and too few places; too many aspirants and too few honours, particularly honours, for both the Kings whom Walpole was to serve jealously guarded the

[1] Although Fryer's letter begins 'My Lord' and he used 'Lordship' twice, the letter is to Walpole. It is addressed in Fryer's hand to 'The Rt Hon Robert Walpole'. Presumably the old gentleman was befuddled by his desire to please and had in mind Walpole's Lordship of the Treasury. *C(H) MSS*, Sir John Fryer, 21 February 1723; 13 January 1725.

[2] Fryer died 11 September 1726, see A. Beavan, *Aldermen of London*, also A. J. Henderson, *London and the National Government*, 1721–42, (Duke University Press, 1945), 19, 21, 33, 81, 112.

titles of nobility. In 1725 Walpole's influence was so great that he was able to resuscitate the moribund order of Knighthood of the Bath. Perhaps when the family portraits were taken down from his old house he noticed the red ribbon across the breast of his grandfather, who had been one of the few knighted by Charles II. Thirty-eight new red ribbons eased the demand on the Garter, always so highly prized, and to demonstrate that one might be the stepping-stone to the other, and perhaps to lend distinction to the new order Walpole himself accepted a Knighthood of the Bath; a year later, much to his delight, George I conferred on him the Garter—the first commoner to be so honoured for generations. He gloried in this distinction and had the Star and Garter plastered into the new ceilings and carved into the chimney pieces at Houghton. Even when painted in hunting costume he displayed his blue ribbon and he went to a vast amount of trouble to have the Garter ribbon, George and Star painted on to old portraits.[1] He took the same full-hearted pride and enjoyment in his titles as he did in his fine pictures and houses—much to the wits' delight—and Sir Blue-String became one of his most common nicknames. His installation of a Knight of the Garter was carried out with such expensive pageantry that it was compared with a new coronation. The next year his feast at Windsor outmatched in extravagance the expenditure of any nobleman who had recently received the Garter. Walpole delighted in the most emphatic demonstration of his wealth and power.[2] But the result was not popularity. The

[1] Portraits of Walpole in the possession of General Sir Henry Cholmondeley Jackson and myself, painted probably about 1721 or 1722, have had the Garter ribbon and star painted in: see Plate II.

[2] Milton Percival, *Ballads*, 1–3. A typical stanza is quoted by Mr Percival in his introduction (xlii):

'In Body gross, of Saffron Hue,
Deck'd forth in Green with Ribband Blue.'

Blue ribbon figures very largely in Walpole's bills and accounts. For a description of the installation see A. Boyer, *Political State*, XXIX, 524: C. De Saussure, *A Foreign View of England in the Reigns of George I and George II*, 97–107. Walpole's new order was not universally accepted. Chesterfield refused the red ribbon and was soon writing witty ballads about it, Milton Percival,

glorification of his wealth and power induced envy and hatred. No skill, no adroitness could have stemmed the criticism which Walpole's power and very way of life were bound to create; and it was equally inevitable that Walpole should consign to the wilderness men of brilliant intelligence who lacked, partly because they were so intelligent, the loyalty, devotion and adulation which his exercise of power led him increasingly to expect. And these first halcyon years also brought into being a new opposition which was to harry Walpole for the rest of his days. Besides, there were deeper causes for dissension.

3

GREATLY AS Walpole loved power, the sycophants who crowded his path were a source of anxieties as well as of benefits. Some he knew to be treacherous; others were too restless, too ambitious, too naturally critical for loyalty. And his eminence needed strong buttresses as well as firm foundations. Rooted in patronage, it was also sustained by Walpole's resolute action and shrewd foresight in political situations in which groups of men rather than individuals were involved. 1725 saw the solution of a number of problems which the destruction of Sunderland's group had helped to foster.

The situation in Ireland had grown uglier after the recall of Grafton as Lord Lieutenant. Swift had followed up his first Drapier's Letter by others, equally satirical and effective. The Brodricks, delighted by Carteret's appointment and confidently expecting his help, aimed to create an intolerable situation for Walpole in Dublin. Walpole and Townshend had, however, judged very wisely. Carteret had been shocked by his dismissal from his post as Secretary of State and he regarded the Lord Lieutenancy, for all its dignity, as little better than exile. He loved Europe and longed for

op. cit., 7. The cost of Walpole's installation feast as a KG was £358 5s. 4d. C(H) MSS, Account Book 22.

great occasions. He lacked, however, stamina for constant and unrelenting opposition and could not face the wilderness for a generation. His immense pride had received a severe jolt by his loss of office. His response, as Walpole expected, was to curry favour. He made it quite clear to the Brodricks and to Swift that he had no intention of playing their game, that his Irish policy would be that of Walpole and Towns-hend.[1] Nothing could have been more admirably suited to Walpole's purpose. Broad hints were given to Carteret that, if he entered wholeheartedly into the ministry's policy, further consideration would be given to his promotion when an opportunity arose. By these means Walpole was able to keep him in an active submission for several years.[2]

Carteret, however, failed to quieten Ireland; the Brodricks, the Archbishop of Dublin and Swift had done too much. The detestation in which Wood's halfpennies were held led to a hoarding of coin and a decline in trade. It proved impossible to reduce the Irish House of Commons to that comfortable subordination to the ministry which had come to be ex-pected of it by the King's servants. Walpole detested changing his policy. He knew the coinage to be of excellent value, far better than the copper coinage circulating in England. The profits of Wood, Walpole argued, time and time again, were modest and no more than any manufacturer had the right to expect. The Irish remained convinced that they were the victims of fraud, that their wealth was being filched to satisfy the greed of the King's whore. Walpole had little use for public opinion; he lived so close to the realities of political management that it seemed an irrelevance, a deliberate exploitation of human stupidity by malevolent enemies. And so, although he was told repeatedly by Carteret that Wood's patent would have to go, if Ireland were to be quietened, he was most obstinate and accepted the decision to withdraw the coins with great reluctance.[3] And, naturally enough,

---

[1] Coxe, II, 422, 435–7; HMC, *Bath MSS*, I, 251.
[2] Coxe, II, 489–90.
[3] RW informed Boulter on 19 August 1725 that R. Edgcumbe, Vice-Treasurer of Ireland, was personally carrying to Dublin the surrender of

though he hated compensating Wood, he had no alternative.

The victory of Walpole's enemies proved brief and illusory. The Brodricks were quickly removed from all positions of influence. They were followed into limbo by a troop of native Irish who had secured places in the expansive days of Sunderland. Hugh Boulter, Archbishop of Armagh, sent an express at the death of every placeman to Newcastle, Townshend and Walpole; he named with unerring accuracy the Irish who had to be stopped and never lacked a nominee —safe, English and Walpolean. Such a policy could only lead as the years passed to resentment and to active enmity amongst the Anglo-Irish of Dublin, but the short term results proved effective. Walpole secured an extension of patronage wherever he could and in the end achieved a reasonably docile Irish government. Much to his amusement, during his next visit to London, Swift called on him in the expectation that his desire for promotion might at last be gratified—a curiously opaque action considering that Swift had recently finished *Gulliver's Travels*, one of the most remarkable and virulent satires ever to be written against Walpole. To no one's surprise but his own Swift got short shrift.

If Ireland was one problem settled, there were others as difficult. Since the Union in 1707 Scotland had never settled down; rebellions, plots, scares of invasion produced a welter of intrigue, double-dealing, divided loyalties, duplicity and chicanery. Neither the representative Scotch peers nor the forty-five Scotch members of Parliament at Westminster were remarkable in any way for their political principles. They kept their eye on the main chance even if, unlike Alexander Abercrombie, they did not beg outright for pensions.[1] Whether they begged or not a surprising number

---

Wood's patent, as a mark of the Royal favour. In the same letter Walpole hoped that in Irish affairs Boulter would always remember that he was an Englishman. *A Catalogue of Books, Manuscripts and Autograph Letters*, issued by Messrs Commins of Bournemouth (1959) item 475.

[1] *C(H) MSS*, Alexander Abercrombie, 2 January 1725; he was in receipt of a pension of £1,000 per annum in 1720. *Blenheim MSS*, D. II. 3.

managed to obtain a comforting addition to their incomes out of the Secret Service Fund. Among those in receipt of pensions around 1721 were: the Earl of Hopetoun, £3,000; the Earl of Leven, £2,000; the Earl of Orkney, £2,000; the Earl of Loudon, £1,000; the Hon Mr Ross, £2,000; the Earl of Marchmont, £1,000; Lord Polwarth, £1,000; Messrs Robert Sinclair, John Scot, John Hay, John Kerr, £1,000 apiece and so on.[1] This expenditure seemed fruitless to Walpole unless the Scots were dependable and loyal and kept Scotland reasonably quiet. They were neither. Ancient loyalties and recent intrigues set the Argyll faction at loggerheads with the 'Squadrone', who, through the Duke of Roxburghe, Secretary of State for Scotland, had linked their fortune first with Sunderland and then with Carteret. Neither Walpole nor Townshend liked Argyll; necessity, however, forced their alliance, for Argyll was not only opposed to Carteret's friends in Scotland but he was also the rival of Cadogan and a close friend of the Prince of Wales. Townshend and Walpole had committed themselves to Argyll before the wild riots in Glasgow in the summer of 1725 gave them their opportunity to break Roxburghe and the Squadrone and place the politics of Scotland into the safe keeping of Argyll and his brother, Islay.[2] Roxburghe had made a foolish calculation. He and his friends, according to Islay, 'believed and do so to this day, that I am acting against the secret inclinations of the King, only to support Sir Robert Walpole, that he is next session of Parliament to fall, and that one Mr Pulteney would have all in his hands in conjunction with Dundas and the Duke of Roxburg'.[3] This

---

[1] *Blenheim MSS*, D. II. 3.

[2] *C(H) MSS*, Duncan Forbes, 29 June 1725; John Campbell, 29 June 1725; Charles Erskine, 29 June 1725; Richard Dowdeswell to John Scrope, 1 July 1725; Anon (Islay?), 27 August 1725. The maltsters at Edinburgh also refused to admit the Excise officers, but riots did not develop as in Glasgow where, according to Forbes, eight were killed and eighteen injured and several houses demolished by the mob, who objected to the imposition of a malt tax for Scotland at the same rate as for England. See also Coxe, II, 438–70: BM *Stowe MSS*, 251, *passim*.

[3] Coxe, II, 457. Dundas had been dismissed from the office of Lord Advocate in May 1725 and replaced by Duncan Forbes. Also *Chatsworth MSS*, RW

must represent almost the nadir of political judgment—even for a Scottish Duke—and can scarcely have been equalled. Never had Walpole been stronger nor was he ever again to give so frequent demonstrations of his power as in the early months of 1725. Perhaps the ease with which he secured Roxburghe's dismissal impressed the dull-witted Scottish politicians. His new allies, however, proved no cheaper than the old and the cost to the secret service fund was considerable, for the supporters of Argyll, like the Squadrone, knew their price. The secret service expenditure rose sharply and Walpole had to send to Herrenhausen for fresh supplies.[1] And it proved a better bargain; the Argylls remained loyal and Scotland quiet through the difficult years ahead.

Ireland and Scotland were brought by a wise use of strength and an unerring judgment of character to a position of quiet subordination, a success of which Walpole could claim to be the sole begetter. Not all of his decisive acts were, however, to prove so effective as these. Naturally Walpole set out to bind to himself as closely as possible the outlying

to Devonshire, 23 August 1725: 'Lord Townshend's letter to Duke of Roxburghe upon this occasion declares the King's resolution to putt an end to the office of the Scottish Secretary of State and not to appoint any other for the future to be the reason of His Majesties taking this resolution and at the same time offers him a Pension of 3000l per ann. for his past services.
I could not but be of opinion that the present state of affairs in Scotland made this measure absolutely necessary, and as it is most manifest and certain that the Duke of Roxburghe's friends and immediate dependents do not only countenance and abett the disorders in Scotland but are the authors and advisers of every measure that is taken to keep up and increase the present confusion, it is impossible to conceive they would act this part if they did not know it to be agreeable to their Patron, and it is as vain to imagine what they have carried matters to this length that they would at all desist untill they were convinced that they had not the support here, which they flattered themselves to have from the supposed creditt and power of the Duke of Roxburghe and your Grace must be sensible how impossible it was for us to carry on the common businesse of Scotland, much lesse to struggle with the present difficulties when we dare not trust the Secretary of State of the Province with any one thought or resolution that was to be executed.'
[1] The amount spent on secret service in 1725 was £103,350 as against £77,450 for 1724 and £42,024 for 1726, *Westmorland MSS*, Scrope Papers, Northants R.O. On 7 September 1725 Walpole sent 3 warrants to George I; in the Scrope Papers there is, however, only one warrant of this date, cashed for £5,000. The Scrope warrants may not be complete.

political systems and areas of patronage in order to build up an unassailable position at Court. The semi-independent and extremely powerful influence of the City of London in the turbulent politics of the seventeenth and eighteenth centuries has, more frequently than not, been overlooked by historians.[1] And few realize that Walpole in 1725 achieved what the Stuarts had, to their cost, failed to achieve—a deliberate reduction in the democratic privileges of the City and a sharp curtailment of the independence of its most influential citizens—a singular triumph for a man devoted to the whig principle of liberty.

For many generations London had given proof of its turbulence. The city fathers were conscious of their power and of their wealth, but they were not all friendly to Walpole nor even to the whigs, and the City's ancient right of addressing the King was used as much to embarrass the ministry as to support it. Furthermore the constitution of the corporation was in many aspects democratic and elections to the shrievalty and to the aldermanic bench involved a wide franchise which reached down to the smaller artisans and craftsmen, amongst whom an amorphous toryism flourished. Great art had been needed to keep the City even moderately quiet during the South Sea crisis and the powers of the aldermanic bench had been stretched to their limit. This tenuous control had been disrupted by the Duke of Wharton, a man of erratic brilliance, restless, exhibitionistic, vain to a degree that bordered on insanity. With his newspaper the *True Briton*[2] he began to exploit and to influence public opinion against Walpole and the ministry. He gave reckless support to Atterbury. He campaigned vigorously at every election for City office and quickly turned every one into a major battle of confidence in the ministry and its aldermanic supporters.

[1] The best discussion of this subject is Miss Lucy Sutherland's 'The City of London in Eighteenth Century Politics' in *Essays Presented to Sir Lewis Namier*, ed. Richard Pares and A. J. P. Taylor: A. J. Henderson, *London and the National Government*, 1721-42 (Duke University, Durham, 1945), is also valuable.

[2] *The True Briton* commenced publication on 3 June 1723 and lasted until 17 February 1724.

Mobs and riots were deliberately provoked and carefully exploited. Pamphlets, ballads, squibs, of unequalled virulence poured forth from the presses. At elections voters were bribed, bullied, suborned, counterfeited, kidnapped and at times polled though long dead. And although Wharton achieved victories and the opposition gained in strength and influence in the Corporation, nevertheless the flagrant dis-order and corruption, wanton even for Walpole's age, finally destroyed him and he fled to join the Pretender and to end his life in frustration and poverty, claiming to the last to be, though a Jacobite, a true whig. This was not such a paradox that it might now seem nor was it merely an eccentric whim of Wharton's. Indeed, in his attitude he showed perception and intelligence, if not judgment. Wharton was acutely and rightly aware of London's radi-calism, of its 'old whig', seventeenth-century sentiment; he failed to realize that it was still strongly puritan, bitterly anti-Catholic and that the Jacobitism which some of its leaders paraded had never taken deep root.

Nevertheless Wharton's irruption into London politics demonstrated to Walpole the dangers which were inherent in the City's constitution. His candidates had been defeated in aldermanic elections and he had failed by a large majority to secure the office of Sheriff for his party. Two tories had been returned to Parliament as members for the City. Both he and Townshend felt that the opposition had gained im-measurably. As early as the summer of 1723 Walpole gave a dinner party at Chelsea at which were present the Attorney-General, the Solicitor-General and the whig aldermen of the City, probably to discuss how London could be managed. Wharton's reckless disregard of all forms of legality at the by-election in March 1724 for the Sheriff, on the death of Felix Feast, played right into Walpole's hands and gave him a strong case for regulating the City's elections. By April 1724 plans for action had been drawn up and Townshend reported to the King that the ministry would be prepared to lay before Parliament 'such bills as may for the future

secure the government of that important place [i.e. London]
entirely in the hands of those who are zealous for your
Majesty's interest'.[1]

The City, however, was very tender of its ancient privileges and Walpole needed to plan his tactics with great care.
Deliberations with his City supporters went on throughout
the summer of 1724 and it was not until 13 December that
Walpole finally struck at London's liberties. He persuaded
several eminent aldermen to petition Parliament for a
curtailment of their city's privileges. The last day before the
Christmas recess was wisely chosen; a thin House agreed to
proceed at once rather than to hear evidence on the petition.
A bill to give the aldermen a veto of the Common Court's
proceedings, to circumscribe the number of liverymen in the
Companies and to raise scot and lot in order to exclude the
poorer freemen from elections was introduced in the New
Year. The opposition in the City fought back and not without
skill. The bill was certain to pass, but every Company petitioned to be heard at the bar against the proposal to limit
the number of their liverymen, a request which could not be
refused; to accept was impossible, so the threat of a filibuster
forced the withdrawal of this clause. In committee, too,
sentiment ran against Walpole, who wanted to see a high rate
of scot and lot; but he got his own way in the end and drove
through an amendment to the third reading. And so the
City Bill passed—3,000 freemen were disenfranchised and
the aldermen confirmed in their powers of veto, which had
always been disputed and never exercised without question
since the reign of Charles I.[2]

Naturally many protested very vigorously against this
reduction of the City's franchise and liberties, though to no
purpose. And the Court was triumphant from Townshend
and Newcastle to young John Lekeux who wrote, 'I hope
that it will prove for the good of the nation. For it is a great

---

[1] HMC, *Underwood MSS*, 429.
[2] *Brabourne MSS, Knatchbull's Diary*, fos. 56, 59, 65-6: A. J. Henderson,
op. cit., 99-113.

shame that the cits should oppose the designs of the government at all elections with so much mutiny and carry themselves with so much ignorant pride, followed by a brutish
behaviour, as they have for several years practised. This will
bring them to reason.' It did. With its aid, and the Duke of
Newcastle's solicitous interest, the Court's candidates were
both elected unopposed to the office of Sheriff two months
later.[1]

Indeed 1725 was proving a glorious year for Walpole;
everything seemed to be going his way. The troubles of
Ireland and Scotland had merely hurt his enemies. Great
fields of patronage had been securely dovetailed into his
system. His luck held even in minor matters. The right
bishops died; the King proved willing to part with old, loyal
friends; Jacobites, convinced of the hopelessness of their
cause, came trooping back, eager to please, docile for a
pardon's sake; the flight of Wharton got rid of a dangerous
and versatile agitator.[2] Even the impeachment of Lord
Chancellor Macclesfield for taking bribes and selling offices
strengthened rather than weakened his ministry. Walpole
had never liked Macclesfield and was particularly glad to
see him go, for he succeeded in replacing him by Sir Peter
King, an old, loyal friend of a generation's standing. And
now with the City subjected, the aldermanic bench was as
pliant as the episcopal.

The change became quickly apparent not only in elections
but in the City's addresses; complaint vanished and flattery
prevailed. The ministry became so delighted by the extravagant terms in which the City continued to address the
King that they celebrated their new-found harmony with a
gigantic feast on 31 January 1727, the greatest, according to
the *Daily Courant*, since the reign of Charles II. 'They [i.e.
the Lord Mayor and Aldermen] were afterwards all of
them most sumptuously entertained in his Majesty's palace
with near a thousand dishes of meat, the most exquisite and

[1] BM *Add MSS*, 32,687, fo. 95.
[2] Realey, *Early Opposition*, 150–2.

most in season, besides a very fine dessert of sweetmeats and fruit. Everything was done in the handsomest manner without the least disorder, to the satisfaction of every person there. The Lord Mayor and Aldermen were honoured with all the Prime Ministers of State at their table, and each other table had at the head of it a great officer of the household. There was a vast plenty of all sorts of the finest wines, and the greatest cheerfulness appeared throughout the whole company that was ever seen upon any occasion.'[1]

In the last minutes of consciousness before they sank into their drunken comas, the aldermen doubtless savoured their curious distinction, but to the other end of the City they presented a more comic picture and one which the ballad-makers relished to the full.

'Now Royal Healths in rank and file full thick and three-
    fold come,
No flinching from the charge, the Word was *Supernaculum;*
Tho' scarcely they till five began, so dreadful was the
    shock,
That many a sturdy *Briton* bold was slain by six a clock.
                . . . . .
For Pipes by gross and Wine by Ton, they called with
    might and main.
They smoaked and drank, and drank and spewed, and
    spewed and drank again.
If ever there was Truth at Court, 'twas then without all
    Doubt,
For would you know a Courtier's Heart? why, turn him
    inside out.
                . . . . .
When Wine was in and wit was out, to Frolicks they
    advance,
The Cits and Nobles changed their cloths, the *Quaker* he
    did dance;
Some Heroes on the Table got, and Victory did crow,
While down among the dead men, more were forced to
    lie below.
                . . . . .

[1] *Daily Courant*, 31 January 1727, quoted Milton Percival, *Ballads*, 11.

Now Wine like Death a Leveller of great and small we
    see,
The Duke of high Renown lay strowed with 'Squire of
    low Degree;
The Common Councilmen were rowled with Peers of
    Council-Board;
The Lords were drunk like any King, the Cits like any
    Lord.

. . . . .

No more ye *Londoners*, go on your Betters to abuse
Or say, the Court debauches all, its Manners are so
    loose;
For never to St *James's* yet was seen such pretty sport
Till citizens from *London* Town went to debauch the
    Court.'[1]

But this is to run ahead. By 1727, Walpole's glory had begun to tarnish a little. He was never to know the freedom
from anxiety, the ease of accomplishment of the two years
that followed Carteret's fall. Nothing went wrong for him.
Money poured in, glory followed. All that he touched
flourished, even riots and rebellions turned to his advantage.
And to cap all he fell in love—wisely, finally and most
successfully.

Little is known of Maria Skerrett's early life. She was the
daughter of Thomas Skerrett, who sported the arms of
Skerrett of Galway, and was born in 1702 in the City.[2] Her
father was said to be a gentleman of fortune. Certainly he
married wisely—rich widows, first a Pleydell, then a Rolle,
and moved on his second marriage to the West End where
his wife, the widow of Sir Henry Winchcombe, had a house

---

[1] *Daily Courant*, 31 January 1727, quoted Milton Percival, *Ballads*, 11.
[2] Maria Skerrett, daughter of Thomas Skerrett by Hester (Stafford),
widow of John Pleydell, gentleman, was born 5 October 1702 and baptised
15 October 1702 at St Bene'ts, Pauls Wharf, London. Her father married
secondly on 7 July 1710 at St James's, Piccadilly, Elizabeth (Rolle), second
wife of Sir Henry Winchcombe of Bucklebury, bt., who incidentally was also
stepmother to Henry St John, Viscount Bolingbroke. Oddly enough the
Pleydell family were clients of the St Johns and two of them had sat for St
John's borough, Wootton Bassett. According to Egmont, Skerrett was a stay-
maker, but Egmont disliked Walpole and his morals. HMC, *Egmont's Diary*, II,
469. *Ex. inf.* Captain T. T. Barnard and GEC *Baronetage*.

in Stratton Street, two doors from old Lady Stafford, the close friend and confidante of Lady Mary Wortley Montagu. Indeed it may have been through Lady Mary that Walpole first met Maria.[1] She was living with her at Twickenham throughout the summer of 1724—near enough to Hampton Court where Walpole spent a considerable part of the summer.[2] Hervey hints that Walpole did not achieve a quick conquest and that this relationship, which was to bring him so much consolation, had a mercenary beginning. Whether his malicious jibe that Walpole paid £6,000 entrance money is true or not, certainly Molly had become his mistress by the autumn of 1724, for their illegitimate daughter, Maria, was born in 1725.

Walpole's eagerness to obtain the Rangership of Richmond Park for his eldest son was in order to provide a retreat for Molly and himself. He rebuilt and furnished the Old Lodge with the utmost rapidity, and installed a housekeeper, Mrs Burton. His weekends there with Molly became the most fixed routine of his life, a routine which not even crises in the Royal Family could break.[3]

Although Walpole had something of a reputation for gallantry and his illegitimate daughter, Catherine Daye, gives substance to the rumour, it is doubtful whether sexual passion was a strong driving force in his character. In

[1] The gossip certainly was current that Lady Mary had procured Maria for him. A scurrilous letter from Paris which denounces Lady Mary ends as follows: 'Must they [Townshend and Walpole] not see by this what a vile person she [i.e. Lady Mary] is and is it not making a jest of and exposing the ministry and particularly Walpole? But his doxie, is seems, can get the better of him in anything where the procuress is concerned.' *C(H) MSS*, ? Morison to Alexander, 19 October 1728.

[2] Walpole was minister-in-attendance on the Prince at Richmond during George I's visit to Hanover. See *C(H) MSS*, Account Book 20a. *Letters of Lady Mary Wortley Montagu*, ed. W. Moy Thomas, II, 493. A codicil, written in a shaky hand, to Thomas Skerrett's will (PCC, Ockham, 44) and probably written in December 1733, refers to the fact that he is putting his will in 'an honest man's hands who I do not doubt will see this, and that which he has, executed and proved. I do this because you [i.e. Maria] have a very ill person to govern which, I could not persuade you to part with this 9 years.' Presumably this refers to Walpole, which would place the connection in 1724. *Ex. inf.* Captain T. T. Barnard.

[3] Hervey, II, 633.

George I's day the women of the Court hardly bothered with the pretence of virtue, and the possession of lovers and mistresses was regarded as commonplace, a matter for gossip but not reproach. And a man who could laugh and joke with his fourteen-year-old daughter-in-law about Lord Stair's attempt to seduce her was unlikely to go to many lengths to hide his attachments.[1] Walpole was nothing if not frank in such matters. Yet Molly Skerrett was his first mistress to arouse widespread gossip; the first whom the whole of London society knew that he was keeping. His previous affairs must have been casual and unimportant. About this one there was nothing casual or unimportant. He loved Molly as completely as he had ever loved anyone and remained devoted to her for the rest of his days.[2] She gave him quiet, ease, affection, probably love. Her portraits display a tall, rather plain girl, inclined to be thin and to show bone. But all contemporaries speak of her wit and charm and excellent common sense.[3] She remains a shadowy figure; no letters between them remain. The depth of Walpole's love can be judged from the eagerness with which he married her the moment his wife died and his sorrow at her death soon afterwards. She gave him the warmth and security which his wife had long since failed to provide. But meeting her and winning her must have given an added zest to the two most successful years of Walpole's life. In 1724 and 1725 all that he touched prospered and the

---

[1] *Letters of Lady Mary Wortley Montagu*, ed. W. Moy Thomas (1893), I, 499.

[2] Naturally Walpole was eager to make adequate provision for Maria and characteristically he did so out of the public funds. Stafford Pleydell of Oxford, her step-brother, was granted by sign manual in 1727 £400 p.a.; he acknowledged this to be a trust in a deed in which blanks were carefully left for Sir Robert to fill in himself, naturally with Maria's name, so that the transaction could be kept completely secret. *C(H) MSS*, Papers 53, 24, 25. This was continued until Sir Robert married her. Maria also had assigned to her £200 p.a. from the office of Inspector and Examiner of Books of Patent, held by Edward Jackson of Richmond New Park and in 1735 she acquired £500 p.a. from the office of Comptroller-General of the Accounts of His Majesty's Customs which has previously been paid to Galfridus Walpole's widow, who forfeited her claim on her second marriage. By 1735, Maria was drawing £1,000 p.a. of public money. *C(H) MSS*, Papers 91–82, 88.

[3] HMC, *Hare MSS*, 238: Hervey, III, 746. See also Plate IV.

anxiety which was so marked a trait in his character was stifled, or at least diverted from his own concerns. His restless suspicions, however, began to focus on Townshend's foreign policy.

CHAPTER FOUR

THE CLOUDS GATHER, 1726-27

IN CONTRAST to England, so quiet, so prosperous, so easy to manage, Europe from 1724 to 1725 was full of drama and excitement. Although its problems remained largely the same, or were merely reshuffled, monarchs and adventurers behaved with more than usual panache. The Congress of Cambrai, which had met in 1722 to settle the problems of Europe, acted as if it had been called for eternity. Two years were spent in examining credentials, in settling the grave problems of precedence, and the inconceivably intricate question of whether a Papal legate might or might not be a member of the Congress. These arduous tasks, which affronted governments and set tempers aflame, were interspersed with gigantic dinner parties in which a spirit of national and ambassadorial competition flourished unchecked. So great was the strain on Lord Polwarth's stomach that his health finally collapsed and he was forced to ask for a separate table at his rivals' banquets where, free from temptation, he could stick to his regimen. After two years the delegates' powers had been either accepted or rejected, the Emperor had brought himself to refer to the King of Sardinia as 'Good Brother', and even the thorny problem of the Eventual Investitures—the acceptance of Elizabeth Farnese's sons as Tuscany's heirs—had been neatly solved. These diplomatic triumphs enabled the Congress to begin, but long before the interminable wranglings reached their conclusions the patience of the great powers had snapped.[1]

The trouble was Louis XV's puberty. He had been caught frolicking with his pages which, for those versed in Bourbon history, boded no good. Worse than his morals, however, was the delicate state of his health. There was no

[1] For Cambrai, HMC, *Polwarth MSS*, III and IV (*passim*).

doubt that Louis was capable of fatherhood, yet he was betrothed to the Infanta of Spain, aged nine; if his potentialities were not realized, it might be a calamity for the duc de Bourbon and for France. Six years' delay could see Louis dead, or with his own solution to a prolonged celibacy. A sudden illness of Louis in February 1725 prompted Bourbon to pack off the Infanta to Spain without further ado.[1] Rash as ever, Bourbon had ordered her return before he had secured an alternative, although probably Fleury, the wily tutor of Louis, who had attached his charge to himself by methods more subtle than those used by his predecessor, Dubois, already had his eye on the obvious choice. However, he proceeded by negatives, opposing first Bourbon's absurd suggestion that Louis marry a daughter of the Prince of Wales, vetoing the second and scarcely less ridiculous proposal of Mademoiselle de Vermandois, and keeping silent when Maria Leszczynska, daughter of the exiled King of Poland and heiress of Lorraine, was selected. To anyone who had the expansion of French power at heart, she was an obvious choice.[2]

The nuptials were concluded with alacrity, particularly by Louis XV, who, the morning after his wedding, informed his courtiers, with the loftiness which, perhaps, comes naturally to monarchs, that getting sons was a pretty easy business. For a time, however, the skill eluded him, and it was some five years later when, to the relief of Fleury and Horatio Walpole, the Queen gave birth, in a room pullulating with courtiers, to what old Horatio in his excitement described to his brother as a 'Dolphin'.

The repudiation of the Infanta caused a sensation. Arguments which seemed unanswerable in Versailles sounded specious enough in Madrid, and Elizabeth Farnese cursed Louis,

[1] Bourbon was motivated partly by jealousy of Philip V as well as by his fears for France. Discussion of the desirability of repudiating the Spanish marriage started as early as 1724.

[2] Paul de Raynal, *Le Marriage d'un Roi*, 1721-5 (Paris, 1887). Coxe, HW., 86-95; A. McC. Wilson, *French Foreign Policy during the Administration of Fleury* (Harvard, 1936), 29-35; *Walpole MSS*, HW to Townshend, 22 December 1723. Mademoiselle de Vermandois was Bourbon's sister.

Bourbon, Fleury and the French Ambassador in language that was far from royal. She was already tired of Cambrai. At its rate of progress the differences between Spain and the Empire were unlikely to be settled for decades, and Elizabeth was not a patient woman. The Golden Fleece, the tumble-down palaces at Rome, dignities and titles, Gibraltar and Minorca, haunted the lunatic world of Philip V and made him as rash as his wife and willing to support any change of policy which could still bring quick results. Lurking on the fringe of the Spanish Court there was a strange, bombastic Dutchman, Ripperda, who had come to Spain as a diplomat. He had changed his nationality and, out for a fortune, undertaken the directorate of Spanish lace-making. He was quite willing to return to his old profession and undertook with alacrity to go secretly to Vienna to negotiate directly with Charles VI an Austro-Spanish treaty that would wreck the Congress.[1]

It is difficult to know whether Ripperda had been sent in November 1724 with truly serious intent. Such an adventurer could very easily have been repudiated, and he may have been intended only as a threat to France and England, to force them into action at Cambrai and to hurry on a settlement. Ripperda was a man who envisaged life in grandiose and dramatic terms. Lacking the caution of the career diplomat, he made such offers to the Court of Vienna that they were quickly dazzled into negotiation with their arch-enemy. Of course, Ripperda's secret mission soon sent couriers hurtling post haste across Europe, and bulky, gilt-edged despatches lay in thick bundles on Newcastle's and Townshend's writing tables, full of speculation and ignorant of fact. The prospect of a separate treaty between Spain and Austria was, however, sufficient in itself to chill Townshend's

[1] For Ripperda see Coxe, II, 572–622: G. Syveton, *Une Cour et Un Aventurier au XVIII Siècle* (Paris, 1896), a brilliant book by perhaps the only historian to have been murdered through discovering that his wife frequented a brothel (see Hicks, *Ces Dames—Psychologie et Pathologie sexuelle de l'Affaire Syveton*, Paris, n.d.). For such a risky piece of diplomacy an adventurer, such as Ripperda, who could easily be repudiated, was more suitable than a career diplomat.

blood, for England had failed to secure the suppression of the Ostend Company.[1]

This thorn in England's flesh had been started by Jacobites with the intention of irritating the East India Company and lowering its profits. Charles VI, who needed trade, gave what encouragement he could and evaded the diplomatic protests which were levelled at him by Dutch and British statesmen. As Townshend had married his son to the heiress of Governor Edward Harrison, a leading figure in the East India Company, he was subject to almost as much pressure as Charles VI. Horatio Walpole in Paris was continuously bidden to hearken to the Governor's complaints and to bring them to the notice of the French Court which, Townshend hoped, would sooner or later use its influence with Spain to curtail the activities of the Ostend Company. A committee of the Commons in 1723 reported on the injury it was doing British trade. Englishmen were forbidden to invest in it; and finally its ships were even harried, though the Company remained unsuppressed and its trade continued. The French were quite indifferent and, like Charles VI himself, prepared to tolerate it for the sake of its value as a diplomatic bargaining counter. An Austro-Spanish alliance, to Townshend, to Harrison, and to a large section of the City, created the instant suspicion that increased trading privileges would be granted to the Ostend Company to the detriment of British commerce. Even the presence of Ripperda at Vienna was enough to alarm the ministry.[2]

The repudiation of the Infanta turned what may have been intended as a manoeuvre into a serious diplomatic exchange. The wanton promises of Ripperda were blindly accepted by Elizabeth and Philip. The Emperor secured commercial privileges and subsidies and in return gave

[1] For *Ostend Company:* G. B. Hertz, 'England and the Ostend Company', EHR, XXII (1907) 255-79. C(H) MSS, John Wordsworth, 30 March 1723: Monsieur de l'Hermitage to Townshend, 5 April 1723.

[2] *Walpole MSS*, William Stanhope to Townshend, 27 December 1725; Coxe, II, 580-1: Wickham Legg, *Diplomatic Instructions, France*, IV, *1721-7*, 108-9.

almost nothing. He moved a step further towards his admission of Don Carlos to his principality, he promised help in case of need and implied, but did not state, that he would accept a marriage alliance. In return Spain offered commercial privileges and subsidies with a profusion that would have done her honour in the days of her greatness. Horatio at Paris, William Stanhope at Madrid, Saphorin at Vienna, Polwarth and Whitworth at Cambrai read in between and beyond the text of the Treaty; and their speculations and suspicions found fertile soil in the cabinet. Gibraltar was to be retaken with the help of Austria. The Ostend Company was to be given a monopoly of trade to the Spanish Main to the ruin of the South Sea Company. And worse, at least in George I's eyes, both Spain and Austria had promised to support the extravagant claims of Russia in the Baltic. In all of these speculations there was naturally a great deal of truth, for they were the perennial problems of the '20s rephrased in a particular situation. And, as ever, it was the impact of the Southern problem on the North which provoked George I and his advisers to action. Russia by bribes and cajolery had obtained strong influence in Sweden, and once more was threatening Denmark with that useful family retainer and pretender, the Duke of Holstein-Gottorp. The Czarina had the effrontery to suggest that, if Schleswig were not forthcoming, Bremen and Verden would make a convenient duchy for him. Naturally this stung George I into action. Townshend revelled in his new and dramatic situation, and his despatches, so crisp and decisive, were a remarkable contrast to the wamblings of Newcastle as he bobbed in his wake like a rudderless dinghy.[1] Fortunately France, whose major diplomatic aim was the isolation of Austria, was also eager for action. By 3 September 1725 Townshend had brought about the Alliance of Hanover,

---

[1] Wilson, *op. cit.*; Wickham Legg, *op. cit.*; Coxe, II, 471–93; Coxe, HW, 97–108: also *Walpole MSS*, Despatches of Lord Townshend, 1725: Despatches of Duke of Newcastle, 1725. Walpole's major worry in all this was that the Czarina would give military aid to the Jacobites and he at once proposed to send a spy to St. Petersburg. Coxe, II, 485–6.

which bound Great Britain, France and Prussia in a defensive system. At once Townshend set about converting Denmark, Sweden and the German princes to his policy— their hunger for English gold made them easy proselytes, for Townshend, much to Walpole's horror, gave with a ready hand. Even before the Hanover Alliance had been concluded, he had complained of the extravagance of Pointz's bribes in Sweden.[1] He hated the thought of war.[2]

The credit of England had never been so flourishing. Money was ready and cheap; stocks firm; harvests bumper; taxation low; commerce flourishing; in all of which Walpole could take a personal pride.[3] He knew all too well that the ease of his control of the House of Commons was in many ways due to this excellent, buoyant prosperity. It was grievous to him that this should be jeopardized by war or threats of war, and his letters to Townshend harp constantly on the need for caution, and dwell repeatedly on the baneful influence of mobilization on credit. Furthermore, he learnt that the Pulteneys intended to use the Hanover Treaty to stir up trouble in Parliament. Their correspondence with the Imperial ministers had been intercepted and opened. They ridiculed the fears of the British ministers; the Austrians stressed the innocence of their intentions, and Walpole saw little hope of a docile Parliament.[4]

And then the sabres began to rattle. A further offensive

---

[1] Coxe, II, 471–3. Actually Pointz proved to be very careful and judicious in his expenditure.

[2] Walpole's attitude to foreign affairs at this time is admirably summed up in a letter of December 1725 to an unknown correspondent who, on account of the unguarded language used, was probably either his brother Horatio or Newcastle: 'You know I do not love to give long opinions nor reasonings upon foreign policies, but your apprehension of any rupture for the next spring does not seem to me so formidable as it appears to others, and as neither the circumstances nor interest of any other powers can make them too hastily fond of a breach, I think the circumstances and true interest of England should have such a share in our consideration as not to be quite carried away by heroism, unless it was as easy really to conquer and reduce kingdoms as tis to magnify our own power in writing and to talk big to one another, to which I wish our swaggering was entirely confined.' PRO, *S. P. Dom.*, 35/60. Dec. 1725, Walpole to ?.

[3] Land Tax in 1725 was 2/- in the £, the lowest for a generation.

[4] Coxe, II, 492.

alliance was secretly concluded by Ripperda at Vienna. True, the Czarina had been momentarily checked in the North, but an onslaught on Gibraltar and war between France and the Empire seemed unavoidable as the year 1725, which had been so big with fulfilment, ended darkly. But it was not only the aspirations of the monarchs of Europe that were to bring tribulations to Walpole. He had made two bitter personal enemies; both in their way were men of genius, both politicians who excelled in and drew deep satisfaction from the destructive pleasures of opposition.

2

BOLINGBROKE AND William Pulteney were two men of exceptional gifts who moved into permanent opposition to Walpole between 1725 and 1726, and began to scheme for his downfall. Although Walpole had only himself to blame for their enmity, he had no other choice—at least in the case of Bolingbroke. Pulteney had never been an easy colleague. Once in opposition with Walpole in 1717, he had objected to his policy of close alliance with the tories on which Walpole had settled.[1] In 1721 he protested against Walpole's settlement of the civil list debts; in July 1723, Walpole and Pulteney were at loggerheads.[2] Pulteney had an excellent head for figures and loved using it; unfortunately the faults of Walpole's financial arrangements were more glaring to him than their merits.[3] Walpole had rather half-heartedly tried to buy him off. After the tiff of 1721, Pulteney had been made Lord Lieutenant of the East Riding of Yorkshire in the following year: in 1723 he had been given the very lucrative post of Cofferer of the Household, Walpole hoping that Pulteney's avarice would keep him loyal when so nobly assuaged. Unfortunately for Walpole, Pulteney was as ambitious as he was

[1] *Walpole*, I, 249.
[2] Realey, *Early Opposition*, 155–67: BM, *Add MSS*, 32,686, fo. 720.
[3] 'He could state and explain the most intricate matters, even in figures, with the utmost perspicacity': Chesterfield, *Letters* (ed. J. Bradshaw, 1926), III, 1415.

avaricious, and an exceedingly rich wife and a large personal
fortune enabled him to gratify both his appetites on the
largest possible scale. He expected Carteret's post in 1724 and
waited for another twelve months without extracting anything
from Walpole apart from promises of future promotion. On
8 April 1725, when Walpole asked the House of Commons,
neither for the first nor the last time, to meet the debts of the
civil list, Pulteney bared his teeth. He made a sharp speech,
hinting at waste, corruption and concealment, and demanded
that a full statement of expenditure on pensions and secret
service be laid before the House. The next day Pulteney
set about Walpole, accused him of providing false figures,
insisted that money was filched from the Sinking Fund, that
the Bank was allowed to make money out of the civil list
debts, that the financial arrangements were thoroughly in-
competent, that money was squandered on pensions,
bounties and gratuities, that Walpole was feathering his
own nest handsomely—a speech which naturally enough
nettled Walpole. He answered Pulteney's criticisms of
figures patiently enough, but once he came to the question
of corruption, about which he was always very thin-skinned,
he gave Pulteney as good as he got. He told him that 'he
thought it hard and unparliamentary and was never his
practice to give the officers of the Crown hard names and
tho' he had increased his fortune he had taken a great deal
of paines, but that he defeyd the greatest enemy he had to
charge him with the least corruption of any kind and if it
were a fault to get an estate in the Treasury he knew some
had got great ones in meaner offices there, than his, but
whether corruptly or no, he did not know, but if it was, he
thought that it might be a blemish to those who possessed
them now that were so ill got'.[1] The last remark was rather
a heavy jibe on Pulteney's expense—his personal fortune was
derived from Henry Guy, Secretary of the Treasury and
manipulator of secret service funds in William III's reign,
who curiously enough bequeathed his entire estate, including

[1] *Brabourne MSS, Knatchbull's Diary*, fos. 67–9.

the parliamentary borough of Hedon, to his young protégé, to whom he was in no way related. Walpole's boasting was a little reckless in a House with long memories, and Shippen was soon on his feet twitting Walpole about his forage contracts. Having shown his mettle Pulteney voted for the Court. If he hoped to frighten Walpole into making him an offer of a better office, he was mistaken.[1] As soon as Parliament rose, Walpole had Pulteney dismissed from his place at Court. He had no further intention of trying to placate Pulteney. He felt himself to be quite strong enough to cashier unreliable subordinates who failed to realize their stations.

The dismissal of Pulteney marks, however, an important stage in the development of Walpole's political career, for Pulteney was to raise up against him a new and formidable opposition, based not on Court politics but on the House of Commons and on public opinion. Pulteney had uncommon literary gifts, a real talent for sharp and biting satire either in prose or light verse. And Walpole's system gave him a sitting target for his witty abuse. He was soon joined by a man even more skilled in political tactics than himself and his equal in literary dexterity—Bolingbroke.

Walpole had failed to break Bolingbroke after the Fifteen. His attainder had remained a gesture. His pardon was being talked of as early as 1717, and once broached, it was only a matter of time before it was achieved. Bolingbroke, eager to please, had insinuated himself in the affair of the dukedom that had brought Schaub's downfall and Horatio's elevation; his wife, rich, elegant and very French, had charmed the King's mistresses if not the King, who thought she talked too much. She was quite irrepressible and urgent little notes arrived for Walpole and Townshend inviting them to a *tête-à-tête à trois* in her little house.[2] She involved

[1] *Brabourne MSS, Knatchbull's Diary*, fos. 69–70. Pulteney maintained in *An Answer to One Part of a Late Infamous Libel*, 37–8, that Walpole had tried to buy off his opposition in the debate by the offer of the first Secretaryship available. There is no other evidence to support Pulteney's assertion.

[2] *C(H) MSS.* Marcilly de Villete, n.d.; *c.* March 1724. She wrote, of course, in French; Coxe, II, 307–45; W. Sichel, *Bolingbroke and His Times* (1902), 148, 511.

Townshend if not Walpole in her struggle with Sir Matthew Decker, the banker, who refused to pay her money on the ground that, as she was Bolingbroke's wife, it was Bolingbroke's property, therefore attainted, and that he might be held responsible and guilty by Parliament if he paid. This was sharp practice, albeit legal, and sharp enough to stir many consciences on her behalf. Finally she got round Decker by swearing that she was not Bolingbroke's wife, much to the ribald amusement of the Court. The absurdity of the situation, however, was used dexterously by Bolingbroke and his advocates to press for the performance of what had long been promised him by the King's personal friends—the full annulment of attainder. Walpole resolutely opposed any such action, but he was alone. Townshend saw no danger in pardoning Bolingbroke;[1] Newcastle, though of course worried by the prospect of making any decision, could not resist his desire to please.[2] The Duchess of Kendal was emphatically in favour; the King indifferent. According to Coxe, Walpole gave way only when he was threatened with dismissal, and Speaker Onslow reports in his memoirs that Walpole was forced to submit. As Coxe never published the evidence for his assertion, it is now impossible to decide how far Walpole exaggerated his difficulties in order to palliate his behaviour in the eyes of his independent friends in the House of Commons.[3] It would seem unlikely that the King or the Duchess could consider parting with Walpole in 1725, seeing that his power in the Commons had never been greater nor his favour at Court stronger. Furthermore, Bolingbroke was only to be partially pardoned, for Walpole insisted that he should not be allowed to take up the broken threads of his political career. Walpole's intransigence was useful to the

---

[1] Coxe, II, 328. *Walpole MSS*, Townshend to HW, 2 April 1724.
[2] *Ibid.*, 'Despatches of the Duke of Newcastle': 28 May 1724.
[3] Coxe, II, 345. HMC, *Onslow MSS*, 515, Coxe, HW, 70–1, where he states that he had recently seen papers which had made him change his view which he had expressed in Coxe, I, 210, four years earlier in which he had underestimated Walpole's reluctance. I have not come across the evidence which Coxe saw and do not know whether it was direct evidence or hearsay such as Onslow's or Etough's.

Court for explaining the meagreness of the pardon, just as the Court's insistence helped Walpole in explaining away his own behaviour. Nevertheless, whether threatened or not, there can be no doubt that Walpole, despite Madame de Villette's blandishments, viewed Bolingbroke's return to England with great reluctance.

Naturally Walpole met with difficulties in the Commons, and the debate on Bolingbroke's petition for pardon, presented by Lord Finch, found him for once in his life in a false position, striving to do his best for a thin case in which he did not believe. He talked about money, charity, rewards for good behaviour, subjects which never came so naturally to his lips—at least when Bolingbroke's future was at issue—as vigorous and brutal denunciation. He was forced to listen to Captain Vernon, who called Bolingbroke a complicated villain, and Sir John Cope, who described him as an enemy to God and man—words that Walpole would have savoured on his own lips. Loyal to the Court, he did his bidding and under his command the courtiers trooped out and carried the day by 120 votes; the opposition vote, however, was a high one—113—for only five tories voted against Bolingbroke, and Shippen and the Jacobites discreetly stayed away. In spite of a strong protest on Bolingbroke's behalf in the House of Lords, the bill which Walpole favoured went through. Bolingbroke got his estates and his money, but failed to win back his seat in the House of Lords. Of course, Bolingbroke spoke of being betrayed, complained long and skilfuly of Walpole's behaviour, and his wife used every art with the Duchess of Kendal to win the King's ear and secure his full restoration. This campaign, even if it wearied the King and frightened Walpole, intoxicated Bolingbroke, who had always felt that great personal triumphs were about to come his way. And when at last he obtained a private audience of the King, his confidence soared. He arrived in the royal presence with a lengthy written indictment of Walpole's ministry upon which he discoursed with his usual wit and urbanity. Naturally Walpole was plunged into feverish anxiety and unnecessary gloom. The King, quite unimpressed, refused to discuss the complaints with Bolingbroke and dismissed them to Walpole as 'Bagatelles'.[1]

At last Bolingbroke realized his defeat: his exclusion from formal politics was final. He turned to opposition, which at least would give an outlet to his resentment and might help to bring about Walpole's downfall, which, if accomplished, could lead to his restoration by those whom he had helped to power. So the summer and autumn of 1726 brought Pulteney and Bolingbroke together. At Bolingbroke's rustic retreat, Dawley Farm, they concocted new methods of attack which were to force Walpole into one of the fiercest political battles of his life.

3

BY THE time that Bolingbroke and Pulteney came together, Pulteney had spent one parliamentary session, that of 1726, in open opposition to the government, and his experience had not been encouraging. Indeed he blundered badly. He suspected that the government would do everything in its power to keep the Congress of Cambrai going and prevaricate about the Ostend Company for the sake of peace, if need be, without honour. So he sponsored a bitter pamphlet attacking the supine policy of the ministry in the face of Austrian threats to British trade. Instead of setting up a train of indignation which was to explode into fury at the next parliamentary session, the agitation fizzled out, for the public in January 1726 was disturbed not by a lack of martial activity, but by an excess of it.[2]

Pulteney spent the summer and autumn of 1725 trying to find evidence detrimental to Walpole. He became very friendly with Count Palm, the Austrian Minister in London,

[1] Hervey, I, 12–17: Horace Walpole, *Reminiscences* (ed. Paget Toynbee, Oxford, 1925), 18: Coxe, I, 208–10.

[2] *Mr Forman's Letter to the Right Honourable William Pulteney:* printed copy is dated 'Amsterdam, 24 Oct. 1724'. A copy in *Arch. Aff. Etr., Corr. Angl.* is inscribed '*Donné au public le 20ᵉ Juin 1725*' (see Realey, *Early Opposition*, 182); a MS copy in *C(H) MSS*, addressed to 'My Lord', is dated 3 July 1724.

and soon promises of mutual aid were flying back and forth between Pulteney and the Austrian Chancellery. Pulteney intended to attack the Alliance of Hanover which, after all, did represent a radical break with traditional whig foreign policy based on friendship with Austria and the Dutch against France and Spain. Any private assurances which Pulteney could obtain from Vienna about the innocence of the Austrian treaty with Spain could be used to underline the argument that the ministry, through the King's fears for Hanover, had behaved rashly and made war more, not less, probable. Pulteney was busily ferreting in other directions. Jacobites reported that he had sent his brother to Flanders to secure evidence that Walpole had received an enormous bribe from the Ostend Company, for Pulteney was quite prepared to attack Walpole both for showing too much enmity to the Austrians and for being too weak about their trading company. Nor was it such a paradox as it looked. Ostend touched British, not Hanoverian, interests; hence its neglect. Whether or not Pulteney was spying in the Netherlands, he was certainly doing so in the Treasury. On 21 September 1725, Walpole received an anonymous letter pointing out that Pulteney had been getting accounts of Treasury transactions: 'as to application of money. Mr Clayton and Mr Merrill are the machines that he works by. The affairs they are most inquisitive after are viz!

The application of the Sinking Fund to the Civil List replaced last Parliament.
Secret Service Money.
The continuance of the allowances for transacting the severall annuities to the officers of the Exchequer'.

And, equally sinister for Walpole, Pulteney had engaged in a little historical research, for the writer went on: 'Mr Pulteney has very lately in a great hurry got copied at the Rolls Chappell the Act of the 14 & 15 of Henry 8th to enable that King during his life to pardon attainders.'[1]

[1] *C(H) MSS*, A. B. 21 September 1725. William Clayton was married to Mrs Clayton, Mistress of the Robes to the Princess of Wales. His action was

Whether or not Pulteney had already got into touch with Bolingbroke is doubtful, but clearly it had already struck Pulteney that Bolingbroke's favour at Court and his failure to achieve a full pardon might be used to Walpole's embarrassment. Hence Pulteney's intentions were clear enough to Walpole, and he did not like them. And he tried, once again, to buy Pulteney off. The King spent two hours with him, trying unavailingly to persuade him of the error of his ways. Pulteney was now resolute for opposition.

The session opened on 20 January 1726, rather late, so that Walpole could organize his credit in the City before the money-market was raised by the augmentation of the forces. He had no wish to go begging for Sarah Marlborough's money, having for seven years managed without it, for Sarah now pursued him with vindictive hatred, quarrelling on the slightest pretext—letters misdirected (after all, there were two Duchesses of Marlborough living), keys for access to St James's Park, or a passage from Marlborough House to Pall Mall, were sufficient to provoke irate letters of complaint.[1] He cannot have relished the session when it came— not that Pulteney proved difficult to handle; he found few converts and his attacks on foreign affairs and corruption fell flat—but because Walpole realized that his speeches would signalize a departure, albeit temporary, from the policy which he had pursued with such success. Increased forces, a semi-mobilized navy, fresh subsidies might for the moment be accepted. Certainly the House took well enough to Horatio's defence of the Hanover Treaty, and his special journey from Paris quickly justified itself.[2] He spoke as usual

not particularly disloyal to Walpole as Walpole was not himself in 1725 on very amicable terms with Leicester House.

[1] *Blenheim MSS.* Walpole, who could hate as hard as the Duchess, did his best to thwart her. He secured a Crown lease on a house on the present site of the Oxford and Cambridge Club for Thomas Ripley (after alterations by Ripley, his son Edward Walpole lived there) in order that the Duchess should be denied her ardent wish to make a back entrance to Marlborough House further up Pall Mall. *Blenheim MSS* and *ex inf.* F. H. W. Sheppard of the Survey of London.

[2] *Brabourne MSS, Knatchbull's Diary,* fo. 80: *Walpole MSS,* Horatio's own draft of his speech.

plainly, in his best broad Norfolk accent, for there was nothing grand about Horatio, and he could play the squire as effectively as his brother. He dressed plainly, even badly, and never looked the courtier, and many a back bencher felt closer to him than to the brilliant, sparkling Pulteney. The majorities proved good ones—the address on the Hanover Treaty was carried by 285 to 107,[1] and yet there was plenty of food for thought. This after all was their first encounter; and if Pulteney had won only ten supporters for his trenchant defence of old whiggery, some were men of competence —Daniel, his cousin, Sir Joseph Jekyll, the Master of the Rolls, and Samuel Sandys, an influential member for Worcestershire. And against Walpole's large majorities were the significant abstentions; 164 members had been absent at the debate in which Horatio spoke, many deliberately withdrawing, like Sir Edward Knatchbull, because they did not wish to commit themselves. It was hardly likely that these new and serious divisions in Europe would be settled in a year; indeed the ministry's difficulties were likely to increase, not diminish, and taxation would keep in step with difficulties. And three years ahead—in 1729—there would be a general election. In his first skirmish, Pulteney was laying the foundations of a campaign, striking out the bold lines of a policy, easy to grasp, capable of endless variation, yet single-minded in purpose—the destruction of Walpole.

Yet Pulteney was immeasurably strengthened by the decision of Bolingbroke to join him. In the session of 1726, when it still seemed probable that Bolingbroke might secure a full pardon, his friends, led by Sir William Wyndham, had frequently refrained from voting against the ministry, and the criticism which they offered had been temperate, far more temperate, indeed, than Pulteney's; and, of course, there had been no concerted endeavour between these two fragments of opposition, and no discussion of tactics. In the House itself, therefore, the opposition promised to be more coherent and better led in 1727.

[1] *Brabourne MSS, Knatchbull's Diary*, fo. 81.

Bolingbroke, moreover, offered more than a few followers in the Commons. He was a naturally gifted writer—lucid, ironic, plausible, with a lively imagination and a gift of phrase which hinted, even if it did not disclose, profundity. He loved wine, good food, and thrived on wit. He drew to him the liveliest minds and readiest pens in London. Pope, Swift, Gay, Arbuthnot were all happy to count him as a friend; Dawley Farm had become since his return a *rendez-vous* of a lively, restless, literary *coterie*. Walpole never relished intellectual society; few crumbs of patronage had been thrown to the men whose society Bolingbroke enjoyed so much. Some, like Swift, were full of hatred, all were eager for satirical, destructive fun. And what a target Walpole and his ministry provided. The King and his two mistresses, his Turkish body-servants, his passion for Hanover; Walpole's vast corpulent body, fat red face, extravagant finery, ostentatious wealth and kept girl; homespun Horatio, apeing the ambassador, and his ugly bourgeois wife; Newcastle, dithering and twittering through his endless despatches; and everywhere corruption and favouritism, all things which could provide endless subjects for ballads and epigrams and allegories and those mocking advertisements at which Pulteney was such a master. And it was just as easy to guy the public policy —Britain the footman of Hanover; the Sinking Fund a fraud; taxation a dodge to fill the King's and Walpole's pockets; and easier still to take the loftiest of moral lines, to be above party and faction, to be ardent for morality in public life, to be the first amongst patriots.

After the delightful, almost reckless, sense of triumph in which Walpole gloried in 1725, the next year quickly dowsed his spirits and brought him back sharply to the sense of strain to which the long struggle for political life had accustomed him. For a man of his suspicious and anxious temperament, the drawing together of Bolingbroke and Pulteney boded an unquiet life ahead. For most of the time he could dismiss them from his mind, for he was secure in the King's favour, even if the Germans were not his friends;

indeed they were no man's friends and shiftlessly they might turn their coats in a day.[1]

His days were, however, darkened by private grief. First his sister Dorothy and then his younger brother, Galfridus, died within five months of each other.[2] Galfridus had, like Horatio, given him what is rare among brothers, uncritical admiration and respect; happy in an inferior station, happy to watch and to applaud from afar; yet by the warmth of his regard Galfridus had added to Walpole's happiness. But Dolly's death proved a more grievous loss. He had long adored her. Her scrapes were always forgiven; her silliness overlooked. He felt for her that protective amorous tenderness which flourishes so readily between a brother and a sister widely separated in age. Until he met Molly Skerrett he had never loved anyone so deeply nor so constantly, and his love for her may easily have been strengthened by the loss of Dolly.

An elegant woman of great charm, she had done much to maintain the friendship between Walpole and her husband, Townshend. Unfortunately she died at a time when that friendship was being subjected to ever-increasing strain. As the opposition grew in the Commons, Walpole viewed Townshend's bold conception in foreign affairs with great distaste. Of course, the friction between the two men had a deeper cause. For long their paths had led towards the same goal—power and influence at Court and the control of their own neighbourhoods in Norfolk. Jointly they had risen to greatness. Throughout Townshend had assumed superiority. His letters to his brother-in-law were normally kind in tone, but they were frequently somewhat patronizing and at times peremptory.[3] Townshend was a nobleman of the second generation, Walpole a squire's son. Townshend,

---

[1] Walpole's favour with George I seemed to strengthen during 1726. The King accepted an invitation to dinner at the Old Lodge, Richmond, where he enjoyed himself so much that he dropped in again uninvited shortly afterwards: perhaps he, too, had taken to Molly. HMC, *Eyre-Matcham MSS*, 4–5.

[2] Dorothy died 29 March 1726; Galfridus, 7 August 1726.

[3] See the tone of his letter to Walpole when he replied to the latter's complaint of the expense of the Swedish subsidies, Coxe, II, 480.

strong and forceful, harsh and even rude at times, nevertheless was very conscious of his birth and blood. He was
scrupulously honest in his dealings, and lost rather than
made money through his service to the Crown. He loved his
wives deeply and stayed faithful to them. He was indifferent
to the full-blooded drinking and lechery that Walpole loved
to parade. The natural temperamental antipathies between
Walpole and himself strengthened as the years passed.
Walpole's growing authority, his tendency to engross power,
his vulgar delight in his new vast wealth, his unconcealed
scorn for Townshend's prudent and prudish life became
harder for Townshend to bear, and far harder with Dolly
dead. She was lovely, careless and gay, and desired to
please, and no one more than her husband; and to her
brother she was as devoted as he was to her. As long as she
lived their mutual antipathy had to find its vent in quips and
sarcasm in society and in forceful debate in the cabinet;
her life bound them to a common purpose; her death made
them forget the long years of mutual endeavour. Dolly
dead broke a link with Townshend; the rift between them
became at once deeper and more unbridgeable; a crisis in
the cabinet might easily link itself with the growing agitation, in which Bolingbroke and Pulteney were beginning
to dabble with such skill. Once the Germans got the scent of
treachery in their nostrils, they would soon be baying for his
blood. So private griefs enlarged public anxieties and Walpole was back again in the wary world of unavowed intrigue;
to survive still needed luck, judgment and the King's regard
and the ability to lead as well as manage the House of Commons. In 1726 it seemed as if events in Europe might
strengthen, not weaken, Townshend at Walpole's expense.

4

THROUGHOUT 1726 Europe was poised on the brink of
war, and crisis followed swiftly on the heels of crisis, flurrying
the diplomats. Couriers hurtled across Europe, bearing the

thick despatches, which even in these troubled days, ran smoothly on, thousands upon thousands of words, so absorbed were the diplomats in the elaborate ritual of their trade. Swift as the couriers posted, they had time enough to sell their secrets or allow their bags to be rifled in a deliberate absence of mind. In the red despatch boxes, alongside the bulky folios of Horace Walpole, Saphorin and Stanhope, lay the deciphered correspondence of Pozzobueno, Ripperda, Palm, Zinzendorff and quaintly enough, the father of the hermaphroditic Chevalier d'Eon, who was, perhaps understandably, dabbing in double diplomacy. The news they contained was always grave, but, such was the confidence of ambassadors in their own craft, never hopeless; argument, negotiation, or even their own strength of character would in the end bring about the necessary adjustments that would ensure peace. As they listened mesmerized to each other's offers, all of which evaded the substance of their problems, the ministries at home wisely took measures for war.

Sir Charles Wager sailed off to the Baltic—a necessary parade of arms that Sweden required. With the British men-of-war riding majestic and unopposed through the Skagerrak, the Swedes could desert their Russian allies, an act for which they had been handsomely bribed. Catherine I had no intention of going to war with Britain alone, and with the defection of Sweden her interest in the hereditary claims of the Duke of Holstein-Gottorp soon diminished. Actions as swift as these gratified George I and enlarged Townshend's vision of the future. They did nothing to relieve Walpole's anxiety; for him the primary danger lay with Spain. He knew from his long years in the House that the Commons could be blandly indifferent to Northern troubles, but the slightest threat to Gibraltar or to the Assiento trade could work them to a frenzy. To be sure, vigorous steps had been taken. Admiral Hosier had been despatched to blockade Cartagena, and Townshend secured the service of 12,000 Hessian troops—at a price. Terrified that they would be plunged into a war they did not want to fight, the

Dutch were more willing to follow the lead of France than answer the trumpet-calls of Britain. Ripperda, still power-drunk with his Viennese successes, attempted to mobilize Spain. With galleons still locked in Cartagena and with no money in the Treasury, the task proved impossible. A ram-shackle army of sorts assembled outside Gibraltar, where no gun was fired except by accident, and a desultory attempt at warfare petered out in a farce worthy of Falstaff's army. By this time, however, Ripperda had fallen. The wild promises of vast subsidies made to the Emperor proved impossible to fulfil, and to save Elizabeth Farnese's face Ripperda was dismissed. To save his skin and maintain his eminence he took refuge in the house of the British Ambassador, where in flagrant violation of diplomatic etiquette he was arrested on the orders of the King of Spain. For some weeks this affront to the law of nations swept graver problems aside, and mem-orials, stately, vast and pompous, passed daily between Stanhope and the Escorial. Ripperda, however, remained imprisoned in the Castle of Segovia.

No sooner had the Courts of Europe adjusted themselves to this dramatic news than they learnt of the dismissal of the duc de Bourbon from the service of Louis XV and his replacement by his aged tutor, the Abbé Fleury, a man of seventy-three. He conducted French policy for the next sixteen years.

At three o'clock on the morning of 12 June, Horatio Walpole was woken up at the British Embassy and given a personal letter from Fleury, announcing the momentous changes which Louis XV had ordered. This gesture en-tranced and bemused Horatio. Sleep was unthinkable, and in the early dawn of that summer morning he sat down at his desk and wrote with a full heart a despatch of inordinate length to the Duke of Newcastle. Although a tribute to his stamina, it betrays sadly his lack of perspicacity. No sooner was it finished than Horatio rushed to his carriage and drove full tilt to Versailles, for Fleury had indicated his willingness to receive him at once. Horatio's heart overflowed at the

unexampled kindness and warmth of Fleury's reception; at
the fact that he was the first ambassador to be so received;
at the unimpeachable sentiments expressed by Fleury of
George I, of his brother, of Townshend, of Newcastle. It was
too much, and he expressed his sense of the honour done to
him and his country in such emotional terms that Fleury
was visibly moved. They dined together. As soon as the meal
(eaten oddly enough with James II's illegitimate son, Ber-
wick) was over, they opened their hearts to each other. As
they made their *tour de l'horizon*—Spain, the Empire, the
Netherlands—they found themselves in complete agreement,
and so it seemed to Horatio that the relations between
Britain and France would be as warm, as intimate, as open,
as those between himself and the Abbé. He could hardly
wait until he got back to the Embassy. The moment he
arrived, he dictated a despatch to Newcastle longer, more
fulsome, than the one he had written at dawn, recounting
all that he had heard and felt at Versailles. His rich Norfolk
voice went on and on, savouring the phrases, reliving the
drama of that astonishing day, until he was too spent to
continue and he drew his despatch to a close in these words:

'I think, in the main, he [Fleury] has shewn a greater
confidence than he has done to any one person whatever,
at least of a foreigner, not excepting the Pope's Nuncio,
who is a great favourite of his; and given me such assurances of his administration being steady to the engagements of France, and agreeable to His Majesty's interest
and sentiments, that his future conduct, he being entirely
the master now of this Kingdom, must prove him the
kindliest man or the greatest knave living; I own I have
still the best opinion in the world of him.'[1]

The waiting courier went away at the gallop and pounded
down the long roads to Calais; the wind was favourable, and

[1] Coxe, HW, 118–32. Fleury's letter is now *C(H) MSS*, Fleury to Horatio
Walpole, 11 June, 1726. *Walpole MSS*, 'Letters to Newcastle 1726' contain the
full despatches. BM *Add MSS*, 32,746, fo. 242 *et seq.*, contains Newcastle's reply.
This has been partly printed in Wickham Legg, *Diplomatic Instructions, IV,
France, 1721–7*, 168–71.

four days later the Duke of Newcastle, in a dither of excitement, rushed to the King, to Townshend and to Sir Robert with the wonderful news from Paris. They all expressed the deepest satisfaction to each other. The King saw the end of his problems; a firm and friendly France would soon bring Spain and the Empire to their senses. Townshend could view the prospect of war with fresh confidence. Walpole could look forward to a peaceful settlement in which his brother would have played a leading role. For Newcastle, the excitement of it all was a sufficient pleasure. Not one of them gave a second thought to Fleury, a man who was to baffle and mesmerize them for years to come. As long as Walpole remained in power his destiny was strangely entwined with Fleury's, for it was Fleury, subtle, skilful, seemingly senile, who was to diminish Walpole's stature as a statesman.

Fleury is not an easy character to understand. His low birth, his profession, his bourgeois habits, did not endear him to Louis XV's courtiers. His power over the King sickened them and their memoirs are full of his faults. His strength lay in the King's regard. Bernis relates how Louis XV, who should have been at his lessons, was usually to be found on his tutor's knee, making ringlets out of the old priest's hair. The marker in the book they were reading remained at the same page for months on end.[1] And so it was Fleury's fault that the King was ill-educated, uninterested in affairs, fond only of hunting and girls. Fleury had kept him immature through his own lust for power. It was not so. Louis XV was profoundly stupid and neither God nor man could change that. Although stupid and lazy, he quickly realized that Bourbon did not wish to rule for his sake; Louis needed an uncommitted minister as a barrier between himself and the greed and intrigue of the princes of the blood. Fleury by birth and by profession was remarkably suitable. He stood outside faction; and although no man's thirst for power was less slakable, his desire for riches was moderate. In personal relations and in the conduct of policy he proved exceptionally adroit.

[1] A. McC. Wilson, *Foreign Policy and the Administration of Fleury*, 25.

He professed humility; emphasized his inadequacies; eagerly admitted mistakes; showed a constant desire to please; no one was more willing, more ready to agree with what was asked of him, no one less a master of doing exactly what he wished. He could twist or turn or lie with charm and with self-abasement. He stressed his limitations—his age, the difficulties of work, his need to consult the King and everyone else at Court so long as it suited his purpose to delay. His long-term aims he shared with none; the years alone revealed them. Yet at all times he carried conviction, and could create almost at will that sense of intimate confidence and warmth of regard which was to prove the undoing of more ambassadors than Horatio Walpole. Aged, gentle, friendly, garrulous, often helpless and distressed by events which seemed too vast for a fragile priest on the brink of the grave, Fleury deceived all but the most perceptive. Beneath the servile and bewildered exterior, there resided a ruthless, vindictive spirit, a lover of power, a lover of revenge; a mean heart linked to a wolfish ambition. He brooked no rival and cheerfully ruined men of ability who sought to be independent of him. He preferred to work with clerks, not equals. He was quite indifferent to public opinion either of the Court or of the nation; the former he despised, the latter he ignored. The steel of his nature was kept for subordinates or for those defeated and rejected courtiers excluded from the circle of power. For those within he exuded a velvet charm. Over Horatio Walpole he was to exert all his fascination, which bred in Horatio a devotion which proved as impervious to satire as to circumstance.

The obligations of the Alliance of Hanover demanded that France should come to the help of England in case of war with Spain, and Fleury's first task was to seem to comply whilst performing no effective act from which there could be no retreat. He encouraged the Dutch to fulminate against the Ostend Company; in every interview with Horatio Walpole, after listening patiently to the enormities of Spain he turned the conversation back to the danger of the Austrian attempt to participate in the East Indian trade. For Fleury the Empire, not Spain, was the danger; for Walpole and Townshend the opposite was true. And so the weeks lengthened to months, and the year passed, and the powers of Europe remained poised on the brink of war.

The Spanish preparations for a siege of Gibraltar made slow progress; Hosier's fleet sailed the Caribbean seas; neither side declared war. Without war declared, Fleury refused to recognize his treaty obligations to Britain. Allies were gained, and allies were lost. The United Provinces acceded to the Hanover treaty, with pertinent reservations; Frederick of Prussia deserted, much to George I's, if not Walpole's, relief. The petty princelings of Germany looked for their bread and butter; some preferred the Emperor's table, others Britain's. And so war looked like a glowering thundercloud on a summer's evening. The storm loomed but did not break. It had blown up fortuitously, caused by personalities and problems of which Walpole had little knowledge and fewer ideas. The dangers to his own work, the difficulties which he would have to face were, however, clear enough to him. Certainly he was deeply suspicious and very anxious. That is why he drank down the heady optimism which his brother sent in such copious draughts from Paris. Walpole was prepared to accept the endless prevarications and delays, the cloudy uncertainties of Fleury's half-given promises were nothing to him so long as the result was peace; outwardly there was much that he and Fleury seemed jointly to desire. But for the first time in his career he had to face Parliament in January 1727 under the imminent threat of war.

5

INDEED THERE was the prospect of war at home as well as war abroad. Pulteney and Bolingbroke had carefully laid their plans, and naturally the threatening foreign situation interlocked with Walpole's domestic problems. His ministry had to explain to and convince the independent country gentlemen that the mobilization of the fleet, and the hiring of 12,000 very expensive Hessian troops were necessary for the security not of Hanover but of Britain.

This purchase of mercenaries, together with the necessary augmentation of the army and navy, had forced Walpole to fix the land tax at 4s. 0d. in the pound—a savage increase which was bound to make the country gentlemen suspicious and critical. There were excellent opportunities here for Pulteney and his friends to exploit to Walpole's detriment, but Pulteney and Bolingbroke nourished loftier ambitions. They had conceived their opposition on broad strategic lines. In January 1727 Parliament had just over two years to run, and by the next general election they hoped to have so roused the country to such passionate hatred of Walpole that his friends and the King would sacrifice him for the sake of political stability. Bolingbroke had learnt his politics in the old uncertain days of Queen Anne when a combination of backstairs intrigue, violent press campaign, and bitter struggle in the Commons had turned out politicians as tough and as dexterous and as well loved at Court as Godolphin and Marlborough. Walpole had grown up in the same hard school, and he had no illusions about his danger. He realized that Henrietta Howard was not being courted at Marble Hill by Bolingbroke, Pulteney, Bathurst and the rest for the sake merely of her intellectual graces and physical beauty. As the Prince of Wales's mistress she might be capable of playing the same game as Abigail Hill; after all, the Prince disposed of considerable patronage and possessed wide electioneering interests which could readily be strengthened by politicians willing to gamble on the future.[1] And George I was ageing. Such thoughts induced a gay optimism, a sense that the future might bring them back to power, and so in the summer

---

[1] See *Historical Journal*, I (1958), 68 *et seq*. A. N. Newman, 'The political patronage of Frederick George, Prince of Wales', which gives an excellent idea of the influence that a Prince of Wales could exercise.

of 1726 Twickenham and Dawley became alive with hope.
Backstairs intrigue was but one aspect of Pulteney's
strategy. The circle of witty, quick-penned men—Pope,
Gay, Arbuthnot—which Bolingbroke had drawn about him
at Dawley naturally attracted men of literary ability—
particularly young men out for notoriety and fame. Outstanding amongst these was Nicholas Amhurst, who had been
expelled from Oxford because of his witty and daring satire;
his expulsion encouraged him to a more outrageous ferocity.
Some time in the autumn of 1726 the decision was taken to
launch with Amhurst as editor a new opposition newspaper.
The moribund *Country-Gentleman* was bought, and on 6
December 1726 *The Craftsman* appeared for sale on the
London streets. For ten years this paper was to play a
remarkable role in English political life.[1] Week after week
Walpole and his ministry were subjected to an endless stream
of vilification and criticism which made not only England
but Europe roar with delight. Walpole hated it, hated it
furiously and bitterly. He could not bring himself to be indifferent, and the more he bellowed the more delighted the
opposition were, the greater grew the sale of *The Craftsman*,
and more widespread became the disrepute in which the
institutions of the Government were held by the middle
class in town and countryside. True, *The Craftsman* started
lamely enough, and several weeks passed before it caught the
popular imagination, but on 27 January 1727, after all the
members had come up to Town for the new session, it
printed 'The Vision of Camilick', probably by Bolingbroke—
a simple, slapstick, personal satire of Walpole.

'In the midst of these execrations entered a man,
dressed in a plain habit, with a purse of gold in his hand.
He threw himself forward into the room, in a bluff,

---

[1] *The Craftsman* did not, however come to an end in 1736 as many historians
have assumed (see C. B. Realey, *Early Opposition*, 201: Basil Williams, *The Whig
Supremacy*, 195, 397). Actually, *The Craftsman* continued publication until 1750:
in 1748 it ceased to be an opposition newspaper, but the change in attitude
brought neither increased circulation nor a government subsidy, and two
years later it failed. See L. Hanson, *Government of the Press*, 120.

ruffianly manner. A smile, or rather a snear, sat on his countenance. His face was bronzed over with a glare of confidence. An arch malignity leered in his eye. Nothing was so extraordinary as the effect of this person's appearance. They no sooner saw him, but they all turned their faces from the canopy, and fell prostrate before him. He trod over their backs, without any ceremony, and marched directly up to the Throne. He opened his Purse of Gold which he took out in handfuls and scattered amongst the assembly. While the greater part were engaged in scrambling for these pieces, he seized, to my inexpressible surprise, without the least fear, upon the sacred *Parchment* itself. He rumpled it unduly up and crammed it into his pocket. Some of the people began to murmur. He threw more gold, and they were pacified.'[1]

Heavy, laboured and obvious as it seems to us, it was outrageous and dramatic in January 1727, and made the more so because the Royal messengers immediately arrested the editor and the printer. Walpole, livid with rage, wanted blood. He did not get it; the evidence proved too slight and Amhurst and Francklin, the printer, had to be released. *The Craftsman* resumed publication and gloried in his defeat; bolder became the satire, more telling the denigration of Court and ministry.[2] Those outside the circle of power loved it; the circulation soared; squires and parsons isolated in their neighbourhoods begged their friends in London to send them copies. They passed them eagerly from hand to hand. Ambassadors sat down at their writing-tables and carefully annotated each item, discovering in the *Craftsman* justifications of their own prescience in prognosticating Walpole's fall.[3]

Journalism of opposition was vitalized, almost reborn. There had been nothing like it since the Duke of Wharton's

[1] *Craftsman* (collected edn. 1731), I, 95.
[2] *Ibid*, I, 127; Hanson, *op. cit.*, 67.
[3] *Arch. Aff. Etr.*, *Mémoires et Documents*, *Angleterre*, VIII, fo. 208. All ambassadors in London, without exception, consistently underestimated Walpole's strength and over-estimated the opposition, and forecasts of Walpole's imminent fall were as frequent as they were wrong.

Free Briton had flamed like a comet across the London politics of the post-Bubble days. *The Craftsman* had come to stay, a new, dangerous, exciting weapon of opposition; in the election of 1729 every wavering voter might be vital to Bolingbroke and Pulteney, and so no abuse could be too vile, no satire too personal or too bitter. There were no conventions, and a tough, aggressive society watched the brutal battle of words with unfeigned delight. It was to last with uninterrupted fury so long as Bolingbroke and Walpole were locked in combat.

The backstairs intrigue, the public attack—these were but two aspects of the opposition's strategy. Both were long term ventures and could not be expected to yield quick results. Pulteney was astute enough to realize that both would gain in weight and effectiveness if Walpole's majority in the House of Commons could be seriously reduced. For this it was essential to unite the opposition, to draw together the miscellaneous fragments of parties with the cranks and individualists and weld them into a united opposition. A solid, well-disciplined opposition, based on a few simple, honourable principles might act as a magnet to the un-committed men, to those who prided themselves (and there were still many) on the independence of their judgment.

It is fairly easy to underestimate the floating vote in the House of Commons of Walpole's day. We possess two highly detailed parliamentary diaries, both of quite exceptional value, for these years and the years ahead, and they give peculiar insight into the working of the minds of two back-benchers. Both diarists developed obligations to Walpole, but both possessed a strong streak of independence, and they could be influenced by political events and swayed in their voting by principles which rose far above immediate self-interest.

Sir Edward Knatchbull belonged to an old Kentish family and his forefathers had served Parliament gener-ation after generation. He was a born leader of his county. His father had been a half-hearted whig, a lukewarm supporter of William III, a man who had flatly refused to allow his place in the Customs to sway his political behaviour. His son had grown up a rabid tory, a keen and ardent supporter of Bolingbroke in 1714 during his last violent bid for power. He had acted as one of Bolingbroke's spokesmen on the front bench. Time and events had cooled his ardour. He remained loyal to his country, accepted the Hanoverians, and as the years passed felt drawn towards Walpole and came to believe that the security of the kingdom was in good keeping. The early years of Pulteney's opposition can be followed in his pages, and it is fortunate that Sir Edward owed neither his seat nor any part of his income to Walpole, for we can see the effect of these great debates on an independently-minded man of middle age.

The other diarist, the Earl of Egmont, at this time Viscount Perceval, is a less simple character than Sir Edward. He regarded himself as a leader of the Anglo-Irish peerage; vain and insensitive, he greatly overestimated his influence. He was acutely conscious of his inferior rank and became very touchy about it. He busied himself with good works. He sat on commissions which investigated the conditions of gaols; he became an ardent supporter of the Society for the Propagation of Christian Knowledge and the Society for the Propagation of the Gospel. He joined forces with Oglethorpe in the promotion of the colonization of Georgia. Elected to the Commons for Harwich by the influence of the Treasury and his brother-in-law, he soon began, much to Walpole's vexation, to refer to 'my borough' and 'my voters'. He was soon at loggerheads with the Government's agents at Harwich, whom he suspected of intriguing against him. Naturally he took a close interest in Ireland, where he had large estates and important electoral interests. He became a self-appointed leader of the Irish interest at Westminster. Egmont liked the image of himself that he saw—a man of high moral rectitude, charitable, benevolent, earnest, a lover of all that was good and just, a man whose principles were founded on and guided by religion and morality. The morsels of patronage which Walpole reluctantly dropped in his lap created little sense of obligation in Egmont, rather indeed resentment that they were small and grudgingly given. Indeed the ties by which Walpole held him to the Government lobby were very tenuous. Egmont prided himself on his judgment and independence, but his conscience could be quickly eased by absence from the scene of combat if the morsel of patronage that Walpole was dangling before his nose was sufficiently juicy. But Egmont's pages are marvellously instructive of Walpole's difficulties with many of the placemen.[1]

An attack such as Bolingbroke and Pulteney were launching could not simply be voted down, with men like Knatchbull and Egmont about, by summoning the ministry's hacks. Every parliamentary session was to prove a battleground of wit, of eloquence, of sense. The vast patronage which Walpole wielded gave him strength and resilience, yet his survival over the next ten years depended on more than patronage. He needed to pursue a policy which he could convince the King, his fellow ministers and the House of Commons was the right one. Above all he had to keep Sir Edward Knatchbull and Lord Perceval in the ministerial lobby, a task for which both subtlety and strength were needed in no uncommon measure.

The difficulties were not all Walpole's. When Pulteney and Bolingbroke came together in the autumn days of 1726, there was little common ground amongst the opposition members. The bluff, hearty Jacobite, Shippen, had a small band of some thirty or forty independents who lived in the dream world of the past and still looked to a Stuart restoration to bring them back to a promised land of place and power. Some were sentimentalists, some merely disgruntled, most were awkward, angular human beings who would have been at sixes and sevens with any monarchy or any ministry. Most were happier cursing Walpole and his world in their neighbourhoods than sitting in the crowded and stuffy chapel of St Stephen's listening to endless debates

[1] Egmont's diaries, atrociously edited, were published by HMC

about the complexities of foreign affairs or the mysteries of
the national debt. With half an excuse they evaded their
duties and stayed away. In close temperamental sympathy,
although possessing very different political ideas, were a
number of rugged individualists and urban radicals—men
like Archibald Hutcheson who held passionately to his own
idiosyncratic views that sprouted like weeds in his fantastical
head; or cross-grained Jekyll, the Master of the Rolls, who
in his own estimation was the one true uncorrupted whig, or
Heathcote, blinker-eyed, indifferent to all problems, all
needs, but the overriding considerations of trade. And then
there was the smug, self-righteous little band of Hanoverian
tories led by Sir William Wyndham, suspicious of Jacobites,
suspicious of whigs, suspicious of radicals. Add to them the
place-hungry and the place-denied, men who had loved
Sunderland too well and too long—the Chetwynds, the
Berkeleys and the Howards—and the ardent youngsters
without connections but with burning ambition and optim-
istic hearts, and there were the ingredients of Bolingbroke's
and Pulteney's opposition. They had to be welded together,
given hope and a common purpose, and a sense of urgency
that could bring them from the hunting field or coffee house
to sit for long stifling hours in St Stephen's. This, too, was a
task which called for the highest political arts. Both Bolingbroke and Pulteney possessed them. Intrigue at Court,
public clamour, a relentless parliamentary opposition, by
such means they hoped to prise open Walpole's formidable
grip on the political life of the nation. Their first united
effort—the session of 1727—might easily have daunted less
resolute men.

The main attack was directed towards foreign affairs.
The ministry was aware that this would be so and Horatio
had been called from Paris. He took in The Hague on the way,
for the reluctance of the Dutch to enter fully into Townshend's policy was a factor on which the opposition were
bound to make great play. Pulteney felt very sunny and
confident. His relations with the Austrian Ambassador, Palm,

had grown very close, and Palm had been instructed to give information to the opposition leader. Pulteney learnt that there was no secret treaty between Austria and Spain and that the Austrians had no intention whatever of supporting the Pretender. They hinted darkly that all this fuss and trouble was due to George I's greedy ambition to extend his Hanoverian territory by the addition of Julich and Berg, two tiny duchies to which he had long made claim but failed to secure formal investiture from the Emperor. *Ergo* the Alliance of Hanover was a trick to make Great Britain pay for Hanoverian interests. As for Spain and the Ostend Company, there were no problems there which could not be adjusted easily enough but for the uncompromising attitude of the ministry. Unfortunately for Pulteney, Palm's letters and the replies from the Austrian Chancellor lay in Walpole's desk, neatly intercepted, neatly decoded, and very valuable not only because they enabled him and his brother to prepare their own case, but also because, if war with Austria should ensue, Pulteney's intrigues with a political enemy would hurt his reputation.[1]

Prepared for what was to come, Walpole drafted the longest King's Speech in living memory, and the two Houses were given a short summary of the ministry's foreign policy and the reason for it; domestic affairs were ignored. The King stressed the danger of the Pretender, the hostility of Spain and the threat of the Ostend Company to British interests. He assured members that there were secret treaties between Austria and Spain. In the debate on the Address the opposition scoffed at the Pretender's threat and

[1] *C(H) MSS*, Emperor Charles VI to Palm, 23 March 1726; Zinzendorff to Palm, 27 March 1726; Palm to Königsegge, 18 April 1726; Palm to Emperor Charles VI, 13 December 1726; Palm to Zinzendorff, 13 December 1726; Palm to Emperor Charles VI, 17 December 1726: Palm to Emperor, 17 December 1736; Palm to Zinzendorff, 17 December 1726; Zinzendorff to Palm, 21 December 1726 (2 letters); Palm to Königsegge, 26 December 1726. Coxe published three of these letters, Coxe, II, 504–11. Those that remain in RW's archive probably represent only a fraction of the intercepted correspondence. RW's Spanish intelligence was equally good. He possessed copies of the correspondence of the Spanish Ambassador, Pozzobueno, with Ripperda, see *C(H) MSS*, Correspondence, 1726.

denied with an air of superior knowledge the secret designs of Charles VI and Philip V. Of course, Walpole could not quote from intercepted despatches and he could give the House Ripperda's disclosures only in the most general terms, as Stanhope had pledged himself to secrecy in detail in order to protect Ripperda's life. Consequently there was a certain lameness in Walpole's defence of the Address, for his brother had to use assertions rather than true facts. Yet it carried conviction with the independents; the vital question was carried by 251 to 81. Sir Edward Knatchbull was with the majority, 'being fully convinced of the danger wee were in, and if wee receded we were undone tho' wee were but in a very bad condition to go on'.[1] Nevertheless, the opposition nagged away, demanding that the ministry produce every sort of paper—correspondence of their secretaries in Vienna and Madrid, Pointz's memorial to Sweden, the secret treaties. Some the ministry conceded, some they refused. Unfortunately, one concession gave the opposition a scent of mischief and they were soon in full cry. Had George I promised to restore Gibraltar in 1721? If he had not, why was his letter not produced? The problem had little to do with foreign affairs as they stood in 1726. Gibraltar was about to be attacked and Walpole had every intention of defending it, and the opposition knew it. That fact proved irrelevant. The House grew excited; anxieties, animosities, personal feeling, the suspicion of betrayal by a foreign King, which independent country gentlemen were quick to sense, suddenly became overriding, and Walpole felt for the first time that his mastery of the House was not as complete as he wished. He himself intervened in the debate, although he preferred to leave foreign affairs to Horatio, in the hope of quelling the growing alarm. He expressed concern for Gibraltar, spoke sternly of the retribution that he felt ought to fall on any minister advising its return, yet in the end admitted that a letter had been written, though merely to induce Philip IV to sign the Quadruple Alliance, and written in guarded

[1] *Brabourne MSS, Knatchbull's Diary*, fos. 92–3.

V. HORATIO WALPOLE AND FAMILY

John Wootton

VI. SIR ROBERT WALPOLE AS RANGER OF RICHMOND PARK

terms and with the proviso that the consent of Parliament would be necessary before Gibraltar could be returned to Spain. But the House could not see the letter for it was a private letter and it would be insolent to demand a sight of the King's private correspondence.[1]

Even Knatchbull's congested précis still carries the flavour of an adroit parliamentary speech in which opposition sentiment was captured and controlled; the effect was spoiled because a flaming row between Pulteney and Horatio had taken place in the Court of Requests and Horatio, carried away by his fury, had told Pulteney that he could call for whatever papers he liked 'the devil of one shall you have'. Foolishly Horatio raised the matter, but Pulteney outwitted him easily enough, and the good effect of Walpole's speech was quite undone. When the previous question was moved Sir Edward Knatchbull strode into the opposition lobby, and Horatio's arrogant tirade was the cause. Not many other independents followed him, but many must have abstained, for the government's majority dropped to 107.[2] This was the best that the opposition could do; the tide in foreign affairs was against them; independents, whig or tory, were very sensitive about Spanish depredations. They believed strongly in the value of the Assiento; they looked askance at the Ostend Company. True, they hated the Land Tax, but they hated Spain more. At this critical juncture they were willing to put their trust in Walpole in spite of Horatio's outburst, which upset a few of them. As far as the attack on foreign policy was concerned, the opposition had failed.

And failure turned to humiliation. Pulteney made a fool of himself. He was baffled and irritated by the government's assertion that there were secret offensive articles to the Vienna treaty between the Emperor and Philip V. He

---

[1] *Brabourne MSS, Knatchbull's Diary*, fo. 95.
[2] *Ibid,* On a later day, Knatchbull himself abstained because he felt that the opposition's motion was too personally directed at Walpole, although he agreed with the sentiments. The whole of his diary gives a remarkable insight into the influences which could sway political decisions.

knew that there were none. He had Palm's word for it, Zinzendorff's word for it, the Emperor's word for it. It maddened him to see good tories and stout independents troop into the government lobby because they feared the Pretender, backed by Spain, Austria and Russia. The government's lying policy must be exposed. Palm, the Austrian ambassador, felt just as keenly as Pulteney. He decided to appeal directly to the people of Britian. He wrote a memorial to George I, couched in very strong terms, denying categorically the secret clauses of the Vienna Treaty, delivered it to the King on 2 March, furthermore printed it and distributed it to the Press. This act of folly created an immediate uproar. George I felt insulted; the Commons felt insulted, so did the Lords, so did the nation at large. To try to retrieve something from the mess, Pulteney and Wyndham fell over themselves in supporting the ministry's address to the King to send Palm packing. Even *The Craftsman* joined the bandwagon, supported the government and denounced Palm, although all London knew that Pulteney was constantly at the embassy.[1] In spite of their protestations of patriotic loyalty, the opposition could not evade the resentment bred by their own misjudgment.

Had this been the whole of the opposition's attack on the ministry it would have made a sorry beginning to their campaign. Fortunately for them they had richer pastures to cultivate. From time out of mind men had deplored the corruption of the government administration, the waste, the graft, the peculation, so that an honest placeman, as far as the public was concerned, was a figure of fantasy as remarkable and as rare as the unicorn or the phoenix. Truth in these circumstances was irrelevant, and every confusion in accounts (and there were plenty), could be used to raise the

[1] The memorial is printed, *Historical Register*, 1727, 149: Coxe, I, 258-9. Coxe regards this memorial as indicating that the Emperor's diplomatic successes in the summer of 1726 amongst the German princes made him indifferent to the possibility of war. This, I think, is very doubtful; in my opinion the Palm affair should be regarded as a genuine, if inept, attempt to influence the British public on behalf of peace.

bogy of corruption. There was a deficit of £125,000 on the previous year's supply. Righteous indignation swelled the opposition's hearts and voices and caught an echoing response on the back benches. Onslow, the member for Kent, full of his own rectitude, joined Pulteney, and they harried Walpole, as he tried to dodge a straight issue of how the money had been spent by exploiting the curiosities of parliamentary procedure, which none knew better than he. The debates went on for hours, but the opposition grew, rising to 110, nearly a third as large again as it could muster on foreign affairs. Worse followed. The Commissioners for Hawkers had drifted into deep financial trouble. No one at the Treasury seems to have taken them to task. The Commons were asked to underwrite their deficits. Encouraged by his previous success, Pulteney's followers tried to twist the debate and so bring in a motion which reflected personally on Sir Robert. 'The Vision of Camilick' had recently been published and was still on everyone's tongue. Walpole had just failed in his attempt to prosecute its printer and publisher, an adverse motion, therefore, could stamp with authority the opposition attack for, even if it failed, as it was bound to do, it would get into the printed votes. Pulteney himself had been more statesmanlike; the previous week (28 February) he had proposed a vote of censure on the Treasury but had allowed it to be overridden. Now his followers wanted blood.

Walpole had been living under great strain. He disliked war. He doubted if it could be avoided. He and Townshend, who had lived and worked so long together, were drifting apart. But above all he was distressed by this new vile abuse which was being heaped upon his head by Bolingbroke and the rest. Doubly hard that a convicted traitor, pardoned by his own consent, should use him thus. And his health, never good, was wretched, so that business was a burden, debates a torment. 'The Vision of Camilick' maddened him and this latest personal attack in the Commons was too much. He lost his temper. He denounced libellers; flung out some bitter words on the *Occasional Writer*, i.e. Bolingbroke; and complained that greater personal enmity had been shown to him than had ever been shown to other men. It was a harsh speech, aimed at Pulteney, and he knew it. He rose at once and gave better than he got. He denounced the ministry as the most corrupt that was ever known; insisted that he had quitted it because he had been appalled by the lavish manner in which it had been carried on. He would, he said, pursue this administration to destruction if he could. This was the challenge. At last the fury of their personal hatred was publicly avowed. And once more Pulteney misjudged the House, which could be so quirkish in its sympathies. They did not respond to him, so robust, so alive, so full of eloquence and wit, so adamantine in his anger. Their sympathy went to Walpole, cross-tempered, battered, querulous and sick. 'I', wrote Sir Edward Knatchbull, 'and Milles in the majority and a few other tories for I saw plainly there was nothing warranted by the evidence to justifie the personal question.'[1] Shortly after this debate Walpole fell gravely ill. He was said to have gout in both legs and fever. He suffered constantly from gravel. Whatever it was, he was so ill that he could not undertake business for many weeks.[2]

As he fought his way back to health, a more cheerful

[1] *Brabourne MSS, Knatchbull's Diary*, fos. 102–3: Chandler, VI, 386–90: HMC, *Onslow MSS*, 468–9. Knatchbull had previously been unable to make up his mind when this attack on Walpole had first been raised and he had abstained from voting. Also *Tickell MSS*, Letters of M. Broughton, Secretary to Carteret, to Thomas Tickell. Secretary to the Lords Justices of Ireland, 14 March 1727. As this is unlikely to be published it is worth quoting in full: 'A publick and avowed attack, Pu[lteney] declaring totidem verbis to the Cha-[ir] that he wd stick to him, till he had expos'd all his corruptions; that as he had been, so he still might have been an associate and ally, if their wrong steps had not rendered it impracticable; to which was answer'd that his seperation [sic] was only owing to his own ill behaviour, which appear'd from other things, as also from a most abject letter of his writing to the K, after his being remov'd; Conduit, in an answer to Sir J. Rushout in that day's debate, was seconded by Mr Clutterbuck, who spoke then for the 1st time, and was well heard and approv'd: Sir Robt being a little heated in some part of the affair, P observ'd upon it, that as temper and coolness was the effect of a good conscience, this argu'd the contrary; but was himself in half an hour reminded of it upon the like occasion, a loud cry arising keep your temper.'

[2] *Mist's Weekly*, 29 April 1727: *Brabourne MSS, Knatchbull's Diary*, fo. 108: *Tickell MSS*, 29 March 1727; HMC, *Elphinstone MSS*, 218; *Chandos-Pole-Gell MSS*, 401; Coxe, II, 515, Horatio Walpole to Pointz: 'My brother Walpole has been extremely ill of a violent looseness', 22 May 1727 (NS).

aspect of affairs greeted him. The danger of war was rapidly receding. Elizabeth Farnese was all too capable of rash and decisive strokes, but she possessed little tenacity of purpose. The galleons locked up by Hosier in the Indies; the warlike preparations of the British to defend Gibraltar and Port Mahon; the accession of the Dutch to the Hanover Alliance; the lunatic craving of her husband for retirement; the loss of Ripperda and the worry of his extravagant promises; all began to unnerve her. And Fleury, subtle, persuasive, Janus-faced, spoke of the family ties between Bourbons, mentioned the continuing absence of sons to Louis XV and let it be known that he looked to Spain for a successor if God should decide to deny Louis an heir. He hinted that the Dutch and English were more worried by the Ostend Company than by Spanish problems, which still might be solved if a Congress could be called. Cupidity, hope, anxiety—the policy of Spain swayed with the moods of its Queen. As her ardour for war cooled, the Emperor quickly began to fear for his own isolation. His weakness, too, was all to well known. If only the great Western powers would guarantee the succession to his only daughter, he would be prepared for any concession. True, he had done well in the summer of 1726 to buy up some princelings with their armies, yet the Hanover powers had done better. Danes and Hessians were the best mercenaries in Europe. England had obtained them. The Swedes had followed suit. True, he had gained Prussia, a power, though hardly to be trusted on an ebb tide. Then the Czarina died. The great subsidies from Spain proved to be a chimera. How would the German princelings be paid? The more Charles VI studied the European scene in 1727, the more he dreaded his growing isolation. Rumours, skilfully strengthened, that Spain might settle without Austria flurried him. The allies perceived his weakness and presented him with an ultimatum on 9 May. His will to resist crumbled. By 31 May the Preliminaries of Paris were signed. The Ostend Company was suspended for seven years, trading privileges were to be as they had been before the first Treaty of Vienna. A Congress of European nations to settle all outstanding problems was called to meet at Soissons. Spain, not Austria, was isolated.

These quick and dramatic events, which lifted the heart of Horatio in Paris and made it swell with pride at the thought of his friend Fleury's skill and goodness, proved a tonic to Sir Robert. He hated war, hated the waste, the expense, the uncertainty. He felt nothing but gratitude to Fleury and believed all that his brother told him. He wanted it so. The Dutch, the British and the French allied together could settle the problems of Europe as they wished. No one would dare to resort to arms against them. Once more the storm clouds seemed to be rolling back, and the days of security and triumph returning. With these good tidings the extravagances of the opposition would be for ever exposed. Life still had its sweetness, its power, its time of hope. As he lay convalescing in the summer sun at Richmond, entranced by Molly and beguiled by their little girl, he felt a new strength and a new purpose. No sooner was he back in harness than he was struck down by a fresh blow. A messenger who had ridden post haste from Germany told him that George I had died suddenly on 11 June of apoplexy at Osnabrück.[1]

---

[1] He had had what Lady Suffolk called 'fits' shortly before he set out, Horace Walpole, *Reminiscences* (ed. Paget Toynbee), 134, 33–4. For the most circumstantial account of George I's death see *Quellen und Darstellungen Zur Geschichte Niedersachens*, LIV, Rudolf Grieser, *Die Memoiren des Kammerherrn Friedrich Ernst von Fabrice* (Hildesheim 1956), 150–2.

BOOK TWO

THE YEARS OF CRISIS

CHAPTER FIVE

NEW KING, NEW FRIENDS, 1727-30

THE NEW King was a short, slight, stiff little man with a high complexion and the bright, bulbous china-blue eyes of his mother. His had not been an easy life. The fate of his mother—her lover killed, she herself a prisoner until her death—had shocked him. He cherished her picture and the moment his father died it was hung in a place of honour.[1] The sense of insecurity which his broken family life engendered in him was strengthened by his father's constant bullying, by the half-veiled threats of disinheritance which he came to fear might be a reality.[2] The years of mockery did their work. He became both quick tempered and weak. He protected himself by a slavish, almost maniac, attention to detail. He possessed an excellent memory. He knew the complicated family trees of all the princes of Europe with absolute accuracy. His knowledge of regiments, uniforms, and orders was equally precise, and never to be faulted. Exactitude was a passion. His day moved with clock-like regularity and his weeks were as ordered as his days. Yet he possessed no confidence; he could say 'yes' or 'no', but he found it difficult to argue a point of view or present a case.

[1] See *Walpole*, I, 210: Horace Walpole, *Reminiscences*, 23.

[2] George I attempted by his last will to bring about an ultimate separation of Hanover and Great Britain. George II promptly suppressed his father's will, thereby to give rise to ugly rumours. See Hervey, I, xxxiv-v: Michael, 'Die Personalunion von England und Hannover und das Testament George I', *Archiv für Urkundenforschung* (1918), VI. Michael corrected these views later, *Geschichte*, IV, 523-7, when George I's will was discovered by Dr Drögereit, see *Niedersächsisches Jahrbuch für Landesgeschichte*, XIV, (1937), 94-199, and Drögereit, 'The Testament of King George I and the Problem of the Personal Union between England and Hanover', *Research and Progress*, V (1939), 83-6. For this last reference I am indebted to Professor G. R. Potter. This problem constantly exercised George I and it was known to several of his ministers. See King, *Notes*, 15-16. By the suppression of George I's will, George II cheated, according to Dr Drögereit, his sister and his father's servants out of their legacies.

He lacked his father's ability to think in general terms. At Raynham in Norfolk there are a large number of private notes that were sent to him by Townshend on diplomatic matters; as soon as they were received George II scribbled his answer. Usually he restated more decisively and emphatically the decisions which his Secretary had drafted. His eye was exceptionally quick to note any slip in a date, and his occasional verbal suggestions are always apposite. He possessed quite obviously a very nice sense of style, and on the rare occasions that he allowed himself a longer comment a sharp intelligence is revealed. He did not, however, very frequently rise above his astounding preoccupation with detail. One of his evident delights was to keep in his mind the possible days of arrival of the couriers that shuttled back and forth across the face of Europe.[1] About all his comments there is the same anxious restlessness that Hervey noted so tartly in his *Memoirs*; wherever he was, he could scarcely keep still or stop talking. He bored the Queen and his Court to distraction. He was, like most kings, very positive and decided in his likes and dislikes, and came to his judgments very rapidly. He hated books, liked music, and loved parades.[2] Yet his tastes were modest. He had no desire to immortalize himself in stone, and the poky little palaces which he had inherited from the Tudors and Stuarts were good enough for him. Yet he was capable of very deep attachments. He wept like a child when, after long years of service, Lord Scarborough quitted his employment.[3] He could bark and snap and jeer at Sir Robert, but once he had grown fond of him his loyalty and trust were unquestioning, and remained unbroken until Walpole died. And so it was with his wife and his mistresses. He was not a lustful man although he took a certain exhibitionistic pride in his virility. When he came to the throne Mrs Howard had been his mistress for more than ten years. She was a cool, witty,

[1] *Townshend MSS* (Raynham); a few were printed by Coxe, II, 520–41.
[2] Hervey, I, 261.
[3] *Ibid.*, 248–9.

elegant creature of modest physical charms who had become slightly deaf as the years passed, a defect which may not have been all loss with a lover as loquacious as George II. He visited her with ostentatious regularity, usually at nine o'clock precisely. Few royal mistresses made so little from their station as Mrs Howard. A small villa at Marble Hill, Twickenham, a few jewels and trinkets, a modest pension and a guinea or so now and then for her private charities, these were the few rewards for her time and person. And she exercised not a scrap of influence; either she was too discreet to attempt to do so, or the King determined never to listen to her pleas. Certainly no friends of hers were preferred. She was a habit to him, scarcely a person—a means by which the fretful days were passed.[1]

If he loved anyone, he loved his wife, Caroline, although love, perhaps, is scarcely the word to use for a strange necessity. Caroline was comely in a soft, flaxen German way. She possessed a lovely pink skin which had escaped, apart from a little roughening, the ravages of smallpox, from which she suffered in 1718. She had magnificent breasts, and she was very proud of them, displaying them to their maximum advantage. She was confident of her charm, and her husband's infidelities irritated rather than distressed her. She knew that the delight he always found in her flesh would bring him back. As the years passed his appetite for her did not diminish. The moment he returned to England after a visit to Hanover, he would rush her off to their private rooms, much to the amusement of the Court. When he died, he left strict instructions that he should be buried by her side, and that the sides of their coffins should be removed so that their dust might mingle in death.[2] Whatever he might do or say, Caroline was the core of his life, the one human being to whom he was absolutely committed. From that thraldom there could never be any escape. Although Caroline realized

[1] For Mrs Howard see Lewis Melville, *Lady Suffolk and her Circle; Letters to and from Henrietta, Countess of Suffolk*, ed. J. W. Croker, 2 vols. (1824): Horace Walpole, *Reminiscences*, 101–46.
[2] Royal Archives, Windsor. *Geo. Add.*, Will of George II.

the strength of his passion, she did not share it. She enjoyed
the power which his love brought her; she grew, at times,
desperately anxious that she might lose it; indeed she need-
lessly endured great pain for fear that his ardour might fade
if he were to discover the rupture from which she suffered.
His personality, however, bored her intolerably, and, in the
deepest sense, George II never possessed her. And this
reticence in love, this withdrawing, this restraint, riveted her
husband to her with unbreakable chains. Angry, frustrated,
beside himself with rage, he could curse her, upbraid her,
insult her before his Court. Yet such tantrums merely revealed what everyone knew, that she enslaved him. She
loved power as her husband loved her—with abandon and
with relish. She wished to dazzle and to dominate. Early in
life she paraded her intellectual interests, corresponded with
Leibnitz, dabbled in theological speculation, and generally
played the blue-stocking—pastimes which she brought with
her to England. Unorthodox divines were quick to solicit her
patronage, and she did her best to pay for their devotion in
preferment—much to Walpole's irritation. And her activities naturally filled Bishop Gibson with consternation. She
thoroughly enjoyed the agitation which her views and
actions created. Yet it was all a game. She did not possess a
powerful mind—her letters are scarcely literate—and her intellectual and artistic judgments were far from sound, as her
ridiculous patronage of Stephen Duck, the labourer poet,
made all too clear. She was far from intelligent and far less
perceptive, far less a woman of taste than Mrs Howard,
although she affected the blue-stocking much more. In the
world of the mind she was obtuse, clumsy, and very con-
ceited; in the affairs of the heart, she was quick, shrewd, and
usually right.

She had been born, like Walpole, an excellent judge of
men and of affairs. And her character, like his, was massive;
it compelled attention and carried conviction even at its
most absurd. Her strength of purpose could so infuriate
George II as to reduce him to impotent rage, but it always

brought him to heel. In the end he did what she told him to do. Naturally it was hard for him to acknowledge that this was so, and a bored, if self-satisfied, Caroline had frequently to listen to her arguments complacently put forward by her husband as his own.

But all boredom, all irritations, all infidelities, all un-shared passions were sufferable for the sweet sense of power, for the gratification of her need to judge and decide and to make the world fear her authority. And probably both her husband and Walpole hoodwinked her a little. Walpole, of course, cultivated her intensely. He was prepared to spend hours with her, deferring to her judgments, praising in extravagant terms her power with the King; he was pre-pared to load her with flattery, and yet it is doubtful whether he ever paid the slightest attention to her opinion—save on Church affairs—unless it chimed with his own. But the illusion of power proved strong enough to hold her to his purpose, to make her his devoted ally, as loyal as he was ever to know. As she in love, so Walpole in power—he was uncommitted; ultimately he was alone, the judgment his. And yet his strength, his power, she seemed to herself to share. And so perhaps her domination of her husband was not quite so real as it appeared to her. The arguments which she stressed so forcibly had often been put to him more cogently by Walpole. George II was a quick man, quick to decide, but he was never opinionated, and his obstinacy was not a part of the fibre of his being, but a matter of emotion and temper that quickly passed. Also, he committed himself in friendship as completely as he did in love. However they might behave politically, he could never disengage himself from the affection that he felt for Caroline, for Scarborough or even for Chesterfield. And so it was to be with Walpole.

As the summer of 1727 turned to autumn, he grew to respect Walpole, then to like him; within a year he had become one of the necessities of his existence, a friend with-out whom the burden of governing would be intolerable. As year followed year, the need for Walpole strengthened, the reliance on his judgment became more profound, the prospect of a life without him more intolerable. And often it must have been vastly irritating to George II to be subjected in the boudoir to a long repetition of arguments he had listened to in the closet, and harder still to endure the self-satisfaction, the adamantine complacency with which Caroline assumed that she was handling him with skill. If from time to time, he turned the tables on her, it was no more than she deserved. And this bullying that was but half necessary went on year after year, and George II's resentment never went deeper than a sudden outburst of temper, for in the last analysis he was entirely hers; at the heart of their relationship he was weak and defenceless. He loved; he ravished; he did not possess. In Walpole this strange pair of lovers found more than a minister. They were drawn to him by needs in their own natures. Time strengthened the bonds between them by giving them a common experience.

2

AS WALPOLE'S coach rattled through the rough country lanes to Richmond, on his way to inform the Prince of Wales of his accession, he had time to take stock of his position. Although the crisis was unexpected, it was not unforeseen, for death was too capricious in the eighteenth century for an astute politician to neglect its possibility. The prospect for Walpole was a dark one. Time and time again the Prince of Wales had called him a rogue and a rascal in the hearing of his Court, for he had never forgiven him for the terms which Walpole had arranged in 1720 on his reconciliation with his father. The Prince of Wales's dislike did not stop at Walpole. 'Scoundrel', 'fool', 'dirty buffoon', were the royal epithets that festooned Horatio's name. At Leicester House there was no need for a gloss when the Prince of Wales referred to the 'choleric blockhead' and the 'impertinent fool'.[1] They were his father's Secretaries of State—Towns-

[1] Hervey, I, 29.

hend and Newcastle. There was a crumb of comfort here
for Walpole. If the Prince gave way to his prejudices, they
would all be out together. In numbers there was a certain
safety, but small comfort—too many politicians, high in the
Prince's favour, were eager for office. Once the Prince
displayed his hand, there would be a circle of applauding
courtiers to keep up his resolution. Few, including Walpole
himself, can have ranked his chances of survival as very
great.

He had, of course, done what he could. For years he had
cultivated the Prince's wife, Caroline of Anspach. He listened
to her opinion on Church affairs in which she took a keen,
if erratic, interest. At times he permitted her to take decisions. He spent hours in her drawing room, encouraging
her interest in politics, flattering her judgment and insight.
He scrupulously avoided the Prince's mistress, Henrietta
Howard. So he boasted afterwards he took the right sow
by the ear. And it would seem the right boar. The Prince
did not make friends easily. The Earl of Scarborough, a
strange, indrawn man with no aptitude for or interest in
politics, was his closest. Walpole secured him the Garter.
And Walpole exploited his luck. The Duke of Devonshire
liked Walpole from the days when they had first met in the
early years of Queen Anne's reign. They became fellow
members of the Kit-Kat. Both loved race-horses, hard
hunting and drink. Nothing had troubled their friendship.
The Prince of Wales approved of Devonshire. He was a
frequent and welcome member of Leicester House. Nor did
George I dislike him, even though he was a friend of his
son's. Walpole took his chance. Devonshire became Lord
President of the Council in March 1725, and through him
Walpole kept the Prince secretly informed of ministerial
policy and connived at Devonshire's showing him despatches.
By these means Walpole had attempted to form ties of
influence and obligation. How strong they might prove, no
one could tell. At least there might be one or two men to
whom the Prince would listen, who could plead his cause

and make the most of his two vital assets—his capacity for business and his strength in the Commons. The last six years had given proof of both.

His arrival at Richmond Palace was most inopportune and gave rise to one of those farcical incidents which had a way of occurring at the more dramatic moments in the lives of the Hanoverians. Dinner was over and the Prince, as usual, was in bed with his Princess. Such news, however, could not wait and the Duchess of Dorset had to disturb them. Flustered, bad-tempered and half-dressed, the Prince came out to discover what Sir Robert wanted. Forcing his huge bulk down on his knees, he addressed the Prince as 'His Majesty' and told him of his father's death. This news, at once so exciting and so distressing, completely confused the Prince, and when Sir Robert asked him from whom he should take his orders, he answered with that rapid, thoughtless precision that was so characteristic of him: 'From Spencer Compton at Chiswick.' The King then darted back to his bedroom to tell his wife the news. Walpole struggled to his feet, climbed into his coach and left, his career seemingly at an end. He returned to London, his worst fears confirmed.[1]

The new King and Queen followed hard on his heels. Back at Leicester House, they received their congratulations as the courtiers poured into the crowded rooms. Lady Walpole found it impossible to force her way to the Queen, for rumours were already flying about, and no one thought it necessary to make way for a falling minister's wife. Caroline, however, raised speculation to fever pitch by calling out: 'There I am sure I see a friend,' thereby compelling the courtiers to fall back and make way for Lady Walpole.[2] The coffee-houses were as confident as the Court that Walpole's day was done,

[1] The best accounts of the accession crisis are to be found in Horace Walpole, *Reminiscences*, 48–52; Hervey, I, 22–34; HMC, *Onslow MSS*, 516–17; Saussure, *op. cit.*, 224–30. Saussure's story, although substantially the same, developed entrancing but not very probable details, as it drifted down to him from the Court. That Sir Robert met the messenger from Townshend by chance is too good to be true.

[2] Horace Walpole, *Reminiscences*, 50.

and people in the streets were full of expectancy and rumour. At Windsor, the tears streaming down the face of little Master Walpole were interpreted as a sure sign of his father's fall.[1] The French ambassador wrote at once to inform his government that a new master would mean new creatures. Newcastle, who always sought solace in ink, wrote a long rambling account of the muddle of it all to Townshend. 'You can easily imagine', he wrote (and doubtless Townshend could), 'the concern and distraction we are all in here for the loss of our dear Master.'[2] His fears for his own future were scarcely controllable. The new King hated him and everyone knew it.

The excitement, however, had unnerved Spencer Compton. Although an adroit courtier and a competent Speaker of the House of Commons, Compton was almost devoid of political ability. At the first meeting of the senior ministers at the Duke of Devonshire's to draw up the King's speech, he had found it quite impossible to cast his distracted thoughts into the appropriate measured prose. Helpless, he had asked Sir Robert to do it for him—and naturally Walpole, with practised skill, slipped in a charming and appreciative tribute to the ability of the late ministry. Though he exploited the few chances fortune gave him, his position on the first day of the new reign seemed hopeless to most people. Everyone (except perhaps the King himself) thought that George II had committed himself to Spencer Compton, and everyone knew that kings do not like eating their words within a few days of uttering them. Newcastle said it would be Compton; and Walpole told Onslow so himself when the latter visited him at Chelsea.

'I went', Onslow wrote, 'to wait upon him at Chelsea, a place he had for retreat, as much as a first minister

---

[1] Horace Walpole, *Reminiscences*, 13. These were so copious because this affected little boy thought that a Prime Minister's son should cry more than the rest at the monarch's death.

[2] BM *Add MSS*, 32,687, fo. 212, 15 June, the day of George II's proclamation. Also *Craftsman*, II, 41 (17 June), where there is a mock advertisement which foretells that Walpole will 'in a short time retire from publick business'.

can enjoy, so near the town. I found him at that time, alone, and he kept me a great while with him. At first he seemed a little shy of talking, and I imagine he thought I came by direction of . . . and to report what he should say in our conversation; but I had no such base view, nor ever was an instrument of that sort for any person, and he soon perceived I had no such motive, and came only out of pure respect and affection for him, as was the truth I really believing that all power was to be in other hands. Upon this he took me into his arms with a flood of tears that came immediately from him, crying out, that this kindness of his friends had drawn a weakness from him, which his enemies never could do. He then made me sit down by him, for I was going away, and entered into a long discourse of his ministry, justi-fying his measures, and defying any charge that could be brought against him, ending with saying, that all he had been employed in would devolve upon Mr. Compton (which indeed everyone believed, and people crowded, during these few days, in their resort to him accordingly), seemed to like this destination for Mr Compton, better than for any other person, and declared he would never leave the Court if he could have any office there, and would be content even with the Comptroller's Staff.'[1]

Even the Comptroller's staff! What a cry from the heart! Anything, anything but oblivion and a return to those grey Norfolk wastes, and the life of a country gentleman, in a house that he could never maintain.

The prospect was not so dark as Walpole feared. Caroline was determined to keep him. Since the days when he had been in opposition she had liked and admired him, even, perhaps, grown fond of him. He had never made the mistake of cultivating the King's mistress, Mrs Henrietta Howard, an attention for which Caroline felt a certain gratitude. The King, of course, had spoken hastily, mentioning perhaps the first name that had come into his bewildered head. Perhaps he only intended that Sir Robert should consult with Compton. This is the interpretation that seems best to fit

[1] HMC, *Onslow MSS*, 517.

the facts, for on 15 June George II had a long and fruitful talk with Sir Robert about the civil list. Sir Robert's own spirits perked up a little from that moment. Gossip of a later generation reported that he had told his crony, Sir William Yonge, that though he would certainly go out, he would soon be back again. It was not long before the world, as well as he himself, expected that he would continue in office. What was more uncertain was whether he would continue on the same footing. Would he and Townshend exercise the same authority, or would they be forced to share it with Compton and the King's friends? Walpole was too realistic a politician to hope that all change might be avoided. For a time the issue remained in doubt, and Compton and Walpole ran in double harness. Compton was not a confident man. Amiable, easy-natured, filled with a desire to please, such a man, pitched against Walpole, had a hopeless task. The Court soon realized it. Even by 16 June the French ambassador had changed his mind and told his government that the old ministry would continue.[1]

This, also, was Fleury's dearest wish. On the news of George I's death Horatio had rushed to consult him. The Jacobites were hooting with joy in Paris, and spies buzzed like flies about the English Embassy, reporting invasion, treason and plot to a horrified ambassador. The Cardinal reassured him. France would be true to her engagements; there would be no acknowledgment of the Pretender. Horatio, though relieved, had imparted some of his anxiety to the Cardinal. No sooner had Fleury left him than he decided that Horatio ought to go to London at once and take a letter from him to George II. Horatio dearly loved a dramatic action and accepted with alacrity. Booted and spurred, he set off without delay and rode post haste for London, which he reached on 19 June. George II flared up with anger at the sight of him. Horatio had broken the protocol. He had left his embassy

[1] *Arch. Aff. Etr.*, *Corr. Angl.* 359, fo. 215. By 20 June, it was common knowledge that George II had asked Walpole to continue. *Tickell MSS*, M. Broughton to Thomas Tickell, 20 June 1727.

without the King's permission. It took him several hours to get the King over this hurdle, but George's temper subsided as rapidly as it had risen. Having read the letter, which stressed the Cardinal's deep affection for England, for George himself, for the Alliance and (here the phrasing was discreet but firm) for Walpole's administration, the King melted and was all charm. He thanked Horatio, he thanked everyone, and sat down and thanked Fleury, exceptionally, in a very long letter in his own hand. Horatio rode triumphantly back to Paris.[1]

This rash action had unnerved Sir Robert. His own position was so delicately balanced that his brother's unheralded eruption seemed to invite disaster. Yet when Horatio left, Sir Robert's position had strengthened. The next ten days confirmed him in power. Compton had to attend Parliament as Speaker to swear in the members; and for the long hours during which they took the oath and signed the roll Walpole had the King to himself.[2] Indeed, as much as he could he left Parliament to Compton during the brief but necessary session before the dissolution. He descended on Whitehall only when he had worked out, to the immense delight of the King and Queen, the full details of their civil list. Walpole knew his duty. Never had a sovereign been so generously treated. The King—£800,000 a year down and the surplus of all taxes appropriated to the civil list, reckoned by Hervey at another £100,000: the Queen—£100,000 a year. The rumour ran that Pulteney offered more. If so, his political ineptitude was astounding. No one but Walpole could have hoped to get such grants through the Commons—a fact which Walpole lost no time in pressing on his Sovereign, and it was a point which his Sovereign was not slow in grasping.[3] Yet when Walpole put his figures before the House, only Shippen raised his voice against them. The rest sat in

[1] Coxe, HW, 150–4: *Walpole MSS*, Letters from Cardinal Fleury. Horatio's sudden appearance in London gave the ballad-makers an excellent opportunity for satire. Percival, *Ballads*, 14.
[2] P. King, *Life of Locke*, II, Notes of Domestic and Foreign Affairs, 46.
[3] Hervey, I, 31–5.

silence—Pulteney, Wyndham, Heathcote, Jekyll, all kept their mouths shut.[1] They still hoped. Perhaps the King would kick out Walpole the moment he got his money. Perhaps he would send for Pulteney and Wyndham and the rest. No hope is too despairing for a politician out of place. The quaint, choleric, peremptory little King, however, was as quick to love as to hate, and there were no surer ways to his heart than through his pocket and his wife. Walpole had reached it dexterously through both. 'Consider, Sir Robert,' said the King, purring with gratitude as his minister set out for the Commons, 'what makes me easy in this matter will prove for your ease too; it is for my life it is to be fixed and it is for your life.' And so it was to be. When Sir Robert drove back in triumph from St Stephen's to tell his master of his success, it was the virtual end of Spencer Compton. What is more, the King overcame his aversion not only to Walpole but also to his friends. 'The choleric blockhead' was confirmed as Secretary and so was 'the impertinent fool'. 'The dirty buffoon' had already left for Paris in a blaze of approval.

The crisis petered out. Yet things were not the same as before. The King had his friends, men to whom he was deeply attached. They had been his constant companions at Leicester House for the past ten years or more, content to enjoy his patronage and to suffer hostility from George I. Their day had dawned. Walpole knew his duty and did it cheerfully enough. To show his eagerness, he kicked his own son-in-law, Malpas, out of the lucrative office of Master of the Robes for the King's German protégé Augustus Schulz. Spencer Compton naturally received handsome treatment. He retained his office of Paymaster-General of the Forces, as Walpole knew there was no office like it for soothing wounded

[1] *Brabourne MSS, Knatchbull's Diary*, fo. 110. The debate took place on 3 July. Caleb Danvers's commentary on Shippen's speech said that it was 'a funeral oration and a monument but he said there would be a resurrection of the just'. There was the next day. Sir Robert and his brother ministers were reappointed to their offices. Pulteney's hopes were well known, see 'When the King died, he again followed the rising sun'. *Remarks on the Craftsman's Vindication of his Two Honourable Patrons*, 54.

pride and thwarted ambition. More spectacularly, however, he was created a baron. Scarborough, the King's closest crony, became Master of the Horse and a member of the Cabinet.[1] But even Walpole, expansive as he was at the moment, jibbed at Chesterfield. Chesterfield's wit, malice and total incapacity to stop intriguing were more than he could bear. The King, however, insisted, and Walpole, still unsure, gave way quickly. Chesterfield became a Lord of the Bed-chamber, but to get rid of him for most of the year Walpole had him appointed ambassador at The Hague. The reshuffle was not an entire loss, for Walpole managed to clear out the last relics of Sunderland's faction.[2]

Many of Walpole's contemporaries (followed by all modern historians) considered that he emerged from the accession crisis stronger than before. This is not true. Before 1727, in order to weaken Leicester House, he had brought Devonshire, whom he could trust, into his ministry and Argyll and his brother, Islay, whom he could not.[3] Now the Campbells were joined by Chesterfield, Scarborough and Compton (all potentially dangerous to Walpole); there was still a very dis-gruntled Carteret in the government, who, although Lord Lieutenant, spent, so Walpole thought, far too little time in Ireland. Here was the nucleus of a possible opposition at Court, and not merely a nucleus of one or two isolated men but of politicians of long standing, men of considerable dexterity and not negligible influence, who had worked to-gether, and to whom George II felt a sense of obligation as well as loyalty. And beyond the circle of the Court the voice of opposition had been raised louder than ever before.

If the death of George I had silenced the opposition

[1] The office had been in commission since 1714; the first commissioner was Colonel Negus, a Norfolk man and a dependant of Walpole's.

[2] Berkeley, First Lord of the Admiralty, was dismissed and replaced by Torrington, 'pitched upon for this post not so much from desiring to show him favour as to embitter Lord Berkeley's disgrace', Hervey, I, 38. The Chetwynds, friends of Mrs Howard, were also dismissed. They did not immediately join the opposition.

[3] Islay had been extremely helpful during the Malt Tax riots in Scotland in 1725, but he and his brother, Argyll, were too powerful in Scotland to be easy allies. Argyll's military interests endeared him to George II.

leaders in Parliament, it had singularly failed to have the same effect on their violent and noisy supporters. The Common Council of London passed a violent address, condemning the late King's ministry lock, stock and barrel— foreign policy, national debt, public credit. It was so outspoken that the Aldermen used their right of veto, recently given to them by Walpole. The Common Council retaliated by insisting on their address or none, so that the Lord Mayor and a handful of Aldermen were reduced to drawing up their own address, leaving it about the coffee-houses until it acquired a sufficient number of signatures to be carried in dignified pomp to St James's Palace.[1] An ugly incident, this, for the new reign and one which Walpole viewed with disquiet. He hated London, loathed its treacheries, its insubordinations, its restless vociferous radicalism, its ferocious xenophobia.

Within and without there lurked new perils. Gone were the unclouded days of 1725 when all troubles seemed reconciled and peace and prosperity for his country appeared as certain as power for himself. For the rest of his political life he was to be harried by constant opposition in Parliament, in the Press, in the nation at large. By itself, this did not matter overmuch; his power might easily be threatened if this external opposition were to fuse with discontent at Court and make a common cause against him. Nor was this a remote possibility, a fantasy of an anxious temperament, for the danger was real and close at hand; the key to it— Townshend. They were no longer brothers. Every month, since Dorothy's death, had witnessed a diminution of their mutual affection. Their common childhood, their long, long struggle, with its failures and successes, were beginning to lose all meaning; sooner or later the fatal words would be spoken, and all would be over between them. Beneath the surface, envy and jealousy were festering. When that moment came, Walpole's career would again be in jeopardy. If these former Leicester House whigs, linked with Carteret and

[1] A. J. Henderson, *London and the National Government*, 117-20.

Pulteney, were to be led by Townshend, they would try hard to find an issue which would rouse the country to secure Walpole's dismissal. His first task was plain: to win the King as king had never been won before.

3

DURING THE long, hot summer days Sir Robert was pursued by crowds of supplicants wherever he went;[1] Arlington Street, Chelsea, even Richmond, were besieged by men and women with hopes of employment for themselves or their dependants, for the posts in the new Royal household were only slowly filled. A nice balance had to be kept between old loyal friends and the hopeful newcomers who were quick to sense a slight. And when occasion demanded it, he bared his sharp, savage teeth. Walpole hated disloyalty. He suffered it in patience and with feigned good nature where he had to—at Court. Towards small men who wavered, he was ruthless, as Sir Archer Croft discovered. Sir Archer Croft of Croft Castle belonged to that class of MPs on whom Sir Lewis Namier has bestowed the adjective 'inevitable'. His family had been settled in Herefordshire for many generations and his ancestors had adorned the back benches, rarely speaking, never seeking office and usually voting against the Court. Times for such gentlemen, as another—Sir Edward Knatchbull—had realized, were changing. London, the Court, a place, entranced them, making an intractable independence of the ministry old-fashioned and slightly absurd. So Sir Archer proposed to make his bow to the new King by moving the Address—and approached Sir Spencer Compton. Walpole took this as an

---

[1] The most charming request that came to Walpole at this time was from an old sea-dog, Sir John Jennings: 'You are senceable when I quitted the Admiralty it was not so much upon account of my indisposition as upon the objection I made to serve there with Lord Beerkley and upon these removes I am not at all sollisatouse to retorne to that board again but must desiar if my pattent for Grenwich is to be renued that it may be for life and that if my Lord Torrington is to be Vice-Admirall of England that I may in my torne be Rare Admirall of the same till the proper time comes for my being created an English Barron. This is all the request I have to make being with unfaingd respect etc.' C(H) MSS, Sir John Jennings, 6 July 1727.

intolerable affront. He was leader of the House and in any case such tit-bits of distinction were foresworn. Croft was written to in no uncertain terms. And the force of Walpole's power can be measured by Sir Archer Croft's reply, and so can the corrupting force of patronage, either in enjoyment or in deprivation.

Sir.

Having too much reason to aprehend that you resent my aplication to the Speaker to open the King's Speech I cant but be encouraged, from the friendship you have been pleased to shew and expres for me, to endeavour to set this matter in a true light and in the most solemn manner to assure you that I had no other thought or intention by aplying to the Speaker, but that I was persuaded it would give the tory party a very sensible mortification to see that honour done to me in every respect so entirely oposite to their interests.

Little, Sir, did I imagine this would have been imputed to a change of principles or party, and whoever knows anything of me, does not want to be told, that there is not a man so little conservant with the Town, or who makes so little inquiry into the changes, that might possibly happen.

If they were my last words I might safely say that I never had any other thought upon the death of the late King but that, Sir, you and the Speaker (if I may take the liberty to say so) would in all things have acted together as one man. No one could be more affected with the death of the late King than myself, more averse to a change, more aprehensive of the tory party prevailing and at the same time more resolved to stand or fall with your self. You will pardon me to say, that not one of all your friends have been more true (however mistaken in this one point) to your interests than I have been; ever since I had the pleasure to sit and hear you in the House of Commons.

I do solemnly declare it, I never would have aplyed to open the King's speech, could I have had a thought it would have been displeasing to you, and the only reason I did not immediately wait upon you, to let you know it, was, that the Speaker told me he had done it and there was no ocasion; so little thought had I to hide it from you or to ask it without your consent.

This, Sir, is the whole truth of this affair and hard is my fate, if I, who have apeared so warm against your most inveterate enemies must be thought to be running into those men; when I solemnly declare I intended nothing but to lend my poor assistance to do honour to yourself and to crush your enemies in the very begining of this reign.

If this be true, Sir, it is hard upon me, that no notice shall be taken of me in the present changes, that are like to be, am I who have ever distinguished my self through the whole course of my life against the tory party, and have, both within and without the house, done my utmost to testifie an unalterable regard for yourself; am I, Sir, (pardon me thus to expostulate with you) to be laid aside, only for a mistake, for not knowing better what some intended or what strugles were like to be; for I solemnly protest I never aprehended there was or would have been anything but the most entire harmony between yourself and the Speaker.

I have only this to add, Sir, that in the last sessions of the late reign when your enemies vented all their malice against you and almost every one of your friends sat silent, I did my utmost to serve you, even when it was not expected for me, at the time you were confined by sickness.

I can hardly, Sir, doubt that after this plain declaration you will not do me the honour which I may justly say not a few think I deserve, to admit me to sit at the Boad of Treasury, Admiralty or of Trade, as there is no man will more sincerely and heartily use his utmost endeavours to serve you.

I am, Sir, Your most obliged
faithfull humble servant.

Croft Castle   Ar Croft[1]

July 29: 1727

---

[1] *C(H) MSS*, Sir Archer Croft, 29 July 1727. Croft learned his lesson and reward followed reprimand. He became a Commissioner for Stamps.

Walpole thoroughly enjoyed the complexity of influence—
and relished the weighty arguments with Townshend, Newcastle, Harry Pelham and the Chancellor, over his dinner-
table at Chelsea. As the Lafite and Margaux rapidly circulated, the last places in the infant princesses' nurseries were
doled out and no doubt they all appreciated the joke of
making the poet, John Gay, Gentleman-Usher to the two-
year-old Princess Louisa.[1] Not even the brightest sparks
could expect favour if they courted Mrs Howard. Walpole,
too, was thoroughly tired of the Twickenham set. It baffled
his straightforward nature to be lampooned one moment and
courted the next. No sooner had he been ridiculed in
Gulliver's Travels than Swift turned up at Richmond expecting preferment. Little Mr Pope had suddenly become
most assiduous in his attendance, exploiting his charm and
wit for all they were worth; yet everyone in London knew that
he had a savage satire on the government scribblers almost
ready for the press. These men expected place, they expected
favours, and they expected to do nothing in return, except to
be allowed to bite with impunity the hand that fed them.[2]
They were not the men with whom Walpole wished to live in
intimacy. They were too complicated, their wit was too
acid, their loyalty too suspect. They spoke the language of
Bolingbroke. Gay—open-hearted, feckless, generous and
kind, a man whom none could hate—was thrown a sop: a
callous gesture by Walpole that was to call forth in *The
Beggar's Opera* a musical satire of wonderful versatility.

The lists drawn up, Walpole got into his chariot and drove
over to Hampton, Kensington and Richmond as the Court
moved restlessly between its suburban palaces. He spent
hour after hour with the King in his narrow, high, dark
closet, going over the names, explaining the web of influence which he had spun with such dexterity during the
last seven years. And, of course, Walpole took advantage of
these long sessions to attach the King more firmly to his own

---

[1] A post which he promptly refused.
[2] Geo. Sherburn, *The Correspondence of Alexander Pope* (Oxford 1956), II, 441.

interests, a task which owing to the nature of George II and his wife Caroline, proved curiously easy.

4

THE DISPOSITION of places, the excitement and delight of new friends and new ministers in a new reign, were not Walpole's sole preoccupations. He had to plan a general election which was held in July and August.[1] The unexpectedness of the King's death found the ministry with its plans but half made and Walpole was swamped with requests for seats, for influence, for money. Although he was unprepared, the leaders of the opposition were in a worse plight. They had hoped to face the election in 1729, after three years of campaign within and without the House; now they found themselves facing an election within a few months of the beginning of their united opposition. They moved into action as quickly as possible. But Walpole and his principal lieutenant, Newcastle, held all the cards, and the administration won, of course, though the victory proved far from cheap. Some of Walpole's devious practices would have startled even his colleagues. There was more 'bare-faced bribery and corruption than was ever known', wrote Abel Boyer in the *Political State*, implying that the responsibility for this rested with the opposition. *Mist's Weekly*, agreeing that there was scandalous corruption, naturally (as became an opposition paper) put the blame squarely on the ministry and excused the opposition expenditure as self-defence. The High Table at Christ Church was full of gossip of incredible sums spent. Bathurst was hard put to it to preserve his family seat at Cirencester from a Treasury candidate said to be well supplied with money. Onslow, standing against Walpole's advice for the County of Surrey, found himself up 'against all the force of unbounded expense,

[1] S. H. Nulle, 'The Duke of Newcastle and the Election of 1727', *Journal of Modern History*, IX, 1–22. A general election had to take place within six months of the demise of the sovereign.

and of party zeal and rancour, with every artifice that could be practised'.[1] Sir Edward Knatchbull, frightened of splitting the government vote and wrecking their chances of getting one candidate home, desisted at Kent, much to Walpole's delight. He quickly found him a seat at Lostwithiel, and another independent had been hitched to his chariot.[2] Although only a minority of elections went to a final contest, there were sharp struggles in the small boroughs amongst the little groups of electors before they reached their choice.

'Every town', wrote John Wolrige, Walpole's agent in the South-West, 'has been tampered with, [for] which reasons the people who have always been bribed do now assemble and cabell to make their market, and this I believe, if you don't send money here beforehand, you may miss your views in more towns than one.'[3] Agents, of course, tried to get their hands on money and their imaginations quickly took fire when they thought of the opposition. Walpole and Newcastle, however, had placed government influence in Devon and Cornwall in the capable hands of Richard Edgcumbe. When he needed to, he paid high. The thirty-five voters at Mitchell only settled at £1,620—but by and large he got ministerial candidates home for less cost to the ministry.[4] Of course, it was delicate work. Lord Falmouth, whom he had replaced,

[1] HMC, *Portland MSS*, VII, 449; Onslow MSS, 518.
[2] *Brabourne MSS, Knatchbull's Diary.*
[3] *C(H) MSS*, John Wolrige, 1 July 1727.
[4] The election did not cause any great rise in secret service disbursements. Walpole had £6,000 in hand at George I's death. £3,683 14s. 0d. was drawn on 31 October 1727 and £11,200 on 20 December, an amount about double the usual amount drawn; this may have been to meet the bills being presented by members coming up for the new session. NRO *Westmorland MSS* (Scrope Papers). Unfortunately there are no detailed accounts in these papers. It is interesting to note that the totals which are available from 1724 do not correspond with those quoted from the *Liverpool MSS* by Sir Lewis Namier, *Structure of Politics*, I, 242. For Mitchell see *C(H) MSS*, John Wolrige, 1 July 1727. Thirty-four votes cost £30. The returning officer, Foss, received £500 for making the return and his son £100. The costs of other boroughs mentioned in this letter of Wolrige's were: Lostwithiel £460 (8 voters at £20 each; returning officer, Johns, wife and daughters £300); Tregoney £770 (150 voters at £5 each; Mrs Bedford for a piece of plate £20); Grampound £1,510 (41 voters at £30; the mayor £100, 3 magistrates £60). The actual costs of the elections, e.g. bell-ringing, vote-taking etc., were additional and were computed at £700.

did his best to spread distrust and to monopolize those little favours by which Edgcumbe hoped to ease his own path.[1] With a cool, appraising eye he saw that death had Thomas Vernon, a land-waiter, in his grip and at once the sweat-flecked horses were thudding along the dusty roads to take tidings to Walpole at Chelsea. Immediately the place was reserved for Edgcumbe's choice and Falmouth thereby thwarted.

In the days of an election the endless prevarication about places had to give way to decision, for ministerial candidates needed to display their power, not merely speak of it. Although decisions had to be quickly made, they were not easy. Because members had received ministerial support, Walpole could not count on their loyalty. Lord Perceval, as the Earl of Egmont then was, and his brother-in-law, Sir Philip Parker, demanded help at Harwich, where the government had large interests. Perceval was greatly concerned about his position at Harwich. Without the government's support he could never have hoped to win this sea-port, where the Admiralty and Treasury were so strong. And, of course, he ran down the chief government agent there, accusing him of plotting against him and undermining his influence. It did not take Walpole long to realize that within a couple of Parliaments Harwich would be under Egmont's thumb and lost to the government, and for the last few years of this Parliament there was more substance in Egmont's complaints than he himself realized. Walpole, with difficulty, kept him on the leash. At the same time, however, he quietly worked to bring the Parker-Egmont influence at Harwich to an end, a task which he successfully accomplished in 1734.

And so it was in many a borough. Could the man with the most material influence be trusted? If the government's power was put at another man's disposal could he carry it against the natural influence? Would money make a difference or a show of favour? Was a candidate exaggerating his standing in his neighbourhood? Here Newcastle's

[1] *C(H) MSS*, R. Edgcumbe to Sir Robert Walpole [n.d.].

wonderful memory and inexhaustible delight in the detailed management of electioneering was a great aid to Walpole.

Of course, in each province—the South West, the Home Counties, the Marches, the Midlands, Yorkshire, Lancashire and Scotland, they had their principal advisers, men of deep political sagacity and powerful local influence. Not much was done at Durham without consulting John Hedworth or George Liddell; Sir Thomas Wentworth advised on Yorkshire; Devonshire could answer for Derbyshire, Rutland for Leicestershire. These men with their vast acres and great commercial interests were Walpole's natural allies, without whom no ministry, not even his, could expect a victory. There were humbler workers; men who could persuade the dissenters not to be lured away by the wild promises of the radical whigs, or tories now ardent for Hanover.

Day after day Walpole had to assess a bewildering number of contingencies and then make up his mind; a decision once made could not be revoked; time was too short, distances too great, correspondence too slow. And each decision, as the unhappy example of Egmont so clearly demonstrates, was a grave one, for Walpole had to live with his Parliament for seven long years. He was, of course, bound to win the election; his array of political allies was too formidable for any other result to be in any way possible; but he needed to win seats wherever he could, with men devoted to him, and that was far less easy to accomplish.

The opposition knew that it must lose. The little boroughs, unless they belonged to a friend, they could never hope to win. Most of the Court were satisfied with Walpole, so were many of the self-electing country gentlemen, even if, like Knatchbull, Egmont, or Onslow, they flattered themselves on their independent judgment. So the opposition set its sights on the great sea-ports, on the populous towns with thousands of voters, above all on London, for a victory there, they argued, would demonstrate the true sense of the nation. They struck up their tune with a mock advertisement in *The Craftsman* on 22 July.

'This week was publish'd
Robin's Panegyrick on Himself and his Friends at Westminster; modestly proving that they were all very honest
Fellows and deserving Patriots; with a full Confutation
of the charge of Bribery and Corruption

Offered to the consideration of the Freeholders; Citizens, Burgesses and Freemen of Great-Britain.

Populus me sibilat, at mihi plaudo. Hor.

Printed for S.B. W.W. and T.W. Printers to the
Robinocracy.'[1]
In the next issue, they discharged a heavier broadside:
'. . . every man, who hath any regard for himself, for
his country, or his posterity, ought to take the utmost
care in the choice of his representatives, and contribute
all his endeavours towards filling that august House with
persons of integrity and ability, who are duly qualified
and properly disposed to execute the great trust, which is
reposed in them: for if corruption should prevail, to any
great degree, in that illustrious body, farewell to all that is
dear and valuable to a free people! Our servants will then
grow insolent tyrants and taskmasters over us; and, instead of being the guardians of publick liberty, will join
with the first bold hand to take it away, for the sake of
sharing in the plunder. Corruption is a poison, which
will soon spread itself thro' all ranks and orders of men;
especially when it begins at the fountain-head. A spirit of
baseness, prostitution and venality will universally prevail. Luxury and extravagance will introduce want and
servility of mind; and the common people, at length, by
the influence of lazy habits, decay of trade, and powerful
examples, will consent to give up their birth-right, like
Esau, for a mess of porridge.'[2]
And so it went on week after week, diatribes, reasoned
essays, heavy jokes, lame dialogues. *Craftsman* after *Craftsman*
urged its readers, if they had votes, to act like true Britons, to

[1] *The Craftsman*, II, 71. Robin's Panegyrick was a collection of anti-Walpole
ballads. See Percival, *Ballads*, 15.
[2] *Ibid.*, II, 73 (29 July 1727).

GEORGE II

QUEEN CAROLINE

VII. TERRACOTTA BUSTS BY RYSBRACK

Frame: *Grinling Gibbons*

VIII. SIR ROBERT WALPOLE AND FAMILY, BY ECKARDT AND WOOTTON

be worthy of their birthright, to protect liberty, to secure freedom, to reject courtiers, placemen, sycophants. Abuse was
heaped on abuse, culminating in the wildly libellous
History of the Norfolk Steward, which began serial publication
in that issue. The ballad-singers too took up the same refrain,
and the coffee-houses, where the opposition gathered, echoed
to the refrain of 'Robin will be out at last'.

> Good people draw near
> And a tale you shall hear
> A story concerning one *Robin*
> Who, from not worth a groat
> A vast fortune has got
> By politicks, Bubbles, and Jobbing
>
> But a few years ago
> As we very well know
> He scarce had a Guinea his Fob in
> But by bribing his friends
> To serve his dark ends
> Now worth a full million is Robin[1]

Only as the election for the City of London drew near
—it was always later than the rest to avoid giving a lead to
the nation—did *The Craftsman* check its diatribes against
corruption, and turn to more serious criticism of Walpole's
policy. Its main charge was Walpole's weakness towards
Spain. It accused the ministry of not being sufficiently determined to retain Gibraltar or to exact proper compen-
sation from Philip V for his depredations on British shipping.
And it revived the South Sea troubles, suggesting that the
directors' estates had not been properly used to alleviate the
distress of those swindled, but had found their way back to
the guilty.[2] This was shrewdly directed. There was much
envy amongst the smaller merchants and the artisans; they

---

[1] Percival, *Ballads*, 15; also *A Miscellany of Court Songs*, published in 1728.
[2] *The Craftsman*, II, 119–87 (*passim*), particularly the *Craftsman Extraordinary* of 9 October, *ibid.*, 154–65.

disliked the great men of commerce who lived like princes and were *personae gratae* at Court. The contest proved desperately close, but the opposition, not surprisingly, gained two seats. *The Craftsman* immediately hailed this as a great victory.[1] Old Dr Stratford at Christ Church was beside himself with joy; 'a great victory', he called it.[2] It was to prove greater, for within eighteen months one of the ministerial candidates, Micajah Perry, had become a leading mouthpiece of the opposition on commercial questions.[3] Nevertheless, the elections were satisfactory enough to Walpole. The great trading towns had not anticipated London's example; and even in some of the counties Walpole had done well. Norfolk was almost entirely his—only one seat, at Castle Rising, going to an opposition member. Jacomb, who had done so much for him during the South Sea crisis (he had been amply rewarded by the office of Deputy Paymaster of the Forces), came in for Thetford by courtesy of the Duke of Grafton, and Walpole's lawyer, Britiffe, won Norwich. And a few months later he used his influence to get in his cousin, James Hoste, for Bramber, thereby healing an ancient feud with his crotchety old uncle, who had so ardently longed to be the member for Castle Rising back in William III's reign, only to be pushed aside time and time again, first by Colonel Walpole and then by Sir Robert.[4] Indeed, as he watched the members signing the roll and lining up to take their oath, Sir Robert felt relief. This could be a good Parliament—his men of business, tried, loyal, and above all, competent in debate, were back in

[1] *The Craftsman.* II, 186. The result of the poll was: Sir John Eyles 3,633; Micajah Perry 3,495 (pro-ministry). John Barnard 3,630; Humphrey Parsons 3,364 (anti-ministry).
[2] HMC, *Portland MSS*, VII, 451–3.
[3] Micajah Perry was a tobacco merchant with large investments in Virginian crops. He proved a bitter opponent to Walpole in the Excise crisis. He was Lord Mayor in 1738 and again very unhelpful.
[4] *Walpole*, I, 100–1: *Brabourne MSS, Knatchbull's Diary*, fos. 112–3. James Hoste was seated on petition and Pulteney's brother-in-law, John Gumley, was rejected. Sir Charles Turner, Hoste's other cousin, presented the petition which gave rise to a sharp debate that nearly ended in a duel between Pulteney and Sir George Oxenden who resented his aspersions cast on Walpole.

force and strengthened with Arthur Onslow in the chair—
his own choice and a welcome one.[1]

Walpole had never liked Spencer Compton, even before
the crisis of the accession; he was far too feeble and indecisive for Walpole's taste: too ready to be all things to all men.
Onslow, practical, business-like, four-square and authoritative, was a man after Walpole's own heart; true, there
was more than a hint of independence in Onslow's manner;
this seemed insignificant, however, beside the obvious
warmth of his heart and his patent capacity for loyalty.
Not that Walpole was entirely free from either irritation or
anxiety as he contemplated the new House. His majority
was certain, but how large it would be no one could tell
until the first votes had been taken, for there were one
hundred and thirty-six new members.[2] The affiliations of
some were, of course, known to Walpole and Newcastle;
others belonged to that self-electing group of country gentlemen who took pride in an independent attitude and whom
Walpole had to woo by a demonstration of his own political
excellence. How far their minds had been made up by the
violent and discrediting propaganda of the opposition remained to be seen. And the old enemies were back, noisier,
more self-confident, ready for the battle. Autumn had
changed to winter, the last places had been filled—house-
keepers at Greenwich, the masters of the Tennis Courts,
ushers and necessary women to the young princesses. No
crumbs came their way. They settled for another seven
years in the wilderness; the opposition, carried on with
such panache in newspapers and ballads, had ended
dismally.

Its leaders probably were realistic enough to hope for little
else. Shippen was quite happy to be as he was without hope of

[1] HMC, *Onslow MSS*, 516–7.
[2] One hundred and thirty-six new members were elected in the original returns; nine were returned to fill vacancies created by members who had been
elected for more than one seat. Six lost their seats on petition but eleven new
members gained seats on petition, so that when the Commons settled down,
many weeks later, there were one hundred and fifty new members. *Ex. inf.* Dr
Aubrey Newman.

office or power. He enjoyed being a figure, delighted in his ostentatious Jacobitism, enjoyed the uproar that his wild, outspoken speeches caused; there was no harm or malice in him, everyone liked him and laughed at his drunkenness. A good row, plenty of vituperation and a scandalized audience could keep Shippen happy enough not only for seven but seventy years if need be. Sir William Wyndham, his rival for tory back-bench support, was a subtler man. He was head of a large, ramified, family group of considerable parliamentary interests and his first and second cousins abounded at Westminster. Since 1716 he had adroitly evaded any stigma of Jacobitism, skilfully piloting himself and his little band of followers through both the Jacobite fiasco of 1719 and the Atterbury Plot, although Walpole had done his best to harry him. He was, of course, intimate with Bolingbroke, and enjoyed his confidence. He loved parliamentary tactics, and lived on hope. His vanity derived great satisfaction from the attention that his oratory always obtained in the House. The roystering, blustering, honest-to-God tactics of Shippen dismayed him. He preferred backstairs gossip, tactical manoeuvres, the unreal hide-and-seek of politics. His vanity and pride did not make him an easy man to work with. Pulteney viewed both Shippen and Wyndham as harsh necessities, useful for their nuisance value, but fundamentally men of straw. A more brilliant orator than either Shippen or even Wyndham, Pulteney also possessed better political judgment and a wider vision of his country's needs. Unfortunately he was too casual, too easily pleased with a victorious quip or happy sarcasm. Nor did he inspire a sense of trust. It was hard for any young ambitious politician to believe in 1727 that the future belonged to Pulteney; a few had been captivated by his wit and by the sharpness of his challenge to Walpole; most, like Lord Hervey, did not remain loyal for long. An opposition led by Pulteney, Shippen, Wyndham, with Bolingbroke in the background and eccentrics such as John Barnard and James Oglethorpe on the fringes, cannot have given Walpole undue anxiety as he watched the Commons assemble. His problems lay much nearer home.

5

THE PRELIMINARIES of Paris, signed just before George I's death, had delighted many besides Walpole and raised in them and in him the prospect of a quick and lasting peace. As so often, however, in eighteenth-century diplomacy, an official and decisive step was followed by a long period of uncertainty. Philip V had gone straight out of his wits almost immediately after the signing of the Preliminaries and Elizabeth had been appointed *Gobernadora del Reyno*. This promptly made Europe bristle with fresh alarm. True, she signed an armistice to bring an end to the siege of Gibraltar. As no shots had been fired in anger by either side and as she now refused to move her troops, the signature proved an ironic gesture, somewhat humiliating to England, for the situation remained exactly as it had been. As a retaliation to Hosier's blockade of Porto Bello, she had seized the British ship *The Prince Frederick*, which she now refused to return until Hosier was back in European waters. As the British refused to recall Hosier until the Preliminaries were recognized by Spain—it had, indeed, been one of the qualifications made by themselves in signing—that was that.

Fleury, subtle, and devious as ever, suggested, without Horatio Walpole's knowledge, that Elizabeth might hand the ship over to a neutral. When this came to light the Walpoles were scandalized. Fleury, however, was giving them a bad summer. No sooner had Horatio got back to Paris from his headlong visit to London at the time of George I's death than he discovered that his old friend Morville, so well bribed that his love for the Walpoles was quite unshakable, had been replaced by Chauvelin of whom Horatio went in terror. He considered him a thorough Machiavelli and a most sinister influence who trespassed on and abused the Cardinal's generosity and weakness of will.[1] It was a brilliant appoint-

[1] In 1720 Morville was already in receipt of £4,000 p.a. from British secret

ment, a masterpiece of political and diplomatic skill. All difficulties in Anglo-French relations were heaped on the willing shoulders of Chauvelin. Fleury escaped the blame and deepened Walpole's obligation by making Chauvelin withdraw from time to time. Fleury's diplomacy acquired an extra dimension. Throughout the closing months of 1727 Walpole was highly suspicious of Chauvelin's authority and terrified of being outwitted. He nearly was. Rottembourg persuaded Benjamin Keene, a young diplomat and Norfolk protégé of Walpole's, who was acting during Stanhope's absence from Madrid, to agree to the question of the *Prince Frederick* being settled at a European congress.[1] Although Keene was promptly disavowed, Elizabeth had been shown that a rift in Anglo-French unity existed and that time and intransigence might be favourable to her. In the hope of having something to show when Parliament met, Horatio had constantly pressed Fleury to break off diplomatic relations with Spain; Fleury listened sympathetically, did nothing, and wrote secretly to Madrid, making it quite clear that he interpreted his role as that of mediator, not ally, of Britain. So when Parliament met, the new King had to address the Lords and Commons in these words:

'I am very sensible of the disagreeable and uneasy situation in which our affairs have been for some time, and have been extreamly concerned to see so many of the inconveniences of a war attending us, without any opportunity of resenting the injuries we sustained, or gaining any of those advantages in return, which the vigorous prosecution of so just a cause and the success of our arms might probably have secured to us.'[2]

Although Shippen cut his usual capers in the debate on the address, few followed his lead; the Court hoped for peace; many members and independents hoped for war; neither could deny the logic of increased armament. Walpole

service funds, *Blenheim MSS*, D. II. 3. Sir Robert also purchased old masters from Morville. For Horatio Walpole's suspicions of Chauvelin see BM *Add MSS*, 32,751, fos. 242–3, and 32,753, fo. 540.

[1] Wilson, *op. cit.*, 181, 189; HMC, *Carlisle MSS*, 53.
[2] Chandler, VII, 16; Coxe, II, 546–7.

increased the land tax to four shillings in the pound—the same high rate which he had found so burdensome as a young Norfolk squire. The land tax had always borne heavily on the small landowners; loud complaints had echoed in his ears throughout his apprenticeship in politics. He hoped that this new imposition would be but temporary, otherwise he knew that many who were content with his rule would grow restive. A settlement with Spain was what he ardently desired. Yet nothing seemed so tantalizingly elusive. There were moments of hope, but these were always followed by renewed anxiety. Before the end of Parliament, Elizabeth Farnese had been forced to ratify the Preliminaries, which she had signed six months previously, and the Congress at Soissons could meet at last.

Horatio was sent as plenipotentiary, aided by Stephen Pointz, one of Townshend's devoted men of business. Long before the ambassadorial coaches lumbered up the long straight road from Paris the old fears were renewed. Horatio always half-expected to be double-crossed. He knew that he was an amateur compared with such professionals as Chauvelin, and probably a clumsy one. He viewed French diplomatic activity rather as many American ambassadors were to view British diplomacy in the twentieth century— as subtle, cynical, sophisticated and utterly selfish. So, when he discovered that the French ambassador had received instructions, about a possible discussion of Gibraltar, which were out of line with England's attitude, he rushed off with Pointz and upbraided Fleury. Pointz reported to Townshend that he 'never saw a man more uneasy in my life'. Fleury, however, extricated himself subtly enough, losing his temper, becoming irritable yet conveying exactly the impression he wished to convey. 'The warmth and passion we put him into, as it turned him inside outwards and putt him off of all sorts of guard, gave us the strongest proof, and, if I may so call it, oracular demonstration of his honesty and sincerity of purpose.[1] The French envoy's credentials, however,

[1] *Bradfer-Lawrence MSS*, Pointz to Townshend, 31 May 1728 (N.S.).

remained unchanged. Within ten days both Horatio and Pointz were making elaborate excuses for Fleury, and writing of him in terms of genuine pity, implying that it was quite impossible to expect such a meek, gentle old man, worn down with the cares of State, to take a strong line about anything.[1] He foxed them completely.

The Congress opened as eighteenth-century congresses were wont to do with a stately examination of credentials, combined with monstrous competitive feasting. 'You guessed right', Horatio Walpole wrote to Tilson, Townshend's under-secretary, 'when you thought we were feasting instead of doing business; we have had two conferences à huit clos that nobody might see what triflers we were. The Cardinal who preached against luxury entertained us with 60 dishes at each course.'[2] There was no one better than Fleury at preaching one thing and doing another—as Horatio found to his cost. His protestation of cordial friendship never prevented him from drifting into the role of mediator and away from that of ally. Horace firmly held to the opinion that this was due to Chauvelin's 'malignant influence'[3] and above all to 'the natural weakness of the Cardinal's mild and pacific temper, joyned with his ignorance of mankind and being too equable of impressions from thinking others as honest as himself, and this leads him into an openness of heart towards enemys as well as friends'.[4] Pointz doubted Horatio's generous interpretation of Fleury's instincts, and William Stanhope, the British ambassador at Madrid, was frankly cynical. Townshend, and George II, reposed enormous faith in Horatio's judgment; age and weakness, not double-dealing, were held responsible; the days, the weeks, the months drifted by, for time was a dimension in which Fleury moved with confidence. He was waiting for the un-

---

[1] *Bradfer-Lawrence MSS*, HW to Townshend, 4 June 1728 (N.S.); Pointz to Townshend, 19 June 1728 (N.S.).
[2] *Ibid.*, HW to Tilson, 20 June 1728 (N.S.).
[3] *Ibid.*, HW to Townshend, 20 June 1728 (N.S.).
[4] *Ibid.*, HW to Townshend, 1 July 1728 (N.S.).

natural alliance between Spain and Austria to break asunder so that he might achieve the isolation of Austria. He was prepared to talk of Gibraltar, Spanish trade, the Ostend Company, the investiture of the Farnese princes, the affairs of Mecklenburgh, anything as long as time passed and he mediated.

Townshend wanted decisions. He needed to impress the new King with the excellence of his judgment and his mastery of the European scene. He disliked intensely the growing criticism of Newcastle, which impelled the Duke to cavil at every letter that he wrote.[1] Sir Robert, too, nagged him. For two years the country had been suspended between war and peace, enjoying the disadvantages of the former and none of the benefits of the latter, and Walpole did not like it. The Hessian troops were expensive, the mobilized fleet cost money, the Swedes and the German princes were monsters of avarice. Something must be done before the next parliamentary session. Townshend possessed a lively imagination. He brooded on the need to get something accomplished at Soissons. Late one night he settled down in his office at Whitehall and dashed off his thoughts to Horatio. They were these. The question of Gibraltar, he realized acutely, was not the real issue nor the most difficult; trade with the West Indies was the running sore in Anglo-Spanish relations. Surgery would heal it. Great Britain must sell back the *Assiento* privileges to Spain. The profit on one ship of 500 tons for fifteen years (the time the *Assiento* still had to run) should be calculated; the sum paid by Philip V to the South Sea Company. After that all British trade with the West Indies would cease. 'This, dear Horace,' he concluded, 'is a sudden thought of my own which I have mentioned to no man alive except my brother Walpole and do it now off hand to you in greatest confidence.'[2] This totally unrealistic

[1] *Bradfer-Lawrence MSS*, Townshend to HW, 10 October 1728; Coxe, II, 521, Townshend to George II: 'If your Majesty approves of the inclosed letter, I will send it privately to Mr Walpole, so as the Duke of Newcastle may know nothing of it.'

[2] *Ibid.*, Townshend to HW, 24 June 1728, '11 at night, Whitehall.'

scheme had clearly been discussed and accepted as a possible policy by Sir Robert. His own personal reaction is unknown. He may, even as early as June 1728, have been quite content for Townshend to make an ass of himself. On the other hand he hated, and was to continue to hate, the difficulties which the *Assiento* created, and he may have been willing to seize any chance, no matter how forlorn. He and Townshend discussed the project in very hypothetical terms with Sir John Eyles, the Governor of the South Sea Company, and with Rigby, one of the directors, who was about to join Horatio at Soissons to watch the Company's interests. They were, of course, averse to this extraordinary plan of Townshend's, and their polite assurances that the Court of Deputies might welcome the scheme cut no ice with Walpole.[1] The project was dropped as abruptly as it was raised, but it remained a strange affair, and had the opposition caught the scent of it, they would have raised the indignation of the City to fever pitch. Both Walpole and Townshend were lucky that it did not leak out, for the opposition was very actively snooping to see what could be picked up to the ministry's discredit.

Bolingbroke sent off his factotum, Brinsden, to Paris in August.[2] Kinski 'intends to play the old game of trying to separate the nation and the King', and he was once more in touch with Pulteney, optimistically believing that he could contrive the ruin of the ministry with a little inside information from Vienna. Spain's demands on Britain were being sent over 'to our enemys here, and will most surely raise a flame against us and our proceedings and be the foundation of parliamentary enquiries next winter, nothing can prevent the latter but a strong, solid and vigorous answer on our part. This will set our proceedings in a right light all over Europe; and for that reason may be a means of securing the Cardinal upon all our main points who by all

[1] *Bradfer-Lawrence MSS, loc. cit.*
[2] *Ibid.*, Pointz to Tilson, 28 August 1728 (N.S.): 'I hear Bolingbroke has sent Brinsden to Paris to see what is going forward.'

I have seen of him looks to be on the popular side of the question, and considering the uncertain state of our affairs as to the event of the present negotiations, it does in my opinion behove us to get the nation as much as we can on our side'.[1]

The tempo at Soissons did not change; the vast complications of diplomacy could not be hurried; draft after draft of political treaties, subsidiary treaties, projected treaties went their stately rounds, each with an *aide-mémoire* as vast as a treatise. Neither Townshend nor Horatio Walpole were patient men, and their anxiety frayed their tempers, led them to exaggerate every difficulty and, more dangerously, to long for any decision. Autumn changed to winter. Horatio with a heavy heart packed up his bags, left Pointz and Stanhope in charge, and set out for the parliamentary session of 1729.

Once more the King's speech was lengthy, once more it stressed the necessity of preparing for war, whilst negotiating for peace. There was, however, one difference from the speech of 1728 and it was significant. The King animadverted on 'the unnatural and injurious practices of some few who suggest the means of distressing their country, and afterwards clamour at the inconveniences which they themselves have occasioned', a subject to which George II returned in even more emphatic terms when he brought the session to a close five months later. The same theme was to be reiterated in speech after speech in succeeding years yet never emphatically enough to please Sir Robert who wanted the King to threaten immediate prosecution of the writers and publishers who were reaping both reputation and fortune by scandalous attacks on the ministry.[2] Of course

---

[1] *Bradfer-Lawrence MSS*, Townshend to HW, 18 July 1728.

[2] *Townshend MSS* contain a draft speech in RW's hand, undated, which runs as follows: 'I thank you for your most dutifull and loyall Adresse and will immediately give the necessary orders for prosecuting and punishing the authors, printers and publishers of all scandalous and seditious libells.

It is too plain that the enemies of my government are indeavouring to make their advantag of the general misfortunes which the nation labours under, but their blind zeal transports them to a degree that will not suffer them

Walpole was the main target of Press scurrility and, hating it so much, he may have exaggerated its effectiveness.

Certainly the session of 1729 must have disappointed Pulteney and his friends. Now and again they scored a witty debating point, tripped up Horatio and poked great fun at Sir George Oxendon, who introduced the debate on the Address. More at home in the boudoir than the senate, Sir George stumbled through his speech and only got to the end of it because his neighbour had a copy of it stuck in his hat so that he could be prompted.[1] The effect of the opposition's mockery, as far as it involved the division lobby, was depressing: the opposition could muster only eighty or ninety against the 250 or so ministerial troops, in a moderate House.

Townshend's anxieties and Horatio's fears, however, proved groundless; supplies were voted; the ministry's arguments accepted; the government remained stable. In one thing only were they embarrassed. The Spanish merchants petitioned Parliament; the Commons listened to the long story of their humiliations and stirred indignantly at the tale of the cruelties of the *guarda costas*. *The Craftsman* waved the flag with patriotic violence, but when the clamour died away nothing had been achieved but an increase in anxiety. Yet the anxiety was real enough. For nearly two years the country had been suspended between peace and war; the financial burden was considerable and men of weight and influence began to feel that a decision must be taken one way or the other. As Townshend wrote to Pointz on 21 February 1729:

to disguise or conceal their black and dangerous designs. This I doubt not will open the eyes of my faithfull subjects, and I promise myself from their known affection, resolution, and prudence to see their vain hopes so intirely disappointed, that they will not be able by fomenting sedition to blow up the sufferings of my people into popular discontent and disaffection.' Presumably Townshend modified this strange language.

[1] *Brabourne MSS, Knatchbull's Diary*, fo. 121. Sir George Oxenden, Bart., MP for Sandwich, Lord of the Treasury and reputed father of Sir Robert's grandson, George, afterwards third Earl of Orford: see Hervey, III, 740–2. After being patronized by Walpole, Oxenden deserted to the Prince of Wales in 1737; naturally Hervey had no use for this renegade. He accuses him of incest, hints that he was a poisoner, and can only find a good word to say for his looks.

'. . . if we are not enabled to give assurances, at least privately to the members of weight and interest in both houses, before they are prorogued, that matters are agreed and concerted between his majesty and France, in such a manner that they may depend either upon seeing an honourable end soon put to our present disturbances by negociation, or that the allys of Hanover have taken measures to do themselves justice by force of arms, the King's credit and influence in this parliament will be entirely lost, which is an extremity the King must never suffer himself to be drove to. The confusions and misfortunes that attended the reigns of King Charles the first, and the second, and King James, in differing with their parliaments, are too recent, and too notorious to be forgot.'[1]

This harking back to the desperate days of the Stuarts illustrates Townshend's fears which had grown monstrous through prolonged anxiety. A note of wretchedness rings through this letter; he needed to open his heart to his protégé, for the bastions of his world were crumbling before his eyes. Walpole hated the Hanover treaty; hated the expense, the uncertainty, and above all, the difficulties which it created for him in the Commons. So far his friends had held firm, but he feared that sooner or later they might swing round to the belief, so constantly urged in debate and in the Press, that England's interests were being sacrificed. Anxiety never made Walpole easy, and Townshend had to listen to the reproaches of his brother-in-law and, perhaps worse, watch the growing friendship between him and Newcastle whose influence waxed as his own waned. As despair echoes in every letter that Townshend wrote during these troubled months, so joy rings out in every sentence that Newcastle wrote to his friend and ally, William Stanhope, and he does not disguise the fact that Townshend was at loggerheads with the rest of the ministry.[2]

Once again the whims of princes had interposed to throw

[1] Coxe, II, 639.
[2] *Ibid.*, I, 641.

the diplomats into a new confusion. This time the Emperor repudiated Don Carlos, whom he refused to have as a husband for Maria Theresa, the heiress of his vast Hapsburg territories, although he had agreed to their betrothal. Naturally Elizabeth Farnese was incensed and it so happened that this repudiation occurred in March 1729, when her husband was showing greater lucidity than he had enjoyed for many months. Owing to Philip's madness, the diplomatic activity of Europe had moved desperately slowly even by eighteenth-century standards. Now it quickened into activity; and, as luck would have it for Townshend, only a few weeks before he set out with the King for Hanover. Naturally, Elizabeth, in her fury, turned to England and to France, for an accommodation with them would be her best way of spiting Charles VI. The final rupture with Austria did not take place until 30 July 1729, for Elizabeth thought that a show of friendship towards the maritime powers might encourage Charles VI to allow Spanish garrisons into Parma and Piacenza, which she was prepared to accept as a sufficient recompense for the snub administered to her son. Charles VI detested the idea of a single inch of Austrian territory passing, even symbolically, into the hands of Spain during his lifetime. Elizabeth was rebuffed again, and with a promptness that often characterized her sudden switches in policy, she despatched draft articles to England that promised so speedy a settlement that William Stanhope was sent at once to Madrid—an act which made Newcastle gibber with delight.[1]

Yet Spain was not Townshend's difficulty. When Newcastle and Walpole had inclined to strong measures, he had been reluctant to follow them. As he saw it, Spain was the minor problem; the major one was Austria. He foresaw that a separate peace with Spain mattered little, might indeed make a concerted pressure on Austria more difficult. He wished to draw away from Charles VI four of the chief German princes, the Electors of Bavaria, Cologne, the

[1] Coxe, I, 651, 654-5.

Palatinate and Trèves, and so increase the Emperor's isolation. This Horatio Walpole strongly disapproved of. The Electors' prices were high, so high that Parliament was bound to resent the expenditure; the Electors were past masters of the double-cross, and furthermore, Horatio argued, the increased isolation of Charles VI might easily drive him back into Elizabeth's arms and on her terms. Horatio thought Townshend's policy bold, rash, dangerous and, worse, expensive.[1]

As the views of Townshend, Newcastle and the Walpoles shifted with the changing circumstances of diplomacy, it became clear to all that there were deeper causes of discontent. The mutual jealousy of Townshend and Newcastle was of long standing. Townshend was apt (not without reason, albeit without tact) to offer Newcastle advice about his despatches. A rough, rather insensitive man, Townshend did not disguise his awareness of Newcastle's shortcomings. And Townshend, who was quick, decisive and to the point in despatches or administration grew increasingly irritated at the ditherings, delays, prevarications and changes of mind by which Newcastle's acute anxiety expressed itself. He was not slow to make his views known to George II, and at times both he and the King deliberately circumvented Newcastle.[2] Perhaps Townshend was more piqued than he should have been because of the obvious warmth of the attachment between Newcastle and Sir Robert. Newcastle was by nature profusely affectionate. He enjoyed hero-worship and a cosy dependence on the great and the powerful as much as some men enjoy independence. And Sir Robert was at this time his hero, an attitude of which Walpole entirely approved.

The links which had bound Walpole and Townshend so closely in the past had snapped one by one. By the defeat of Carteret, they had lost their last powerful common enemy.

---

[1] Coxe, I, 659–65, where Horatio gives an excellent exposition of his attitude to affairs to Stephen Pointz, who inclined to Townshend's view. Townshend was Pointz's patron.

[2] See p. 189.

By the alliance of Hanover they lost confidence in each other's judgment. By the death of Dolly they lost their deepest bond of mutual affection. The accession of George II and, perhaps, more particularly of Caroline, left Walpole far less dependent on Townshend than he had been during George I's reign. In these years the ties of mutual regard and obligation dissolved, only to be replaced by sharp resentments. For generations the Townshends had been incomparably the greatest family in Norfolk. Their day was passing. At Houghton a squire's house was giving way to a nobleman's palace—grander far than Raynham. And the Walpoles lived with a profusion that Townshend could never have emulated even had he wished to do so. At Arlington Street the crowded *levées* with their throngs of sycophants and supplicants showed where the world thought the real power lay. Few made their way to Cleveland Square. All this had been common gossip, and their rows were the talk of the Court. Walpole could not refrain from baiting Townshend. As a joke, he suggested to the Queen, and in the presence of Townshend, that Townshend was laying siege to Lady Trevor's honour; actually he was caballing with her husband, and Walpole knew it. Instead of turning Walpole's coarse irony against himself, Townshend flew into a rage and bellowed that he had neither the appetite nor the money nor the conscience to support such immoralities. Polished by Hervey, who pointed up the phrases and adjusted their balance, this incident was soon going the rounds.[1] This occurred in 1728 yet it was two years before Townshend brought himself to resign. Walpole carefully avoided pressing the issue. To have done so would have been too dangerous. There were men about the Court who disliked him; in 1728 the King was showing increasing confidence in him, but the days of his dislike were not remote. With the opposition raging out of doors, Walpole could not afford a crisis either in the Court or the Cabinet. If Townshend went, he must go alone.

[1] Hervey, I, 86–7.

This was a problem that made great demands on Walpole's political skill; and here perhaps, too, ancient obligations, the sense of all the years of their shared triumphs and defeats, took the edge from his rancour and made him patient. The long friendship did not, however, distort his vision or render him less supple. He moved with measured dexterity. Above all he was careful not to obtrude his own views, particularly when the King and Townshend were in Hanover. When opposition was offered to any of the measures projected by Townshend, it came not from one, but from many; Walpole saw to it that his colleagues were unanimous. He who had formerly despised cabinets, repeating with relish George I's dictum that no good ever came from them, now discovered their value. True, he still disliked the large cabinets, but except for formal business they rarely met, and even the Lords Justices, who were legally charged with advising the Queen, were managed by a smaller and more discreet body, usually known as the Select Lords.[1] These ministers—Devonshire, Newcastle, Grafton, Trevor, Wilmington, King, Scarborough, Godolphin and Walpole—formed an inner cabinet, and their principal task was to advise the Queen on all foreign negotiations. Of these only Trevor and Wilmington and, more doubtfully, Grafton, were allies of Townshend.[2]

Once Townshend had departed for Hanover in May 1729, this Council, with Walpole very much its guiding spirit, took charge of the negotiations with Spain. Indeed, no sooner had George II landed in Holland than he gave full powers to the

[1] King, *Life of Locke* (1830), II, Notes of Domestic and Foreign Affairs, 86. The Diary kept by the Lord Chancellor is of exceptional value for this period, especially if taken in conjunction with PRO, *SP Regencies* for these years.

[2] Meetings of the chief ministers about foreign affairs were, of course, a commonplace of business before 1729, and King himself had attended them, see King, *op. cit.*, 50, 84. Both George II and Walpole disliked large formal cabinets, *ibid.*, 52, but from King's words it is clear that this body of 'Select Lords' was intended to have a more formal recognition than private meetings of the chief ministers. 'The Duke of Newcastle told us that the King being to go to-morrow, and having appointed the Queen Regent, he desired that we would meet, as there should be occasion, and that we would not tell any one either of the message or of this, or of any other meeting that we should have, because there were some others that might expect, to whom it was not fit that every thing should be known.' *Ibid.*, 86.

Queen to negotiate with Spain, on the grounds that it lay in England's sphere of interest and scarcely concerned Hanover. It also lay within Newcastle's department, for he was Secretary of State for Southern Europe. These arguments were strong; that they isolated Townshend made them overwhelming. And so Newcastle was able to send William Stanhope to Spain, to insist on it in spite of his cousin's reluctance and to obtain the Queen's orders for it. Once in Spain, Stanhope had little difficulty in concluding the Treaty of Seville. By 9 November 1729 it was signed, and Newcastle and Walpole enjoyed their first diplomatic triumph. Walpole celebrated the occasion by one of his rare appearances in print. He drew up a short pamphlet entitled '*Observations upon the Treaty between the Crowns of Great-Britain, France and Spain*'. It bubbles with self-satisfaction. All troubles are at an end; the hopes of the opposition destroyed; the wickedness and profligacy of Bolingbroke demonstrated. These hateful men had clamoured for war because secretly they desired their country's ruin. But England, France and Spain were now bound in friendship and all differences would be settled. The terms of the Treaty were that England and France agreed to Parma and Piacenza being garrisoned by Spanish and not neutral troops. All problems arising from seizures and confiscations of shipping engaged in the West Indian trade were to be dealt with within three years by commissioners, and the old privileges of the *Assiento* restored. Nothing was said of Gibraltar; the Treaty simply ignored its existence.

All the ministry's writers followed Walpole's example. The Treaty was a triumph of reason, of patience; a justification of the French alliance, a denial of England's subservience to Hanover, a demonstration of English strength and English resource. Above all, it was Newcastle and Walpole's treaty, particularly Walpole's. Retrenchments could be made at once, the army cut, the navy laid up, the taxes lightened. The expensive burdens laid upon the country by the Hanover alliance were at last at an end. The quick and easy success of the Seville Treaty profoundly influenced Walpole. His convictions were strengthened; there was no need of war, no need for a parade of armed might; patience, determination, a constant readiness to negotiate, would secure that balance of interest which would maintain peace in Europe. The case against Townshend was complete.

Yet Townshend drifted on. And Walpole did not face the issue. He and Newcastle steadily pressed their view that a strong bullying tone towards the Emperor would not bring the final accommodation which England desired. Townshend waited on events, hoping that Charles VI's intransigence would supply the justification for his policy. As a last throw, he tried to undermine the King's confidence in Newcastle. The end came when the King, faced with two despatches, one drafted by Newcastle, the other by Townshend, chose the former. On 15 May 1730 Townshend resigned. In 1717 his resignation had split the whig ministry from top to bottom; in 1730 no one quitted office for his sake.[1] Lonely and defeated, he retired to Norfolk to devote himself to the estates which he had so long neglected. He proved magnanimous, though not so magnanimous as historians have believed. He did not cabal against Walpole. He refused to join forces with Bolingbroke or Pulteney in their day-to-day struggle with the ministry, but his vote was at their disposal either by proxy or in person. He neither spoke nor wrote to Walpole again; with Horatio he maintained a tenuous friendship. To both Townshend and Walpole the situation cannot have been other than painful. Childhood, youth and middle age had been spent together; side by side they had risen to greatness, known together defeat and anxiety; fought the same battles; shared the same hopes. Now there was nothing left but resentment, guilt and silence.

---

[1] Hervey, I, 81. 'He either conferred fewer obligations or met with more ingratitude than any man that ever had been so long at the top of an administration, for when he retired he went alone.' What was equally rare for an early eighteenth-century statesman, he left office no richer than he entered it. Herts RO., *Panshanger MSS.*

CHAPTER SIX

THE CRISIS ABROAD, 1730-31

THE TIDE was no longer running with Walpole. The Treaty of Seville, acclaimed at Court as a masterpiece of Walpolean diplomacy, was viewed with suspicion not only by the City merchants but by many country gentlemen. Knowledge of the rift between Townshend and Walpole had led the opposition to redouble their efforts in the session which opened in January 1730. And significantly they began to gain converts. For three years Pulteney, Wyndham, Shippen had railed at Walpole and his ministry. The House enjoyed their oratory, roared its approval at the jibes and quips and neat debating points. Occasionally the hard core persuaded one or two independents to venture into the opposition lobby, but more often than not they trooped in alone. Numbers were rarely more than eighty or ninety; once or twice, on very controversial issues, 110 members had voted against the ministry. But these were trivial numbers and the sessions of 1727, 1728 and 1729 saw no change. The bulk of Parliament agreed with Sir Robert's policy, and if they did not always turn up either to listen to his speeches or to vote for him, they were quite prepared to accept his government and to let his men of business get on with the work of the Commons. Furthermore the disappearance of the Prince's household on his accession as King had naturally increased the Court party. Walpole could now rely even on Chesterfield's dependants. In 1729, there was a slight but significant change. A number of wealthy and influential merchants—Francis Child and Micajah Perry being the best known—allied themselves with the opposition. In 1730, the drift of merchants into the opposition corners strengthened, and they were joined by a number of country gentlemen, mainly knights of the shire, who had been bred to regard

independence as their birthright. They could, and did, refrain from voting if they thought the issue doubtful.[1] They
could, and did, support the ministry when they thought the
ministry deserved it. But some if not all, more often than not,
found themselves in the opposition lobby, and the ministry's
majority fell noticeably if never dangerously, in the session of
1730. Once or twice it fell below one hundred even on important issues. This had not happened for years and it put
new heart into the opposition. There is a life, a vigour, an
élan about their attacks which marks the birth of new hope.
Furthermore, half the life of this Parliament had already
elapsed. With an eye to the future, the opposition needed to
intensify their attacks. And so long as Townshend remained
in the ministry and remained at loggerheads with Walpole,
their hopes could fasten on the prospect of a ministerial
crisis. A rumpus at Court, the defeat of 'the Great Man', a
change of heart in George II and Caroline, a ministry
headed by Carteret, such delusive dreams warmed the
spirits of those condemned to sojourn in the wilderness. Yet
behind the leaders were men of resolute intention. Without
hope of office or interest in place, they pursued courses at
once altruistic and selfish. For them Walpole's policy had
failed. It had failed to bring Spain to heel; had given in too
easily to France; had rattled sabres meaninglessly and
burdened the country with expense. They regarded such
weakness with suspicion and subjected Walpole's acts and
speeches to a closer scrutiny.[2]

Walpole had sufficient indications of this new temper

[1] This is based on a comparison of two division lists; those who voted against
the addition of £115,000 to the Civil List in 1729 and those who voted against
the Hessian troops in 1730; both of these were unpopular back-bench measures.
These lists are not entirely reliable, but some of the changes which they indicate can be substantiated by the parliamentary diaries of Knatchbull and
Egmont. A precise and accurate picture of changes in the nature of the Parliamentary opposition to Walpole cannot be drawn until Mr Romney Sedgwick
has completed his section of the Parliamentary History.

[2] There are two excellent sources for the session of 1730; the diary kept by
the Earl of Egmont, printed HMC, *Egmont's Diary*, I, 2–96, and that of Sir
Edward Knatchbull, *Brabourne MSS, Knatchbull's Diary*, fos. 152–85. Hervey,
I, 111–20, deals briefly with this session.

before Parliament met. He drafted the King's speech with some care, and it reflected clearly enough his firm belief that the Treaty of Seville was a masterpiece of which he had every right to be proud. Besides the satisfaction in this accomplishment, there was the promise of further benefits. 'That my subjects', said the King, 'might reap the earliest fruits of this advantageous peace, I gave orders for the immediate reduction of a great number of my Land Forces, and for laying up and discharging a great part of my Fleet.' This economy was intended to reduce taxation. To make doubly sure that this desirable and longed-for benefit should be conferred on the nation, the House was recommended to consider the Sinking Fund. 'You are the best judges', George II told the Commons, 'whether the circumstances of the Sinking Fund, and of the National Debt, will as yet admit of giving ease where duties are most grievous.' Here was the nub of Walpole's policy: peace abroad, low taxes at home. For more than five years Walpole's intentions had been frustrated. Armies, navies, subsidies had kept taxation high; trade depression had intensified the burden of taxation. He had fought by argument, by intrigue, by an adroit choice of colleagues, to bring about a fundamental change in British policy. He had isolated Townshend and convinced the King. Peace achieved, he was in a hurry to enjoy its fruits. No sooner was the Treaty signed than he launched his campaign to reduce taxation and to reorganize entirely the system of its incidence and collection. Master as he was of the nature of the country's finances, he can have seen no danger to himself or his ministry in the plans which were taking shape in his mind. The dangers, as far as he was concerned, lay in diplomacy and these he was in a fair way of overcoming. Ironically enough, the greatest perils he was ever to face, until his final fall from power, were to spring from over-confidence in his supreme gifts as a financial administrator.

Yet for the time being the opposition were as preoccupied with foreign affairs as Walpole himself. Pulteney, of course, denounced the Treaty. He hinted at secret articles; expressed patriotic horror at Commissioners going to Madrid to discuss outstanding problems with the Spaniards; and then treated the back-benchers to a little homily on whig theory, showing how iniquitous it was to thrust Don Carlos on Parma and Piacenza without the inhabitants' consent. More cogently, he demanded to know what decisions, if any, had been taken about Gibraltar or Port Mahon. Until these questions were settled, any peace with Spain would be illusory. Old Horatio, brought back from Paris for the occasion, spent an hour going over the old ground, repeating the arguments which the government's Press had already made trite. Everyone was bored. The debate drifted on. Not one of the speakers, Egmont thought, was this day equal to himself, which he attributed to 'the evident reasonableness of supporting this address, the question whether two and two make four admitting neither art, nor wit, either to prove or to contend against'.[1] Along with 268 other members he trotted dutifully into the ministerial lobby; conscience and self-interest for once were happily united. But, surprisingly enough, for many members it was not quite so simple a piece of arithmetic and they found the merits of Seville no more beguiling than Horatio's prosy defence—129 members went into the opposition lobby, a small but marked increase on previous sessions.

It was sufficient to put heart into Pulteney. Walpole and his men of business were kept in the Commons day after day, hour after hour; debate after debate dragged on far into the night. And yet about the reports of these debates there is a curiously ramshackle air—almost as if Walpole were using time as an emollient, allowing those critical of his regime to talk the back-benchers into boredom or exhaustion. His interventions in debate were few, although he was most assiduous in attendance, when attendance often meant difficult and wearying hours of listening to complaints or to pleas for place, as Egmont's diary all too plainly shows.

[1] HMC, *Egmont's Diary*, I, 5.

Throughout these days Egmont, and his brother-in-law, Sir Philip Parker, were nagging Walpole about Harwich, demanding the dismissal of one Philipson, the Master of the Packets, and therefore an employee of the Post Office. Parker constantly referred to 'my borough', which, considering the Treasury, Admiralty and Post Office influence at Harwich, must have galled Walpole intensely. Sir Robert turned Horatio on to them, to little avail; they became more suspicious, offered a few threats of greater independence, asked more for their poor relations. They increased their nuisance value by pouring out their woes to Lord Grantham who cornered Sir Robert; from him he had to listen to another endless tale of the iniquities of Philipson, the sterling values of Egmont and Parker, and the desperate plight and deserving necessities of their brother-in-law, Dering. Ever suspicious, Egmont thought that Walpole was maintaining Philipson as a rod, to keep them devoted and loyal to the ministry, or putting off the day of his expulsion so that the blame could be pitched on Carteret when he returned from Ireland, for it was Carteret's brother, the Postmaster-General, who was primarily responsible for Philipson. Fearing the worst, Horatio became assiduous in his cultivation of Egmont, listening with sympathy to his inordinately long complaints and then gently discoursing to him on the virtues of ministerial policy. Sir Robert repeatedly promised that Philipson would be expelled. The Queen, no doubt primed by Sir Robert, listened graciously to pleas for brother Dering. The King paid Egmont marked attentions at the Drawing Room, so marked that Egmont's vanity got the better of his judgment. He confided to his diary 'that the Court are returned to those favourable thoughts it had of me a year ago, and I look upon this gracious regard of me now as proceeding from a desire in them that I should perceive their sensibility of having wronged me in their opinion'.[1] However, they needed to bare their teeth a little

[1] HMC, *Egmont's Diary*, I, 14–24, 33. Egmont's account of Harwich, Philipson, Sir Robert and a more important place for Dering is the best and most

before they secured Sir Robert's final promise to eject Philipson. On 25 February Dering, Parker and Egmont held a family conference at which it was decided that 'They were of opinion that as the Court had lately showed me particular civilities, I should do right to answer their expectations in the House as far [as] my judgment and conscience would suffer me, but that my brother Parker, not being in the way of meeting the same civilities, was not obliged to attend the House with equal assiduity'.[1] Egmont's judgment and conscience loomed very large in his own estimation and needed to be treated with a proper respect. The ministry, however, were as well aware of his self-righteousness as his cupidity, and Horatio had him high on his visiting list and brain-washed him thoroughly before any important debate.

Of course, all members who supported the ministry were not so difficult as Egmont to handle, but there was an important fringe of quasi-independent, self-seeking members whose reliability fluctuated so sharply that they demanded the most careful attention and added enormously to Walpole's labours in the House. There were few other labours he loved so well. Enemies as well as friends had to acknowledge his superb mastery in debate, his subtle sense of the moods of the House and his unrivalled knowledge, based on nearly twenty years' experience, of the procedure of the Commons. Indeed he loved it all so much that Bubb Dodington sneered that he dressed with more care and with more finery to go to the Commons than he did to go to his mistress.[2]

In this session he needed all of his skill. The back-benchers were restless; the opposition cock-a-hoop; Pulteney more acid than ever. And there were disturbing rumours that the opposition had a trump card up its sleeve, and for once Sir Robert's intelligence service was totally ignorant of

detailed revelation of the ambivalent attitude of the ministerially favoured and of the corroding nature of influence. Egmont prided himself on his independence of mind; yet he was totally preoccupied with what he could get or might fail to get out of politics, and his independence of mind was largely a forcing bid, even if an unconscious one.

[1] Ibid., 60.
[2] Ibid., 31–2.

what it was. An air of expectancy hung about the Commons as the opposition kept the ministry hard at it through the long debates on supplies. Shippen baited Sir Robert, saying that it was good to rub ministers up. They shone brighter for it. No minister, said Walpole, could shine brighter than he, subject as he was to constant libel and slander. At which Pulteney leaped up in his place and said only brass and pewter grew brighter through rubbing. The House laughed heartily at this quip, for everyone knew Walpole's nick-name of 'Brazen Face'. Feeling the House with him, he let himself go in a bold, almost 'brazen-faced' speech of self-justification, but skilfully clothed with an expansive warmth. Of course, he told them, he had got a great estate, a very great estate, and having held some of the most lucrative offices for nearly twenty years what could anyone expect, unless it was a crime to get estates by great offices; if so—and here he turned the tables on Pulteney, much to the House's amusement—if so, how much greater a crime it must be to get an estate out of lesser offices. Everyone knew he referred to Henry Guy, William III's Secretary of the Treasury, who had left his fortune to Pulteney. Walpole's speech was forthright, good-humoured and adroit, for it neatly turned the tables on his adversary. Susceptible to irony, the House, when it came to divide, gave the ministry a large majority, and the opposition lost rather than gained a few votes by their display of bad temper.[1] Indeed Walpole often exploited their sharp tongues to their own disadvantage. In this session Shippen, drunk as usual, let himself go on the Army estimates and said that the large standing army showed that the constitution was to be germanized, that force and violence were the resort of usurpers and tyrants. Then, seeing that he had gone too far, he tried to cover up with a compliment to the King, explaining that he did not refer to George II, who enjoyed so much of his subjects' affection. This did no good: the House was profoundly shocked; a fact which Walpole quickly

[1] HMC, *Egmont's Diary*, I, 9: *Carlisle MSS*, 65: but the fullest and best account is *Brabourne MSS, Knatchbull's Diary*, fos. 156–8.

sensed. Instead, however, of calling Shippen to book, as Sir William Yonge suggested, Walpole mentioned that the proper course, and one which showed a proper respect for the King, was to close the debate at once and vote the King his army. Aware that the alternative was the Tower for Shippen, the opposition knuckled under and concurred, for there was no going against the loyal sentiment Walpole had so neatly aroused. It is on occasions such as these that Walpole's dexterity in handling the House is demonstrated so clearly.

Rumours that the opposition were planning a major debate led many to expect that the greatest battle of oratory would take place on the question of the subsidy of the Hessian troops which the ministry had hired from the Duke of Hesse during the alarms of the previous year. The understanding was that they should be employed for four years, but Walpole realized that these mercenaries were far from popular. They could so easily be condemned as a burden inflicted on a declining country, not for its own protection, but for Hanover's. But when the debate came, although Walpole was subjected to biting criticism, neither Pulteney nor Wyndham nor Shippen spoke. They left the field to Gilbert Heathcote, who made a few tart references to the parliamentary limitations of British Kings, particularly in regard to standing armies, and to Thomas Wyndham, who fulminated against the Hessians. Both of these interventions were mortifying for Walpole as, according to Egmont, Heathcote had received ministerial support at his election, and worse still, Wyndham had been given two places. Naturally he did not keep them.[1] On such a topic it did not require the opposition leaders to rouse the back-benchers; they cherished deep suspicions of Hanover and detested mercenaries. Walpole's majority fell to seventy-nine, the lowest in a major debate for ten years—an ill omen. And naturally this result deepened Walpole's apprehension. He knew that the major attack was still to come—Pulteney's

[1] HMC, *Egmont's Diary*, I, 27–9.

and Sir William Wyndham's silence made that clear. Their oratory might influence even more waverers, and the prospect of a seriously embarrassed ministry emerged for the first time for many a long year. He did not, however, know whence the attack would come or what its subject would be.

Wyndham rose and asked the Speaker to set aside a day to debate the state of the nation, a request which, by custom, could not be refused. Both Horatio and Sir Robert learned that tory leaders, extremists like Shippen and Sir Watkin Williams Wynn as well as moderates like Sir Thomas Hanmer, were holding secret meetings. Pulteney, Wyndham and Bolingbroke were equally active. Naturally the Walpoles lost no time in putting all possible pressure on their friends and supporters to be present on 10 February, and when the House met it was crammed with members, and throughout the day and far into the night the tiny gallery in the lantern was packed with spectators. Everyone knew this to be a great occasion, the first serious trial of strength that Walpole had had to meet during his ministry. But only the opposition knew what the trial was to be about. Their discipline had been admirable; not a word had leaked out. Nevertheless Walpole had taken counsel with Onslow and when the House met the Speaker rose and declared that 'before the House resolved itself into a Committee, gentlemen should call for the papers they judged necessary for a foundation of their proceedings, that they might be referred to the Committee, for that whatever was not so referred could not be made use of'.[1] The intention was to force the opposition to disclose its hand and give the ministry a precious breathing space to prepare its case. Naturally the opposition resented this procedural trick, and said so at length. Both Pulteneys spoke, so did Wyndham, and they were fortified by the intervention of Sir Joseph Jekyll, the eccentric and learned Master of the Rolls. Pelham and Walpole replied. Sir Robert appealed to the good sense of the House; he hoped that 'it was not the intent to ask for papers, or recur to the journals that relate to

[1] HMC, *Egmont's Diary*, I, 34.

past transactions already determined; that on the conclusion of a session the matters which passed that session are over, and not to be overhauled, so as to render the papers and journals concerning them a foundation of new enquiry and resolutions; if that were so, nothing could receive a final determination, but the most important things, and which have long ago been decided, would be rendered uncertain, and set into a fluctuating condition'. Here spoke the administrator. To Walpole's admirably practical mind, decisions once taken must be kept; enquiry, flux, uncertainty, these were the bug-bears of good government. But he forgot his own past, which Pulteney did not. Were not the ministry of Queen Anne's reign, he asked Walpole, impeached by a subsequent Parliament although the former Parliament had approved their actions? Perhaps, he sneered sarcastically, some were afraid of impeachment; their minds could be at rest, he had no such thoughts. A sentiment which did not entirely appeal to crotchety Colonel Oglethorpe who, insisting on the absolute sovereignty of the Commons to do whatever they wanted, and to call for whatever they needed, thought that this debate might end in an impeachment. The Speaker, who prided himself on fairness of mind, generously admitted his mistake; the Commons should have what they wanted even if called for in Committee. For once Walpole lost on a point of procedure.

Pulteney in his speech of protest had demanded papers on the Treaty of Seville and the Dutch accession to it; if the ministry took his hint, they realized within an hour or two that they had chased a red herring. As soon as the House had resolved itself into a committee and put Edgcumbe into the chair, an action in itself very welcome to the ministry, Sir William Wyndham rose in his place to open the debate. He held the House in suspense as he listed the grave state of the nation's affairs at home and abroad. He stressed the decay of trade, the falling-off of woollen manufactures, the adverse balance with other countries, the low state of the coinage, the mismanagement of the revenue—too long, he maintained, in the hands of one man—and the wretched administration of justice. In foreign affairs, the position was no better. And he gradually worked up the House as he related the indignities which Britain suffered through the weakness of her ministry. Merchants were neglected; the colonies knew no security. And worse. The honour of the Crown was insulted by the French, who never acknowledged our flag even in our own ports. Indeed, a lieutenant who fired at them to compel them to do it was immediately turned out of his employment. The French were encircling the plantations and stealing away the Spanish trade. Yet there was a matter more grievous still, one that would fire the breast of every Englishman. The harbour of Dunkirk had been restored, and he had masters of ships at the door of the House, ready to be examined, to give proofs of it.[1] So the bomb exploded. Horatio sprang to his feet at once, seeing himself as the target for the opposition's animosity, for any deceitful actions by the French could be laid at his door; ambassadors were not sent abroad to be hoodwinked. Naturally he opposed sending for the ships' captains. Representations had been made many times to the French by himself; if the House must hear the captains then it should wait until the ministry's papers on this matter were available. Pulteney demurred. What was the point, he asked, of sending for Armstrong, the British representative at Dunkirk; he was paid by the Crown and he would say what 'the Ministry should dictate'. Naturally Sir William Wyndham also insisted on an immediate hearing. Horatio received support from another government front-bench speaker, but the indignation of the House mounted so quickly at this attempted delay that Sir Robert intervened, realizing that a tactical blunder had been made.[2]

[1] HMC, *Egmont's Diary*, I, 35–6. *Brabourne MSS, Knatchbull's Diary*, fos. 168–70. Knatchbull's account is brief, differs little in substance from Egmont's which is much fuller and individual members' speeches are more clearly differentiated in it. I have followed Egmont.

[2] There is confusion in Egmont at this point. He makes Sir William Wyndham support both sides of the question. The account makes sense if the 'Sir

He calmed the House. He spoke with his usual clarity
and good sense. The captains should be heard at once. The
House must receive the fullest light on this affair—but, of
course, from both sides; and so it would be quite improper
to pass any resolution until Colonel Armstrong had been
heard and the record of the ministry's effort on this subject laid before the House. And he deeply regretted that
Colonel Armstrong should have departed for Dunkirk the
very day that Sir William Wyndham received his information. (He wisely refrained from pointing the moral of
this which would have been clear to the meanest intelligence
on the back bench.) Now he must send for Colonel Armstrong to come back. It was a pity that he and the captains
could not be heard together, but there it was. In this briefly
reported speech, Walpole's dexterity in the Commons is
abundantly clear. It illustrates his quick sense of the mood of
the members and displays the skill with which he could make
a fighting withdrawal that appealed to common sense,
decency and fair play. To relish fully the adroitness of his
manoeuvre it is necessary to remember that the members
that crowded the benches on that dark February afternoon
were not his sworn, avowed enemies, pledged to oppose him
at every turn; many prided themselves on the independence
of their attitude and the fairness of their judgment. They
could be wooed and won, and of this art Walpole was a
master. The captains were called in and examined at length,
and it was six o'clock before they had finished giving their
evidence. That done, another procedural wrangle followed.
Should the House debate the evidence? Or defer to another
day? Pulteney, Sandys, Vernon and peppery Oglethorpe
were all for proceeding; Wyndham was for another day, so
long as no new matter was entered upon by the House until
Dunkirk had been fully debated. Sir Robert, glad of a rift in
the opposition's ranks, and sensible of the value of time,
pushed the House a little further along the road that he

William' on p. 36, line 34 is taken to be a slip for the name of a Government
supporter (? Sir William Strickland).

wanted it to go. He stressed the gravity of the accusation, but recalled that Sir William Wyndham had made others equally serious. He wanted them all to be sifted; he wanted everything plainly enquired into. But too much time would be lost if Dunkirk had to be dealt with first. He proposed that every other day should be set aside for these enquiries, beginning on the following Thursday. Though the House was reluctant to do so, Walpole got his way in the end.

His ministry was in trouble. Walpole had been deeply perturbed by the strength of the feeling against the ministry. His friends and agents reported on the unreliability of many independents and even of those who had obligations to the ministry. He and Townshend were scarcely on speaking terms, and Townshend might exploit this embarrassment to Walpole's disadvantage.[1] Nor could Walpole have been encouraged by the friendly social relations of Wyndham and Wilmington (Spencer Compton). There were others, too, in his ministry who would regard his fall with equanimity. As always in his political strategy he relied on time—time which could cool tempers, engender boredom, and permit the art of management to flower in all its complexity. Egmont's diary provides fascinating glimpses of Sir Robert at work both in the House and outside it. Egmont was a critical figure. He nursed resentments; Philipson was still *in* at Harwich, his long-promised dismissal still delayed; brother Dering still lacked the employment that Egmont felt he deserved. And Egmont carried weight with the Irish peers in the House and with other members who had large Irish interests. He was neither solitary nor negligible. And at the same time, he possessed ferocious pride, allied to a monumental self-righteousness, qualities which were very much in evidence when Walpole's first agent, Duncombe, called on him shortly after the first Dunkirk debate.[2]

[1] This quarrel was common knowledge, see HMC, *Egmont's Diary*, I, 50.

[2] The caller, Anthony Duncombe, MP for Salisbury, was a firm supporter of the Ministry. Although no placeman, he had received support from the ministry in his election at Salisbury in 1727, *C(H) MSS*, Correspondence 3238/9, n.d. His sense of obligation was greater than Egmont's and he remained a very loyal friend of Walpole's.

Duncombe, who had been primed by Horatio, went over the ground very carefully with Egmont. Egmont, however, was convinced that there would be a majority of honest men and lovers of their country against the government. And even if 'the Ministry should by the weight of places, pensions and promises carry a division', it would be the end of them next session. He protested his attachment to the ministry; he thought them capable and honest. 'But though I had all the attachments in the world for the Court, and all regard possible for the ministry, yet I had a greater person than King or ministry to serve and that was God.'[1] Nothing daunted, Duncombe went on arguing and probing, chewing over all the popular back-bench grouses—standing armies, George II's avarice, heavy taxes, the extra votes of credit, selling of commissions, the King's indifference to the gentry and his neglect of ancient families. But Egmont was too wary; he entered only very guardedly into the discussion, for he knew where Duncombe's loyalty lay and guessed that he was bent on observing what discontents Egmont would support. Yet Duncombe's visit did not prove useless, for Egmont was persuaded to agree that Sir Robert should be allowed to put off the debate until he was ready for it. That at least squared with Egmont's conscience. And it suited Walpole admirably. Time was what he was after.

His other men of business had been equally assiduous, and the opposition less skilful. When the debate was resumed two of its supporters—Dundas and Plumer—were quite prepared to give Walpole all the time in the world because they thought he could never find excuses for France's behaviour—a fatuous intervention that Pulteney, though his allies were not at their best, did his utmost to counter. Sandys, supporting him, boasted of the effective action the tories had taken in Queen Anne's reign by insisting that Louis XIV should be pressed to make a more effective demolition at Dunkirk. Indeed such was his sense of self-righteous glory that he proposed that the Clerk should read the Journal. His confidence

[1] HMC, *Egmont's Diary*, I, 38.

turned to anxiety when Sir William Yonge, one of Walpole's leading supporters, quickly seconded the motion; the anxiety changed to shame and confusion as the Clerk read the Journal. The whigs, not the tories, had pressed the Queen. Sir Robert, in his corner, roared with laughter. Much piqued, Charles Cesar, a rabid old Jacobite, started a heated defence of the Queen's last ministry. The speaker ruled him out of order. This put Shippen in a passion, never a difficult thing to do; the Speaker roared back at Shippen, who tried to continue, but the House shouted him down. His place was taken by Captain Vernon, wild, eccentric, bad-tempered, who launched into a passionate harangue and 'brought in the Pope, the Devil, the Jesuits, the seamen, etc'. The House would not give him a hearing. He shouted himself hoarse, but to no avail. Nothing could have suited Sir Robert better, and he was able to bring this pitiful display to a satisfactory end by getting the debate adjourned for a fortnight.

The fortnight was well spent if Egmont's diary is any indication of ministerial activity. Lord Grantham had a long talk with Egmont on the iniquities of Philipson at Harwich, blaming Lord Townshend for Sir Robert's delay in doing anything about it. And Philipson was put out at last, but only after the Prince as well as the King had spoken to Egmont of Harwich and their desire to help. The ministry took the sensible precaution of not dispatching Philipson's successor until the great Dunkirk debate was over. Royal condescension, however, was not the only attention which Egmont received in those strenuous days. William Sloper, Deputy-Cofferer of the Household, called on him, discussed Ireland, listened sympathetically to all Egmont's pet theories and hinted that the ministry was likely to receive them kindly. This was followed by an invitation to dinner from Sir Robert himself; no doubt one of many such dinner parties during these Dunkirk days. It was a snug party—Walpole's son-in-law, Malpas, Lord Palmerston, an Irish peer who sat in the Commons, Sir John Shelley, Mr Butler and Sir Edward Knatchbull; and once the ladies had retired Walpole, ably supported by Malpas, Palmerston and Knatchbull, set about Egmont's views on Dunkirk. Shelley and Butler listened. These attentions bore good fruit for, by the time the great debate took place, Egmont was safely back in the ministerial fold, his conscience either appeased or squared. And not only safely back but ardent; the Prince himself acknowledged how valuable his work had been in winning over independents; and when Egmont was confined with a cold on the Queen's birthday and Sir Robert sent to enquire of his health, he reflected on the recent past. 'How busy', he wrote in his diary, 'is mankind about vain and transitory things, while we all forget, at least, neglect the one thing useful.' He soon recovered from both his introspection and his cold, and took himself as quickly as possible to Arlington Street for a long if inconclusive talk with Sir Robert about a place for Brother Dering. Even if he had a thousand places, Walpole complained, he still would not have enough. Dunkirk had stretched his promises to the limit.

Yet Sir Robert's methods worked; the individual lobbying combined with astute handling of the Commons saw him through. Time and time again he outwitted them. One day he and Horatio were seen in their corner wreathed in smiles, spreading the good news far and wide, heartening their friends, dismaying their enemies. They had a letter from Fleury in their hands. He had consented to order the Dunkirkers to destroy whatever had been clandestinely repaired. Then Walpole deluged the Commons with Dunkirk papers, masses of them that a bevy of clerks had worked throughout the night to copy. Pulteney made a false move and demanded the originals, pleading the precedent of Atterbury's trial. Walpole immediately put him on the wrong foot. Could Pulteney possibly conceive that Walpole would deceive the House? He regarded his honour as insulted. He did not speak angrily, only with deep feeling. Indignation was left to Edward Gibbon's grandfather, who told the House he would not have treated his meanest servant as Pulteney had treated Sir Robert. The originals were kept locked up, and Pulteney received a rebuff for his pains. Most of these skirmishes Walpole won hands down. He made only one false move. He tried to throw out the perennial Place Bill, but he failed by ten votes. Sir Edward Knatchbull thought that it was folly to oppose such a popular measure in the midst of the Dunkirk difficulties. Place bills were dear to independents, and the independents were in a difficult mood. The bishops could always be relied upon to throw out any Place Bill in the House of Lords. Knatchbull marked his disapproval of this policy by slipping out of the House before a division was taken. Many followed his example, and the Court could muster only 134 votes. But this was Walpole's sole error of tactics. The opposition were battering him on a number of other issues—gaols, the renewal of the East India Company charter, the Africa Company, the complaints of London shopkeepers, the peculiarly difficult by-election petition from Liverpool—and he was forced to spend long, long days in the Commons. He was always there in his corner, resplendent in his Garter, cheerful, good-humoured, watchful, strong, as subtle in his tactics as the serpent.

He was never better than in the great debate itself, which took place on 27 February. The House met at noon. After prayers, Wyndham proposed a motion, but before it could be seconded, Dr Sayer sprang to his feet and proposed another, of course Walpole's, and the moment he sat down up popped Bromley and seconded it. The Speaker had kept a blind eye on Sandys, who was frantically trying to second Wyndham's. The opposition had no alternative but to debate Walpole's motion; theirs could not be placed before the House until this had been disposed of. No one knew better than Walpole both how to exploit parliamentary procedure and the friendliness of the Speaker. His motion, of course, was a mild one, to address the King in terms that were unlikely to disturb Fleury's calm indifference. But the House was packed with back-benchers, and Walpole had to earn his majority. There could be no certainty until the members filed through the lobby. He spoke supremely well. He was simple; he was homely; and he did not bother much about details of fortifications or protests to Versailles. He went to the heart of the matter. This was simply an agitation of an evil man— everyone knew he meant Bolingbroke—and he told a little parable that the most dull-witted, port-fuddled squire could follow.

'A farmer going home from markett saw, as he thought, a dead body in the road and observing some life in it, took it home in hopes to bring it to life and by his care and humanity did and kept him in his house but as soon as he was well instead of returning the person thanks he was of such a turbulent spirit that there was no peace in the family ever after till the farmer hanged him up and then all was quiett again . . .'[1]

Foolishly Wyndham sprang to the defence of Bolingbroke, a man in no way loved by the solid gentlemen on the back benches, who sat patient and dumb in the flickering candle-light as the debate stretched on through the night. Sentiment here was with Walpole. The independent supporters of the ministry boggled slightly at one phrase in the motion. Walpole took it out at once. No man knew better how to compromise in inessentials.

The debate dragged on until three in the morning—and Walpole, when the vote came, got his majority—270 against 149. The crisis was over—but only for the time being.

This had been the most difficult session Walpole had faced since the South Sea Bubble. The opposition had grown by at least fifty on important and vital issues. And the source of the trouble was, as Horatio declared to Lord Waldegrave, the City.[2] That, of course, had been the point of the Dunkirk debate, as Bolingbroke made clear, as soon as Parliament rose, in his pamphlet: *The Case of Dunkirk Considered*. There the old theme was reiterated. Subservience to France meant the loss of trade; Seville would be the ruin of the British merchant. Every opportunity that the ministry's business

[1] *Brabourne MSS, Knatchbull's Diary*, fo. 179.
[2] Coxe, II, 669.

217

gave them was exploited by the opposition to win new ad-
herents in the City. And they aimed not at great merchants
or rich bankers but at the middling men. They opposed
strongly the government's motion to prevent money being
lent to the Emperor on the London market—a wise precaution, as war with the Emperor could not be ruled out of
account. They attacked the East India Company's charter;
they sneered at the Sinking Fund and attacked Walpole's
fundamental views on taxation.[1] All was done with an eye to
the City. So, too, were the increasing laments in the opposition Press of the decay of trade and the lamentable state
of British manufactures. And there was substance in this
growing tide of opposition. The economic life of the nation
was temporarily depressed; recent harvests were below
average, with the usual repercussions of high prices, unpaid
rents and moribund markets.

To this Walpole had one simple answer: to secure peace
and reduce taxation. Whatever the opposition might say,
Seville had reduced the tension with Spain. The Emperor
must be won over as quickly as possible. That done, peace
would be secure, the land-tax reduced and financial reforms, long contemplated, put into operation. So the dark
clouds would be dispelled, the rancorous clamour quietened,
and Walpole and his friends would be as secure as they had
ever been. At fifty-four Walpole felt that he had many years
service ahead. He loved power. He thought he knew how to
use it. He had little or no regard for the opposition. His
mastery of the Commons, the strong personal regard of the
King and Queen, and the ease of his private circumstances
are reflected in the serenity, almost the amusement, with
which he faced the Dunkirk crisis. The libels irritated him,
but the opposition did not breed in him the same anxieties

[1] In order to ease the burden of taxation Walpole proposed to relieve the
country of a tax appropriated to the Sinking Fund as this fund had a surplus.
He wanted the removal of the tax on candles, but did not press his preference
strongly and agreed finally to the removal of the tax on salt although it created
patronage difficulties for him (his son-in-law, Malpas, and others among his
friends and supporters were involved in salt production). The opposition
preferred salt as it eased the poor.

as the difficulties at Court, which were now in a fair way to being resolved. Townshend was to go at last and Walpole could reshuffle the ministry a little nearer to his heart's content. After a dark winter, the summer promised fair. By the time that he faced the Commons again he hoped to be able to offer them peace, low taxes and a united ministry. In the summer of 1730 he could never have expected that he was to be confronted with years of increasing crisis. And his self-deception was made worse by the ease and success of his first attempts to guide the country's foreign policy.

2

THE PROBLEM was complex. Could a quick settlement be achieved with the Emperor Charles VI? Peace with Spain had been accomplished; a firm alliance with the Emperor would mean a permanent settlement of England's difficulties. Townshend, ever rash in his undertakings, had favoured strong measures. Time was short. In December 1729, at the signing of the Treaty of Seville, the Emperor had been given four months to accept Spanish troops in Parma and Piacenza; the alternative would be war. The Emperor firmly maintained that this was an infraction of the Quadruple Alliance, and concentrated troops in Tuscany. War rather than a settlement seemed likely. To this neither Fleury nor Chauvelin objected; after all, the defeat and humiliation of Austria had been the secret end of French policy since Utrecht. Townshend, also, viewed war with equanimity; indeed, his fervid imagination and need to win George II's admiration had led him to contemplate seizing the Austrian Netherlands in the event of war, and not only seizing them but insisting on the British retaining them at the peace. Their possession would reduce Dunkirk to insignificance and abolish automatically the Ostend East India Company. With these large ambitions baffling his judgment, he pressed for a strong alliance with the Wittelsbachs' Electoral Union with its consequent threat to the Emperor in Germany. Both

Walpoles opposed this. They did not wish to adopt Townshend's policy for both personal and public reasons. The opposition had raised the clamour that Seville meant a threat of war to the Emperor, England's traditional ally; it would be nonsense politically to add further justification to their criticism.[1] And, of course, at this time both Walpoles saw immediately the weakness rather than the strength of anything that Townshend suggested. Their powerful criticisms of this dramatic policy of Townshend's, so much at variance with the traditional pattern of England's European alliances, were represented by him to George II as a want of zeal for the King's Hanoverian interests.[2]

But all these difficulties were resolved by Townshend's resignation, which marks a vital stage in the evolution of Sir Robert Walpole's own foreign policy as well as of his political position as Prime Minister. It enabled him to recast his ministry with the intention of completely reshaping British foreign policy. Few historians have realized the exceptionally critical nature of the moves which he made during the summer of 1730. They mark as critical a moment in his career as 1717 or 1720, and again, as in those earlier crises, the decisions were entirely his. Not only the quarrel with Townshend, but also the dangerous successes of the opposition led him in the previous session to take his decision to change British foreign policy fundamentally, and to bring to an end the policy which Townshend had inaugurated at Hanover in 1725.

His first aim, naturally, was to secure a complaisant Secretary of State. He had long marked out William Stanhope, whose success in negotiating the Treaty of Seville had earned him the Earldom of Harrington. 'He was absolutely nothing,' Hervey wrote of him, 'nobody's friend, nobody's foe, of use to nobody, and of prejudice to nobody.'[3] The Queen said that he needed six hours to dress, six hours

[1] Coxe, II, 659–60, 663–4.
[2] Coxe, II, 678, 'Hanover is Lord Townshend's great merit, and we have all been represented as wanting *zeal*.' Newcastle to Harrington, 23 April, 1730.
[3] Hervey, I, 174.

to eat, six hours with his mistress and six for sleep.[1] Such indolence did not trouble Walpole; complaisance was what he was after. True, the name Stanhope had been highly suspicious to him in the first place, and his brother, Charles, was far from being on the best of terms with Walpole, but Newcastle had sung his praises for so long and Walpole himself had been impressed by Stanhope's readiness to comply. Certainly the appointment made Newcastle dithyrambic with joy; as he wrote the glad tidings to Harrington, his pen flashed across the paper in an illegible, hysterical scrawl. 'God bless Sir Robert— 'tis all his doing: and let us in return, resolve to make him happy as we can.'[2] They were soon to have a chance to put their gratitude to a test.

In addition to complaisant Secretaries of State, Sir Robert needed devoted ambassadors. Horatio had grown tired of Paris; he was on bad terms with Chauvelin and was shrewd enough to know that it would always be so. Furthermore, his brother's plans required a change at the French Court, and as Horatio could serve him better in the Commons he was appointed Cofferer of the Household. His place was taken by Waldegrave, whose mother was a bastard of James II by Arabella Churchill. He had been educated in France as a Jacobite, then had changed his Court, and become a career diplomat. He was a man whose experience of life had taught him the art of simulation. To Walpole, however, he was absolutely loyal; with his shaky past he could not afford to be otherwise. His removal from Vienna enabled Walpole to replace him by Sir Thomas Robinson, a monumental humbug of a verbosity equalled in the eighteenth century, perhaps, only by Archbishop Wake. Like most humbugs he worshipped the protocol and adored authority. If Walpole had kicked him, he would have whinnied with joy. To do his master's bidding was one of the few pleasures of his arid existence. Walpole knew that he would be both meticulous and obedient.

[1] P. Vaucher, *Robert Walpole et la Politique de Fleury* (Paris, 1924), 34–5, n. 2.

[2] Coxe, II, 689–90; also *ibid.*, 696, 'Sir Robert is pure gay and does like an angel; Mr Cofferer (i.e. Horatio) the same.' 25 May 1730.

These changes greatly strengthened Walpole in the pursuit of his foreign policy. Yet a man of his political sagacity was not merely concerned with the placing of his friends; enemies, known or potential, needed to be handled with equal skill before he attempted one of the most dangerous and critical moves of his life. He disgraced Carteret. When not in Ireland, Carteret's position as Lord Lieutenant brought him too closely into the counsels of the King for Walpole to relish his presence at Court. For six years he had behaved with circumspection, expecting the reward of a Secretary- ship to come to him in the fulness of time. His disappointment at Harrington's elevation could only breed envy; envious men were, as far as Walpole was concerned, best in oppo- sition. So Carteret went. Others of Carteret's clique had to be prevented from following him either out of fear or friendship. So Wilmington, ever on the verge of disloyalty, was kept in favour. Walpole tossed him an earldom and promoted him to Lord Privy Seal;[1] Chesterfield, equally dangerous and far less guarded in his enmity, was kept at The Hague. Walpole tried to soften him by making him Lord Steward.[2] Walpole certainly disliked Chesterfield; he found his malice, his vanity, his total incapacity to hold his tongue or restrain his sarcasm, unbecoming qualities in a statesman. Nor could any man accuse him of loyalty. Yet despite Chesterfield's politically dangerous nature, Walpole had to tolerate him. He could not afford an abundance of enemies, nor jettison all the King's friends at once.

At the same time, Walpole strengthened his team in the Commons. Horatio, freed from his ambassadorial duties, could be relied upon to discharge with efficiency the minutiae of time-wasting consultations that pressed so fiercely on all eighteenth-century politicians who were men

[1] On Trevor's death, shortly afterwards, Walpole kicked him further up- stairs and made him Lord President of the Council.

[2] Carteret had been offered this post. For Carteret it was demotion—more or less a gratuitous insult by Walpole. It did not carry with it, as the Lord Lieutenancy of Ireland did, an automatic seat in the cabinet. Coxe, I, 338 is wrong in assuming that Chesterfield went into opposition to Walpole in 1730. He did not do so until 1733, see p. 272.

of business. No one, except Sir Robert, could match Horatio's stamina in arguing with waverers or spinning a web of hope about the place-hungry. Henry Pelham, long singled out by Sir Robert as an administrator and politician after his own heart was promoted to be Paymaster-General of the Forces, which gave him a firm and dependable ally in Treasury business and one who could handle figures as skilfully as himself. Sir William Strickland, a tough and persuasive orator, took his place as Secretary at War; he had been a firm whig and a loyal friend since the far off Junto days. His promotion also strengthened Walpole. These changes were completed by the middle of June. About a month later, Walpole set out as was his custom for Norfolk—to view his estates, check his rents, glory in Houghton's growing magnificence, and plot with his cronies in the high-panelled library. There, too, he could rest his vast bulk on the elegant *chaise-longue* designed for him by Kent; lying there, staring at the broad acres of his park, he had time enough to contemplate the dangers that lay ahead and to take his measures.

He decided to placate the Emperor; to prevaricate as long as possible on any decision to use force to compel him to accept Spanish troops in Parma or Piacenza; to offer him the bait of guaranteeing the Pragmatic Sanction; and to secure in return the suppression of the Ostend Company. Straightforward as these measures may seem, they were both revolutionary and complex. Under the terms of Seville, France and Britain were to declare war on the Emperor if after six months he had not received Spanish troops into the duchies. That date had passed. France proposed attacking the Austrian Netherlands, a project which struck both the English and the Dutch as highly undesirable, and they urged Sicily as an alternative. In this conflict of views between the allies the leisurely pace of eighteenth-century diplomacy aided Walpole's scheme, albeit fortuitously; months might melt into years before any concerted plan of attack could be drawn up. One obvious danger lay in Spain's impatience; Elizabeth Farnese might be rash enough to tear up the Treaty of Seville and attempt direct negotiation with the Emperor. Yet the greatest obstacle to the success of Walpole's policy could easily be George II himself. As Elector of Hanover, he had his own quarrels with the Emperor. For years Charles VI had delayed formal recognition of his right, as Elector of Hanover, to the Duchies of Julich and Cleves. This enormity loomed far larger in the eyes of his German advisers than the activities of the Ostend Company and it was more than likely that the King would insist on a settlement of the Duchies question as a prerequisite of any new peace treaty with the Emperor. The suppression of the Ostend Company was no *quid pro quo* in Hanoverian eyes. They were not interested in placating the growing hostility of a merchant class to Walpole's management of Parliament. Walpole had, therefore, two delicate and difficult tasks, firstly to secure the King's acceptance of his policy irrespective of his Hanoverian interests, and secondly to negotiate with the Emperor without France's knowledge.

This crystallization of Walpole's policy did not take place in a day. The difficulties which Walpole had faced in the Commons during the session of 1730 and the slyness of French diplomacy had, in a sense, been responsible for the evolution of Walpole's policy. Although it is not possible to state precisely when Walpole fully clarified his ideas, his correspondence with Horatio in August 1730 enables us to gain a rare glimpse of his detailed thoughts about foreign affairs. Quite clearly he had been deeply disturbed by the Dunkirk disclosures of the previous Parliamentary session and he repeatedly pressed Horatio to obtain a categorical promise from the Cardinal to destroy its sluices and jetties. In a memorandum which he sent to Horatio in August 1730, he wrote:

'If, therefore, this summer is to be spent in negotiations and inactions, and we must purchase the demolition of Dunkirk at that price, one may attone for the other; and, after the clamour and expectation that is raised upon that subject, the effectual demolition of Dunkirk may contribute as much to the making things easy, as the contrary will certainly make them impracticable—I mean it is impossible to stand both; but one may make the other go down. And if France will do what is right upon that point, other matters, though troublesome and disagreeable, may be got through.'[1]

Indeed, it is quite clear from this correspondence that Walpole did not wish to face the next session of Parliament without being able to tell the Commons that he had received satisfaction about Dunkirk or that the Treaty of Seville had been put into operation. The constant prevarications of Chauvelin and the Cardinal rendered the latter unlikely; by the height of summer discussions as to where the campaign should be fought were still meandering on; indeed, by the end of August, Walpole had reconciled himself to the prospect of inaction until the summer of 1731. That being so, demolition at Dunkirk was imperative.[2] By early September, Fleury was almost convinced that something would have to be done there, but to those who had had long experience of the Cardinal, eternity could easily be contained in *almost*. Walpole was impatient for results. He saw matters with clarity. He knew, as he always did, what should be done. By the time he returned to London and saw the King at Windsor, he had made up his mind. Fleury and Chauvelin were, he decided, using Britain for their own ends: a direct approach to the Emperor must be undertaken in order to have results to show the Commons. And so the needs of

[1] Coxe, III, 24, from the *Walpole MSS*. The paper is without date or signature, but it is in RW's handwriting: presumably he drafted it to get his own thoughts clear and then sent it to his brother. Their correspondence, printed by Coxe, III, 1–31, is an invaluable guide to RW's thoughts during these months. It has been checked with the originals at Wolterton.

[2] RW's views may be inferred from HW'S letter to him on 10 September 1730 (N.S.), *C(H) MSS*, printed Coxe, III, 29; 'You cannot be more sensible than I am of the great importance that the demolition of the works of Dunkirk is, and in particular with respect to yourselfe and me; and how necessary it is that it at least appear in parliament that there has been no neglect, coolness, or indifference in the King, or any of his ministers, in demanding, and in endeavouring to procure satisfaction.'

Walpole in parliamentary affairs had come to dominate his diplomatic conceptions.[1] The furious opposition had wrought better than they knew.

When Horatio learnt on 1 September of his brother's decision, which now had the support of the King and the Secretaries, to negotiate directly with the Emperor, he was, naturally enough, horrified. For years he had laboured for Anglo-French understanding, and he could scarcely bear to see his work placed in jeopardy. He possessed an immense respect for his brother's judgment even in fields where he knew his intimate knowledge to be small. But even he was shocked by the knowledge that a separate negotiation was on foot with Vienna. He felt that such an action must ruin the diplomatic position of Britain in Europe and he begged to be allowed to return home.[2] His wish was granted and by the middle of September he set out from Paris for the last time, too late, however, to influence his brother. All he had worked for had been destroyed almost without consultation, and it says much for the largeness of his spirit that his complaints were muted and that within a few weeks of his arrival he was, once more, working for his brother, with undiminished energy and enthusiasm. There are few periods in the life of Horatio Walpole that bring into such shining relief his loyal and generous spirit.

His brother had acted in diplomacy with that same absence of hesitation with which he acted in politics or

[1] Nor was this the only success of the opposition. Horatio Walpole thought that Chauvelin's reluctance to take action was due to the fact that the French ministry wished to wait for the next parliamentary session to see if the new ministry was really secure; Coxe, III, 6. No foreign powers estimated properly Walpole's strength either in the Commons or at Court; ministerial revolutions were often confidently predicted. Because Walpole survived for so long, there is a natural tendency in historians, perhaps, to overestimate his security as in contemporaries to underestimate it.

[2] Coxe, III, 30-1. ' . . . give me leave to tell you, that I am very apprehensive that you are going on too fast upon a fixed principle as if all was *over with France*, and, upon that notion, without having any certain scheme of friendship or security with any other considerable power. Your measures, as far as I can guess, are vague and inconclusive and will, if care is not taken, bring us to a quarrell with France, while at the same time we are destitute of any reall friend.'

administration. Sir Robert loved decision, hated prevarication, and loathed an atmosphere of hesitation and prevarication. He wanted above all to win back his huge majorities in the Commons. That was the personal aim of his diplomacy, but not the *raison d'être* of his policy. Walpole believed in what he did. His solution, convenient as it was for himself, would, he thought, solve England's and Europe's problems. His brother's disappointment he could understand but not relieve. Quick though he was to make up his mind, Walpole was no fool. He knew the risks that he was running. Disclosure of his negotiations before they had matured could have ugly consequences. France could easily force Britain's hand by coming to a decision as to when to exert military pressure on Austria in order to force the Emperor to implement the Seville Treaty. To engage in secret negotiations with a prince with whom one is on the verge of war without consulting one's allies is always a desperate gamble. Walpole hoped for secrecy. The conditions of eighteenth-century diplomacy, as he should have known, did not permit it. The close alliance between the servants of the Imperial Court in London and Pulteney and other members of the opposition created a dangerous channel down which truth as well as rumours might too easily flow. So thought the Walpoles, but betrayal came from another quarter. Pulteney, Bolingbroke and others discovered—from France—just before Parliament was summoned that separate negotiations were on foot with the Imperial Court. Chauvelin, by the usual methods of interception, cryptography and bribery, knew Walpole's policy by Christmas 1730. He instructed his ambassador in London to get in touch at once with the opposition. He did so, and on 13 January 1731, a few days before Parliament met, *The Craftsman* published a letter purporting to come from The Hague, exposing the entire negotiation.[1] Sir Robert Walpole's interference in diplomacy now wore a desperately amateur air.

This was a hazardous moment for Walpole. No progress

[1] P. Vaucher, *Robert Walpole et la Politique de Fleury*, 39–40.

had been made with the Vienna Court. The trouble lay with Hanover. George II insisted on a settlement of his quarrels with Charles VI on his own terms. Charles VI would not budge. So it looked as if the career diplomats would be right —with France indignant, Spain infuriated, Austria unsecured. After the Dunkirk exposure, this could be disastrous. The decisions which Walpole had taken with such abrupt confidence in the summer now seemed fraught with peril. The offices of *The Craftsman* were raided and the publisher, Francklin, clapped into gaol on a charge of sedition.[1] Revenge eased the heart but solved no problems. Yet Walpole survived the new session of Parliament better than he could have expected. Several factors helped. The most important was the mood of the House itself. Opposition in the eighteenth century was always difficult to organize. Wyndham, Shippen, Pulteney and its leaders could appreciate the excellent tactical advantages occasionally offered them by the drift of events. It was far harder to make the ordinary members of the Commons realize the need of constantly harrying the ministry and keeping the pressure at full cock. In the previous session, the entire Commons had been roused by the Dunkirk question. It swept them like a prairie fire. But that emotion had burnt out and it was not easy to rekindle the imagination.

Besides, the new drift of affairs matched their mood more closely. Hatred of France and Spain went deep; alliance with Austria appeared natural. That France had been duped pleased as many as it had disturbed. After all, Walpole knew the moods of Parliament better than any man, and his foreign policy had been formulated with the House of Commons very much in his mind.[2] The opposition had attacked Walpole and his brother for years on the ground that they were sacrificing Austria and that they were dupes

[1] Walpole's own personal interest in the matter may be judged from the fact that Francklin's papers, seized on this occasion, are not amongst the Secretary of State's papers but at Houghton with Walpole's, *C(H) MSS.* Papers 74/1-79.
[2] A fact noted by Sir Adolphus Ward, but ignored by many subsequent historians; see *Cambridge History of British Foreign Policy*, I, 83.

of the astute Fleury. It proved more difficult for them than for Walpole to change their line of criticism and maintain an air of consistency. Also there was a vast difference between indignation at the non-fulfilment of a treaty and condemnation of a policy. Many back-benchers felt that foreign affairs demanded a united and not a divided Commons.

And then Castelar, the Spanish ambassador at Paris, played into Walpole's hands. He denounced the Treaty of Seville on 28 January 1731 (N.S.) to the French. The opposition seized on this in order to attack the handling of British relations with Spain. All the old bogeys were trundled out—attacks on British shipping in the West Indies (pirates, said the ministry) and Spanish fortifications against Gibraltar (exaggerated and useless, the First Lord of the Admiralty maintained), and now the insult that, without consultation, Seville had been torn up. This Sir Robert denied. Castelar's declaration had been made to the Court of France, no intimation had come from Spain to St James's. Castelar was merely attempting to sow division, particularly in Parliament. And Walpole finished his speech boastfully and proudly. Seville was an excellent treaty; it would be achieved. All the ministry needed was a little time. Most believed him; the opposition mustered only 121 in the lobbies. The ministry obtained a large and comfortable majority in a thin House. Many members put patriotic interest before opportunism. They knew difficult negotiations were in train; they were prepared to wait for the outcome, then judge it. Before they broke up the outcome was known. Walpole secured his treaty with Austria.[1] Spanish troops were to be allowed in the Duchies; the Ostend Company was to be suppressed; no Archduchess was ever to marry a Bourbon or a member of the House of Brandenburg; Leghorn became a free port. In return England guaranteed the succession of Maria Theresa to her father's lands, much to the astonishment of Chauvelin and Fleury. Elizabeth Farnese and her husband greeted this treaty with delight and joined it with surprising alacrity. By

[1] Treaty of Vienna signed 16 March 1731, see J. Dubois, *Corps Diplomatique*.

September 1731, France, not Austria, was isolated and without allies. Walpole had secured, with a speed unusual in eighteenth-century diplomacy, a complete settlement of Austro-Spanish relations, which had threatened war in Europe for more than ten years. Nothing demonstrated his strength so absolutely, for this settlement had been achieved not only by reversing a policy pursued for six years, but by persuading George II to lay on one side his outstanding Hanoverian claims against the Emperor; or as Sir Thomas Robinson, the ambassador at Vienna, grandiloquently phrased it: 'I as boldly suspended His Majesty's electoral affaires for the sake of Europe.' No single act in the whole of Walpole's career marks his ascendancy at Court so clearly as this deferment of Hanoverian questions by George II for the sake of Walpole's immediate diplomatic needs. Nothing so clearly demonstrates the unshakable confidence of his master in his judgment.

By the summer of 1731 Walpole had achieved a most remarkable *tour de force*. He had not only jettisoned Townshend and his foreign policy, but broken entirely with the ideas and attitudes which his brother had steadily inculcated. He had behaved with his usual ruthless efficiency, caring nothing for the outcries of the outraged professional diplomats, who saw the work of years being thrown overboard with brutal realism. Walpole approached the problems of foreign policy as he approached all problems, with simplicity and with desire for decision. He reduced the complications to their clearest expression and drove with formidable directness to a solution. When he met intransigence, he put up his offer. Emperors and kings as well as more humble men had their price which, as soon as stated, Walpole paid, if they could give him what he wanted. And as with all he did, this simplicity and directness hid subtler motives. His foreign policy brought peace, but in terms which were dear to the hearts of the self-electing, independent country gentlemen whose goodwill or neutrality was so necessary for his power. Walpole had realized that it was no longer possible to pursue a foreign policy that was in essence European and continue to ignore its repercussions on the stability of his ministry in Parliament. Fear of war, high taxation and, above all, the growing belief that England had been duped by France, had turned the mercantile interest against his government and started to corrode the support that he had enjoyed amongst the back-benchers. By the Treaties of Seville and Vienna those fears had been scotched. France had been isolated. She was without friends or allies in Europe. The commercial gains were as obvious as they were great; the Ostend Company suppressed for ever; the outstanding problems of Spanish trade under debate at Madrid. These triumphs, Walpole felt, could not be ignored even by the most fractious merchants of London. And to commercial advantage were added the blessing of peace and all that peace meant to Walpole—lower taxation at once and the introduction of those reforms in finance and administration which he had long contemplated but had never, owing to the exigencies of the time, had an opportunity of putting into practice.

Yet those with hostile eyes thought they saw the weaknesses of Walpole's policy. France would never remain isolated and, instead of acting as an intermediary with Spain, was more likely to become Spain's ally. The formal and solemn guarantee of Maria Theresa's succession could only have one consequence in the event of a general European war— Britain would be compelled to enter it as a principal. And if Ostend were suppressed, that was but a minor advantage to the monopolistic East India Company. The real problem– Spanish trade—was unlikely to gain either a solution or an advantage from negotiations carried on with Spaniards in Madrid. Instead of being the dupe of Fleury, Walpole had become the dupe of Spain. For the sake of an immediate advantage Walpole had lost the future. These criticisms, which echoed from pamphlet to newspaper, have been absorbed into the canons of historical criticism, and Walpole's policy has been denounced as amateur, pacific and oppor- tunist. There were, of course, tides in European affairs that

Walpole could not control; Prussian needs and ambitions, the rivalry of France, the temptation of the Spanish Empire, these were matters for Time, not for a statesman. Some, like Chatham, who discerned the course of the great currents that were bearing humanity along, could achieve a symbolic role by giving moral force to inevitable conflict between France and Britain over Spain. That was not Walpole's way. He saw immediate problems and solved them. He hated war, muddle, loss. He felt that the problems of nations, like the problems of men, could be solved by hard bargaining. To seek peace and not empire, to look for prosperity without plunder, to yearn for stability and to shun glory may be the work of an amateur whose policy can be stigmatized as opportunist. For those who love life, and are indifferent to fame, Walpole's policy is both consistent in aim and distinguished in purpose. The tragedy lay in its ultimate failure, and for that only the follies and avarice of mankind with its uncontrollable and thoughtless lust for wealth and power are to blame, not Walpole.

CHAPTER SEVEN

THE CRISIS AT HOME, 1732–34

THE COURT, the cabinet and the Commons absorbed most of Walpole's time and energies. They were the focal points of his power, the moulders of his policy. They could be difficult to the point of intractability. They each contained enemies, avowed and unavowed. They all required patience, skill, knowledge and above all stamina in the man who was to manage them. Only a statesman possessing an exceptional political skill could have lasted so long in power as Walpole had done by 1732. His authority derived strength from many sources, but few were so important as his skill as an administrator. Indeed the foundation of his power lay in the Treasury. In 1732 the Treasury was the only department of State which possessed a complex organization and involved a large number of established civil servants.[1] This controlled the entire financial fabric of the country and Walpole had intensified Treasury influence where before his day it had been weakest, in the quasi-independent departments of Customs and Excise. He enjoyed administration as well as power and he wanted to bring the entire financial system under his own direct supervision. In this he succeeded. And he made his departments work with a greater efficiency than was ever again achieved until William Pitt the Younger took over the Treasury.

Walpole was a born administrator. His work as a member of Prince George of Denmark's council, nearly thirty years earlier, had been marked by its efficiency. He could absorb and remember detail with ease. He knew how to delegate to trusted subordinates. He enjoyed laying out the shape of a

---

[1] For the Treasury see S. B. Baxter, *The Development of the Treasury* (London, 1957), and E. Hughes, *Studies in Administration and Finance 1558–1825* (Manchester, 1934).

problem and propounding a scheme at once, neat, simple and comprehensive, to solve it. His memoranda, where they survive, demonstrate these qualities over and over again. Lucidity and obvious common sense are the hall-marks of his work. His scheme of conscription when Secretary at War was a simple answer to a simple need—so long as the irrational nature of men was not taken into account. His reorganization of the National Debt showed the same technical competence, the same clarity, the same simplicity, and the result harmonized with the mood of those with money to invest. That was accidental and not the result of Walpole's insight. The mathematical, provable side of administration attracted him and controlled his judgments; he did not, like Lloyd George, bring the same rich imagination to problems of human organization as he did to personal relations.

Walpole's love of administration, his desire to see it based efficiently on knowledge, was very much in tune with the more advanced opinion of his age. Political arithmetic, particularly in relation to commerce, had been enthusiastically adopted by professional administrators after the Revolution. Charles Davenant, the great propagandist on problems of trade, had been appointed Inspector-General of Imports and Exports with an adequate staff of clerks, so that both the Board of Trade and the Treasury could be supplied with the statistical information which they required for the proper formulation of policy. William Lowndes, the Secretary to the Treasury, who profoundly influenced Walpole, had the same passion for exact detail as Davenant. Both belonged to a generation of highly cultivated civil servants, often fellows of the Royal Society, who believed in applying rational methods and calculation to problems of administration as well as to those of nature. By the time Walpole achieved high office some of these men had died, but others survived, possessed of immense authority and unrivalled knowledge of the working of English government, which they had revolutionized.[1]

[1] Lowndes remained Secretary of the Treasury until his death in 1724.

The immense achievements of the Civil Service between 1689 and 1715 are only just beginning to be recognized. In a smaller, more closely interlocked society these achievements were widely appreciated and widely discussed. *The Spectator* discussed political arithmetic as well as fashion or literature. Dr Arbuthnot, poet and wit, wrote a passionate plea in its support. Walpole was deeply sympathetic to this attitude and to these men. They worked in mutual harmony. Nothing gave Walpole greater pleasure than a solid wad of statistics or a well-grounded argument about trade and its organization. Only a fraction of his papers survive—perhaps no more than a tenth. Yet the largest proportion of what remains are the papers which deal with his administrative work at the Treasury as Chancellor of the Exchequer; and amongst these volumes statistics, giving detailed comparisons of the yields of various taxes year by year, are the most frequent items.[1]

Scattered amongst these accounts as well as amongst Walpole's correspondence are scores of projects for reducing taxation but increasing yields, designed, of course, to appeal to Walpole, for everyone knew that he cherished the ambition to reduce taxation. As a young man his life had been harassed with debt, and like other country gentlemen he regarded the Land Tax—the chief source of public revenue— as a grievous burden and largely responsible for the plight of him and his kind. Yet to all who lived at this time, it was clear that England's trade was flourishing as never before. There were lean years. There were times of over-production, low prices and unemployment. Yet the forest of masts in the Port of London grew thicker. Liverpool, Glasgow, Bristol

---

Henry Martyn, who succeeded Davenant in 1714, was a brilliant writer on economic problems. Walpole was no sooner at the Treasury than he was involved in discussion with Martyn on the volume of certain aspects of the Customs. *C(H) MSS*, Henry Martyn, 3 March 1716, 14 January 1717. For Martyn see G. N. Clark, *Guide to English Commercial Statistics*.

[1] *C(H) MSS*, 27, 1-33, Duties on Coffee, Tea, Chocolate; 28, 1-31, Wine, spirits and brandy; 29, 1-35, Tobacco; 30, 1-11, Salt; 31, 1-21, Malt; 32, 1-16, Offices; 33, 1-12, Beer; 34, 1-47, Miscellaneous. They have been sadly neglected by economic historians.

were building great docks to take the huge volume of shipping that traded with Africa, the West Indies and the American plantations. A constant stream of colliers, Whitby- and Yarmouth-built, plied between Newcastle and London. Luxuries abounded and the new wealth was mirrored in a prosperity which touched the working class as well as the owners of property. Naturally Walpole wished to see this increasing volume of trade contribute its quota to the Treasury and so ease the burden on land. At the same time, he realized that the utmost circumspection must be used to avoid any taxation that might check or divert the nation's trade. He did not wish to increase taxation, but simply to render the operation of existing taxes efficient.

In 1724 Walpole had sketched the main lines of his policy in a series of acts. He had freed English manufacturers, but not produce, from export duties.[1] At the same time he had experimented with excise. Tea, chocolate and cocoa had been exempted from customs duties.[2] They were taxed only when bought for sale within the country. Until then, they could be kept in bonded warehouses and re-exported. This system had many advantages. The shopkeeper, selling tea, chocolate and cocoa, could be asked to produce the certificate showing that the goods which he was offering for sale had been taxed. Hence it was not sufficient for smugglers merely to evade the customs officials. Re-exports were facilitated because merchants were not held up by having to pass their dutiable goods back through the customs and claim the return of the tax already paid—a lengthy process and one which absorbed clerical time and labour. Also, this helped to stop fraud. Many dishonest merchants—not a rare

[1] Wool was not freed and its export was regarded as deleterious to the manufacture of cloth; also it was regarded as important to starve French manufacture of English wool, and the most stringent regulations were laid on the export of Irish as well as the English wool. Walpole, of course, did not consciously follow a policy of free trade. Expediency rather than theory moulded his attitude to economics as to politics.

[2] These were largely East Indian products and Walpole may have been influenced by Governor Harrison, Townshend's relation, in adopting these goods for excise. Townshend was constantly pressing Walpole to take Harrison's advice in 1723. See BM *Stowe MSS*, 251, *Bradfer-Lawrence MSS*.

phenomenon in an age in which there was a frank acceptance of public corruption—used to re-export commodities which appeared to be genuine and were often frauds. A layer of tea would be laid over a chest of sawdust, the tax drawback claimed, and the chest then dumped in the Thames. Simple frauds such as this, and there were scores of others, proved much easier at a time when the acceptance of a bribe carried little stigma.[1] Of course, excise did not eliminate corruption—excise officers were no more virtuous than customs officers—but many of the avenues of smuggling and cheating were blocked by it.

It is difficult for us to comprehend the immensity of eighteenth-century smuggling. Walpole had first-hand knowledge. Not much of the linen used at Houghton during his early life there had passed through the customs. Even when Secretary at War he had been engaged in smuggling his wines up the Thames. In an excess of zeal the customs officers at Lynn had confiscated brandy that he was running in. His mother wrote to him cheerfully and unabashedly in her old age about the way she neatly foxed customs men at Wells. He knew that the whole country soaked up smuggled goods like a sponge. But whatever he did or had done in his private capacity did not influence his judgment as an administrator, and his regime saw a steady increase both in the number of laws that dealt with smuggling and in their severity. For Walpole, like his chief legal advisers, believed in the efficiency of harsh laws, both as a retribution and as a deterrent. During this period of office some of the most savage laws relating to crimes against property ever passed by Parliament were placed on the Statute Book. The Waltham Black Act, by which any man found disguised or with his face blackened was guilty of felony and liable to be put to death, became law in 1726. Hardwicke, Walpole's close friend and the man upon whom he relied most heavily in legal matters, was responsible for judicial interpretation of the utmost severity of this Act. Savagery and efficiency

[1] C(H) MSS, Papers 29/4, 1-2.

became correlated in the minister's mind. In consequence, Walpole constantly sought to increase the powers of customs and excise officers and to pile up the penalties for those who attempted either to evade them or to obstruct them in the performance of their duties. He was in no way squeamish about the liberties of the individual or the privacy of a man's home. He struggled to suppress smuggling, to increase the yield of taxes, to encourage trade, to diminish the burden on the gentry. If the necessity arose, he was quite prepared to use harsh measures, savage punishment, and the full authority of the Crown to make the public conform to his system.[1]

Naturally such methods bred resentment. One Reynolds, swinging by his neck at Gloucester for having done no more than blacken his face, aroused pity and resentment. The powers loaded on the excise officers were not easily accepted in an age which cherished personal liberty. The Press never tired of lurid accounts, some true, some invented, all heightened in effect, of the brutalities of excise officers. Goods were stolen, bribes extorted, wives raped, without redress. A favourite time for excise officers to strike appears to have been the early hours of the morning, much to the terror of those supposedly honest shopkeepers whom they plundered.[2] For a humble trader, these depredations had to be suffered or evaded by bribery, for redress against an excise officer was hard to come by; the processes of the law were slow, expensive and unlikely to err on the side of the weak. In a world in which smuggling was almost second nature to all classes, the activities of the excise officers were more often than not justified. This did not make them any the less hated. Although evasion was easy, which probably increased the resentment of those caught, nevertheless the net of the excise and customs gradually tightened. Between 1724 and 1727 the yield on tea, chocolate and cocoa had

---

[1] *C(H) MSS*, 41/20, for the use of troops in Suffolk to aid customs officers.
[2] *The Argument Against Excise; The Second Part of an Argument Against Excise*, 1733. For an actual case of malpractices, *C(H) MSS*, 41/19.

risen by £125,000 a year, a very considerable sum in an eighteenth-century budget. At the same time the volume of export trade, no longer encumbered with the complicated drawback system, had grown. It was clear enough to Walpole that merchants as well as the Treasury gained by his sensible methods of taxation. The greater the range of excise, the wealthier the country would become, the richer the government and juster the incidence of taxation. These by 1731 had become Walpole's profound convictions, based on experiment as well as upon deeply inculcated beliefs. And yet the other side, exaggerated as many of the stories may be, must not be forgotten. The brutal extortions, the violence of privileged officials, the harsh judges, the severe penalties inflamed men's minds and fostered hatred against excise. The Press, so novel, so fresh and exciting in its attitude, was not slow to exploit these passions with a lack of restraint extravagant even in England of the 1730s.[1]

Such was the background to the greatest crisis of Walpole's career. On his side, determination and conviction; in the public at large, fear and loathing; both attitudes were soundly based on experience. Too many historians have dismissed the popular rage which Walpole's excise scheme produced as hysteria conjured up by wanton political opportunists. It was rather the expression of a profound and cumulative hatred of a system that seemed oppressive, tyrannical and corrupt.

2

WALPOLE, HOWEVER, had to face more immediate difficulties. In 1730, he had reduced taxation with a great flourish. The yield of the taxes appropriated to the Sinking Fund had, in his opinion, grown too large. The National Debt provided the country with an admirable investment. Everyone hoped for its ultimate liquidation; no one desired

---

[1] These paragraphs are based on the large volume of papers dealing with smuggling and repression in *C(H) MSS*, 41.

that that event should take place too rapidly. So Walpole, with peace secured, had money to spare. Which tax should go—candles, soap, leather, salt? Walpole left the decision to a free vote of the House of Commons, although he and the Treasury much preferred candles. The House, led by his own son-in-law, Malpas, who had large salt interests in Cheshire, went bull-headed for salt.[1] The result, which Walpole must have foreseen, proved chaotic. The salt duties were raised by commissioners and an army of local collectors.[2] By the repeal these men lost their places and Sir Robert was beset by mendicant place-holders and outraged patrons. As he complained to Egmont, 'he never was so troubled and encumbered with applications as at this time, and the more so that now the salt duty is to be taken off, there are five commissioners to be provided for at such employments that there does not fall five such in a year'.[3] Of course, the ministry hurried slowly; six months elapsed before anyone set to work to dismantle the Commission. Many could be kept going for another eighteen months collecting back duties; others could be absorbed into the Customs to look after the duties on foreign salt. Nevertheless the majority faced dismissal. To diminish patronage always appeared wanton to Walpole, a crime against nature. Furthermore he preferred salt taxes on general grounds. He believed in taxing the poor; it kept wages low, and low wages encouraged the working man to work. This attitude, so foreign to later thought, was

[1] This, at first sight, seems fantastic, and quite out of character for Walpole. It was not so. Ways and means of taxation were always more a matter for a free vote than any other part of the Commons' business. Hence Walpole was neither surprised by, nor resentful of, his son-in-law's opposition. The Court and Treasury party enjoyed a large measure of independence on such questions. This, too, helps to explain Walpole's *sang froid* about his dropping majority on excise. Historians have failed to grasp this point, although a comparison of the behaviour of government supporters during the debates on the Salt Duties, the Excise Duties and later the Cider Tax should have led them to it.

[2] The best discussion of the salt tax is by E. Hughes, *Essays in Administration and Finance, 1558–1825*, 291–304. He judges Walpole harshly and to some extent anachronistically; nor does he give due weight to the political considerations which influenced Walpole's economic policy. Walpole's own papers on the salt duties are in *C(H) MSS*, Papers 30/9–10; 65/40a–b.

[3] HMC, *Egmont's Diary*, I, 79.

generally held by economists as well as statesmen. Indeed, to the bulk of the population, it was a self-evident truth. The poor did not use candles, hence Walpole had wanted the candle tax removed. And Walpole's antipathy to the removal of the salt duty had been strengthened by political events. Doubtless the repeal of this duty had helped the poor, but it had helped the manufacturing classes even more. Bulk quantities of salt were used in many industries. The merchants gained more than the poor. And Walpole disliked merchants as a class. They opposed him in the House and in the City. He was not a man to make expensive gestures to the irreconcilable. And then, he had been troubled by the growing uneasiness of the independents who supported him in the House. The conviction, always strong in him, that the country gentlemen were his chief support, that they needed further encouragement if their loyalty was not to be overstretched, became overwhelming. He decided to restore the salt tax, reduce the land tax to one shilling and, on the wave of popularity he confidently expected, bring in the extension of the principles of excise to tobacco and wine.[1] That done, and war avoided, the squire might look forward to years of ease and plenty.

Discussions at the Treasury and the tables of comparative statistics demanded of its clerks soon quickened the interest of the political world. Walpole's intentions were well known before the debate opened in the House of Commons on 6 February 1732[2] and, in consequence, the opposition were well primed with arguments. But so were the ministry. Walpole

---

[1] His choice of these two commodities may have been made on general financial grounds, but with Walpole it is always as well to look for personal factors as well. The Governor of Virginia was the brother of the Bishop of Ely, both belonged to the Norfolk family of Greene, and, of course, were friends of Walpole. This helps to explain the ease with which the planters' representative, Randolph, obtained access to, and sympathy of, Walpole.

[2] HMC, *Carlisle MSS*, 99: Hughes, *op. cit.*, 297-303: Vaucher, *La Crise du Ministère Walpole en 1733-1734* (Paris 1924), 14-15. It is interesting that Hervey did not regard the Salt Debates as of sufficient interest to report them in his *Memoirs*. The best modern account of these debates is in W. Kennedy, *English Taxation 1640-1799*, 99-109, a neglected book of quality. N. Brisco, *Economic Policy of Robert Walpole* (New York 1907) is almost valueless.

foresaw that opposition might be intense and he remembered
the debates of 1730 when the vociferous Mr Plumer had
accused him of wanting 'to grind the face of the poor in order
to relieve a few of the rich' because he preferred the relief or
tax on candles to that on salt. The same emotional appeals
were likely to be made again. They sounded well within the
House and even better in print. Not trusting his henchmen,
particularly Newcastle, to answer such a case as cogently as
it required, Walpole drew up a lengthy memorandum for the
guidance of his colleagues so that when the debate came on
the ministry, both in the Lords as well as in the Commons,
spoke with one voice—his own.[1] And the burden of it was
this. Firstly, the salt tax was freer from fraud, cheaper to
raise, more equable in distribution than other taxes. 'The
salt no burthen either on the merchant, the farmer, the
manuring land, the curing fish and price of provisions in the
home consumption or exportation! An equal and reasonable
tax, every man must share, and every man can afford.'[2] 'The
Land Tax falls on 400,000 men out of 8 millions. Since 1688,
they have paid £65,000,000. Great towns and moneyed men
pay little or nothing.'[3] Of course, Walpole admitted that the
Land Tax was easy and cheap to raise, but neatly turned the
argument. Because it was so, it would always be required in
time of war, therefore ease it in time of peace. And he added
a good scattering of subsidiary arguments, mainly designed
to appeal to the plain gentlemen in broad-cloth on the
back benches, that Land Tax had ruined smaller gentry;
that the constant drain on the gentry's income made them all
want places. Walpole, too, knew that many felt that this was
but the beginning and that the end was to be a general
excise. This was to be dismissed as totally without foundation. The opposition in both Houses failed to be impressed

[1] This memorandum is in BM *Add MSS*, 33,052, fos. 124–34; it is printed
in extenso by Hughes, *op. cit.*, 299–303.

[2] Hughes, *op. cit.*, 300.

[3] *C(H) MSS*, Papers 65/40. Section three of this MS is almost identical with
the MS quoted by Hughes. This MS belonged to Lord Islay and is a stray
from the Campbell MSS. It is fuller than the MS quoted by Hughes.

by these arguments, nor were their fears allayed by Walpole's denials of a general excise. Their conviction was as deep or as expedient as Walpole's, and their ancient arguments were trundled out. Plumer appealed for the poor; Vernon mocked at Scotland (exempt from the duties) and sneered at the servility of Scottish members and bishops, without whose support Walpole could never do his monstrous work. Wyndham beguiled the House with the by-ways of arguments—the corrupt nature of the management of salt duties, the way its officers were used in elections, the encouragement it gave to perjury, the discontent it would arouse would only lead to an increase of the standing army and so to greater taxation and greater discontent. And he threaded his enchanting oratory with a few shrewd popular blows— salt would raise the price of food; expensive food spelt a decay of trade; a fall in trade meant unpaid rents, and once again the gentry paid. Dundas, to prove at least one Scot unbought, made a trenchant and irrelevant speech on the theme that this revival was a deliberate and wicked conspiracy to undermine the independence of the Commons. To all of which Walpole replied at inordinate length and with astounding vigour, only to be outmatched by Pulteney in a speech of even greater length and greater eloquence, in which the absence of fact was hidden by the warmth of his passion.[1]

Altogether it proved a great debate, full of studied oratory, all leading speakers in excellent fettle; yet the House, for a royal contest, was ominously thin, a mere 412. And Walpole scraped home by only thirty-nine votes—225 to 186. This compared most unfavourably with the great Dunkirk debate, when the ministry obtained the support of 270 members, and the opposition in spite of unprecedented efforts raised but 159.[2] And the next day, much to everyone's surprise (for in eighteenth-century parliaments the first

[1] Chandler, 1727–33: 159–209. *C(H) MSS*, 65/40 a. b.
[2] HMC, *Egmont's Diary*, I, 75, states that thirty members paired, which would give the ministry 285 and the opposition 174.

division on a question was usually the critical one), Walpole did worse. When the report stage was taken, the ministry's vote dropped to 205 and their majority to twenty-nine; another ten of Walpole's supporters thought it prudent to stay away or could not, after hearing the debate, bring themselves to vote for the renewal of the salt duties.[1]

These figures did not worry Walpole overmuch. After all, the debate was about Ways and Means, and he had never expected his placemen or his friends to show the same absolute loyalty on such questions as they did on foreign affairs, the army or navy estimates, or matters which closely touched the King's business. For the opposition, however, these figures naturally told a different story. They pointed to the truth of Vernon's bold assertion, quickly repeated in gossip, in pamphlets and in the newspapers, that these detestable duties that would weigh so heavily on the poor had been imposed by Walpole's paid hacks in the Commons and in the Lords. Every man of independent judgment, they claimed, had been against Walpole. Without these hirelings—the Scottish members—Walpole's measure would have failed. There are no division lists for this debate, so whether or not the Scottish members gave him his majority cannot be known. Yet a mere majority of twenty-nine at a time when place, pension and influence were believed to carry so much weight was bound to make Vernon's assertions carry conviction for those who knew nothing of the inner working of the Commons or the ministry. And the theme, so endlessly reiterated by *The Craftsman*, that a ruthless statesman was forcing a minority policy through the Commons by means of corruption, seemed to acquire a new justification.

The opposition realized that they had stumbled into rich pastures. If these duties had passed the Commons with such reluctance on the part of its members, clearly the public would give an even colder welcome to them. Almost before the debate was over, Pulteney's extremely able *The Case of the Salt Duties Considered* was a best-seller. The government

[1] HMC *Egmont's Diary*, I, 220.

IX. WALPOLE COMPARED TO HERCULES. A PRINT IN SUPPORT OF WALPOLE

BRITANNIA Excisa:

Britain Excis'd.

FOLKS talk of Supplies
    To be rais'd by *Excise*,
Old *CALEB* is bloodily nettl'd;
    Sure *B——* has more Sense,
    Than to levy new Pence,
Or Troops, when his Peace is quite settl'd.
    Horse, Foot, and Dragoons,
    Battalions, Platoons,
Excise, Wooden Shoes, and no Jury;
    Then Taxes increasing,
    While Traffick is ceasing,
Would put all the Land in a Fury.

II.

From whence I conclude,
    This is wrong understood,
From his Cradle *B——* hated Oppression,
    And our King Good and Great
    Would have us All eat,
Then dread not, good People, next Session.
    Horse, Foot, and Dragoons,
    Battalions, Platoons, &c.

III.

See this Dragon, EXCISE,
    Has Ten Thousand Eyes,
And Five Thousand Mouths to devour us,
    A Sting and sharp Claws,
    With wide-gaping Jaws,
And a Belly as big as a Store-house.
    Horse, Foot, and Dragoons,
    Battalions, Platoons, &c.

IV.

This Monster, Plague rot him!
    The Pope first begot him,
From *Rome* to King *Lewis* he went;
    From a *Papist* so true,
    What Good can ensue?
No Wonder he'll make you keep *Lent.*
    Horse, Foot, and Dragoons,
    Battalions, Platoons, &c.

V.

From *France* he flew over,
    And landed at *Dover,*
To swill down your Ale and your Beer;
    Now he swears he can't dine,
    Without Sugar and Wine;
Thus he'll plunder you Year after Year,
    Horse, Foot, and Dragoons,
    Battalions, Platoons, &c.

VI.

Grant these, and the Glutton
    Will roar out for Mutton,
Your Beef, Bread and Bacon to boot;
    Your Goose, Pig, and Pullet,
    He'll thrust down his Gullet,
Whilst the Labourer munches a Root.
    Horse, Foot, and Dragoons,
    Battalions, Platoons, &c.

VII.

Besides, 'tis decreed,
    The Monster must feed,

C

X. BRITANNIA EXCISED, THE MOST POPULAR OF ALL THE EXCISE CRISIS
SATIRES

replied, Walpole's brother leading the attack, but little impression was made by them, for the opposition were able to play astutely on fears, doubts and dire experience of long standing. It should have been clear to a politician of experience that the renewal of the salt duties had not only undermined the confidence of the Commons in the ministry, but had unleashed a public clamour of ugly proportions. Nor was the moment propitious for such battles. Within two years a general election would have to be fought; in many constituencies discussions had already started and the process of selecting candidates begun. That Walpole should have been prepared to divide and alienate his supporters at such a time or that he could ignore the seething popular discontent, requires explanation.

Firstly it must be stressed again that Walpole's insensitivity to the mood of the public and of the House was due partly to the nature of the business. On such questions he expected diversity of opinion among his supporters, and narrower majorities. Yet that is far from being the whole explanation. Walpole persisted in his determination far longer than was expedient or reasonable, even allowing for the nature of the question.

Walpole had become too great a man. For ten years he had dominated the political life of the country, defeating intrigue, grinding down opposition, surviving all crises, growing ever stronger in the regard in which he was held by the King and Queen. Everywhere he was treated with God-like respect. Dukes, bishops, millionaires crowded his levees as suppliants. At Court he met the same servility. Years of fawning adulation dulled his political perception, or at least made him more indifferent to danger that was not immediate or at the centre of his political world. In the Cabinet or the Closet he was still quick to sense the first shift of movement against him. The gross clamours of the public irritated but did not frighten him. Wyndham, Pulteney, Shippen he could patronize, even praise their oratorical performances, but every grand design to embarrass him in the Commons had ended in their defeat. How could he conceive of the possibility of their victory? And he had worked this constant miracle by lobbying men of authority, the great men of their localities—Hedworths of Durham, Crofts of Hereford, Archers of Warwick. What had they to offer? A Plumer against a Hedworth, a Vernon against a Croft, mere wasps against elephants; how could such irritable, baseless, excitable creatures stand up to men who lived as if God had made them to sit in the seats of power? All patronage was his; every mite that could be grasped did his will. And what had they to offer? Nothing but the unseeable future. And where was their knowledge? His mastery of facts and figures and the contingencies of affairs was quite unrivalled. Such ignorant men could never prevail. The world was his, its power and its glory. Everything proclaimed it. The time had come when the timidity of a few placemen, the honest doubts of a few supporters, the fears of loyal friends hardened his intention to an obstinate resolution.

Furthermore he had committed himself, both by action and by word. Early in the session he had called for an independent investigation by a parliamentary committee of the frauds practised on the Customs. His friend, Sir John Cope, sat in the chair and Walpole had seen to it that the Customs commissioners did their part. The evidence deluged the committee; 103 folio pages were insufficient to describe the ingenuities of merchants and traders in defrauding the revenue, and the committee apologized for not providing the Commons with a thorough and complete exposure of the iniquities practised. They pleaded shortness of time in the face of monumental evidence. Perjury and forgery abounded, so did brutality, manslaughter and murder. The crime wave, universal and violent, proved as expensive as it was vast. The Port of London alone lost £100,000 a year. 'The smuggling of tea and brandy was conducted so openly and so audaciously that since Christmas 1723, a period of only nine years, the number of custom-house officers beaten and abused amounted to 250; and six had been murdered.

251,320 pounds weight of tea, and 625,924 gallons of brandy had been seized and condemned; and upwards of 2,000 persons prosecuted; 229 boats and other vessels had been condemned, 185 of which had been burnt, and the remainder retained for the service of the Crown. The smuggling of wine was managed with so much art, or the connivance of the revenue officers so effectually secured, that within the period of nine years, only 2,208 hogsheads had been condemned, though it appeared from depositions on oath that in the space of two years 4,738 hogsheads had been run in Hampshire, Dorsetshire, and Devonshire only, and on inquiry 30 officers were dismissed, and informations entered against 400 persons; 38 were committed to jail, 118 admitted evidence, and 45 had compounded.'[1] FRAUD, indeed, was written in vast letters across English trade. This could not be ignored nor did Walpole wish to ignore it. In his heart he hated merchants, hated them with all the intensity of a debt-loaded squire. Barnard, Perry, Heathcote—they were the bane of his life. He detested the obstreperous Common-Councilmen of London; loathed their constant clamours and wearisome petitions. They smeared his name with corruption easily enough and ranted about his greed. Here was his answer, a huge indictment of the dishonesty of the entire merchant community. A strictly enforced and efficiently run excise system held for Walpole the promise not only of increased revenue but also of satisfying personal revenge. The merchants were to be reformed in their own best interests.

So Walpole was committed, and he had admitted as much. In the Salt debates, although strongly denying his intention of introducing a general excise, he had admitted his intention of reforming the customs and, if need be, excising specific items, particularly luxuries; and the prominence given, in Cope's investigation of frauds, to tobacco and wine showed where his intentions lay. Therefore the world knew his purpose; to withdraw meant defeat, a confession that the opposition in alliance with London's merchants were too

[1] Coxe, I, 380; *C(H) MSS*, Papers, 41/81.1–9.

strong for him. Of course, Walpole could make no such admission. He had embarked on a policy, staked his power, ability and influence upon it, and it was a policy that lay close to his ambitions both private and public. It would enrich the Crown, whose unswerving loyalty pillared his own greatness; it would mortify his enemies and bring the hot-headed rabble of merchants to heel. Clamour had pursued Walpole all his life; since the South Sea Bubble, he, the Screen-Master-General, had been the best-hated man in England; vulgar squibs, licentious satire, cruel libel and the pain of truth exposed had been his daily lot for ten years. His broken marriage, his liaison with Maria Skerrett, the friendship of the Queen; his houses, pictures, clothes; his brothers, his sons, his cousins, nothing was too private or too remote for Grub Street. Nothing was too gross for the public; the French ambassador sent the cartoons and caricatures back to amuse Versailles, and many remain among the despatches at the Quai d'Orsay. There he is down on his knees licking the Royal backside or stuffing his breeches full of guineas or brutally treading on the necks of his supplicants.[1] To understand the furious passions of the excise crisis, it is necessary to recall this unrelenting propaganda; the years of hate, constantly fostered, the deliberate misrepresentation of all that Walpole attempted or achieved. The country was not swept by a sudden hysteria in 1733; excise merely produced the culmination of a long campaign of hate. The obstinacy with which Walpole fought on against ever mounting odds derived its strength from the same causes. He, too, had accumulated hate which could only be discharged by success.

3

THROUGHOUT THE last weeks of the Parliamentary session of 1732 the pamphlet battle over the salt duties for a time grew in fury. The summer heat soon killed it, for members drifted home and the King left for Hanover. As soon as he

[1] *Arch. Aff. Etr., Mem. et Docs., Angl.*, XXXIX, fo. 127.

could Walpole cleared off to Norfolk, refreshing himself with a sight of Godolphin's splendid horses and stables at Gogma-gog.[1]

Back at Houghton, he could dismiss the fury and the vituperation and draw comfort from the splendour about him. Houghton was nearly complete, opulent with walnut and mahogany, brilliant with crimson and gold, studded with pictures of magnificence. In these hot summer days the vast Stone Hall offered a cool retreat, made cooler still by the soft grass-green velvet of its furnishings. About him were the busts of Roman Emperors and there shamelessly amongst them was his own head, as imperious as the rest. Beyond the great windows stretched the huge park set with thousands of trees; the old village uprooted, the old parish church masked. This was all his work, created by his force and cunning, and achieved through a brave and obstinate determination to succeed and to remain successful. The greatest men in Norfolk humbly paid their respects to his power. His colleagues—dukes, earls, barons—rode post haste to Houghton at his call. The couriers sped from Hanover, and the Queen in London waited on his advice. For years it had been so, his greatness growing as Houghton rose in glory. Here, the triumph of his life was more immediate and more striking, for it was on this plot of ground that his needy boyhood had been spent. He had obliterated all vestiges of his homespun past and built in this place the dream of his childhood's ambition. Such success, so absolute and so visible, had drawn his character into a harder mould. He became so used to his own greatness that he no longer bothered to adjust himself to circumstances. His sensibilities hardened. His language, always coarse, became brutal; his attitude to friends and foes franker, more unguarded. Flattery, no matter how gross, sweetened a vanity grown monstrous with a decade's sycophancy. The bright,

[1] He lay there on 1 July 1732 (Coxe, III, 127). Godolphin's house has disappeared, but his splendid stables which housed the Arabian still remain. Walpole often stayed with him in July for the Newmarket races.

gay, ever-laughing Robin Walpole of the Kit Cat had vanished in the vast, square-jowled hulk of a man who talked and acted as if power were his to eternity. He alone had triumphed. As he looked down the years, death or defection had destroyed all who had opposed him: Harley, Bolingbroke, Stanhope, Sunderland, Pulteney, Carteret, Townshend; not one had survived his enmity or his victory. Some in their impotence had cursed him, and stirred the mob to clamorous hate. To no effect. His decisions, his measures had constantly prevailed. And in contrast to the squibs and satires and jeers to which he had always been subject, there was the atmosphere of greatness in which he lived and the adulation which greeted him as day followed day. As certain of royal favour as a Buckingham, and enjoying the confidence of the Commons that Pym sought but never achieved, he had reached a height of political power unequalled in English history. It was unthinkable that a sharp debate or a moment of doubt among his supporters should deter him from his purpose. He made that clear enough during the summer months; and at the November Congress at Houghton, he unfolded his plans to his staunchest allies—Newcastle and his brother, Henry Pelham, and the rest.

His intentions, if not accurately known, were correctly surmised. And from October, *The Craftsman* unleashed a press campaign of unparalleled fury and unprecedented success. It started, mildly enough, on 28 October 1732 with a revival of the debate on the salt tax, condemning it, in accordance with Pulteney's view, as a burden on the poor. The following issue of 4 November opened the attack on general excises and argued that such a tax would destroy British liberty; the slavery of the French, the despotism of their monarchy was easily traced to their excise duties. And on it went week after week, plugging the same theme, to the effect that excise destroys trade, destroys liberty, breeds intolerence, brutality, despotism, poverty.[1] The Crown would become so rich that

[1] *The Craftsman*, X (1737). This volume of the collected edition which re-

Parliaments would be unnecessary. The additional excise officers appointed by the King would add vastly to Crown patronage and subvert the Constitution and render elections in the small seaports even more farcical.[1] These criticisms were all couched in terms of reasonable argument. The more lurid and popular Press, particularly *Mist's Weekly Journal*, lacked such restraint. They dwelt with relish on the brutalities of excisemen. More of these notorious villains would go about their devilish tasks and their monstrous cruelties would go unheeded. No justice could be expected from special juries or from summary trials by commissioners. Excise would extinguish the Englishmen's liberty. His house would be broken open, his wife and daughters violated; robbed without redress, he would be indistinguishable from a Frenchman. Excise would end in Popery and slavery. 'Excise, Wooden Shoes, and No Jury': this slogan emblazoned across newspapers, pamphlets and ballads was chanted uproariously by the mob. Where *Mist's Weekly Journal* left off, the cartoonists and the balladmakers took over. Walpole sits arrogant in his coach, drawn by a vast, evil, many-headed dragon that gulps down life's necessities and evacuates a stream of gold into Walpole's lap. This is excise; and together with two other woodcuts of equal malice 'fit to be framed', it could be bought for a penny. With the woodcuts went the ballads. Pasted on the walls of the alehouses, they spread their message as swiftly as a modern jazz hit; and scores of drunken voices were soon roaring in unison:

'See this Dragon Excise
Has ten thousand Eyes
And Five Thousand Mouths to devour us
A sting and sharp Claws
With wide-gaping Jaws
And a belly as big as a Storehouse.

prints the leading articles is almost entirely concerned with the iniquities of excise. The major part of every issue was devoted to this subject. See also E. R. Turner, 'The Excise Crisis', EHR, XLII (1927), 34-57, which deals with the pamphlet literature.

[1] *An Argument Against Excises, passim.*

This Monster, Plague rot him!
The Pope first begot him,
From *Rome* to King *Lewis* he went;
From a Papist so true,
What good can ensue?
No wonder he'll make you keep Lent.'

And so on, through twenty stanzas, each punctuated with this resounding, foot-stamping chorus:

'Horse, Foot and Dragoons
Battalions, Platoons,
Excise, Wooden Shoes, and No Jury;
Then Taxes increasing
While Traffic is ceasing
Would put all the Land in a Fury.'[1]

As the beer went down, and the frenzied voices rose up, the alehouse politicians got to work and soon had the mob out in the streets, bellowing its mindless hatred to a terrified London. A quick-witted merchant imported crates of clogs (probably from Holland) but maliciously dubbed them French. Stuck on poles they became the mob's emblem. Advertisements, full of tendentious mockery, plastered the walls. Never before had the printing press been used on such a scale or with such violence or ingenuity.[2] The excitement spread; the mailbags bulged with newspapers and ballads, and the pot-houses of the provinces were soon full of the drunken songs that echoed in London's streets.[3] The pace grew hotter as the session of Parliament drew nearer; the conductors of this public agitation moved from propaganda to organized protest. On 22 December 1732, a large number of London merchants met at the Swan Tavern in the Corn-hill and solemnly and unanimously passed the resolution 'That the Merchants, Traders, and Citizens here present will act with utmost unanimity, and by all dutiful and lawful

[1] M. Percival, *Ballads*, 63–4.
[2] E. R. Turner, 'The Excise Crisis', EHR, XLII (1927), 39.
[3] M. Percival, *Ballads*, 61–80.

methods, strenuously oppose any new excise, or any extension of the excise laws, under whatever name or pretence it may be attempted.' What is more this meeting elected a body of twenty-five, including some of the most influential merchants of the city to call on the members of Parliament for London to press them to oppose excise to their utmost endeavour. Vintners, Brewers, Grocers, Merchant Taylors, Tobacconists all made the same protest. Provincial towns were not slow to follow suit. Before Parliament met, Carlisle and Leicester had instructed their members to oppose any scheme that extended excise. According to the Press, scores of towns followed their example, but the opposition never allowed the agitation to be diminished for the sake of truth. The wild, irresponsible Nathaniel Mist reported that King's Lynn had ordered Walpole and his brother-in-law, Sir Charles Turner, to oppose excise.[1] But truth or fiction, no one could deny that the whole country was in an uproar. Foreign ambassadors filled their despatches with excise gossip and crammed their bags with ballads and newspapers. As Delafaye wrote to Essex in Turin: 'Your Excy. will have seen in the Prints what caballing there has been all over the Kingdom to stir up people against it. There is not a cobler but is made to believe that he is to pay an excise before he eats his bread and cheese and drinks his pot of beer.'[2] This vast clamour naturally deluded Walpole's ill-wishers; long before the debate came on in Parliament, they told themselves that his credit was dwindling.

Walpole viewed the scene without concern—indeed, with complacency. He worked hard, but hunted harder. He had a sharp attack of the influenza which held London in its grip early in December, but he was soon about again, and off he went to Richmond to enjoy his hounds and to be solaced by Molly.[3] His confidence and *sang froid* communi-

---

[1] E. R. Turner, *op. cit.*, 37.

[2] BM *Add MSS*, 27,732, fos. 93-4.

[3] *Ibid.*, fo. 74b. It was an exceptionally mild, damp winter. The influenza epidemic struck London very hard in December and January. HMC, *Carlisle MSS*, 93, 95, 98.

cated itself to his colleagues. Delafaye was certain that excise would not be attempted unless success was assured; Henry Pelham thought nothing of the clamours which would 'be easier quelled than even those they have formerly been foiled in', and he scoffed at the machinations of the opposition leaders, who were concerting their plans at Cassiobury.[1] His brother's confidence matched his own. 'Excise will be the grand affair,' Newcastle wrote, 'but as it is right in every respect, it gains every day, and will certainly be carried by a great majority in both houses.'[2] As in all the battles of the past, the ministry would win. The narrowing majorities in the salt debates had taught Walpole nothing. And his sycophantic colleagues mirrored his own complacency.

Complacent Walpole might be, but he was not idle. When he was not hunting or frolicking with Molly, he was at his desk. He intended his case for excise to be based on irrefutable facts and overwhelming arguments. He saw to it that the Treasury supplied the ministerial newspapers with impressive figures and with stories of excisemen beaten to death by smugglers that were quite as horrifying as anything the opposition could produce. The Post Office did its duty and an infuriated opposition saw ministerial ballads, handbills, advertisements and newspapers distributed free throughout the country. The government's propaganda became as great in extent if not in effect as that which the opposition poured out. This alone would have taxed many a man's energies, but Walpole naturally was more concerned with Parliament than with the people.[3]

The officials of the Customs and Excise and the Treasury clerks had never been so harried. Demands for statistics rained on them as fresh ideas and fresh needs sprang up in Walpole's mind. Here are some of the requests. One day he needed to have:

---

[1] BM *Add MSS*, 27,732, fos. 80, 94–5.
[2] *Ibid.*, fos. 95, 125, 126.
[3] L. Hanson, *Government and the Press*, 109–110; HMC, *Carlisle MSS*, 118.

'An account of the annual importation of tobacco into Scotland, and exportation from thence for seven years. To be immediately sent for. Could any account be had from France of the quantity of tobacco annually imported there from England? An account from the Customs House in England and Scotland what is now due upon bonds for tobacco.'

Another brought requests for:

'What failures have been upon securities of bonds for tobacco? What failures in tobacco merchants for seven years past and what losses? And what frauds and abuses.'[1]

And another:

'What time is allowed for payment of the duties upon wine, if the allowance for prompt payment is not given. Ditto for tobacco. Upon entries of tobacco for exportation. Are the particular places mentioned for which the tobacco is designed? Is the duty upon tobacco charged in the levy before manufactured or not? If so charged what check upon the manufacturer before 'tis sold to the retailer.'[2]

But perhaps only the extensive quotation of one paper of these memoranda will give the proper sense of the range of Walpole's enquiries and the keenness of his perception of where the weight of the argument might lie.

'Q. Manufactured tobacco for exportation
In what manner the samples are taken?
What seizures have been made by excise-officers
in druggists shops or houses upon stocks?[3]
Printing the Virginian Petition.[4] Memoranda the old debt standing out upon desperate bonds.
At what time and in what manner is the subsidy payable
upon tea at the Custom House now paid?

[1] *C(H) MSS*, Papers, 43/1, 43/5. These memoranda are all in RW's own handwriting. They are undated but obviously they were made before the debates.
[2] *C(H) MSS*, Papers 43/4.
[3] One of the major attacks of the opposition was concerned with the violation of privacy by excise officers.
[4] *The Case of the Planters of Tobacco in Virginia, as represented by themselves, signed by the President of Council, and Speaker of the House of Burgesses*, together with *The Vindication of the Said Representatives*, 1732. Sir John Randolph was the author of the latter, and probably of the former. See Milton Percival, *Ballads*, 69. This helps to date this memorandum to the autumn months of 1732.

Is coffee putt into warehouses? yes. Is the duty paid and secured?

Did the publick prosecute upon the socking [*sic*]? Did the merchants abuse?

Does the E.I.C.° now give security for payment of the subsidies upon tea when they are carried into the warehouse?

The new subsidy to be paid down upon importation not the 10 p. ct. discount or to be paid by the buyer of it to the Custom House officer according to the weight taken upon importation, and to be marked upon the hogshead.

All fines, forfeitures and Penalties to the publick.

Q the most usual times of importing and exporting tobacco?

Q The annual medium for the Kings Civil List out of the excise

Q Mr Fowles and did Mr Sandys apply to take off a prosecution and to be tried by Commissioners?[1]

The landwaiters books to be examined at what weights at a medium a hogsh^d is entered inwards, at what weight exported from the searchers books.

The old numbers marked upon importation, are allways cutt off before exportation.

Upon exportation the merchant takes the crocquett in the Long Room indorses upon the back, the number of h^g h^ds and weight against each of them.

The officer viz. dep. searcher weighs one in ten, if they answer the proper weights, the whole parcell is allowed.

Mr Jacksons seizure in Scotland: 10 hgsh^d full of stalks and dirt.

The prosecution of Perrin hogsh^ds marked sworn to be new bought to discharge old bonds. serv^t swore.

it was the same tobacco in the new casks.

Bonds given in London are annualy about £550,000, clear annualy to about 50 or 60,000.

What money has been paid upon debentures over and above the discharge of bonds?"[2]

[1] John Fowle of Broome, Norfolk, Customs Commissioner, was a second cousin of RW.

[2] C(H) MSS, Papers, 43/10.3.

And, as if this was not enough, he set about making his own digest of the ancient laws that dealt with customs on merchandise. There survives among his papers a detailed précis from Davies's *Le Primer Report des Cases* and many extracts from statutes as far back as the reign of Henry V. Some of these documents were in Norman French, but this held no terrors for Walpole; his notes, in his own unmistakable handwriting, are in the same language—further proof that Walpole knew French well.[1]

Mastery of the subject was not enough. Walpole, knowing that opposition were determined, wished to make certain that his scheme would have the approval of the tobacco producers, if not of the merchants of London. For a long time Virginian merchants had resented the monopolistic control which the London tobacco brokers exercised over their trade. In June 1732 they had appointed John Randolph their agent and paid him £2,200 to go to London to represent their plight as strongly as he could to the ministry.[2] His criticisms of London tobacco merchants were outspoken and phrased in bitter language. He proved to be a man after Walpole's own heart and peculiarly apt for his present purpose. He recognized this by obtaining a knighthood for Randolph in November 1732.[3] He spent long hours with Randolph, discussing every aspect of his excise scheme; indeed, he saw so much of him that some came to believe that Randolph and not Walpole drew up the bill to excise tobacco.[4]

In addition to these extra labours on excise Walpole had

---

[1] *C(H) MSS*, Papers 43/3. *Le Primer Report des Cases* of Sir John Davies, the Attorney-General of Ireland from 1606-19, were published in 1615. Davies was very interested in problems of taxation, and his reports among other things dealt with matters arising from Irish excise laws. These reports are written entirely in Norman French and require a good knowledge both of the language and legal terminology to understand them. They were not translated until 1762.

[2] McIlwain, *Journals of the House of Burgesses*, I, 160.

[3] W. A. Shaw, *Knights of England*.

[4] *C(H) MSS*, 43/11.1. This is the only draft of the Bill in RW's papers. It is in a clerk's hand with queries in the margin by RW. Oblique references to Randolph were made by RW in the Commons: Coxe, I, 388, also Chandler, VII, 306.

his usual burdens—the preparation of the supplies, which involved long calculations and the consideration of reams of figures—for in his day the Chancellor of the Exchequer was expected to do a considerable amount of computation that would now be done for him by his secretaries. Foreign papers never ceased streaming in, and the successful conclusion of the Treaty of Vienna in 1731 had not suddenly released Walpole from the drudgery of reading those monumental if urbane considerations of affairs that flowed so easily from ambassadorial pens. Nor, of course, did the petitions, supplications, threats and cajolery of patronage-seekers suddenly ease for excise's sake. The vast network of spies which Walpole had created to keep a check on Jacobitism needed constant supervision. And to these matters must be added the formal meetings at the Treasury with his brother Commissioners, the daily audiences with the King on business, the occasional privy councils and cabinets; and then the informal work, time spent with the Queen making certain that she grasped his policy, the hours with his men of business preparing them for the oncoming session, the long conferences with Newcastle, Harrington, Hardwicke and the rest on the drafting of despatches. Walpole had little secretarial assistance; clerks there were, of course, to help him in his Treasury business, but no private office to arrange the vast mass of his informal work and more often than not, no one to write his letters. Sharp, terse and to the point, these were frequently written in his own hand. Yet he carried his prodigious burden without complaint and with obvious enjoyment. He worked fabulous hours, starting often at dawn, but always finding time for the things he loved—hunting, his visitors, heavy eating and hard drinking. To his strenuous working day was added a new and threatening crisis, which doubled the load on his shoulders, for not only had he to master his subject but he would require all his arts of persuasion—those time-consuming attentions to all and sundry—if he were to overcome the prodigious clamour that had now been raised against him.

Already some of his supporters doubted his success. 'Some of his friends,' wrote Hervey, 'whose timidity afterwards passed for judgment, advised him to relinquish it, and said, though it was in itself so beneficial a scheme to the public, yet since the public did not see it in that light, that the best part he could take was to lay it aside.'[1] Such advice Walpole spurned. Everyone knew that he was committed to excise. To withdraw would mean acknowledging the power of the clamour he despised, and forever after finding himself at the mercy of public opinion, no matter how misinformed, so long as it was noisily expressed. To give way would be dangerous to the Constitution as he saw it. After eleven years of unbroken triumph in Parliament he did not doubt for a single instant his capacity to carry his measure in the Commons. So long as the Court stood fast, he was confident of victory, confident, above all, of being able to persuade by argument and force of personality sufficient of the back-benchers to secure a majority. Once the excise tax became law, by no matter how small a margin, the political world would quickly revert to normality—a disunited opposition and a contented ministry. So Walpole reasoned, but he took care with his tactics.

The King's speech at the opening of the session was noncommittal. No more than ordinary supplies were demanded; there was a little self-congratulation on the state of affairs at home and abroad, a few heartfelt platitudes on the need for unanimity and the avoidance of controversy, the hope that supplies would be raised in the easiest manner[2]—and the King left the gladiators to spar for position. The initiative lay with Walpole. At first he needed to solve the problem of immediate supplies. The revived salt tax had produced far less than expected and unless Walpole either raised the land tax again from the much vaunted shilling in the pound or found a new source, he would be faced with a gross deficit. His solution was neat. With the taxes appropri-

[1] Hervey, I, 134.
[2] *Ibid*, 135; Coxe, I, 381.

ated to the Sinking Fund steadily increasing their yield, Walpole argued that the National Debt might be paid off too quickly. After all, the National Debt provided the one safe investment for widows, orphans and trustees of all kinds. He would therefore take from the Sinking Fund what was wanted (£500,000) for current needs. Otherwise all the landed gentlemen, and that meant the vast majority of the Commons, would have to dig their hands in their pockets for another shilling in the pound on land. Robbery, sheer robbery, Pulteney fumed. He had always maintained that Walpole's Sinking Fund was a mere blind; that he had no intention of paying off the National Debt which, he maintained, had steadily increased during Walpole's ministry. Now Walpole had taken away the merest pretence and brazenly acknowledged his hypocrisy. Sir John Barnard, a London merchant, whose independence of mood and persuasive skill in debates always drew from Walpole a reluctant admiration, told the Commons that the author of such an expedient must expect the curses of posterity. Sir William Wyndham treated the House to one of his more mellifluous oratorical exercises. The opposition taunted and badgered Walpole to their hearts' content, but he took it well enough, giving as hard as he got, and shrewdly at the height of the debate, frankly admitted that he intended to introduce a new scheme of taxation so that this temporary expedient would not be required again. Of course, he was testing the temper of the House and it must have been peculiarly satisfying to win the day with a comfortable majority of 110. Such numbers augured well. Walpole, however, was in no hurry. He let the opposition keep up their own spirits. To keep them up required ingenuity, and the opposition brought out their usual measures designed to embarrass the ministry and convince the independents of their public virtue. In addition to another Pension and Place Bill, once more sponsored by the indefatigable Sandys, they were presented with a demand for land qualification for members. Another public scandal mentioned on this occasion was the

York Building Company, to add to the Gaols and the Charitable Corporation of other years. Ecclesiastical courts were also attacked and ridiculed, and the translation of bishops denounced as political corruption. All of these matters proved set occasions for the measured oratory of the opposition. They failed, however, to ruffle Walpole's calm or to diminish his majorities. As for excise, he bided his time. He knew how difficult it was for Pulteney, Wyndham and Barnard to keep their forces intact and expectant. Also, of course, he was testing opinion.

There were few weathercocks half as reliable as the Earl of Egmont. Horatio, who was doing a great deal of private lobbying on his brother's behalf, had him round to dinner. Of course Egmont had his doubts; he was never free from them, for he enjoyed making life difficult far too much to be a complacent supporter of the ministry. He admitted that excise was a good scheme, *but* an increased yield of tax meant an increase in the civil list, which, he thought, would be resented. Sir Robert had thought of that, Horatio hastily interpolated. The general election was very near, Egmont pointed out; already members were approaching their constituencies and everywhere excise was hated; even Harwich had written urging its rejection. Good as the measure was, could it be wise to press it when within a matter of months those who supported it would have to face their angry electors? Shrewdly Egmont placed his finger on Walpole's most grievous misjudgment in this affair; men who might be indifferent to public clamour at the outset of a seven-year Parliament, could not help but be sensitive to the outcries in their constituencies when they would shortly be up for election.[1] So the soundings went on; and Walpole's men of business worked over the well-known *doubtfuls*, presenting their master's case as skilfully as they knew how, soothing the piques and irritations, arguing away doubts and difficulties,

[1] HMC, *Egmont's Diary*, I, 311–12. Sensing that the Walpoles needed him, Egmont was soon on the warpath for promises about support at Harwich and a place worth £200 a year for his brother. There was nothing like a crisis to excite his appetite, and stimulate his conscience.

and raising hope and expectation. And still Walpole bided his time. Much provoked, the opposition accused him of unfair trickery, of waiting until the end of the session when members were worn out, an accusation which Walpole repudiated with affronted dignity.

4

WALPOLE'S FABIAN tactics had not diminished public excitement. The printing presses poured out pamphlet after pamphlet; handbills were scattered broadside; advertising was used on an unprecedented scale; the air was filled with the catchy tunes of the ballad-singers and the windows of the printsellers were crammed with obscene cartoons. 'Excise, wooden shoes and no jury' echoed through the land. Such ferment was beyond men's experience, for the violence of the days of Sacheverell's trial was nothing to it. About the excise clamour there was a voracious hate, as if the pent-up emotion of a thwarted and oppressed people had at last found a vehicle of expression. It was by no means a mere Press campaign: private and public correspondence bears witness to the widespread excitement.

'Besides the regular infatuation from daily and weekly papers, little hand bills were dispersed by thousands all over the City and country, put into peoples' hands in the streets and highways, dropped at their doors, and thrown in at their windows; all asserting that excisemen were (like a foreign enemy) going to invade and devour them, and ready to enter their houses; into all houses, private or public, at any time, by day, or by night. They might as well have asserted, that these excisemen were to be invested with the power of life and death.

Such as could not read, were informed by such as could; and all were ready to inform, and mislead, and enrage one another. It was the theme of coffee-houses, taverns, and gin-shops, the discourse of artificers, the cry of the streets, the entertainment of lacquies, the prate of wenches, and the bugbear of children.'[1]

[1] *A Letter from a Member of Parliament from a Borough in the West*, 9–10, quoted Turner, *op. cit.*, 38–9; also *Historical Register, 1733*, 282.

Naturally the fever caught the Commons, for the wind of public opinion could stir the complacency of eighteenth-century politicians, and this was a gale.

About Walpole, however, there was an elephantine complacency that led him to disregard the danger signals that flashed about him. His past victories, and the absolute confidence of his King and Queen, still made him certain of success. Once his plans were completed he gave the Commons ample notice of his intention and on 14 March the House was alive with members. The galleries were packed; the Prince of Wales was present with his gentlemen; the French and Spanish ambassadors were conspicuous in the dense mass of diplomatic representatives. The peers crowded in to listen and the heat in St Stephen's was almost insufferable.[1]

About a quarter to one o'clock, Walpole rose in his place by the Speaker's chair and spoke for two hours on his scheme to excise tobacco. His advisers thought that he excelled himself and that this was one of the greatest speeches of his career.[2]

He was well-prepared. He presented the House with the facts and figures about smuggling; discoursed on the plight of the tobacco planters; stressed the gain to the revenue; and forecast an increase in commerce. With his exceptional lucidity he made it all so crystal clear that the meanest intelligence could grasp the full implications of his figures. There were no tropes, no flights of imagination or oratory, but a massive indictment of fraud and a plain statement of how to avoid it. The solid, impressive detail of Walpole's speech ruffled Perry, the City merchant, who answered him, and who complained that he had not expected such a deluge of facts—the accuracy of many of which he impugned. The debate grew furious. Heathcote saw the end of liberty.

---

[1] Coxe, III, 129. Four hundred and seventy-three were present.

[2] *Ibid*, Delafaye to Waldegrave. The debate 'was opened about a quarter before one, by Sir Robert Walpole, who spoke two hours and a quarter, explaining and shewing the advantages of his scheme with such perspicuity and strength of argument, that everybody that heard him allows that he never made a better speech in his life': also BM *Add MSS*, 27,732, fo. 137.

Methuen spoke for the opposition, but Pelham, Yonge and Dudley Ryder were a match for Pulteney and Wyndham and Barnard. Jekyll, the Master of the Rolls, who prided himself inordinately on the independence of his mind, came out on Walpole's side. Everyone knew that Jekyll was quite unyielding to pressure and he carried weight with the independents. The debate surged on until Walpole brought it to a close just after midnight. His voice throbbed with confidence and high spirits, for victory was certain. The House divided and his majority was sixty-one—265 against 204. Delafaye hurried back to the Cockpit to scribble the glad tidings to the ambassadors abroad. 'This event will shew that neither the ministry nor the Parliament are to be deterred by popular clamour from doing of what is for the King's and the Country's service.'[1] Walpole, to avoid the mob, slipped out through the Speaker's chamber to eat a well-earned supper and drain a well deserved bumper with Lord Halifax. Hervey went off to St James's where the King was waiting for him. He took him to the Queen's bedchamber and together they went over and over the debate until the King, meticulous as ever, got everything right. It was not until three o'clock that Hervey crept off at last to his own rooms.

All seemed set fair for another triumph for the Court, another rebuff for the opposition, another defeat for public opinion. Everyone at Court knew that the King was firmly behind Walpole. His civil list funds were bound to increase if smuggling was to be checked and with simple-minded egotism George II came to regard opposition to excise as a personal insult. And yet all was far from well. The brief parliamentary recess at Easter failed to diminish tension, which, indeed, contrary to Walpole's hopes, increased. Instead of petitions, boroughs sent deputations; ministerial pamphlets were solemnly burnt by city corporations; in many districts tumult and disorder, so long as it was directed against excise, was winked at by the authorities. Yet this

[1] BM *Add MSS*, 27,732, fo. 139; Coxe, III, 130.

noisy, obstreperous propaganda was not Walpole's main danger. The uproar was neither better nor worse than it had been for months: a majority of sixty, to be sure, was far lower than Walpole had ever known except in the salt debates, but then there had been far less public agitation. Sixty, however, must have seemed safe enough on a matter of Ways and Means and when the members dispersed for the Easter recess, Walpole can only have expected a comfortable passage for the bill itself, whose first reading was arranged for 5 April.

Yet Walpole was in peril. An attempt was being made to spring a mine under the Court, the citadel of his strength. The rattle that the excise made in the world at large and the violence of parliamentary debate have distracted the historians' attention from the heart of the matter. Trying to soothe George II, Hervey recalled the year of Dunkirk and suggested that the spirits of the opposition were far higher then. 'Phoo!,' the King snorted, 'you talk of a time when my servants lay under all the disadvantages it was possible for a ministry to be exposed to. In the first place, it was so early in my reign that nobody knew whether I had any resolution in my temper, or any steadiness in my counsels, or not. In the next place, the ministry were divided and torn by contention among themselves; that was a time when Townshend was in place, and was giving Walpole all the trouble he could, both in the Parliament and in my closet; Carteret was not yet discharged, there were a thousand different parties among my ministers, and nobody knew whom I would support.'[1] This excellent analysis shows that George II, if the words and ideas are his and not Hervey's, had a realistic grasp of a political situation even if he could not deduce its proper consequences. The factors which he so accurately described did not make for weakness so much as strength even though the strength could only be temporary. In 1730, the half-discontented in the ministry could savour the future and hope perhaps to gain from it. The King's final resolution was not known; Townshend had not been de-

[1] Hervey, I, 151.

feated; Carteret had not been dismissed; power, therefore, might still be gained at Walpole's expense. By 1733, Townshend was in retirement, Carteret in opposition, Walpole supreme, and the King dominated, as no recent monarch had been, by a single minister, who controlled diplomacy, finance, patronage. Many who professed to be Walpole's friends hated him. In 1727 he had found places for all the members of George II's former household. Wilmington, Chesterfield, Scarborough and a score of lesser men had been accommodated. The years passed; their lot did not improve; the King paid less and less attention to their views or needs. They could not fail to take pleasure in Walpole's difficulties or to be attracted by the brilliance of Cartaret, for whom, everyone knew, both George and Caroline had a sneaking admiration. At the time of the Townshend crisis Horatio had feared this group, but Walpole had skilfully detached Wilmington, who in his heart, preferred ease as a courtier to glory as a politician.[1] But these men had never been fully reconciled and their jealousy of Walpole grew monstrous as the years strengthened him at their expense.

So, the whispering started. Weighty heads were bent together at Court; sedan chairs sped through the dark streets; solemn conferences argued the possibilities endlessly. Could the clamour about excise be used to break the King's confidence in Walpole? Could he be defeated in the Commons if their friends or henchmen discreetly absented themselves? The rash and the choleric were the first to show their hands. Stair told the Queen that his conscience could not stomach excise, a statement which she greeted with hilarious scorn.[2] He stuck to his decision and others soon followed. Chesterfield, far too sharp and critical to admire Walpole, saw, not for the first time or last time, the prospect of revenge. The Stanhopes of his ilk deserted the ministry and went into opposition. More serious for Walpole was the fact that Scarborough, the King's closest and oldest friend, told the

[1] Coxe, II, 673, 687, 693; also HMC, *Egmont's Diary*, I, for Wilmington.
[2] Hervey, I, 137–43.

King that he could not give the measure support. Scarborough's defection was symptomatic of the rot that was setting in.[1] The Duke of Bolton and Lord Cobham, both of whom were influential in the Commons as well as the Lords, let their hostility to the Bill be known. Wilmington dithered more violently than ever, and it was only a matter of time, perhaps, before he would go the same way. And the last straw of all—even the Bishops began to wobble.[2] Before a bewildered and astonished Walpole, there opened the prospect of a loss of his majority not only in the Commons but in the Lords too. Walpole could show indifference to public clamour; he could risk a sharp drop in his majority in the Commons; but a defeat in the Lords, combined with the desertion of the politicians at Court, was more than even he could brazen out. Nevertheless the drop in his majority in the Commons was spectacular enough. On the first reading on 4 April it was fifty-six, the next day it had fallen to a mere sixteen. This was dangerous, if not disastrous. Certainly it was sufficient to scare his friends and to excite his enemies. Happily, he still possessed sufficient judgment to know that he might be defeated.

Promptly and without hesitation, he hurried down to St James's to tell the King and Queen that the bill must be dropped. Their respect and admiration for Sir Robert had never been higher, and both were deeply touched when he offered to resign his offices, if they thought it better for their affairs. When he left the Palace the Queen was in tears, and the King, for whom opposition to the measure had been tantamount to treason, determined to support Walpole to the last.[3]

Naturally enough Walpole was reluctant to give up his measure, but he had to bow to political necessity if not public

[1] HMC, *Carlisle MSS*, 107, Hon. Charles Howard to Lord Carlisle, 10 April 1733. 'Lord Scarborough, Lord Stair, Lord Chesterfield, Lord Cobham, Lord Marchmont, Duke of Montrose have declared against it.' Scarborough saw Walpole on 9 April, in the morning, so the news of his defection spread rapidly.

[2] *Ibid.*, *Egmont's Diary*, I, 356.

[3] Hervey, I, 156–8.

opinion. Nevertheless he was determined to conduct his retreat on his own terms. His greatest concern was to try to avoid the appearance of giving way to the City's clamour. He believed that a surrender which seemed to be due to outside pressure would be a dangerous precedent for the future. It would be the end of good government if a minister's actions were influenced by any body but Parliament or the Court. So for some hours he kept his decision a secret.[1] He was determined that the petition of the City of London against the bill which was to be brought in great state from the Guildhall to Westminster, should be rejected unheard and no counsel allowed. The work of the Commons could be hamstrung by endless petitions and a ministry strangled through lack of funds if the right were established that cities and corporations could demand to be heard against taxes. In many ways this was the crux of the excise crisis. It would have been far easier for Walpole not to have faced this issue; to have called off his bill; to have left the question of the petition unresolved. However, he hated the City of London, despised the opposition, and felt that the initiative must remain in his hands to the last both for his own sake and for the sake of his country.

He was a great parliamentarian and he sensed an opportunity to rally his friends amongst the independent backbenchers. Little touched them so keenly as an implied threat to their special privileges as members of the House of Commons. The raising of taxes was their business, not the City of London's; on this issue at least the opposition could be put on the wrong foot. And Walpole's decision to reject the City's petition before withdrawing excise reveals the shrewdness of his political judgment and his unfailing sense of the mood of the Commons.

On Tuesday, 10 April, the petition was brought with pomp and panoply by the City Corporation from the Guildhall to St Stephen's. By immemorial custom it had to be received;

---

[1] He may have told a few intimates. Horatio certainly knew that he had taken the decision on Monday, 9 April. HMC, *Egmont's Diary*, I, 359.

but it was left to lie on the table and the House dismissed the City's plea that their counsel should be heard on its behalf. The majority of seventeen, though desperately small, was sufficient for Walpole. The opposition had exerted themselves to their utmost to secure a hearing for the City; victory for them would have meant that Walpole had lost control of the Commons, and the crisis could have been prolonged to his ruin. At the time, the smallness of the majority elated the opposition and drove Walpole into a gloom which even he could not conceal; yet the peak of the crisis had passed and decisions that could lead to recovery were now open to him. His course was clear. After the debate a few friends went to supper with him in Downing Street. Hervey was there.

'After supper, when the servants were gone, Sir Robert opened his intentions with a sort of unpleased smile, and saying "This dance it will no farther go, and to-morrow I intent to sound a retreat; the turn my friends will take will be to declare they have not altered their opinion of the proposition, but that the clamour and the spirit that has been raised makes it necessary to give way, and that what they now do is not owning what they have done to be wrong, but receding for prudential reasons from what they still think as right as ever." On this text he preached for some time to this select band of his firmest friends, and then sent them to bed to sleep if they could.'[1]

If sleep came to Horatio, it was slight, for by nine o'clock the next morning he was with Egmont pressing him to get down to the House early and to make sure of having his brother-in-law with him in order to prevent the opposition coming to 'any ill-natured resolutions' on Sir Robert's withdrawal of his scheme. Later that morning, to a crowded House, Walpole spoke with all the art he could muster. To show his authority, the bill was to be postponed until 12 June, when, of course, the House would not be in session: at all costs, he wished to avoid the bill's rejection, which would have meant defeat in the House, which as yet he had

[1] Hervey, I, 162–3.

avoided. The debate flared up with its customary violence, the opposition pressing for out-and-out rejection. In the hope of drama, crowds swarmed into Westminster. The Court of Requests was packed with men and youths half-bent on violence and although the Justices read the Riot Act and deployed additional constables, they were helpless in the face of an angry, noisy and expectant mob. His friends tried to dissuade Walpole from braving this mob and urged him to slip out as he had done in the past through Lord Halifax's house. But Walpole was as bitter and as angry as the mob itself; his pride deeply stung, he insisted on leaving the Commons through the Court of Requests. His son Edward and his close friends—Islay, Hervey, Churchill—formed a bodyguard. His presence fired the mob, and both the constables and his friends had difficulty in getting him away. Imprecations, insults and threats mingled with blows. His son Edward received a severe blow on the arm, little Hervey got a bump on his head for his bravery and Walpole himself, once clear of the Court, had to rush in and out of a coffee-house like a hunted highwayman. Imagination set to work, emotions swelled the next day at the recollection of the night's drama; urgent consultations between Walpole, Henry Pelham and Hervey resulted in the natural decision to make the most out of this fracas. The hysteria in the Court of Requests had spread to the City at the news of the Bill's withdrawal. Walpole and Queen Caroline were burnt in effigy; fireworks, bonfires, drink and a rip-roaring mob of apprentices kept the town in a tumult throughout the night. Not for decades had the City given itself up to such an orgy of hatred.

It was easy for Walpole the next day in the Commons to point a solemn finger of warning. If such riots went uncondemned it was the end of good government. The voice of the mob would replace the voice of Parliament. This rallied the back-benchers who had little love for City merchants. So quick was the sympathy for Walpole, so obvious his case, that Wyndham and Pulteney were forced to echo his words and even Barnard and Perry, the leaders of the City faction, dissociated themselves from the violence of the previous night. Unanimously the House condemned the mob, unanimously they directed the City members to carry their resolution to the Lord Mayor. And so the master-tactician recovered a little of his lost ground. Those of Walpole's friends who had been against the Bill, though not against him, rallied once more to his standard. The noise and the tumult died away, but the crisis was not over. It was transferred from the Commons to the Court.[1]

5

THE COMMONS were swinging back to their loyalty; independents, so active in a crisis, dwindled away when confronted with the drudgery of day-to-day business. Walpole needed, however, to be certain of the loyalty of his inner core of men of business; and this, in turn, hung on the dependability of his brother ministers, great and small, and their relatives and friends at Court. And furthermore, government in Hanoverian England did not depend on the Commons alone: the Lords played an active part. The Lords, and the Lords alone, could be relied upon to check the constant endeavour of back-bench squires in the Commons to thwart the executive by introducing measures to make land-qualification of Members effective, to reduce place-holders and pensioners, to make elections less corrupt, or to prevent the translation of bishops; all of them measures that embarrassed the Commons and could best be dealt with in the Upper House. And it was so easy to give a direction to foreign affairs by a well-timed address in the Lords. Majorities in the Lords also reflected to some extent the disposition of influence at Court. Because most ministries were reasonably secure in the House of Lords, historians have tended to neglect its influence and to overlook the occasional crises

[1] Hervey, I, 164–8: HMC, *Egmont's Diaries*, I, 361–2: Vaucher, *La Crise du Ministère Walpole*, 38–41.

there, which could be as dangerous to a minister as a momentary loss of control of the Commons, for it meant the loss of the Court.

Thus it was for Walpole in the spring of 1733. The great public clamour aroused by excise and the dwindling majority in the Commons have obscured the fact that he faced defeat in the Lords. He had experienced hair-breadth majorities on questions of taxation (in which so much liberty was permitted by custom to members, even to place-holders); never before, however, had he faced such a situation with an unreliable House of Lords. It was the desertion of his noble friends in the early days of April, together with the threat that even the bishops were not to be depended on, that had finally persuaded Walpole that 'the dance would no farther go'. Although Walpole could draw back, it was more difficult for his enemies to do so, at least for those who knew that Walpole had long realized their detestation of him. And this was particularly true of Chesterfield, who had led others more stupid than himself to cherish the hope of their own rise in Walpole's imagined fall. The envy which they felt towards him erupted during this crisis. He could not ignore it. As a warning, on 13 April the King dismissed from office Chesterfield and Clinton, the alpha and omega of the Court opposition.[1] It should have been sufficient. George II's attachment to Chesterfield had long been his protection from Walpole's disfavour; that it could no longer save him demonstrated that Walpole's standing in Royal counsels had not been diminished. This sharp lesson was lost on all save the docile and the timid. Wilmington, who had tottered on the verge of committing himself, sank back with relief into his natural subservience. Dorset followed suit.[2] Others were less judicious. Uncertain of their fate and confident of their strength, they determined to make a final effort to force Walpole from office. What had been lost in the Commons might be gained

---

[1] BM *Add MSS*, 32,688, fo. 3: Vaucher, *La Crise du Ministère Walpole*, 38–9; Coxe, I, 46, is unreliable on the dismissals.

[2] Hervey, I, 172–4; Sundon, *Memoirs*, I, 218–223.

in the Lords. To this action they were urged by Chesterfield, by Carteret and by their active friends in the Commons who, naturally enough, did not intend to remain idle or silent. Indeed they showed their usual skill in raising embarrassing issues.[1]

In many ways Henry Pelham was Walpole's most reliable colleague in the Commons. Solid, dependable, shrewd, he possessed a comprehensive knowledge of men and procedure; usually he could be trusted to do his best to keep the House within the bounds that Walpole marked out for it. On 20 April he tripped up badly. He accepted an enquiry into the abuses and frauds practised on the Customs House. That was harmless enough; the folly lay in accepting a ballot as the means of choosing the members to serve on it. In a trice, Sir William Wyndham had persuaded Pulteney (against his better judgment) to present a list consisting of Walpole's most determined enemies. This alarmed Walpole. He hated secret ballots. All malice, envy, secret hatred could be discharged against him in perfect security. He acted promptly. His men of business got into their chairs and coaches and scurried through Bloomsbury and the West End, receiving many an ironic bow as they passed the opposition bent on like errands. Persuasion, cajolery, promise, the sheer fun of political excitement brought the lobbied members crowding to the Cockpit on Monday, 23 April to hear Walpole.[2] He had decided to harangue his friends, supporters and well-wishers on the necessity of utterly defeating the nefarious designs of the opposition. Indeed it was essential that he should. He had not been foolishly or unduly disturbed; there was a real menace in this move. He was acutely aware of the growing danger to himself in those circles whose strength lay in the Lords. He could not afford another long drawn out crisis in the Commons. He needed to trounce the opposition

---

[1] They had attempted to keep the Commons roused about excise by presenting a petition from the tea and coffee merchants, praying for an investigation of the tribulations they suffered because their commodities were excised. The ministry easily secured its rejection.

[2] HMC, *Egmont's Diary*, I, 365–6.

His henchmen had done their work well. The Cockpit was crowded to overflowing and Walpole made a brilliant fighting speech, denouncing the crisis as the malicious work of discredited tories led by Bolingbroke, and professing his life-long devotion to whig principles.[1] Its reception was excellent and Walpole's spirits soared; even Egmont, cap in hand as usual in a moment of crisis, later received from him a warm-hearted welcome and rich promises of future benefits. That afternoon over 500 members crowded into St Stephen's and cast their lists into the great glass ballot-jars. The result was a majority for Walpole's list of eighty-five. And that was that. The opposition had failed for the third time in a House in which scarcely a back-bencher was absent. Despondency set in and the discontented members trooped off to their country houses. The future had the same dreary aspect as the past. Hope would continue to be deferred.

Although this quick victory gave Walpole great advantage in the struggle which was developing in the Lords, yet he still had to win that battle. Historians have largely neglected this development of the excise crisis—the most difficult of all for Walpole—for the influence and power of the House of Lords has been consistently overlooked.[2] From 1689-1714, it was the immense strength of the whig party in the House of Lords that prevented utter chaos developing in English politics. Time and time again they checked excesses of tories and independents alike who, if they had their way, would have reduced Parliament to the impotence of a Polish Diet. So long as the whig Lords controlled their House, the structure of government remained unassailable. After 1714 the role of the Lords was not so vital, but it remained im-

[1] Hervey, I, 179–84. Egmont was not present, in order to show his independence; he had already decided to vote for the ministry. Earlier on the Tuesday morning, he nobbled Walpole at his levee and demanded a place for his brother; judicious timing, as the crucial vote took place in the afternoon. HMC, *Egmont's Diary*, I, 366.

[2] A. S. Turberville, *The House of Lords in the Eighteenth Century* is a most unsatisfactory book. The Lords need to be studied as Sir Lewis Namier and his colleagues have studied the Commons.

portant, and with the growth of oligarchy and patronage its indirect influence grew. Certainly it was unthinkable that any minister, no matter how warmly supported by the King, could remain in office for long if he lost the confidence of the Lords. The first servant of the King had to control Parliament, not merely the Commons.

The ground upon which the opposition Lords decided to fight Walpole was an old grievance—the use to which the confiscated estates of the South Sea directors had been put. Chance had favoured the Lords in bringing about such an excellent opportunity. The South Sea Company's affairs were in a far from flourishing condition, partly owing to continued difficulties with Spain. The directors wished to reduce its capital, and for this they needed parliamentary sanction. Suspicion, bitterness, a sense of betrayal, still coloured many men's minds whenever they were reminded of the South Sea and of fortunes lost in 1720 and never regained. Ugly whispers had gone on from year to year. Aislabie, the guilty Chancellor, continued to build and embellish his palatial house at Studley Royal and to squander a fortune on its wonderful gardens. Janssen and Gibbon, men who should have been bankrupt and ruined, maintained establishments, below perhaps their former standards of elegance, but still far too sumptuous for those who had been condemned to a life of penury by criminal carelessness. Walpole, men knew, would not consent to the return to England of Robert Knight, the cashier at the time of the Bubble. He knew too much. And men talked of Houghton, of Chelsea, of Richmond, of the profusion and extravagance of Walpole's life; *The Craftsman* and the informed whispers of the malignant courtiers had taught everyone to look for the explanation in corruption. For years the story had gone around that many of the downiest features of Sir Robert's well-cushioned nest had come from the bribes paid by the directors to get back their estates. So frequent, so circumstantial had this story been that for many it had the certainty of established truth.

In a thin House of Lords, Bathurst secured an enquiry into the management of the South Sea directors' estates in spite of a desperate attempt by Newcastle and Islay to get the debate adjourned a day in order to muster their allies. This defeat took place on 3 May. Between this date and the first trial of strength on 24 May 'many Lords were closeted, schooled and tampered with by the ministers, some by the King and more by the Queen'.[1] Nevertheless, hard as the Court worked to secure its majority it failed to carry its wishes. The opposition wished to interrogate De Gols, a director of the Company; the minority tried to prevent this by moving the previous question. The voting was 75–75, and by custom of the House the motion was negatived—the first defeat any ministry had suffered in the House of Lords within living memory.

So grave a situation called for urgent action. Walpole, with Newcastle and his chief advisers, carefully worked over the division list. Only ten lords without office or place had turned up to vote for them,[2] and one or two of these were so idiosyncratic in their political behaviour that no firm reliance could be placed on them for the future. The ministry's utter defeat had, of course, been prevented by the serried ranks of the bishops; seventeen had appeared in person, six had sent their proxies; only one of their brethren, Lincoln, had voted with the opposition. Even bishops might rat; bruised ambition irked many of them. Indeed, knowing this, Walpole had had Hoadly, Bishop of Salisbury, whose failure to obtain Durham rankled, closeted by the Queen, for the defection of Hoadly the most consistent sycophant of the Court, would have spelt disaster.[3] Nevertheless, bishops and courtiers were not quite numerous enough to control the House of Lords with absolute certainty, and the danger for the ministry was

[1] Hervey, I, 190.
[2] Timberland, *Lords*, IV, 147–8. They were the Dukes of Ancaster and Chandos, Earls of Warwick, Clarendon, Jersey, Lords Abergavenny, Lovelace, Byron, Manson, Lovel.
[3] Hervey, I, 190–2. Hoadly got his reward for standing steadfast in this crisis; in 1734 he was translated to Winchester.

XI. EXCISE IN TRIUMPH, 1733

XII. A SATIRE ON SIR ROBERT WALPOLE'S TRIUMPHAL ENTRY INTO NORWICH, 1733

greater because of the aftermath of fury and resentment aroused by the excise crisis. Failure in the Lords meant fundamentally failure to control the Court, and it was the realization of this that reduced both Walpole and the Queen to a state of acute anxiety.

Walpole and Newcastle brooded on the list and weeded out the irreconcilables—the men like Chesterfield, Stair and Cartaret, who were risking everything to secure Walpole's defeat or those permanent members of the opposition whom no arts could wean from their intransigence—Berkshire, Coventry, Oxford and Strafford—men for whom opposition had become a part of life itself.[1] There remained thirty-three men who had, sometimes for years, sometimes occasionally, given Walpole support, or who had obligations through which they might be reached.[2] Then the remorseless pressure began: threats, exhortations, appeals to ancient loyalties; the wearying, will-corroding arguments that dragged on through the long summer evenings. Some were easy enough. Sutherland, that pitiful, impecunious Scotsman, could be ordered to make certain of his attendance; Saye and Sele would be unlikely to risk the secret service pension, so long enjoyed that it

[1] Timberland, *Lords*, IV, 147–8.

[2] *C(H) MSS*, Papers, 66.5. This list was also used by Newcastle, when writing to Walpole about the outcome of the debate of 1 June 1733: *C(H) MSS*, Newcastle, 2 June 1733, where he lists for Walpole how each one of these voted. Walpole's list has certain names ticked, which may indicate those lords whom he himself had been able to see between 24 May and 1 June. If it indicated those noblemen whom Walpole hoped had been won over, it betrays a wild optimism. This list, which is of exceptional value, is as follows—(Walpole's ticks are given in brackets).

'Against.
Dukes. St. Albans (√), Bolton, Montrose, Kent, Argyll (√), Manchester (√)
Earls. Denbigh (√), Westmorland (√), Burlington, Scarborough (√), Rochfort (√), Rothes (√), Buchan (√), Haddington (√), Marchmont, Uxbridge, Harborough (√), Macclesfield (√), Pomfret (√), Fitzwalter.
Viscounts. Townshend, St John, Falmouth, Cobham
Lords. Hunsdon (√), Cornwallis (√), Haversham (√)
Bishop of Lincoln.
Absent.
Earl of Sutherland (√)
Viscount Saye and Sele
Lords Hertford, Guilford, Onslow.'

must have seemed like a part of the family's inheritance.[1] For some, and certainly for the Duke of Manchester, the promise of future pickings was enough to make them doubt the strength of the arguments that had led them into the opposition lobby. Others were great enough to make their own terms. Argyll had to be won. His immense influence in Scotland was too great for Walpole not to exert every effort to get him back, especially since the desertion of some of the Scottish lords— Buchan, Haddington, Rothes—had been largely responsible for Walpole's difficulties. Fortunately Argyll's brother, Islay, had steadily supported the ministry: yet Argyll was too proud a man to reverse his conduct in a trice, no matter how cosseted with promises. In the end Walpole had to accept his abstention and be grateful for it. There were few men in 1733 who could treat Walpole with such a lofty display of independence and not only retain but increase their honours and dignities. Even Walpole, accustomed as he was to the drudgeries and humiliations of political life, could not bring himself to beg for Townshend's vote.

After a week of strain, agitation and anxiety, the decisive clash came on 2 June 1733, when the opposition peers tried to extend the crisis to the House of Commons by a motion which called for an inquiry by both Houses into the affairs of the South Sea Company since 1720. Bathurst made a good fighting speech in favour of the motion; Devonshire bounced up, in opposition, spoke of his honour and conscience, and sat down. The Bishop of Winchester, his duty clear, spoke trenchantly for the seventeen bishops who sat in a solid phalanx on the crowded benches. His plain exhortation was soon forgotten as Chesterfield followed Carteret, both scintillating, witty, fluent, fighting with all their art to persuade those few noble voters who could give them victory, and perhaps power. Islay attempted to destroy the effect of their brilliant speeches, but it was

---

[1] *Blenheim MSS*, D.2. In 1720, Lord Saye and Sele was in receipt of a pension of £1,000 p.a. The same sum was being paid yearly to his successor in the title in 1761: Namier, *Structure of Politics* (1st ed. 1929), I, 221–2.

Newcastle, anxious, determined, muddled, churning up facts and ideas in a lengthy chaotic speech, who enveloped the angry House in a warm soothing fog, and so blunted the sharpness of difference, giving those men who loved the establishment an excuse to creep back to their natural allegiance.[1] And so the Court won, albeit by a narrow margin. The blandishments, threats and cajoleries of the ministry secured the absence of Argyll, the presence of Sutherland, Saye and Sele, Hertford and Onslow, and changed the minds of St Albans, Manchester, Harborough, Falmouth and Cornwallis. Although the opposition, too, had not been idle in trying to undermine the confidence of the government supporters, its success had been small. Only Ancaster and Clarendon turned their coats.[2]

This was the end of the crisis which had raged since March. The battle had been fought with a furious disregard for all standards of decency. Vile libels, obscene cartoons, wild lies had bespattered the Press week in week out, creating a storm of anger and hate that bordered on national hysteria. Yet the real crisis lay neither in the public riots nor in the intense struggle in the House of Commons. More crucial than either had been the attempt at a *coup d'état* at Court and in the Lords by the friends of the King when he had been Prince of Wales. It had almost succeeded, and for the first time since 1722 Walpole's power had been in jeopardy. He had been saved, by one thing and one thing alone—by the loyalty of the King and his inner group of advisers, who showed on this occasion a unanimity, a willingness to submerge private ambition as remarkable as it is unnoticed in the annals of English politics at this time.

The King and Queen were quite unshakable. 'I never saw', wrote Newcastle to Walpole immediately after the critical debate of 1 June, 'my Master and Mistress in such

---

[1] *C(H) MSS*, Newcastle, 2 June, contains the most reliable report of this debate.

[2] These changes can be inferred by collating Walpole's list, *C(H) MSS*, Papers, 66/6, with Newcastle's letter, Coxe, III, 135–6.

joy as they were last night.'[1] Overbearing, coarse, at times impatient, Walpole was nevertheless their man. He had rooted himself in their lives, and never for a moment did their confidence in him waver. His triumphs were theirs. And so it was with Newcastle, Devonshire, Henry Pelham, even Harrington; the deviation of one of these might have brought Walpole tumbling down, and the loyalty of his junior supporters—Sir Philip Yorke and Hervey and the rest—proved equally reliable. Most of the men whom Walpole had made stayed with him and stayed loyal; and these were the men who were to be called the Old Corps, the backbone of his party that was to prove unbreakable until its leaders grew too old to face a new King and a new generation in 1760. They had their baptism in the crisis of 1733.

Had this been all, the crisis would have been all victory; but there were losses which took away some of the strength his party had gained in battle. Walpole's position in the Lords had been seriously weakened. The determined opposition in these crises of so many Scottish peers opened up a grave threat—the possible loss of all ministerial control in the election for representative peers of Scotland that would take place in 1734. The defection of Chesterfield, not important in itself, weakened still further Walpole's debating strength in the Lords. More sinister than this, however, were two grave facts. There was now enough ability in opposition, of proved loyalty to Hanover and of unshakable whig convictions, to provide an alternative ministry to his own, a situation which had not existed since the deaths of Stanhope and Sunderland. His narrow victory had been won with the help of men like Wilmington and Argyll, who had shown a glimpse of their treacherous instincts. Such a situation was full of danger and Walpole met it, typically enough, with bold decisive action.

There was to be no return to Court of men who had opposed him, to intrigue with the wavering and the unreli-

[1] C(H) MSS, Newcastle, 2 June 1733.

able. Every honour they possessed should be taken from them. Montrose, Stair, Marchmont, Bolton, Cobham lost their places, the last two their regiments. This astounded society. A colonel's regiment, purchased for hard cash, was regarded as his freehold. To be so deprived for a political offence looked like robbery.[1] Nothing could have demonstrated Walpole's power with the King so clearly, for George II regarded the Army as peculiarly his own. To those who had suppressed their instinct to treachery, Walpole was all grace, all charm, all benevolence. Promotions went to Argyll, to Islay; the Garter rewarded Wilmington's complaisance. And Walpole picked his way carefully along the thorny path which the re-deployment of minor offices created for him. With his usual skill he avoided the ambitious and selected men of considerable electoral influence and no capacity to shine at Court. To this there were two exceptions. The madness of the Lord Chancellor enabled him to promote Talbot and bring into the Lords as Lord Chief Justice the ablest young lawyer of his day, Philip Yorke, afterwards Earl of Hardwicke. Already Walpole, Newcastle and Hardwicke formed a triumvirate of mutual trust, and the accession of Hardwicke's powerful, weighty debating skill on the ministerial side in the House of Lords to some extent counterbalanced the loss of Chesterfield. The other exception makes a vivid contrast to the sombre, dull and learned Hardwicke— John, Lord Hervey, who was given a barony; and nothing shows Walpole's remarkable judgment as the selection of these two men of so widely different characters. Hervey, witty, malicious, extravagantly feminine in looks and manner, possessed a tongue as sharp and as poisonous as a viper's tooth. Furthermore, he was supremely careless about what he said of those whom he disliked, and that covered most of

[1] *C(H) MSS*, Montagu, 3 July 1733, reported the rumour current in Hampshire that all men of rank were to be turned out of the Army. Montagu got Bolton's job as Governor of the Isle of Wight, worth £1,500 p.a., and so, according to Hervey, 'took this opportunity to sell himself for full as much as he was worth', Hervey, I, 205. Stair did not lose his regiment; the reason being, according to Hervey, that he would have starved without its emoluments.

the House of Lords. His sharp, outrageous wit was more than a match for the irony of Chesterfield or the lofty sarcasm of Carteret. His great advantage for Walpole lay in his unerring ability to uncover those discreditable human motives which are so often obscured by the platitudes of political morality. Such men, of course, are dangerous. Neither Newcastle, Hardwicke nor Argyll felt comfortable in Hervey's presence; and his malice could corrode the friendship and loyalty of simple men as well as scarify enemies. For the moment the latter were Walpole's deepest preoccupation.

And so the crisis ended. Unable to restrain his bitterness, Walpole wrote a sharp reference into the King's Speech, when on 11 June this momentous session came to an end.

'I cannot pass by unobserved the wicked endeavours that have lately been made use of to inflame the minds of the people, and by the most unjust representations to raise tumults and disorders that almost threatened the peace of the kingdom; but I depend upon the force of truth[1] to remove the groundless jealousies that have been raised of designs carrying on against the liberties of my people, and upon your known fidelity to defeat and frustrate the expectations of such as delight in confusion. It is my inclination, and has always been my study, to preserve the religious and civil rights of all my subjects; let it be your care to undeceive the deluded, and to make them sensible of their present happiness, and the hazard they run of being unwarily drawn by specious pretences into their own destruction.'[2]

The rapturous reception given to members who had opposed excise as they returned to their constituencies told Walpole clearly enough that the battles of this year would reverberate for many months throughout the land. To sweeten his bitterness his Norfolk friends planned a public demonstration of their regard which would surpass anything ever shown before to a King's minister.

[1] The city were much annoyed by this expression and said 'truth' must have been a misprint for 'troops'. HMC, *Egmont's Diary*, I, 387.
[2] Hervey, I, 203–4; see also HMC, *Egmont's Diary*, I, 387.

On 10 July Walpole and his brother approached Norwich in their coaches as evening shadows began to lengthen. The gentry of Norfolk, together with the leading citizens, rode out to meet him. More than a thousand men were drawn up three miles from the City to pay their homage. The Hobarts, Cokes, Harbords, Turners escorted his coach to the deafening cheers of the mob. 'At eight in the evening they entered the city midst the loud acclamations of all sorts of people, the higher and the lower gentry. The crowds were so great, that within the memory of man there were never so many people seen in the Market Place together, on any occasion whatsoever.' After spending the night in the Bishop's Palace, Walpole was received in state by the Corporation and presented with a gold box. Quick to respond to the public affection thus shown him, he captivated the company with an admirable, warm-hearted speech. Here, at least, he was known and respected. Naturally feasts followed. Horatio pledged the Corporation and promised to exert all his efforts to promote their shrinking woollen manufacture. Then, with his party around him, Walpole took opinion and the county candidates were chosen for the election that was to take place in 1734. Down went the bumpers, and meat and wine and good fellowship bred security and banished memories of those howling mobs that had threatened him with insult and injury.[1]

The next day his cavalcade rode out across the heaths towards Houghton; still the galloping horsemen circled and cheered; the villagers rushed to gape and wonder. Never before had a Norfolk man received such marks of esteem from his countrymen. So long as men felt thus, all was secure. Well satisfied, he could give his undivided attention to the urgent problems of Europe. Peace was once more in danger.

---

[1] *The London Journal*, 21 July 1733; *The Norwich Mercury*, 11, 12 July 1733. This visit naturally stimulated the London wits, and ballads guying the reception of the Walpoles were quickly on sale, see Milton Percival, *Ballads*, 81-5; Coxe, III, 136.

CHAPTER EIGHT

THE AFTERMATH, 1734

WHEN WALPOLE reached Houghton, he found a pile of red despatch boxes awaiting his attention. Once more the danger of war threatened the stability of Europe, and for Walpole the causes and issues were singularly remote from the interests of England. The crisis had been caused by the death of Augustus II of Poland on 1 February 1733. The throne of Poland was elective; the nobles who chose their monarch were notoriously corrupt, the majority in the pay of France. The great powers—Austria, Russia, France—wished the King to be a creature of their own choice. Austria's candidate was Augustus's son; Louis XV demanded the election of his father-in-law, Stanislaus Leszczynski, who had been deposed long ago. Russia favoured the young Augustus. It was a matter of complete indifference to Walpole who wore the crown in Poland.[1] His preoccupation was with the complicated treaty obligations which Britain had with France and Holland and many of the German states. If France fought Austria, he was determined that a diplomatic chain reaction should not drag England into the conflict.[2] His view was simple, cogent, blinkered. George II understood the European situation far better, even if he was less apt to formulate his ideas either clearly or forcibly. What troubled the King was the possibility of a radical shift in the balance of European power. Defeat of Austria could only mean the aggrandizement of France and Spain. This prospect frightened other

[1] Vaucher, *Robert Walpole et la politique de Fleury*, 85 n., and authorities there quoted proved that Townshend and, after his fall, Walpole's ministry had told the British minister in Poland not to oppose Stanislaus, but this, of course, was long before the crisis and before the British ministers had given serious thought to the problem.

[2] The danger lay in the Second Treaty of Vienna (1731) by which Britain was pledged to help Austria in case of war. As with most treaties, there were holes in it.

members of the cabinet as well as the King; neither Newcastle nor Harrington was entirely happy about the complete trust which both Walpoles placed in the intentions of France. The siren voice of Fleury was beginning to ring hollow in their ears.

Owing to the distractions and tribulations of the excise crisis, the ministry had been willing to suppress their anxieties and put their trust in Walpole's bland optimism.

'Your court', wrote Delafaye, the Under-Secretary of State, to Waldegrave, the ambassador at Versailles, 'blusters and threatens, makes encampments, and marches their militia; but I take them to be mere bullys, at least during the Cardinals life, whose business at his age should be to keep and leave the kingdom in peace. When he is gone, it cannot be Chauvelin's interest to go into a war, and give some military man an opportunity to get into the saddle. There can be but one reason for them to desire a war, which is the hopes it would divert the minds of their people at home from their attention to affairs of religion that give them so much trouble. The time for France to go to war is, in my mind, when the emperor dyes without heir male, in order to have his succession decided: and so the house of Austria, their rival, brought to nothing, and France remain the first power in Europe. Till then, they should save their men and money, and endeavour to grow rich by trade.'[1]

This comment was shrewd enough to convince. It has about it the air of Walpole's plain common sense, embroidered with a few of the half-witted fancies about religion that may have flitted through Newcastle's head. And its weakness too is characteristic, that ineradicable belief that Fleury, old, tired, pacific, would never, never risk war in Europe. It is quite astonishing how deeply embedded their faith in Fleury was.

Throughout the excise crisis the antics of the French ambassador in London had vastly irritated the two brothers. Horatio felt a personal responsibility for all things French:

[1] Coxe, III, 136.

Robert detested any man who consorted with his enemies. Chavigny, the close friend of Horatio's dreaded *Garde des Sceaux*, Chauvelin, delighted in the company of Boling-broke, Pulteney and Wyndham. He entered whole-heartedly into the spirit of opposition, and did all that he could to help it. He filled his despatches (read of course by the Wal-poles) with prognostications of the imminent ruin of the ministry. To all and sundry he gloried in the prowess of France, confidently prophesied a war and spoke largely of France's predestined victories. The Walpoles protested about his behaviour to the French government, but wrote him off as a jackanapes sent by Chauvelin to plague them. They did not for one moment consider that his views and actions might be connected with the grand design of French diplomacy.[1]

In a rage Horatio wrote to his old crony, Baron Gedda, the Swedish ambassador in Paris; thereby making sure that the enormities of Chavigny would be brought to the private ear of the Cardinal.

'Mo^r Chavigni,' according to his letter of 30 July 1733, 'dabord trompète par tout que c'est nous qui avons excité l'Empereur, et qui l'avons encouragé à user de force en Pologne, et que nous sommes engagés à le soutenir par raport à cette election—quelqu' eloigné que cela soit de notre pensée et de notre interêt. Si nous marquons du deplaisir de voir l'Europe en danger d'une guerre generale, à l'occasion d'une dispute qui interesse si peu l'equilibre de cette partie du monde; et de l'empres-sement à maintenir la paix et à prevenir une rupture; il va aussitost representer à ceux qui le veulent bien ecouter les bonnes intentions du Roy et de ses ministres comme l'effet de leur faiblesse et de leur timidité, se trouvant dans l'incapacité de remplir leurs engagemens; d'où il

---

[1] Coxe, III, 137–41. Wickham Legg, *Diplomatic Instructions, France, 1727–44,* iv, 108–9, 113. *Walpole MSS*, Letters of Cardinal Fleury, Mr Walpole, Baron Gedda: particularly Walpole's letter to Gedda of 30 July 1733 (N.S.); 'Quand on s'addresse au Cardinal, ce fonds de sagesse et d'integrité qui accompagne tous ses discours et toutes ses actions, et qui le dispose à peser toutes choses dans la balance de la justice et de la prudence, donne une entière satisfaction à tous ceux qui ont l'honneur de conferer avec lui' etc., etc.

infere qu'il n'y a rien à craindre de l'Angleterre ni de la Hollande dans l'abaissement où elles sont presentement. Enfin on voit par toutes ses demarches et tous ses discours que ce qu'il a le plus en voüe [*sic*] est d'allumer une guerre en Europe . . . La guerre, selon lui, est necessaire pour retablir la gloire de la France et l'election en Pologne en peut fournir l'occasion aussi bien qu'autre chose . . .'[1] It took another four folios for Horatio to discharge the bitterness of his feelings for Chavigny, whom he conceived as ruining the greatest glory of his diplomatic career—the friendship between France and Great Britain.

Neither Horatio nor his brother could believe that this outrageous ambassador could represent the real actions of the Cardinal and of France. It proved far less easy to convince George II than themselves.

George II did not like the Emperor. He resented, as most German princes did, his vestigial rights over their territories. He had been quite prepared to threaten the Emperor through alliance and diplomatic manoeuvre in order to get his own ends. In the event, however, of an Austro-French conflict, George II knew his duty. It lay with the Emperor. George II had never been enamoured of the Walpoles' policy towards France. He had consented to it; he had permitted himself to be half deceived by the persuasive blandishments of Fleury; but his suspicions had never died. That France would sooner or later provoke a war in order to recapture the supremacy in Europe which she thought to be hers by destiny, he never doubted. So for him Chavigny's wanton behaviour with those elements of the opposition which George II detested were all part and parcel with Chavigny's outrageous boastings and posturings. He was a better guide to the true policy of France than the foxy, evasive Fleury. And so, thought George II, Britain should be prepared to fight, and to support Austria with arms as the Treaty of Vienna stipulated. No one would be happier than he to blood his troops in battle.[2]

[1] *Walpole MSS*, loc. cit.
[2] Hervey, I, 217.

During their brief stay in Norfolk the two brothers had time to consider both the situation in Europe and its dangers for the policy which they had pursued for so long. Back at Hampton Court, where the Court had gone for the summer in order to escape from the stench of London, Walpole took over the duties he had delegated to Lord Hervey. Hervey, as Vice-Chamberlain, was constantly in the presence of the King and Queen, indeed at their beck and call, and Walpole expected him to use whatever opportunities any turn in the conversation gave him to damp down the King's martial ardour and to wean his wife from her firm sympathy with Austria. Strongly believing, like his patron, that the fate of Poland and of Stanislaus was not a direct concern of England, Hervey tried his uttermost to bring the irascible King to his own way of thinking. It proved an uphill task, and Walpole himself was forced to spend hours first with Caroline and then with George, going patiently and gently over the arguments for the policy of disengagement which he wished to pursue. The situation was fraught with danger: Russia had massed an army; Austria's had moved into Silesia; France was mobilized along the Rhine. In September, French gold triumphed at the Polish Diet and Stanislaus was proclaimed King of Poland. The Russians marched on Warsaw; and Stanislaus and his supporters had no alternative but to flee to Danzig, after which the Imperial party in the Polish Diet elected the Russian candidate, Augustus III. France absorbed Lorraine; besieged Austrian strongholds on the Rhine; concluded a most satisfactory alliance with Sardinia which enabled her troops to attack the Austrians on the plain of Lombardy; then set about enticing Spain to implement the Family Compact and left Stanislaus to rot in Danzig. The despatches poured into Hampton Court, as one dramatic event rapidly followed another. Austria made no bones about her desire for British help; and considered that anything short of immediate aid would be a breach of treaty obligation. This seemed entirely reasonable to George II.

Walpole patiently argued against the King's desire to

fight. Continental war was always unpopular with the country and with the Commons. The gentry hated increased taxation. War without the Dutch, who had signed a treaty of neutrality with France, would give them a chance to seize a larger portion of the world's carrying trade to the detriment of British interests. War against France might give the Jacobites their longed-for chance and the possibility of an invasion could not be ruled out. These were the old arguments, but there was also a new one: in 1734, a general election was due to be held. Already the constituencies were stirring, candidates were sounding opinion, and Walpole's post-bag was swelling with demands. The furore engendered by the excise would be kept alive by every device and no one expected the election to be either peaceful or easy to win. The addition of an unpopular war to the opposition armoury might seriously endanger the success of the ministry.[1] The King was therefore cajoled into accepting delay. He agreed in October that Horatio should be sent to The Hague— ostensibly to bring over the Prince of Orange for his marriage to the Princess Royal, but in reality to try to smooth away the suspicions which this marriage project had aroused in the Netherlands and to attempt to bring about a greater degree of agreement between the Maritime Powers on the Polish question. Deeply suspicious of the House of Orange, their High Mightinesses had viewed their prince's marriage to George II's eldest daughter as an attempt by the British to resuscitate the Stadtholdership; their opposition to war sprang partly from a like fear; and their irritation with the British had been sharply revealed by their independent action in signing a treaty of neutrality with France. Naturally the French ambassador had exploited Dutch suspicions and Dutch fears and nourished them with French gold.[2]

Horatio rushed about The Hague, renewing old friend-ships, and exuding that radiant common sense and simplicity

[1] Hervey, I, 216–7, 225; Vaucher, *Walpole et la Politique de Fleury*, 83–4.
[2] P. Geyl, *Williem IV en Engeland* (1924), Letters of Queen Caroline to Princess Royal, ed. P. Geyl, *Bijdragen en Medeelingen van het Historisch Genootschap*, XIV; *Receuil des instructions, Hollande*; Coxe, HW, 172–93.

of heart that made him so easy to like and so easy to deceive. The Dutch, however, had gone as far along the line of independent action as they wished to go. Their neutrality was established; they had cocked a snook at kings and princes. And after a few days had passed, Horatio's ebulliently confident despatches began to stream towards his brother's desk. The Dutch were quite willing to join with the British in offering mediation to the warring powers. Along with this welcome news came exhortations for the Princess Royal and her parents. Dutch susceptibilities must be quietened at all costs; public honours paid to the Prince should be kept to the minimum—one sentiment at least which chimed with the King's intentions. George II hated the expense of the marriage, regarded the House of Orange as scarcely fit for his daughter, and the dowry excessive. No matter how distasteful Horatio's advice was to the Princess Royal, it was more welcome to her parents than the fruits of his diplomacy.

By the time Horatio returned with the Prince, the King had been brought so closely into line with the Walpoles' policy that he himself told Kinski, the Emperor's ambassador, that a war, which had arisen from the affairs of Poland, could not be regarded as a matter which called for British aid within the terms of the Treaty of Vienna; but that with Holland the British were willing to offer their services as mediators. This was a triumph for Walpole, a triumph for the hours of patient argument. Yet it pleased few at Court. Harrington, Newcastle, Grafton agreed, though reluctantly; instinctively they felt that aid should be given to Austria, England's only powerful ally in central Europe. They wished, too, to gratify the King; their natures led them always to comply rather than oppose, and they were less certain than Walpole that he could control so complex a diplomatic situation.

Years of power had given Walpole a monolithic confidence in his own judgment. He pooh-poohed the misgivings of Grafton, rode roughshod over Newcastle. He had brought the King round; and what was even better still, he thought, started a train of negotiation—the prospective marriage of an Austrian archduchess with a son of Elizabeth Farnese—that might detach Spain from her alliance with France. The acute danger of war had passed. He collected Grafton, the Pelhams and the rest of his cronies, and the huge cavalcade of statesmen and servants set out for Houghton on 18 November to enjoy yet another Norfolk Congress. They were, wrote Hervey, 'to hunt, be noisy, jolly, drunk, comical and pure merry'.[1] No one enjoyed these carousals in Norfolk more than Sir Robert. He sniffed up the adulation of his colleagues and enjoyed the devotion offered by his neighbours. He could give himself up wholeheartedly to the glory that he had achieved; relish the magnificence, toss down bumper after bumper, drink until his guests sprawled stupefied in their chairs. Early the next morning, well mounted on one of those rare great horses that could carry him, this huge gross man would be galloping across his fields and heaths, his hounds in full cry after hare or fox. After a full day in the saddle, he returned to gargantuan meals, deep drinking, and the affairs of state. Day after day the couriers rode into Houghton from Whitehall, bearing despatches not only from ambassadors abroad but also those confidential reports about the Court which his absence required. Naturally these did not add to his peace of mind. With usual Walpolean foresight he had collected the major doubters of his policy at Houghton, well out of the way of the royal family, but there were others who were only too eager to exploit his absence. Hatorff, the King's Hanoverian minister at St James's, in particular made all the mischief he could. A man of first-class ability, Hatorff was sincerely attached to the Emperor's cause and he played with great skill on the deep love of Germany which both George II and Caroline felt. For the next twelve months Walpole waged a continuous battle with Hatorff in order to prevent his views prevailing with the King.[2] His ideas

---

[1] Ilchester, *Lord Hervey and His Friends*, 180.
[2] Hervey, II, 342–3: 'a clear-sighted, artful fellow . . . a man of great temper,

proved far more dangerous than the doubts and anxieties of Walpole's colleagues in the cabinet; their fears were never formulated with the cogency and precision of Hatorff's arguments. Indeed, the need to counter Hatorff's steady and brilliant advocacy of the Austrian cause led Walpole to spend far longer in the preparation of the arguments for his own policy than was his wont. So what hours he could save from hunting and feasting he spent in his library, drawing up memoranda in favour of the policy of neutrality which he wished to pursue.

If the secret reports of Hatorff's activities disturbed the carefree conviviality of these November days, the antics of the opposition brought nothing but amusement, and doubtless many an ironic toast was drained at their expense. Of course, they were in close contact with Chavigny, the French ambassador, and Carteret had had him to stay at Haynes during the summer months. He gave Chavigny every encouragement and approved warmly of France's resolution to go to war, if need be, on Stanislaus's behalf. He left Chavigny in no doubt that the opposition would follow a policy which called for peace; his encouragement of France's intransigence was merely a desperate hope that it would so provoke George II that he would override Walpole and insist on help being given to the Emperor. Walpole, who read Chavigny's correspondence before Fleury received it, knew that if he succeeded in holding George II and Caroline in check then he could expect little or no trouble in the House of Commons on foreign affairs, and this, in itself, would help to justify his policy to his sovereign. The dilemma of the opposition played straight into his hands. Pulteney had been in Parliament long enough to know that a call to the backbenchers for war on Austria's behalf for the sake of the Polish crown would fall on stony ground. Indeed, realizing that the Commons were being manoeuvred into a bi-

and could reason with decency, and yet as full hard to be either convinced or persuaded as his master.' It is probable that the paper printed by Coxe, III, 147–8, was written by RW to rebuff Hatorff.

partisan foreign policy by Walpole's skilful handling of the
Court, Pulteney tried to evade the snare by composing an
indictment of the ministry's foreign policy from the time the
Walpoles' influence had become paramount. As Parliament
assembled, he published *The Politicks on both sides with regard
to Foreign Affairs:*[1] and with the neatness and adroitness which
made him so formidable a debater and pamphleteer, he held
all policies to blame, all action calamitous, and the Walpoles
responsible for everything.

'In short whichever way we turn ourselves, or whatever
side we take, if we take any, we shall not only involve our
selves in a dangerous and expensive war but likewise incur
the reproach and resentment of *one side* or the *other:* since
both of them think themselves intitled to our assistance.

If, to avoid these difficulties, we choose a state of
absolute neutrality, and leave the *opposite powers* to dispute their
own quarrel among themselves, the consequence may be
fatal to Europe, and at length involve *Us* in the common
calamity.

The question therefore recurs, *what is to be done?—Or
is anything to be done?*—Ought we to involve ourselves in a
war in which we have *no particular interest* concerned?—Or
shall we sit down in quiet, and run the hazard of seeing
Europe become a prey to the arms of the *conqueror?*—For
my part, I cannot pretend to answer these questions; and
the present situation of affairs is surrounded with so many
difficulties on every side, that I believe the wisest man in
England, as I said before, would be at a loss to judge what
is most expedient in *such a crisis.* But one thing seems to be
very obvious; that *those persons* who have intangled us in
the *present difficulties,* are the most unlikely to work us out of
them again: . . .'[2]

One of the main reasons why Pulteney wished to be in a
position to argue for either war or peace was his uncertainty
about the ministry's intentions. Rumours reached him in
plenty. Newcastle's anxiety, Grafton's desire to please,

---

[1] Vaucher, *Walpole et la Politique de Fleury,* 81, establishes the authorship of
the pamphlet.
[2] [W. Pulteney], *The Politicks on Both Sides,* 69.

Harrington's flaunting of independent judgment were common enough knowledge: George II never kept his opinions to himself. After the grave crisis of excise, it scarcely seemed possible—at least to Pulteney—that Walpole could force his own opinion on a reluctant Court and sovereign. So he could write, even as late as 17 December 1733: 'This nation never was in a more extraordinary situation. The ministers themselves are, I believe, even at this time as undetermined what part to take as they are fearful of taking any . . .'[1] When, however, he attributes this indecision to the lack of the ministry's knowledge of the opposition's intentions, he betrays both his vanity, his prejudice and his credulity. He should have known that the opposition's views, as far as they had any, had circulated in the red despatch boxes which conveyed the deciphered foreign correspondence to the inner Cabinet.[2] It was even more ludicrous for him to assume that Walpole, lover of expedients as he was, would permit his policy to be guided by men in opposition.

The overriding consideration which Walpole kept before his colleagues and his master was Parliament—Parliament which had been so disturbed by excise and whose life drew to an end in 1734. Everything must wait on the election. Indeed the election had begun. County after county had chosen candidates; every post brought Walpole new problems of influence and patronage. All the electors, great and small, knew that they were unlikely to be so eagerly courted for another seven years; candidates felt that any refusal by Walpole might jeopardize their chances of success. Mr Tizzard, aged seventy, scarcely able to read or write, must, wrote Thomas Pearce of the Navy Office, be promoted the next Surveyor of Customs at Weymouth, otherwise Pearce himself might very easily be out of Parliament. On no account, wrote Gordon, must Mr Tizzard, the incom-

---

[1] HMC., *Mar and Kellie MSS*, 529.
[2] For proof that despatch boxes were already in use for the circulation of secret papers to the Cabinet, see HMC, *Egmont's Diary*, I, 371.

petent creature of Turner, whose influence, due to his ownership of the Portland quarries, was far too great at Weymouth, be allowed to be the next Surveyor of the Customs at Weymouth. It would ruin the government interest and spoil Gordon's chances.[1] Nicolas Wenn, clerk to the common brewer of Peterborough, offered to transport himself and friends to Norfolk and vote for any candidate so long as in return Walpole could find him a place in the excise. John Hedworth insisted on immediate promotion for a Lambton; the party situation in Durham called for quick action. His friend Liddell, not to be outdone, sent in a sheaf of requests. Ralph Jenison, scared about Northumberland, insisted that his client succeed as manager of the forfeited Derwentwater estates. Samuel Pleydell, Molly's cousin many times removed, felt himself fully qualified to discharge both the land surveyor's and tide surveyor's job in Greenock, and, of course, he reminded Walpole that his father, himself and his friends voted for Robert Hucks at Abingdon, where votes were few and competition severe. George Dennis insisted that he must have the lease of the lodge and deer park of Liskeard, property of the Duchy of Cornwall and now in the Prince of Wales's gift; otherwise he trembled for Liskeard's fate in the coming election. An unknown correspondent from Edinburgh demanded the immediate recall of Charles Lesley, 'one of the bloodyest mouthed of patriots', to his regiment which he had not seen for two years, otherwise the elections in Fife would go against the government. The Duke of Richmond, unwilling to face the deep Sussex mire, asked Walpole to negotiate about Shoreham with Frederick, his rival. It was most important, Richmond thought, that Frederick should agree to his paying half the cost of the votes. (Obviously Richmond feared that he would make a deal with someone else for the second seat.) Lord Berkshire demanded a pension for an aged spinster relative; Jenison never slow to ask, a promotion for his son in the army.[2]

[1] *C(H) MSS*, Thomas Pearce, 29 November 1733; Mr Gordon, 4 December 1733.
[2] *C(H) MSS*, Letters, Nos. 1984–2097.

And so it went on, mainly simple, straightforward demands but sometimes as odd and as strangely devious as this from Henry Bromley, the MP for Cambridgeshire:

'I received two petitions for application to you, the one in behalf of Mr Underwood to be a commissioner in bankruptcy, the other from Mr Dixon to be clerk of the estreats. They are both particular friends of Shepheards[1] and encouraged by him in order to put me under the necessity of disobeying the people of the country or unseasonably fall out with you but as I design not to fall into either trapp, I shall ask both these favours and desire you to grant me neither, and if I should have any more demands, as I expect many, of the same nature I shall take the liberty of making my application in the same manner.'

Naturally he wanted the refusals to be 'as agreable as refusals can be' and, displaying a delightful finesse, he went on to suggest that the vacant prebendary's stall at Norwich should go to Dr Towers, Master of Christ's College, who would be thereby effectively fixed in Walpole's and Bromley's interest. Walpole, however, was not to be so easily had and evaded the claims of the sour, morose, irascible Master of Christ's.[2] Nevertheless, the rest of Bromley's letter must have given him real pleasure. To create obligation by not granting offices was a rare experience for Sir Robert.

Each of these demands, and, of course, these represent only a few from a list which could be almost endlessly extended, required the most careful consideration of contingencies. There was far too little patronage; each decision meant a refusal for someone and the possibility of enmity: the reactions of all involved needed careful assessment. Where gratification was not possible, hope for the future must take its place, and it required a nice judgment to decide when hope was turning sour. This was all a familiar game to Walpole, as familiar to him as the crowds that thronged his

[1] Samuel Shepheard of Horseheath was MP for Cambridgeshire, 1724–48.
[2] *C(H) MSS*, H. Bromley, 11 December 1733; J. Peile, *Biographical Register of Christ's College*, II, 137. Towers was known to be an ardent whig and at loggerheads with the University tories, so needed no fixing.

doors on his return from Houghton. But the pace was more furious, the sense of conflict more urgent throughout the country; anxiety greater, and the need to avoid all risks stronger than ever before. Walpole needed more than dexterous exploitation of patronage to see himself safely secure in the Parliament to come; every bit of good will, every shred of ancient loyalty, needed to be cossetted.

'I received the favour of your letter', wrote the Duke of Kent, old, neglected, forgotten, on 15 December 1733, 'and am very much obliged to you for thinking I have any interest in this county[1] worth being desired or wished for; but I have more to say on that subject than I can put into a letter and as I shall be in town in about ten days, shall reffer myself 'till I have the honnour of seeing you there. As for Sir Rowland Alston,[2] tho I have no reason to like him, nor his behaviour to me, yet my resentment would not carry me so far but I would give it up if the publick required it, and I have no fear that the country will goe at any time against my inclination, having never lost any ellection here these 30 years but I have been thought of late a person of so little consequence that I think the less I have to doe in any of these matters the better, and only desire to live well with all my neighbours.'[3]

The overtones and undertones of this letter must have depressed Walpole, for they reverberate with self-importance, a sense of neglect, reluctance to please, a desire to arouse anxiety. Yet no matter how urgent foreign affairs might be, no matter how long he needed to spend with George II and

[1] Bedfordshire.
[2] Sir Rowland Alston, 3rd Bt., MP Beds., 1722–41, had endangered his position as Knight of the Shire by voting for the Excise Bill, hence Walpole's concern to prevent Kent becoming a declared enemy. Also Alston was not an easy man to deal with, as may be seen from this letter written to RW shortly afterwards. 'I humbly beg you'l please to turn out the person who hath the Post Office in Bedford; she is the wife of Alderman Okely who was bribed by the tories to put the corporation into their hands, and I do assure you there is a general complaint against her in the county for misbehaviour in her office. The person I would recommend in her room is one, Mr John Day, brother to Alderman Day.' C(H) MSS, Sir Rowlnd Alston, Bt., 15 February, 1734.
[3] C(H) MSS, Kent, 15 December 1733.

Queen Caroline, all the vast unfolding complexity of the election had to be kept in the forefront of business and never neglected. Walpole was used by long training to carry an almost intolerable weight of business, but never in his life did he shoulder a heavier one than during these months that saw a crisis at home followed by a crisis abroad, and both overshadowed by a general election as critical as any that he had so far faced.

These were special circumstances for which, however, Walpole's daily work did not stop. A new session of Parliament required a budget—a highly elaborate, time-consuming business which required hours of work in going over the figures provided by the Treasury clerks as well as in endless discussions with departmental chiefs. And as the session drew nearer he needed to prime his men of business on the details of policy to be pursued in the Commons. In all these things his own personal intervention was vital. Furthermore, throughout his career as the King's chief minister Walpole had personally supervized the vast web of anti-Jacobite intelligence which he had created in Europe. His principle was never to reject the slightest offer of help and to encourage the merest flicker of treachery, although this frequently led to a waste of time and money on the broken-down riff-raff who drifted about the capitals of Europe in the hope of trading gossip and mystery for the sake of a crust. Unfortunately, at one of the busiest moments of his life, the brother of Sir Roger Martin, a popish priest, offered to make disclosures about Jacobite plots, hinting even at the possibility of an invasion from St Malo, but hinting so evasively that no one could tell what he really meant. 'I tryed him and turned him all ways I could think of', wrote Waldegrave, who interviewed him in Paris, 'to fix him to any one single point relating to the plots that he says are carrying on in favour of the Pretender, but to no purpose; he rambled from one thing to another.' The one thing that Martin was quite adamant about was that he should be allowed £50 to go to England to see Walpole. On 31 January 1734, after some weeks of correspondence with Waldegrave and Thomas Pelham, his secretary, Walpole finally ordered the £50 for Martin's visit to England.[1] It was, of course, a matter which he could not neglect; a threatened Jacobite invasion, based on the flimsiest of rumours, could be turned into grist and emerge as a telling argument for avoiding the entanglements of European war.

More deadly, however, both for Walpole's peace of mind and for his work, was the trouble about Dr Rundle. Sydall, Bishop of Gloucester had become a sick man. Someone— Caroline, Lady Sundon, goodness knows who—had let it be known that Rundle would succeed him, for when Walpole returned from Houghton in the middle of December, he found the Bishop of London in umbrage. Appointments were the Bishop's province, a part of that pact sealed long ago between Gibson and Walpole and Townshend. Rundle was a light-hearted man who spoke gaily of Revelation and was not at all sound by Gibson's standards, on miracles or the Trinity; nevertheless his unorthodoxy and his lively social charm had impressed Caroline sufficiently to make her wish to assert herself and to get a bishopric for him. Walpole had scarcely settled into Downing Street for Christmas when a polite but ominously firm letter reached him from Gibson.[2] 'My own judgment and the regard I owe to my character and the general sense of the bishops and clergy will not permit me to concur or acquiesce in it either of which in my present situation would be interpreted as sacrificing the cause of the Church to my own private views'; therefore Gibson begged to withdraw from all Church matters; the only way, he felt, to avoid displeasing the Court and the Lord

---

[1] This affair, which Coxe, III, 143, muddled with an earlier scare about a plot to assassinate RW, stretched from 10 November 1733 to February 1734 and the considerable correspondence can be followed in *C(H) MSS*, which contain Martin's letters to RW (missed by Coxe); Waldegrave, 17 and 27 December 1733, 17 January 1734 (N.S.); also *Waldegrave MSS*, RW to Thomas Pelham, 10 and 15 November 1733; RW to Waldegrave, 31 January 1734. See also Coxe, III, 141–3.

[2] Printed with some slight omissions and without date by Sykes, *Gibson*, 414. The letter was written on 18 December 1733, *C(H) MSS*, 18 December.

Chancellor, who was as keen as Caroline to get Rundle in.[1] This put Walpole in a quandary. He was having trouble enough in keeping his colleagues, as well as his sovereign, steadily in line with his foreign policy. Both George II and Caroline had grown bad tempered at his refusal to budge an inch from his declared policy of neutrality. He did not relish bullying them about a minor Church appointment. And yet he could not lose Gibson, whose well-drilled cohorts of bishops had saved him from disaster in the previous parliamentary session. If they deserted him now, he would be lost—a calculation which, of course, Gibson was as capable of making as he was. For once Walpole must have prayed for a bishop to live; so long as Sydall clung to life at Gloucester prevarication might be possible. Sydall, however, did not oblige; he died on Christmas Eve.[2] Unfortunately the meeting of Parliament would bring the bishops together and enable Gibson to marshal them on a common front. Walpole knew he was caught. Rundle could not go to Gloucester. Sooner or later Walpole would have to face that fact; he preferred later to sooner and prevaricated.[3]

He prevaricated because there was nothing else he could do, for despite the welter of business in which he found himself, he had to devote most of his time after his return from Houghton to recovering ground at Court which he had lost during his absence. Under the constant and cunning pressure of Hatorff both George II and Caroline had begun to waver again in their allegiance to Walpole's policy. They had been won over to it reluctantly and Hatorff knew as well as anyone how to exploit their German prejudices. Over-confidence, a reluctance to break the habits of a lifetime, may have been responsible for Walpole's folly in leaving the Court for Houghton at such a critical juncture. The election, the budget, the Jacobite scare, the crisis in the Church,

---

[1] *C(H) MSS*, Gibson, 18 December 1733. From 'either of which' to end of quote omitted by Sykes, *loc. cit.*

[2] *Handbook of British Chronology*, 149.

[3] He persuaded both the Lord Chancellor and Gibson to let the matter rest until after the general election. Sykes, *Gibson*, 270.

were each enough to absorb the energies of one hard-
working man; and now his foreign policy once again required a major effort. The sympathies of the King and Queen
had been effectively undermined and Walpole needed to
muster all his powers of persuasion. Hatorff, who wrote
as well as he talked, drew up at the Queen's suggestion,
for she was tired of endless argument, a memorandum
stressing the overriding reasons for intervention. It impressed both George II and Caroline. Hatorff could not have
timed his intervention more perfectly—a day or two before
Christmas 1733. Only a few working days remained for
Walpole before Parliament met. The King's Speech needed
to be drafted and the speech must give some indication of
policy. If the King refused to commit himself to neutrality,
Walpole could expect a renewed crisis. Fortunately the
Queen gave Walpole Hatorff's memorandum, and on
Christmas Eve he drew up a masterly summary of what he
thought British policy should be. It displays Walpole at his
best—clear, concise, realistic, single-minded; his aim to
seek peace by all expedients and not to contemplate war
until all were found to be barren. In its simplicity and cogency it evokes the arguments to which their Majesties were
daily subjected; the King cross, fidgety, impatient, and by his
side the vast, ornate bulk of Walpole, the red, authoritative
face, the firm, even voice, the sense of immovable power
against which the irritation of George II or Caroline broke
in vain.[1] Steadily, remorselessly, day after day, Walpole
went over the arguments which he felt compelled neutrality.
He never wavered, never tired, never allowed other business
or other anxieties to distract his attention. His authority, his
experience, the full weight of his personality were called into
play; this was the crisis of his relationship with his sovereign
and he could not, dare not, lose. All his instincts told him
that no minister who called for war could survive in the
Commons. His greatness depended on harmony between the
Commons and the Court.

[1] Coxe, III, 147–8.

BY THE time Parliament met on 17 January 1734, Walpole had, at least temporarily, won his battle against Hatorff and the secret waverers in his own cabinet. He phrased the King's Speech with great skill. Terse by nature, Walpole required more words than usual to stress the delicacy of the diplomatic situation: the determination of the ministry not to act alone but to seek to mediate with the Dutch; to call for increased supplies in case war proved unavoidable; to insist on unanimity and to plead for a choice of new representatives at the coming general election that would impress Europe by the unity of the Crown and the nation. Long as it was, the Speech gave nothing away, and the opposition were driven to particularly obvious tactics to try to elucidate the policy which the ministry were pursuing in Europe. Day after day one opposition member after another got to his feet and demanded information. Sir John Rushout demanded that instructions sent to British ambassadors in France and Spain relating to the execution of the Treaty of Seville be laid before the House; Sandys wanted those given to the minister in Poland; Waller proposed that the King be addressed to know how far he was engaged, by his good offices, in the causes of the war against the Emperor; Sandys tried again, asking for an account of what application, if any, had been made to the King by the parties engaged in the war. Walpole brushed these aside with contempt—two without a division, and on the other motions the opposition could only muster 114 and 104. As Horatio jibed, to the amusement of the House, the opposition wanted to know the ministry's policy so that they could decide on what to oppose. If Walpole wanted justification for his policy of patience and a demonstrable answer to the pleading of Hatorff, it was ready at hand—the independent country-gentlemen did not want war. They were content to let Walpole pursue his policy; indeed his skill in controlling the King, whose views everyone knew, for George II was not the man to dissemble his opinions, had done much to re-establish Walpole's political ascendancy in the Commons.

Conscious of this, and knowing how bitterly resented and feared excise still was throughout the countryside, the opposition attempted to revive the controversy by engineering a petition of tea-dealers against the excise laws on their merchandise which, however, they had suffered without complaint for fourteen years. Barnard did his best and the old arguments reverberated once more through St Stephen's. Time, however, had staled them. A few with a keen eye on the coming election joined the opposition lobby, which mustered 155, but there was no danger here for Walpole. So far the opposition had failed to inflame the Commons, or to arouse even a reflection of the passions which had stirred it in previous sessions.

More warmth was engendered on 13 February 1734, when Lord Morpeth moved, in the Committee stage of the annual mutiny Bill, that officers in the army should not be removed except by courts martial or by an address by both Houses of Parliament. The third Duke of Marlborough, who had recently succeeded to his dukedom, moved a similar motion in the House of Lords—much to the satisfaction of old Sarah, who hated Walpole with the full force of her turbulent spirit. These motions gave vast offence to the King, who fumed and stormed at Court, cursing Marlborough, Bedford, Morpeth and all who gave them countenance. The fact that the Court would be agitated spiced the debate; in any case it touched some of the most cherished attitudes of eighteenth-century gentlemen. Pulteney sat silent in his corner, but as the debate grew warmer he could restrain himself no longer and spoke sooner than he intended. With his usual skill, urbanity and wit he touched on the deep-seated prejudices of the uncommitted—the power which dismissal gave to a ruthless minister, the monstrosity of depriving a man of what after all was as much his freehold as the land that he had purchased, and this, too, for following his conscience and the public good, and he scoffed at the ministry's plea that security of tenure would lead to a third estate—for surely both brother officers and the two Houses of Parliament could be relied upon to maintain public liberties. This was the sort of performance that an eighteenth-century parliament enjoyed, a cunning mixture of principle and prejudice done with grace and clarity. Yet it was done too soon; by the time Henry Pelham had methodically, competently, decently and dully answered not only Pulteney but all who had spoken before him, the effect of his speech had worn off. Not even the charm and wit of Sir William Wyndham could revive it: in any case, the cause was lost. The ministry, early in the debate, had expressed their strong disapproval of any lessening of the King's prerogative; on the face of it this seemed foolish, throwing tricks into the opposition whigs' lap, who were quick to display the unsullied nature of their whiggery and to accuse the ministry of being crypto-tories. However, such pleas were not meant for whig ears. Shippen heard the siren's note, never stirred from his seat and, as ever, more ardent for his principles than the defeat of the ministry, made sure by his defection that the opposition was resoundingly defeated on a motion upon which it commanded a great deal of independent support.[1]

Naturally, with an election almost at hand, the opposition trotted out all the old saviours of the constitution; a qualification bill was introduced and quashed; the yearly place bill met with a like fate, yet this year Walpole preferred to kill it in the Commons rather than leave it for the bishops to destroy in the Lords, an action which as usual exercised the conscience of Lord Egmont. Naturally Egmont approved of place bills in principle; naturally he disliked such disturbers of public tranquillity as Shippen, Wyndham, Pulteney. If he voted against the Bill, on grounds that the time was not expedient, he would be thought to be a pensioner, an idea which filled him with horror, for he was conscious of his rectitude in such matters (true, a few weeks before he had demanded a sinecure for life for his brother from Walpole,

[1] Chandler, VIII, 88–120; HMC, *Carlisle MSS*, 132–3.

but at such moments uncomfortable recollections rarely came Egmont's way). So Egmont cut the Commons that day, and with smug self-righteousness deplored the fact that the ministry stopped the Bill at its second reading and did not permit its committal. It is fascinating to observe how the fine-meshed net of patronage entangled a conscience as subtle as Egmont's. Those with less hope of place proved of greater courage and went into the opposition lobby to register their disapproval of what they were unlikely to enjoy.[1]

However, these were preliminary skirmishes, debates which had become almost a part of the formal ritual of the parliamentary session; in this election year the opposition had decided to make their set piece for the display of oratory the demand for the repeal of the Septennial Act, a favourite not only of those independent members of small fortune but also of multitudes of voters who thought their freehold should receive its reward more than once in seven years. To those few austere men of principle it was a self-evident truth that frequent parliaments would end corruption. Knowing that the opposition would deploy their finest talent in this debate, Walpole started his counter-moves early, lobbying Egmont and many another self-styled independent, for he knew that seven-year parliaments lay uneasily on many a conscience.[2] He was also fully aware that more would be needed for such a debate than the point-by-point refutation of the enemy's case to which so many of his earnest but dull colleagues were addicted.

Gossip had so well advertised the debate that the Commons was crowded to overflowing: the repeal of the Septennial Act was proposed by young William Bromley, the heir of an incorruptible tory tradition.[3] His short, pointed speech stressed

---

[1] HMC, *Egmont's Diary*, II, 37–8. Egmont, of course, was in no way unique; as well as his brother, Parker, the two Towers, Moore and Page all thought that discretion and conscience demanded their absence from the Commons.

[2] *Ibid.*, II, 39.

[3] His father, William Bromley, MP for Warwickshire and Oxford University, had sat in Parliament from 1689 to his death in 1732; he had never

the old precepts of parliamentary independence; recalled that clause of the Bill of Rights which demanded frequent parliaments; reminded the House that the Septennial Act had been passed because of the emergency caused by the Jacobite invasion of 1715-16; and maintained that his motion had the support of the common people. Sir John St Aubyn, who seconded the motion, naturally, as he was a Cornishman, dwelt on the increase of bribery and corruption that a seven-year tenure engendered. The government speakers raised the ogre of Jacobitism, laying at its door all the difficulties and tribulations (not excluding excise) which had overtaken the ministry. And, of course, it was just as self-evident to the Court that long tenure created independence as it was to the country that it encouraged subservience. And so the hours passed—blunt statements from back benchers followed by long, ornate, self-satisfied, tedious speeches of ministerial hangers-on, like Sir Thomas Robinson, who hoped to enlarge their reputations; and every hour or so a brilliant, well-turned, carefully set piece of oratory brought relief—Barnard, Wyndham, Shippen at their best, and Pulteney as witty and as persuasive as only Pulteney could be; these, and the abrupt short statements of squires unused to speaking, gave the opposition the run of the debate. And, although the conclusion was perhaps foregone, the extent of the ministry's majority was of importance to Walpole; a narrow victory would strengthen the opposition's propaganda, and this Walpole could not tolerate.[1] He held himself in reserve to the very end, speaking only after all the great orators of the opposition had had their say. As soon as Pulteney sat down, he rose in his corner by the Speaker's Chair and made one of the most dramatic speeches of his parliamentary career. He

deviated from his 'country' principles. He was Speaker from 1710-13 and Secretary of State 1713-14.

[1] The best account of the arguments used in the debate is to be found in HMC, *Egmont's Diary*, II, 35-58. Egmont does not mention Walpole's attack on Bolingbroke; Coxe, I, 426-7 based his account on Chandler, VIII, 203-09. See also HMC, *Carlisle MSS*, 133.

used what was rare for him—surprise and rhetoric. He began
with a blistering denunciation of Bolingbroke, whom he
accused, in the thin disguise of the 'Anti-Minister' of not
only raising up factious opposition out of disappointment and
malice but also of trading secrets with his country's enemies—
both remarkable activities for a pardoned traitor. This, of
course, was so unexpected in its intensity and savagery that
it electrified the House, and made them doubly attentive to
the short discourse which Walpole gave them on the mixed
nature of their Constitution, the danger of strengthening
the democratic part of it and the necessity for any ministry
to have security for longer than three years if any stability in
policy was to be achieved. As for bribery and corruption, he
brushed it aside with his usual healthy realism: he did not
deny it, but made the shrewd point that it was easier to
bribe when there was no strong political passion to divide a
nation, when therefore it was largely irrelevant; and of
course, he larded his harangue with well-judged phrases on
the country's need for security and tranquillity. It was a
splendid, forceful speech—realistic, hard-headed yet passionate—on this occasion, in the sincerity of his convictions and
his hatred of Bolingbroke. It carried the day, comfortably,
if not overwhelmingly, by 247 votes to 184.

In this speech and in this debate, Walpole had done far
more than repel a threat to the Septennial Act. His attack
on Bolingbroke was not the mere expression of long-felt
resentment. As always with Walpole, it was the result of
deliberation and meant for a purpose. Walpole knew his
enemies better even than his friends. He watched them
tirelessly; every shred of gossip, every letter that he could
intercept was seized upon, sifted, digested, remembered. He
possessed the patience of Fabius and the capacity of a
Marlborough for surprise and attack. Wyndham, with his
sneers at his position in the State, with his mockery of
the evil minister and the deluded King, had given him the
opening he sought to drive deep and hard between whigs and
tories by the exposure of Bolingbroke's secret communi-

cations with Chauvelin and the French Court, and his acceptance of presents from the French for the information which he passed on. There was little unusual in this: Walpole was at the moment buying, if the right price could be found, the services of a highly-placed member of the French Court. Probably such activities of Bolingbroke could not be adjudged treasonable, for the information that he passed on was mere gossip and his own interpretation of the direction English policy was likely to take with regard to the affairs of Poland. England was not at war with France; indeed they were allies. On the other hand, Bolingbroke had been convicted of treason in the past, and this fresh evidence of his deceit might be used by Walpole to pay off old scores. Certainly in Walpole's savage irony lay a threat even if undefined. Yet the purpose of his speech was political rather than personal; to expose to men such as Barnard, Pulteney and other dissident whigs the nature of their allies. Walpole knew that the leaders of the opposition were at cross purposes and he wished to exacerbate their divisions.[1]

According to Hervey 'Lord Carteret and Lord Bolingbroke had no correspondence at all; Mr Pulteney and Lord Bolingbroke hated one another; Lord Carteret and Pulteney were jealous of one another; Sir William Wyndham and Pulteney the same; whilst Lord Chesterfield had a little correspondence with them all, but was confided in by none of them.'[2] Even after allowance has been made for Hervey's delight in symmetry, much truth remains; the alliance between tories and dissident whigs had been uneasy for some time and was strained further by Pulteney's line of attack in the Septennial debate. As Pulteney himself wrote: 'I urged that the people had but two ways of helping themselves, if they found the government attacking them or their representatives betraying them, and these two ways were re-election and re-

[1] For Bolingbroke's intrigues with the French see Vaucher, *La Crise du Ministére Walpole en 1733-4*, 64-5, and the evidence quoted there: see also *Waldegrave MSS* for Waldegrave-Walpole negotiations about suborning a leading French minister.
[2] Hervey, I, 256.

sistance . . . the torys did not much approve of it, being so
contrary to their notions of passive obedience and seeming to
justify the Revolution. You see, therefore, how hard it is in
this critical situation to conduct oneself to the satisfaction of
both sides. It is this jealousy that makes the well meaning
dissenters fearful that what we are doing may establish their
enemies the tories in power.'[1]

These were all symptoms, not causes. The excise crisis had
been as disastrous for the opposition as for Walpole. Bolingbroke, perhaps, was alone in perceiving this. That bitterly
fought battle had pushed Chesterfield, Bolton, Cobham and
many another life-long whig into opposition. Naturally they
drew together with Pulteney, but even then their alliance
never became so warm-hearted as it was with each other. The
majority were peers: in the House of Lords they had come
within a vote of defeating Walpole. They were well aware of
his new weaknesses in their house—the dissatisfaction of
Gibson and many bishops over the long struggle about the
diocese of Gloucester and the heretic Rundle. They were
even more keenly aware of Walpole's dependence on the
Scottish peers for his certain majority. At once they drew
together and began an elaborate campaign to try to secure
sixteen opposition Scottish Lords in the coming election, and
to this end met with great regularity in order to set up a
most elaborate organization, which involved a secret postal
service to Scotland. (They knew too well Walpole's control
of the Post Office to trust it with their correspondence.)[2]
From these secret meetings Bolingbroke and the tories were
excluded. For Chesterfield, Cartaret, Bolton and the rest,
with their eyes on the Court and ministerial office, tories

---

[1] Edinburgh Register House, *Mar and Kellie MSS*, W. Pulteney, 24 February
1734.
[2] The postal service was set up by December 1733: on 15 January 1734 they
founded the Liberty or Rumpsteak Club: the chief members were Bedford,
Bolton, Carteret, Chesterfield, Queensberry, Marchmont; they met every
Tuesday during the session of Parliament to keep up each other's spirits and
to plan tactics: *Papers of the Earls of Marchmont*, ed. Sir George Rose (1831), II,
12, 19. For the origin of the name and George II's reaction to it, see *Egmont's
Diary*, ii, 14, 53.

could never be allies. They wished to avoid the odour of
Jacobitism which many of them exuded; neither had they
much belief in Bolingbroke's ability. They preferred to
direct their own campaigns; the tories would be in the
opposition lobby in any case.

Bolingbroke realized this with clarity. Writing many years
later, he said: 'Long before I left Britain, it was plain that
some persons meant that the opposition should serve as *their*
scaffolding, nothing else; and whenever they had a glimpse
of hope, that they might rise to power without it, they showed
the greatest readiness to demolish it.'[1] Nor was this an
arrière pensée; in his *Letters on the Spirit of Patriotism,* written no
later than 1736, he expresses himself even more bitterly.

'Whilst the minister was not hard pushed, nor the
prospect of succeeding him near, they appeared to have
but one end, the reformation of government. The destruction of the minister was pursued only as a preliminary
but of essential and indispensable necessity to that end.
But when his destruction seemed to approach, the *object*
of his *succession* interposed to the sight of many, and the
reformation of the *government* was no longer their point of
view. They divided the skin, at least in their thoughts,
before they had taken the beast: and the common fear
of hunting him down for others made them all faint in
the chace.'[2]

Except for the last phrase it was all true: they did not
grow faint in the chase, the hunters had become exclusive. It
is, however, a mark of Bolingbroke's fine intelligence that he
was so quick to perceive these subtle changes in the nature of
the opposition to Walpole. There remained no future for him.
He was nearly sixty. His long battle with Walpole had resulted not in a prospect of a mixed ministry, should Walpole
ever fall, but of an alternative whig government. Long before
Walpole exposed his intrigues in the Commons and published
them abroad in the pamphlet *The Grand Accuser—The
Greatest of All Criminals,* Bolingbroke had realized that his last

[1] *Papers of the Earls of Marchmont,* ed. Sir George Rose (1831), II, 273.
[2] *Letters on the Spirit of Patriotism,* ed. A. Hassall (Oxford, 1926), 25.

throw against his lifelong rival had failed. He waited to see
the outcome of the election, but shortly afterwards made his
plans to withdraw to France, where he played the philoso-
pher as he had played the politician with the same curious
mixture of subtlety, banality and fraud.

Walpole detested Bolingbroke, a man far cleverer than
himself, and one possessing more subtlety, more insight, more
skill in political analysis. Bolingbroke, even if he exaggerated,
realized the dangers of corruption for an elected assembly,
realized, too, the growing chasm between government by
oligarchy and the tide of popular opinion. The dangers of
isolation, the duplicity of France, the renewal of the conflict for empire, all of these matters were clearer far to
Bolingbroke than to Walpole. Yet it is the men of plain
common sense, who can fill all who know them with a sense
of security and authority, who govern; the Bolingbrokes are
born to oppose and to fail. Bolingbroke did not possess the
temperament of a martyr. He displayed the brilliance of his
mind at his dinner table; wrote with splendid venom for the
fashionable newspapers, fathered pamphlets that sparkled
with debating points good, bad and fraudulent. He could not
dedicate his life to simple political principles and pursue
them year in, year out, and accept the trials and tribulations
that come to men committed to simple attitudes of mind.
Bolingbroke could not convince anyone that this demand for
a change of measures as well as men was made with true sincerity. For Bolingbroke could not forbear to cheat; there was
a twist, a bias in his nature, that drew him irresistibly to
duplicity. The secret game was all his delight; his lust for
intrigue would have been dangerous in a man of unassailable
authority, for a pardoned traitor opposed to his country's
government it was fatal. And yet this devious character
wrings a reluctant admiration from all who study his life.
The quickness of his intellect, the clarity of his prose, and the
skill with which for nearly ten years he raised, led, and controlled one of the most brilliant oppositions in the history of
English politics, are the astonishing attributes of an astonish-

ing man. Fate has not been kind to his name. Many have come to regard his drunkenness, his lechery, his atheism as reflections of the essential weakness of his character, forgetting that Walpole drank as deeply, wenched as ardently in word if not in deed, and paid as scant respect to the Almighty as any Bolingbroke; yet the fibres of Walpole's temperament were as strong as rope, Bolingbroke's as frail as gossamer—at least in the eyes of those commonplace, dull, unremarkable men who through luck of birth drifted into Parliament. Perhaps the insight into politics which Bolingbroke undeniably possessed was all the more penetrating because he could never, in his heart, belong to a party, or a cause. Loyalty was as alien to his nature as honesty of purpose: neither is important in the diagnosis of politics; both are essential for the acquisition of power. The strategy of parliamentary politics demands consistency to a few simple, fixed principles no matter how devious the tactics may be in order to get them established. And it demands endurance, not merely for a few years, but if need be, for the best part of a lifetime. Bolingbroke lacked both. By the time the hammer-blows of Walpole's invective fell upon him, his interest in the political struggle had already waned.

3

WALPOLE HANDLED the last session of his second Parliament with great skill. He had hamstrung the opposition on foreign affairs, which remained at the end where they were at the beginning. The interminable negotiations proceeded; sometimes George II grew exasperated, fumed that Horatio, who had now returned to The Hague, was more the ambassador of the Grand Pensionary than of the King of England. Mostly he saw the force of Walpole's arguments and was content. Of course, there were alarms and excursions; fears that Sir Thomas Robinson in Vienna was encouraging the Emperor and not pursuing Walpole's policy of neutrality with the fervour that Sir Robert required.

Walpole even worried lest his brother might fail to hold Britain and Holland to a common policy.[1] Yet war was held off, and when the King came to dissolve Parliament, Walpole put first things first in the speech which he drafted for him. After thanking them for the money voted, he pointed to their duty.

'I must in a particular manner,' the King told them, 'recommend it to you, and from your known affection do expect, that you will use your best endeavours to heal the unhappy divisions of the nation, and to reconcile the minds of all, who truly and sincerely wish the safety and welfare of the kingdom. It would be the greatest satisfaction to me to see a perfect harmony restored amongst them that have one and the same principle at heart, that there might be no distinction, but of such as mean the support of our present happy constitution in church and state, and such as wish to subvert both. This is the only distinction that ought to prevail in this country, where the interest of King and People is one and the same, and where they cannot subsist but by being so. If religion, liberty, and property, were never at any time more fully enjoyed, without not only any attempt, but even the shadow of a design, to alter and invade them, let not these sacred names be made use of, as artful and plausible pretences to undermine the present establishment, under which alone they can be safe.

'I have nothing to wish but that my people may not be misguided; I appeal to their own consciences for my conduct, and hope the providence of God will direct them in the choice of such representatives, as are most fit to be trusted with the care and preservation of the protestant religion, the present establishment, and all the religious and civil rights of Great-Britain.'[2]

[1] C(H) MSS, Letters 2153, 2153a, for the careful summaries of his brother's views which RW made presumably in order to be in complete control of the Dutch situation when he argued with the King: also Hervey, II, 346–54. Hervey was wrong in thinking HW pro war and RW's correction of Hervey on this point, p. 354, is in accordance with HW's despatches, see Walpole MSS, Despatches from The Hague, 1733–4.
[2] Chandler, VIII, 248–9: C(H) MSS, 65/49.1–3.

Fires which had been assiduously stoked for two, three or even four years, were not so easily quenched. Rarely had preparations for a general election been so elaborate. The Yorkshire tories, looking for a justification of their former history, hit on the memoirs of Sir John Reresby, an honest cavalier devoted to Charles II and James II; suitably edited, they were published in York to warm the faith of the old tory families. Not to be outdone, the whigs riposted with a massive inditement of tory iniquities, produced in eight parts (a relatively new method of publishing) so that it could be purchased by the poorer freeholders.[1] Pamphleteers had been as active as historians and an unending stream of caricatures, ballads, letters, arguments, appeals, inquiries, remarks, cases, considerations from the opposition presses swamped the modest vindications that attempted to calm the rage and passion that the word 'excise' still engendered.[2] Walpole, however, possessed one advantage over his enemies: his protagonists might be dull, though some like Malachi Postlethwayt were worthy enough,[3] but at least they could use the Post Office to make certain that every man jack employed by the government got the ministerial arguments for use in his local ale-house. Once a week, from 11 March to 8 June 1734, 2,050 copies of *The London Journal* were despatched, at a cost to the government of £272 1s. 8d., of

---

[1] *Memoirs of Sir John Reresby*, ed. A. Browning (Glasgow, 1936), x, n.1. *Revolution in Politics: being a compleat collection of all the Reports, Lyes and Stories which were the fore-runners of the Great Revolution in 1688 commencing from the Death of King Charles II. And from thence regularly continued to the settlement of the Prince and Princess of Orange upon the Throne. Wherein the several views and designs of all parties are exposed: and divers Jesuitical and Fanatical Intrigues are detailed and set in a true light. The complete 8 parts in 1 vol. London 1733.* For the publication in parts see R. M. Wiles, *Serial Publication in England* (Cambridge 1957).

[2] A full list of these pamphlets is to be found in EHR XLII (1927), 34–57, E. R. Turner, 'The Excise Crisis'.

[3] *C(H) MSS*, M. Postlethwayt, 10 June 1734. He asks for payment for the 3,000 pamphlets sent through the Post Office on Walpole's order; his letter ends: 'I have completed an answer to the piece called Politics on Both Sides etc. which I hope will meet with your Honours approbation and be a fresh testimony of my laborious endeavours to recommend myself effectively to your favour and regard'. This is the first known reference to Postlethwayt. *The Ministry and Government of Great Britain Vindicated*, which appeared in July 1734, is probably the pamphlet referred to by Postlethwayt.

which payment to the hack writers amounted to the modest sum of £50 for the three months. *The Daily Courant*,[1] however, was more extensively subsidised, for it printed Walpole's best amateur journalists—Bland, Hare and his brother, Horatio. Most expensive of all, however, was William Arnall's *Free Briton*. From January 1733 to January 1734 (for which the figures exist) Arnall was paid £3,435 for printing and distributing his newspaper. And as if this were not enough, Walpole countenanced the launching of *The Corn Cutter's Journal*, for which the Treasury paid out about £200 a quarter.[2] Naturally this enraged the opposition whose newspapers and pamphlets had the unhappy knack of lying about the Post Office for weeks on end and a positive genius for getting misdirected. Pulteney himself fulminated against the brazen use of the Post Office at this time to deluge the country with the Ministry's views.

'A multitude of select hands, in ministerial pay have been employed to frame apologies for him, of various kinds; and the poor hackney beasts of the Post Office have crouched under their burthen. Circular letters have been sent, in the name of Mr Jos. Bell, to all the postmasters in the kingdom, with orders to make these papers as publick as they can; to send up the names of all persons within their delivery, who keep the coffee houses, where gentlemen resort to read the news, that they likewise may be furnish'd with them gratis; and even most private

---

[1] Ralph Courteville was the principal hack journalist of the *Daily Courant:* his delight in his own efforts led him to send a copy of the *Daily Courant* personally to RW to make sure that he read it. C(H) MSS, Letters 2388 n.d. c. 1734.

[2] L. Hanson. *The Government and the Press*, 110–114. He is in error, however, in thinking that the *Corn Cutter's Journal* lasted only for eighteen months, see *Yale Edition of the Correspondence of Horace Walpole*, ed. W. S. Lewis, Mann Correspondence, I, 475. Nor was Hanson aware of the considerable correspondence on the government and the press in the C(H) MSS. The *London Journal's* bill is C(H) MSS, W. Wilkins, 11 June 1734. Wm. Arnall pestered Walpole, besieging him at levees and calling on him at eight o'clock in the morning in order to get money. He was an inveterate place seeker, in spite of what he himself called 'noble returns', and he deserved Pope's couplet;
'No crab more active in the dirty dance
Downward to climb or backward to advance.'
For his letters to Walpole: C(H) MSS, 26 March 1730, 27 April 1731, 6 December 1732 (where he speaks of his five years' service to the government), 12 April 1733, 10 August 1734.

families of any note have them crowded upon them by the same hands.'[1]

Not even in the days of Sacheverell had the Press played so vigorous a role in electioneering, and it certainly helped to exacerbate feeling which had almost come to boiling point. There was a widespread belief in the country that Walpole would fail. Bad harvests and falling trade had made his government exceptionally unpopular with the lower classes; the effect of the Excise Bill encouraged all tories, Jacobites, and dissident whigs to make a violent effort in their constituencies; while the uncertain temper of the times created a hothouse for all personal emotions and family feuds. The upshot was the most violent general election of the mid-eighteenth century, and the last for many decades in which a great public issue played some part. The triumph of the opposition Press was its consciousness of political principles—excise, corruption and the complete domination of government by one man.

The battles began early. At Stamford races, held in the fields near Burleigh House, the Earls of Exeter and Gainsborough, 'the Lords of the Confederacy' as the local historian named them, reviled the supporters of their whig enemy, Cust. Stones were soon flying through the air. Cust's men were driven off with bruised and broken heads, nor were their womenfolk spared.[2] Indeed, the story of the Stamford election reveals both the depth of feeling which this election engendered and the utterly unscrupulous nature of the methods used to win it. The Cecils' great house of Burleigh dominated this small Lincolnshire town, but the Custs of Friary Gate had tried for generations to maintain an in-

[1] W. Pulteney, *A Review of the Excise Scheme*, quot. Hanson, *op. cit.*, 109–110.
[2] *C(H) MSS*, Papers, 68/11. 'The Historical Part of Stamford Election, 24 April 1734 or Part I. *Manus haec inimica Tyrannis . . .* Lucan.' This anonymous MS history is written by a whig: nevertheless many of its allegations can be substantiated from other sources. Dr William Stukeley, the antiquarian, who was vicar of St Martin's, played a prominent part on the whig side. This pamphlet was used by Vaucher, *La Crise du Ministère Walpole*, 56. He misdates the pamphlet, however, and gives the impression that it is a printed pamphlet. It is not.

terest in it against both the Cecils and the Berties of Uffing-
ton.[1] In an electorate of five hundred they found enough
voters who disliked the domination of the great families
nearby to give them a chance, and furthermore they could
count on support from Walpole and the government. Secure
in a mayor of his own choice, Exeter had gone to work with
a will. He let it be known that no tradesman who supported
Cust could expect custom either from Burleigh or from any
of his supporters. The town's charities were used to show his
favour or displeasure. His supporters' sons, even at the tender
age of three, had their apprenticeship premiums paid out of
the town's charities; the sons of his enemies found themselves
expelled from Stamford school; likewise the hospital only
succoured the loyal; and leases of town property found their
way only into tory pockets. Friends of the mayor, and
therefore of Lord Exeter, paid nothing for being made free
of the corporation.[2] To make certain that Exeter's views had
proper publicity, *The Stamford Mercury* was brought into
being. As the election drew nearer nothing was left to
chance; surreptitiously at night men and women slipped
across the river from the suburbs in Rutland, bringing their
beds and household goods; these were taken in by 'chiefly
tenants of Lord Exeter and Lord Gainsborough' who
lodged them 'in garrets, closets, and cellars' and built them
'extempore chimneys' and so qualified them to vote, which
they did and thereby swelled the poll by a 100 more votes
than ever before. Drunk with the prospect of victory,
Exeter and his men paraded the streets of Stamford on
session day, taunting all the well-known supporters of Cust
until tempers broke and blows were exchanged. Naturally
Exeter quickly had Cust's men clapped in gaol for a breach
of the peace and kept there in spite of the protests of Dr
Stukeley, who offered to go bail, with the result that they
lost their chance to vote. In the end Exeter's followers got

[1] *Walpole*, I, 19; Lady Elizabeth Cust, *Records of the Cust Family*, I, *passim*.
[2] This gave them a vote, but also made them eligible, amongst other things,
for town charities.

out of hand and swarmed to Friary Gate, Cust's house, just out of town, threatening to tear it down. In the end they were repulsed, but not before several men had been badly injured by stones and sword-thrusts. Naturally it was not Exeter's men who paid the penalty for this riot. Noel and Proby, the candidates sponsored by Exeter and Gainsborough, naturally gained the majority and sat in the Commons.

Prejudiced though the source is, other evidence points to the extreme rowdiness of the 1734 election. At Knighton, in Radnorshire, the disappointed tories burnt Walpole in effigy before the houses of his chief supporters, broke their windows with stones, and threatened their lives to such an extent that the whigs there begged Walpole to quarter a troop of horse on the town.[1] Troops were in great demand, for Lord Hertford wished to bring the town of Marlborough back to its senses and allegiance by quartering six troops of horse on it, after the Corporation had deserted his patronage for the tory side.[2] At Steyning races, the Duke of Newcastle's supporters were hustled by a mob roaring 'No Excise', and burning Walpole in effigy was as popular in Sussex as in Flint.[3]

Wherever Walpole was in the heat of the electoral battle, the results followed him, brought by hard-galloping couriers from the four quarters of Britain. His men of business kept him posted, quick to report success and full of optimism. Most small boroughs behaved as their patrons wished; and naturally their elections were quickly despatched when a handful of voters had already pledged themselves. These

[1] *C(H) MSS*, Sir Humphrey Howarth, 11 June 1734. The troop was sent and by September 1734 not only were the inhabitants petitioning to have the troop removed back to Shrewsbury but so was its commanding officer, who complained that half the public houses had shut in order to avoid billeting, with consequent overcrowding and sickness. The inhabitants also kept back fuel. *C(H) MSS*, Duke of Chandos, 21 September 1734; J. (?) Malcolm, 28 September 1734.

[2] *Ibid.*, Hertford, 9 June 1734: see also George Wynne, 16 June 1734; 'I presume, Sir, that my good Lord Cholmondeley hath informed you my numerous opponents at Flint behaved with the utmost violence and inveteracy'.

[3] EHR (1897), XII; Basil Williams 'The Duke of Newcastle and the Election of 1734', 466–75.

out of the way, the difficult corporations could be tackled. This often meant rousing distant freeholders, bringing them with fife and drum and brandy in a great cavalcade across the breadth of the county, as Sir George Treby brought his through the red clay lanes of Devonshire to make certain that Walpole's loyal supporter, Sir William Yonge, should get the whig candidate home at Ashburton.[1] And no election took place in any borough large or small without great treats of beer and beef, wine and music, an orgy of heartiness in which the victorious revelled with unabashed glee and the defeated roared and ranted and plotted revenge.

These quick victories in Cornwall, Devon, Dorset and Somerset were sweet music to Walpole, struggling in Norfolk as he had never struggled before; but there were discords in plenty. The reports from the great cities and populous counties were ominous. In Yorkshire, the tories and independents had thrown all their resources into a battle that was the result of two years of campaigning.[2] Unfortunately for Walpole, the whigs were at sixes and sevens; Burlington, one of the greatest landowners in Yorkshire, had gone into opposition; Cholmley Turner, a popular independent, prevaricated for months before joining forces with Sir Rowland Winn, the official whig candidate, whereas the tories were united in their support of Sir Miles Stapylton. They divided up their county into canvassing areas, devoted close attention to the truculent and independent freeholders of the clothing towns of the West Riding, subscribed with a will, and used every artifice of propaganda—feasts, balls, solemn mayoral receptions, processions with banners, advertisements, handbills, food, drink, and earnest argument. Every race meeting saw them there in force. In a close contest (and the divisions amongst the great landowners had made that certain) the little man had a chance of registering his protest against the entrenched establishment, and he did

[1] C(H) MSS, Sir George Treby, 30 April 1734.
[2] For Yorkshire, see the excellent article by C. Collyer, 'The Yorkshire Election of 1734', *Proceedings of the Leeds Philosophical Society*, VII, Pt. I, 53–82; also *Wentworth Papers 1705–39*, ed. J. J. Cartwright, 482–98.

so. Sir Miles Stapylton headed the list, Walpole's 'wrong-headed' Cholmley Turner came next, the ministerial Winn well behind in third place, and last of all Lady Mary Wortley Montagu's husband, who had been put up at the last moment by the tories as a red herring. Naturally the ministerial whigs were utterly dismayed; they had the poll-books copied out, subscribed an immediate £2,300 to contest the result by petition, briefed lawyers and set in train the whole vast expensive machinery of an appeal to the Commons. They were met with equal determination; the tories countered by subscribing £5,000, and set to work to discover whig mischief. To celebrate their victory off they went in cavalcade to Leeds races, where Sir Miles was to greet his supporters from a specially prepared husting; alas, the carpenter was a whig, for no sooner had Sir Miles and his friends mounted the platform than it subsided, amidst hoots of derision from his enemies.

Yet Walpole had to suffer harder blows than Yorkshire.[1] John Scrope, on whom he depended more than any other man at the Treasury, was thrown out at Bristol. Worse still, Norfolk deserted him. This was the greatest blow of all, as well as the most unexpected. Both Sir Robert and Horatio knew that they were in for a hard fight at Norwich itself, where Crossgrove's *Norwich Gazette* had been busy publishing anti-ministerial propaganda.[2] And Walpole's anxiety about

[1] Coxe, III, 168, Newcastle to HW: 'We are returned very victorious from Sussex, and you may imagine are not a little pleased with it, considering the violent and strong opposition we mett with, and the bad success of our friends in other counties, as Kent, Cheshire, Hampshire, Yorkshire, Gloucestershire, Essex etc.'

[2] *Walpole MSS*, John Fowle to HW, 31 December 1733. Fowle, who had a place in the Customs, was a cousin of the Walpoles. He lived at Broome Hall in the Waveney valley and managed this distant part of the county for the Walpoles as well as keeping an eye on their Norwich interests. Horatio Walpole had countered Crossgrove's propaganda by having ministerial pamphlets sent to his supporters: 'I have duly received,' wrote Thomas Vere to him about 4 March 1734, 'the *Letter to the Craftsman* under your address and desire you'd believe I would not have deferred my acknowledgments had I not been burdened by illness. I have read it over several times with great pleasure and think the reasoning upon the posture of the present state of affairs in Europe not only extremely just but the best expedient that could have been produced to the publick at this time to calm the minds of the giddy multitude and blunt

the city itself can be gathered from a note he dashed off
to Newcastle, before even the final count was done.

'My dear Lord,

'Ten at night, the poll just closed and two books now
casting up; we have carried it for both,[1] the exact numbers
you shall know, if before the post goes. Great expenses made,
great threats ushered in the day, but a due provision to
repel force by force, made it a quiett election. I think the
county a much more secure gain and the successe of this
day will not much animate our antagonists.

I am ever and sincerely
Yours most affectionately
R. Walpole.'[2]

The same optimism filled the hearts of his supporters, who
had been telling him for months that Sir Edmund Bacon, the
leading tory candidate, and sitting member, had been losing
voters even 'in those parts of the county where he hoped to
have had his interest very entire'.[3] A week later, on 22 May,
these hopes were dashed: the two tories Bacon and Wode-
house narrowly triumphed over Coke and Morden, the whig
candidates. For both elections, Walpole had spent money
like water, and the county defeat was a bitter blow.[4] He
would not accept it. He set up his dependable Quaker
friend, John Gurney, to organize a petition. Gurney with the
thoroughness of his sect immediately set out to scrutinize
every vote. This success naturally made the tories cock-a-
hoop; life, after all, in Norfolk had been depressing enough
for them for decades, and they celebrated to the full. Their

the points of a pungent pamphlet intitled *Politicks on Both Sides*.' The pulpit
was also used, for Parson Shuckford's sermon was printed and sold to good
effect: HW also promoted a petition from the Norwich merchants complaining
of the decay of their woollen trade owing to competition from Ireland which
of course received an affable welcome from the ministry and wide publicity.
Walpole MSS, Letters of Thomas Vere, March–April 1734.

[1] Waller Bacon was HW's partner. He died shortly after his election and
was replaced by Thomas Vere, a strong supporter of HW.

[2] BM *Add MSS*, 32,689 fo. 241. Norwich, 15 May.

[3] *Walpole MSS*, loc. cit.

[4] *C(H) MSS*, John Gurney, 27 May 1734. RW was paying for the transport
and lodging of freeholders from as far away as the Walpole villages on the
borders of Cambridgeshire, where he possessed no estates.

celebrations were, of course, interpreted by the jaundiced whigs as Jacobite outrages.

'Our opposers now take off the mask and besides oak bows,[1] several gentlemen, who I may believe, assured me that the day after they were chose at Norwich they cryed "No Hanover Succession, King James the 3rd for ever and King James health was also drunk at Hempton fair . . . Fakenham is more outrageous and insolent than any time." And the gaiety of Fakenham on Walpole's defeat was hardest of all to bear, for it lay between Holkham and Houghton and close to Raynham, where Townshend kept his tenants loyal to the old whig cause.[2] By 4 June, Lovel thought it was useless to continue the fight, but Gurney, undaunted, went on with his methodical examination of the poll-book, trying to set up a small committee of whig gentlemen in each hundred to investigate the veracity of each tory voter's claim to a freehold.[3] But the interest had died: Lovel had gone to Derbyshire; Walpole was back in London; no one had any interest, save the tories in trumpeting their victory, and the publicans in getting their bills paid. Even such a sharp blow as this did not, however, affect Walpole deeply. He remained utterly sanguine of the result: each day at his levee, he and his cronies went over the lists;[4] generous with doubtfuls, he gave himself a more substantial majority than in the previous parliament, and boasted of his triumphs to the Queen. Whether he really believed this or not can-

---

[1] i.e. oak boughs, these were tory emblems to recall their part in the Restoration to offset the whig glorification of the Revolution.

[2] *A Copy of the Poll for the Knights of the Shire for the County of Norfolk, 1734*, 131–2; all eighteen freeholders of Raynham voted for the whig candidates: Fakenham's twenty-three freeholders divided twelve for the tories, eleven for the whigs (*ibid.* 59–60), so Lovel's view was somewhat jaundiced.

[3] *C(H) MSS*, I. Leheup, 4 June 1734; 'I found by Ld Lovel that no proceedings on the scrutiny was made, and I fear by what I know and hear that both cannot be carried, so submitt to you whither keeping up the spirit as tis called now that Parliament is actually chosen, is equal to the insolencies the Jacobites use towards us in all parts of the country,' and J. Gurney, 22 June. Gurney was tougher than Lovel and was still working at the poll books in July. Coke and Morden sent out circular letters to their supporters to keep up their spirit. *Ibid.* Hen. Bedingfield, 13 July 1734.

[4] Coxe, III, 167.

not be known, for the truth, as Newcastle realized, was different. He knew the majority was smaller, but the new parliament would be 'a good one; but by no means such a one as the Queen and your brother imagine'. He wrote to Horatio: 'It will require great care, attention, and management to sett out right, and keep people in good humour.'[1]

The Craftsman vaunted opposition victories in London and the great towns, sneered at ministerial triumphs in the 'beggarly little seaports'; but with a clear majority in the Commons, Walpole cared little about popular sentiment.[2] His confidence in his own ability had not weakened with the years and he had, moreover, repelled the danger where he had feared it most. The loss of Norfolk was an irritating personal insult, Yorkshire annoying, but the complete victory in Scotland offset these petty defeats. A most elaborate attempt had been made by Chesterfield to secure the return of sixteen Scottish Lords who would be opposed to the ministry.[3] A victory would have endangered Walpole's grip on the House of Lords, for everyone knew that Gibson and the bishops were very unhappy about the way Church offices were being handled and the contest about Rundle and the diocese of Gloucester had shown them their strength. A restless, unmanageable House of Lords could have been as disastrous to Walpole as an uncontrolled House of Commons, so he and Islay left nothing to chance; every artifice that the ministry possessed was used to secure the return of sixteen loyal peers and to the infinite chagrin of Chesterfield and his cronies, the ministry got their way at Edinburgh. Of course, they threatened a petition, but Walpole realized that the first round in electioneering was usually the vital contest so long as it was the ministry that was victorious. This triumph in Scotland boosted his confidence. With the House of Lords docile, and a good majority in the Commons, he could look forward with pleasure to seven more years in the

[1] Coxe, III, 168.
[2] The majority was estimated variously at about 75.
[3] Vaucher, *La Crise du Ministère Walpole*, 60; Register House, Edinburgh, *Mar and Kellie MSS*, 628.

handsome new Treasury buildings which William Kent had just completed for him, and to enjoying the house in Downing Street recently given by George II to the Treasury for the residence of its First Lord. For years he had lived in private splendour, now his public offices and official residence provided a fitting background to the 'Great Man'. He had taken risks, made enemies, driven through crises, foreign and domestic, and still the power was his—Parliament was firmly in his grip; his favour at Court was unshakable; and his view prevailed on all questions foreign and domestic.

CHAPTER NINE

AN APPRAISAL

THE YEARS 1733 and 1734 form the watershed of Sir Robert Walpole's career: yet the slope towards defeat and retirement was so gentle that few of his contemporaries perceived it. To his royal masters, to the members of the cabinet, to his family and friends, to the public at large, and even to the opposition, his authority after the election of 1734 seemed as great as ever. In the Court, in the cabinet and in the Commons he was still the master, still 'the Great Man'. Yet this moment in his career is more appropriate than any other for assessing the influence which his twelve years of power had had not only on the affairs of his country but also on his own nature. His favour with the King and Queen had never stood higher; he had shown that he could manage them even against their natural sympathies, for he had brought them to accept a policy in foreign affairs, a field which they regarded as peculiarly their own, that conflicted with all that they had been taught to believe and cherish. In domestic arrangements at Court, his word was law. The King had dismissed, for his sake, old friends of a lifetime and taken into his confidence servants whom he despised. There was hardly a place of profit under the Crown or in the Church, the Army, or the Navy that could be disposed of without prior consultation with him. His interference in elections was as constant and as authoritative as his disposal of patronage. He dominated his cabinet with more ease than he dominated the Commons. In twelve years of government he had suffered one check and one check only—the Excise crisis—for the fiasco of Wood's halfpence had no influence on his political position in England. His control of the financial affairs of the nation was, apart from the methods of taxation, absolute, and he ruled his Treasury with an efficiency unmatched throughout the eighteenth century. These things were more obvious to Walpole than to us. He had pursued power and found it; he had enriched the nation by fostering commerce, by efficiency of management, by low taxation; he had kept the King on the throne. These were the avowed objects of his political life and he had achieved them.

He took most pride in establishing the Hanoverian succession and defeating Jacobitism. His great speech on the Septennial Bill makes this clear enough; and the alarms, excursions and even rebellions of the Jacobites were dealt with so easily and the solemn succession of Georges seems in retrospect so inevitable that Walpole's constant pre-occupation with the dangers of faction, ferment, public criticism and disorder, because of the opportunities they gave for the Jacobites to exploit them, appears like one of those common delusions of men of power, who conjure up phantoms of public danger in order to suppress criticism. And this element is not entirely lacking. When Walpole sees the hidden hand of Jacobitism in the spontaneous crit-cisms which excise engendered, he becomes the dupe of his own obsessions. Yet his preoccupation with Jacobitism can-not be written off as a convenient bogy with which to secure the destruction of tories and to stifle public agitation. He had in his own lifetime witnessed one rebellion and two attempted invasions, and uncovered a widespread plot. The flight of James II was one of the most vivid recollections of his early childhood. He had grown to manhood as the civil wars of Ireland and Scotland had brought fresh strife and blood-shed and almost ruin to the nation. These were the actuali-ties upon which his fears were grounded. They were kept alive by the monstrous rumours, lies and grains of truth that his elaborate espionage system revealed. In Brussels, Calais, Boulogne, Paris, Rome, Walpole placed his spies and agents. His correspondence teems with as much rumour and conjecture as the vast mass of the Stuart papers themselves. For the Jacobites the flicker of dissatisfaction in a politician spelt a promise of a return to his Stuart allegiance; for

Walpole, the unguarded action of the son of a tory on the Grand Tour hinted of conspiracy and plot. An atmosphere such as this fostered that inclination to deceive, to betray, to undermine, which threads the lives of all who seek power; minor betrayals abounded and suspicion festered as men smeared each other's reputations. The money which Walpole spent, the time which he consumed, the secret meetings which he contrived, all demonstrate, however, that this world of lies, rumour and suspicion was a real world of fear to Walpole himself. The need to circumvent Jacobitism was one of the fundamental principles that guided Walpole's decisions in domestic and foreign affairs. And the invasion of 1745, after his death, showed clearly enough that exaggerated as this fear of invasion might be, it was never groundless. Walpole was completely committed to the service of the Georges, upon whose survival, he maintained, depended both the whig party and whig principles.

All the arts of his political management were therefore directed to the maintenance of the Hanoverian succession. The more men who were tied to the Court, the greater the strength of the dynasty. The means Walpole employed were not simple and they have been misunderstood. By strict attention to all appointments at Court, in the Church, in the Army and in the Navy, by the same rigorous supervision of all officers in the counties and boroughs, Walpole set about achieving a loyal establishment. Such was the rigorous nature of his selection that by 1734 there was scarcely a tory bishop, general, admiral, or deputy-lieutenant to be found in the land and tory courtiers never cast a shadow on a Drawing Room. For better or for worse the toryism that had flourished so vigorously in Queen Anne's day was by 1730 without political significance. There were no converts and constant defections; it had become the creed of squireens, Oxford-bred parsons and a few families dedicated to their ancestral past. In the whig triumph patronage had played its part as Walpole intended it to do. There was never enough, but what there was paid whig dividends. Aristocratic and gentle

families were taught to look to the Court and to the politicians for their economic and social advancement. What was
intended to secure stability through loyalty rapidly became
a scramble for place, in which personal vendettas, greed,
ambition and devotion to principles became hopelessly
mixed. These things were, perhaps, the inevitable consequences of an aristocratic and oligarchic society yet the
slide into factional politics with all their tragic consequences,
was undoubtedly made quicker and easier by the methods
which Walpole employed. Few can doubt that ambition to
enjoy the social prestige and financial fruits which came with
a place in the establishment, helped to give stability to the
regime: nevertheless it was not in itself sufficient.

There were men who prided themselves on independence
of spirit, others who were intractable or incalculable friends
and enemies by fits and starts, men who cared little for the
drudgery of politics and lacked sufficient influence or estate
to secure rewards without work. There were a large number
who were uncommitted, but inclined to accept authority
so long as it was in the hands of their neighbours and
friends. Upon these men Walpole used his persuasive arts,
and his cunning lay not so much in parliamentary rhetoric
or dazzling oratory as in facts, figures and clarity, with an
adroit use of all the advantages in parliamentary procedure
that ministerial power gave him. Unless he was really ill his
attendance in the Commons was exceptionally assiduous;
he intervened in most debates, displaying an astonishingly
detailed knowledge of the whole range of affairs, domestic
or foreign. This ability to dominate the Commons, to
defeat the attacks of the opposition, week after week and
year after year, was one of his principal duties as the first
servant of the King. Naturally this had made him responsive—not to the clamours of the opposition—but to
the ideas and opinions of those who supported him with
little hope of reward.

The authority which Walpole acquired in the Commons
was derived not only from his favour with the King, the

disposal of his patronage, his skill in debate and the adjust-
ment of policy to back-bench sentiment, but also from the
authority which comes to a first-class administrator, the
fruits of whose work are there for all to see. Walpole governed
well; the financial system of the country worked better in
his hands than ever again in this century; customs, excise,
land-tax, ran quite efficiently; relations with the Bank of
England and the great chartered companies were exceptionally smooth; interest rates fell; government stock
maintained its price. A great deal of this was due to economic
causes over which Walpole exercised no control; much also
was due to that tireless attention to detail that sent him
hurrying through the wintry gloom to the Treasury to be
at his desk before eight o'clock in the morning. Walpole's
energy was directed to making the machine work. He was
not averse to innovation. Regular issues of Treasury bills,
payment of interest on a daily rate—these show his shrewd
grasp of detail and his willingness to accept innovation. Yet
his long rule at the Treasury was not marked by any radical
reforms. No antiquated office was abolished, no cumbersome
procedure reformed; he preferred to keep every office in being
so long as it could be used to further the stability of ministry.
Efficiency within the old framework of government was all
that Walpole desired to achieve. And this he accomplished.
And yet paradoxically he was as responsible for the inefficiency of the administration which followed his as for the
efficiency of his own. Deeply rooted in Walpole was the
belief that men had a prescriptive right to rewards from the
institution they served. It was as natural to him to establish
generations of Popples in the Board of Trade and Cardonnels
in the Salt Office as to give places for life to his own children.
Loyalty, the prescriptive right of birth, weighed more with
him in the end than efficiency.[1]

[1] By these methods he created, of course, the Court and Treasury party
which was to be the core of the old whigs and the greatest factor making for
political stability for the next thirty years. But political stability was achieved at
the expense of administrative efficiency. After Walpole's death many offices—
like the Land Tax Office—were run badly or—like the Board of Green Cloth—
lapsed into desuetude.

An excellent administrative ability, an outstanding parliamentary skill, the unshakable favour of the King, these factors gave Walpole an eminence in English life unparalleled since Burleigh.[1] They brought crowds of sycophants to his door; dukes and duchesses begged his favours; bishops waited for his commands; such constant attention, such constant sycophancy, did not leave his character unmarked. He grew impatient of criticism, regarded with hostility men of strong will who would not accept his yoke, bullied weaker characters with a coarseness and brutality that shocked. Naturally he did not relish formal or semi-formal meetings by which his authority appeared to be diminished and preferred to work through private interviews with individuals or secret discussions with his tried and loyal supporters. He quoted with approval George I's dislike of large cabinets and agreed with him that no good ever came of them. He preferred the closet to the cabinet except when others appeared to have more of the King's sympathies than his own; then he favoured a small, 'efficient' cabinet in which he could be sure of a majority. And, of course, he found it difficult to brook rivals; his career is littered with the broken careers of gifted men who crossed his path—Pulteney, Carteret, Townshend, Chesterfield, Cobham—and apart from Hardwicke, a man of massive moral integrity and great intelligence, and one or two others, he surrounded himself with faint replicas of himself or fools and flatterers. At least, by 1734 he had come to that and it is a measure of how power had hardened his character.

All that he does and says in the early thirties argues a growing inflexibility of temperament, a greediness to grasp and exercise power; the anxiety lessens, and the future is contemplated less than the present. As a young man his contemporaries spoke of his gaiety, of his ebullient life, of the

---

[1] A comparison noted also by contemporaries:
Such the great *Parallel* as here behold
Walpole is now, what Burleigh was of old.
William Musgrave, *Genuine Memoirs of the Life and Character of Sir Robert Walpole* (London 1732), 50.

warmth and spontaneity of his nature. Some of this he never lost. Although he could be the most affable of men, quick to respond even to his defeated enemies, this should not blind us to the essentially ruthless nature of his political actions. Where he differed from many great men who have wielded political power as great as his, is this: he did not require the death or even exile of men who had vainly crossed his path. Their complete political impotence was all he desired. Nor did great power make him secretive or remote or grossly suspicious of his close friends. He went on giving the same trust and loyalty to his brother, to Hardwicke, to Pelham, even to Newcastle, that he had always shown towards them. He was available to all from field marshals to ensigns, admirals to midshipmen, archbishops to curates, princes to merchants, so long as they were prepared to wait patiently in the throng that daily besieged his doors. And to his colleagues, and to the Court, he remained open-hearted, generous almost to a fault, retaining his delight in ostentatious display, in gargantuan meals and vast potations; his coarseness, his love of a lecherous sally, grew rather than diminished with the years, so that even Queen Caroline, no prude herself, had to rebuke him for his language before the princesses. His frankness, his lack of all pretentiousness, were nevertheless tinged with vulgarity, with a gross enjoyment, with almost a delight in stimulating the envy of men.

Certainly that envy was stirred, more profoundly, more publicly than is the common lot of great men of state. He was hated more for being himself than for his conduct of affairs. Not only was his power resented; and his royal favour loathed; his whole manner of life bred detestation wherever he went. He paraded his wealth with ever greater ostentation. He bought pictures at reckless prices, wallowed in the extravagance of Houghton, deluged his myriad guests with rare food and costly wine; his huge ungainly figure sparkled with diamonds and flashed with satin. And he gloried in his power, spoke roughly if not ungenerously of others, and let the whole world know that he was master. Such a way of life invited criticism on a personal level. All the opposition Press revelled in portraying the grossness of Walpole's life; ballads were sung of his ill-gotten wealth; obscene caricatures illustrated his relations with the Queen; bitter pamphlets laid bare the graft, the corruption, the favouritism of his regime. The Chelsea Monarch, Bob of Lynn, The Quack Triumphant; year in, year out the gutter Press squirted its filth over his reputation. His friends did little better; the institutions by which he governed worse. The Court was corrupt, his ministers feather-witted, his Treasury a swindle, his Parliament bought, the Church a political trade. He was the dupe of France, of Spain, of the Dutch. His sole aim in life was to amass gold and aggrandize his family. Day after day, week after week, month after month, year after year through the two decades of his ministry this twisted and malicious criticism never ceased: and embedded in the heart of the sludge was a grain of truth, enough indeed for this uncontrolled propaganda to carry with it a certain conviction. The good that he did—the stability, the peace, the prosperity, were taken for granted—the evil magnified to phantom proportions.

Public life and the institutions of government were thereby brought into disrepute: by 1734 Parliament had lost much of the respect it had enjoyed in the early years of the century; an ever franker acceptance of the greedier side of human nature strengthened self-seeking, weakened altruism and vulgarized politics, until critical issues of state became a matter of personal vendetta. In 1734, this had not yet gone so far as it was to go at the time of the War of American Independence, but each year that Walpole remained in power lowered the standards of public life, for the vituperation and criticism were as responsible as the long years of power for hardening his nature and coarsening his response to life.

By 1734, his life, his attitudes, his methods had been clamped into an iron mould; the years had hardened and coarsened the fibres of his personality; and as his vision narrowed into a desire to retain power for its own sake, as intolerance of criticism grew, as the fluid, sensitive feeling of the realities of men and politics were smeared by success and calloused by power, so too did Nemesis creep upon him. Time no longer favoured him; the dashing young sprigs in the Commons—the hooting patriot boys—calculated his age and drank to the future. No longer could he regard the years ahead as a time of promise or fulfilment; the unfolded years were his consolation and delight. The future would bring the death of friends, the decline of powers, age, sickness and defeat.

A NOTE ON SOURCES

The major source for this volume, as with the first, is the papers belonging to the Marquess of Cholmondeley. They are deposited at the University Library at Cambridge. Although they are not rich in letters of a personal nature, they contain a mass of valuable political papers and correspondence that was only partially used by Archdeacon Coxe in his life of Walpole. The most important source, after the Cholmondeley (Houghton) Manuscripts, has been the papers at Wolterton Hall of Sir Robert's brother, Horatio, now belonging to Lord Walpole. It was Horatio's intention to write a diplomatic history of his own time and he carefully preserved and bound a large number of diplomatic dispatches as well as correspondence. They have proved invaluable for foreign affairs. The Townshend papers at Raynham are not extensive but I have had the good fortune of being able to use the valuable and interesting collection of Townshend papers in the possession of Mr H. L. Bradfer-Lawrence of Ripon. The Newcastle papers at the British Museum become increasingly rich in this period, but, as these are comparatively well known, I have drawn my examples of patronage and electioneering from Walpole's own papers when an opportunity presented itself.

For parliamentary affairs the most important new source, used extensively in this volume, is the diary of Sir Edward Knatchbull Bt. in the possession of Lord Brabourne. It fills an important gap that is not covered by Lord Hervey in his memoirs or by Lord Egmont in his diary. For printed sources the reader is referred to the 'Note on Sources' in volume one of this *Life*. In addition to those books listed there, there are three others that I have used extensively and I feel a special debt of gratitude for the authors of them. They are:

A NOTE ON SOURCES

A. McC. Wilson, *Foreign Policy and the Administration of Fleury.*

P. Vaucher, *Walpole et la Politique de Fleury.*

L. Hanson, *The Government and the Press.*

ABBREVIATIONS

Add. MSS.	Additional Manuscripts.
Arch. Aff. Etr. Corr. Angl.	Archives des Affaires Etrangères, Correspondance d'Angleterre. (Quai d'Orsay.)
BM.	British Museum.
Chandler.	Richard Chandler. *The History and Proceedings of the House of Commons from the Restoration to the Present Time*, London 1742–44 (14 vols.).
C(H)MSS.	Cholmondeley (Houghton) Manuscripts. *Note:* as letters are chronologically arranged, all references are by writer and date. The addressee, unless otherwise stated, is Sir Robert Walpole.
Coxe.	William Coxe. *Memoirs of the Life and Administration of Sir Robert Walpole, Earl of Orford*, London 1798 (2 vols.).
Coxe, HW.	William Coxe. *Memoirs of Horatio, Lord Walpole*, London 1802.
DNB.	*Dictionary of National Biography*.
EHR.	*English Historical Review.*
Hervey.	John, Lord Hervey. *Some Materials towards Memoirs of the Reign of King George II.* ed. Romney Sedgwick, London 1931 (3 vols.).
HMC.	Historical Manuscripts Commission.
HW.	Horatio Walpole, brother to Sir Robert Walpole.
PCC.	Prerogative Court of Canterbury.
PRO.	Public Record Office.
RO.	Record Office.
RW.	Sir Robert Walpole.

S.P.Dom.   State Papers Domestic.

Timberland.   Ebenezer Timberland. *The History and Proceedings of the House of Lords from the Restoration to the Present Time*, London 1742–43 (8 vols.).

Trans. R. Hist. Soc.   *Transactions of the Royal Historical Society.*

Walpole.   J. H. Plumb. *The Life of Sir Robert Walpole, The Making of a Statesman*, London 1956.

INDEX

Abercrombie, Alexander, MP, 104

Africa Company, 216

Aislabie, John, MP, estates of, 275

Albani, Cardinal, 86

Alberoni, Giulo, Cardinal, Prime Minister of Spain, 14, 27, 30–1

Alliance of Hanover, cf. Hanover

Alston, Sir Rowland, 3rd Bt., 297 and n.

Americas, battle for empire in, 13: English power in, 36: American trade, 236

Amhurst, Nicholas, 141–2, 151

Amsterdam, 17–18

Ancaster, Peregrine Bertie, 2nd Duke of, 279

Anglo-French alliance, 35

Anne, Queen, 15, 140: patronage, 92: whigs and tories, 94: ministry impeached, 209

Anne, Princess, project for marriage, 74 n.

Answer, An, to one Part of a Late Infamous Libel, 124 n.

Arbuthnot, Dr John, 131, 141, 235

Archers, of Warwick, 246

Argument, An, against Excises, 251 n.

Argyll, John Campbell, 2nd Duke of, 38, 50, 52, 71, 105, 106, 170 and n., 282: and Cadogan, 94: and Townshend, 105: and Walpole, 105, 277–81

Aristocracy, European, 9, 10, 11, 15, 16: English, 9: family alliances, 16: French, eighteenth century, 33: Irish, 66: Peerage and parliamentary government, 79

Arlington Street, 87, 91, 172, 196, 215

Armagh, Archbishop of, cf. Boulter, Hugh

Armstrong, Colonel, British representative at Dunkirk, 210–1

Army private, 9: commercial power

and, 11: professional armies, 13: England and, 13: Cadogan and the mustering of the troops, 54–6: patronage, 92, 94: increased forces, 129: Hessian Troops, 134, 140: reduction of army, 202: army estimates, 206: Bolton and Cobham deprived of their regiments, 281: officers not to be removed except by courts martial, 303–4: troops and election of 1734, 318

Arnall, William, journalist, 315 and n.

Art collection made by Walpole, 85

Artari, plasterer, 83, 84

Ashburton, 91, 319

Assiento, 17, 31, 32, 36, 134, 149, 189, 190, 198

Atterbury, Francis, Bishop of Rochester, 40, 44: character of, 45: imprisonment of, 45–7: trial of, 48: relations with Walpole, 48 n.: death, 48: Sunderland's intrigues with, 48 n.: attitude of the ministry, 49: exiled, 95: Wharton's support, 107: Atterbury plot, 184

Augustus II, of Poland, death of, 284

Augustus III, son of Augustus II, 284: proclaimed King, 288

Austrian Empire, 24, 25: Austrian armies, 25: French policy towards, 29, 219: Austrian innocent intentions, 121: war with France unavoidable, 122: threat to British trade, 127, 139: Austria and the Pretender, 147: Austro-Spanish relations and treaty, 51, 118–20, 122, 128, 147, 149–50, 153, 189: rupture with Spain, 194, and Fleury, 189: isolation of Austria, 194–5: Walpole's direct negotiations with Charles VI, 226, 227, 228: secures Treaty with Austria, 229, 230: succession to throne of Poland,

Paris, 74: attitude to Townshend's foreign policy, 77: appointments in army and navy a royal prerogative, 94: titles of nobility, 100, 101: and Roxburghe, 106 n.: feast to the City of London, 110–2; and Austro-Spanish treaty, 120: and Bolingbroke, 125, 126: audience with George I, 126, 127: Anglo-French relations, 137: Pulteney's memorial to, 150 and n.; views on Cabinets, 197: death of, 154 and n.: his will, 157 n.: and Walpole, 1, 2, 52, 76, 80, 101, 129, 131–3, 154: and Townshend, 52–4, 64, 108, 134

George II, accession, 162–5, 167, 196 and n.: character and personality of, 157–61, 213: his mistresses, 158–9: quarrels with George I, and reconciliation, 79, 157, 162: George I's will, 157 n.

Army, his personal responsibility, 281: removal of officers debate, 303–4: Civil list revised, 167: Excise debate, 264: Excise Bill, decision to support Walpole, 267: European situation, 1733, 284: France, intentions of, 285: Austro-French war, 287, 288: George II favours British aid, 288: delay, 289: willing to mediate, 290: attitude to Walpole's neutrality policy, 300–1, 312: France, his policy towards, 287: Hanoverian interests, 220, 224, 230: his analysis of the situation upon accession, 265: King's Speech, 191, 202, 259, 282, 302, 313: marriage of Prince of Orange to Princess Royal, 290: visits to Hanover, 159, 194, 197, 248.

and Queen Caroline, 159–62: and Carteret, 265: and Charles VI, 224, 226, 228, 287: and Chavigny, 287: and Chesterfield, 161, 272: and Spencer Compton, 164–6: and Devonshire, 163: and Egmont, 204, 214: and Fleury, 287: and Hatorff, 300; and Hervey, 264, 287;

and Mrs. Howard, 158–9: and Newcastle, 163, 165: and Scarborough, 158, 161, 163: and Townshend, 156, 158, 162, 189 n., 195, 197, 199, 219–20: and Horatio Walpole, 162, 167–9, 188: and Walpole, 113 n., 158, 161–5, 167, 172, 175–6, 199, 201, 218, 230, 245, 258, 264, 279–80, 288, 290, 294, 301–2: accession of George II, 162–4: Civil List, 167–9: crisis in relationship with, 301

Georgia, colonization of, 144

Germany, aristocracy in, 15: German princes, Townshend's policy, 121: German princes, policy of, 139, 150: Electors of Bavaria, Cologne, Palatinate, Trèves, 194–5

Gibbon, Edward, Director of the South Sea Company, 275

Gibbon, Edward, historian, 215

Gibbs, James, architect, 82, 84 n.

Gibraltar, English possession of, 31, 32, 36, 77, 118, 120, 122, 134, 135, 139, 148–9, 153, 181, 187, 189, 198, 203, 229: armistice signed, 185

Gibson, Edmund, Bishop of Lincoln, and London, adviser on ecclesiastical patronage, 95, 97: character of, 96: and the Universities, 96: case of Dr Rundle and Gibson's offer of resignation, 299–300, 309, 323: and Queen Caroline, 160: and Townshend, 95, 299: and Walpole, 95, 96, 299–300

Glasgow, riots in, 1725: 105 and n.: shipping at, 235

Gloucester, Bishopric of, see Rundle, Dr Thomas

Gloucestershire, election 1734, 320 n.

Godolphin, Sidney, 1st Earl, 81 n., 140, 197, 249

Goertz, Georg Heinrich, Baron, von, 14

Golden Fleece, Order of, 26, 118

Gordon, Mr, 294–5

Government, Mr, 294–5

Government, institutions of, 332